Frida Kahlo

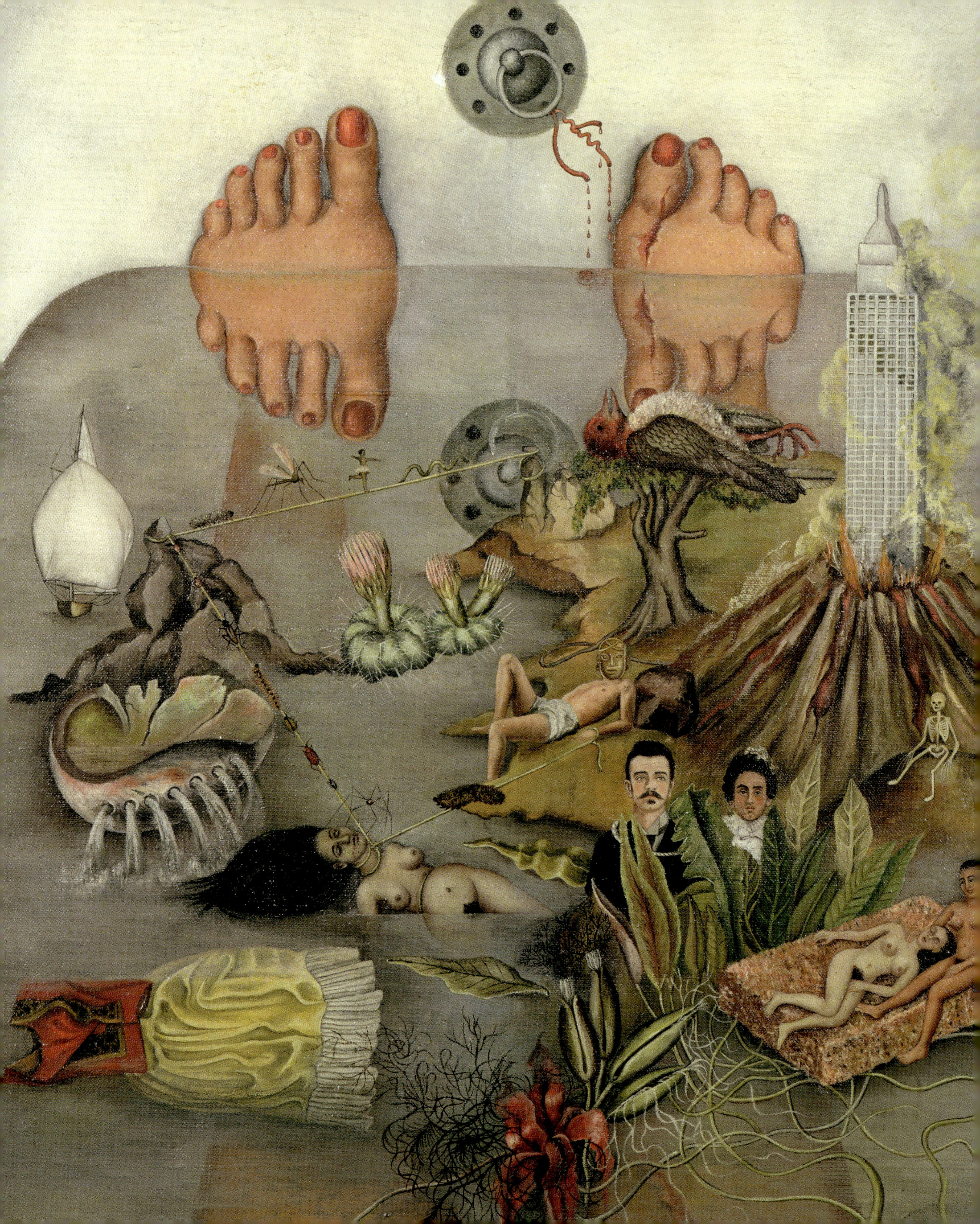

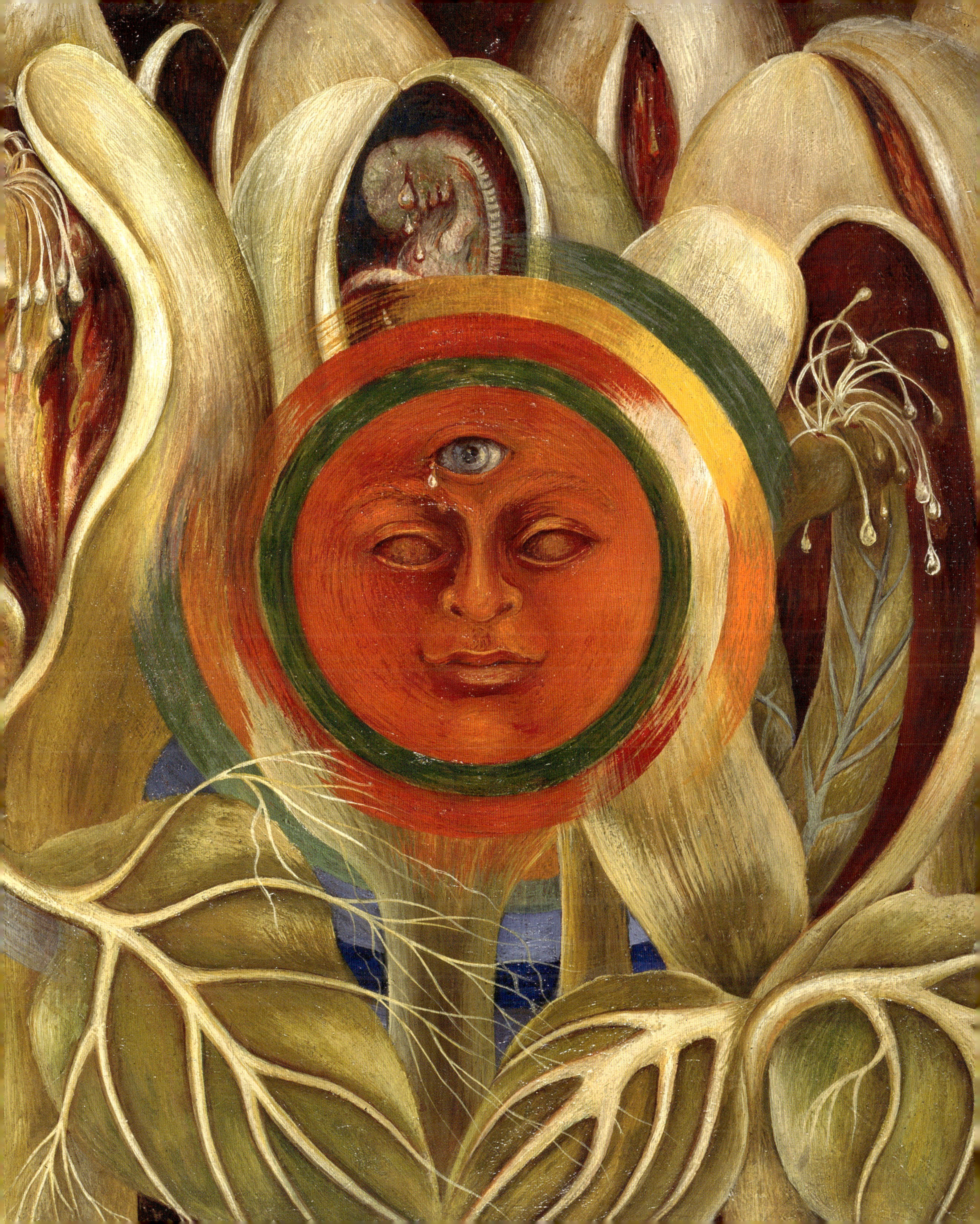

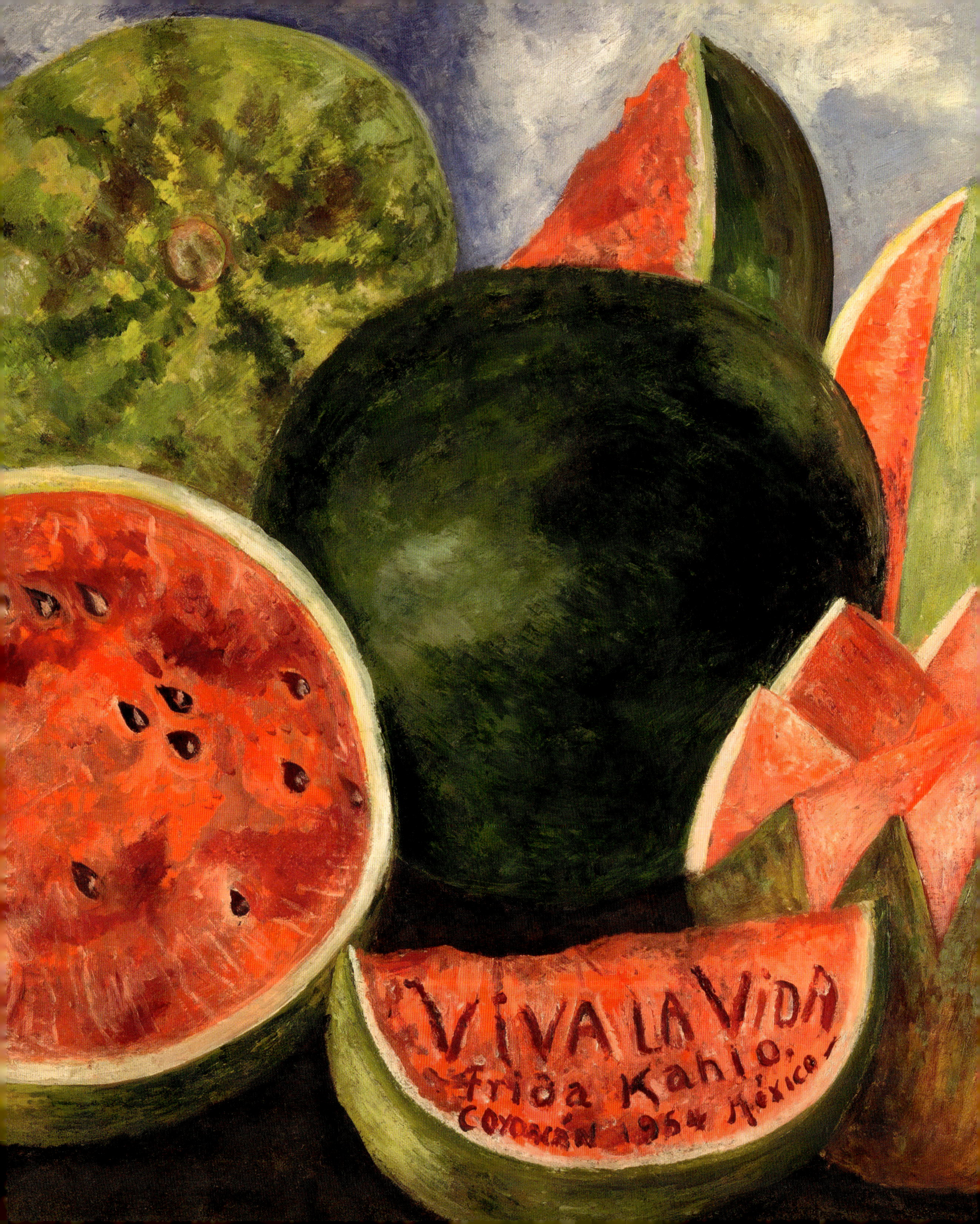
VIVA LA VIDA
Frida Kahlo.
COYOACÁN 1954 México

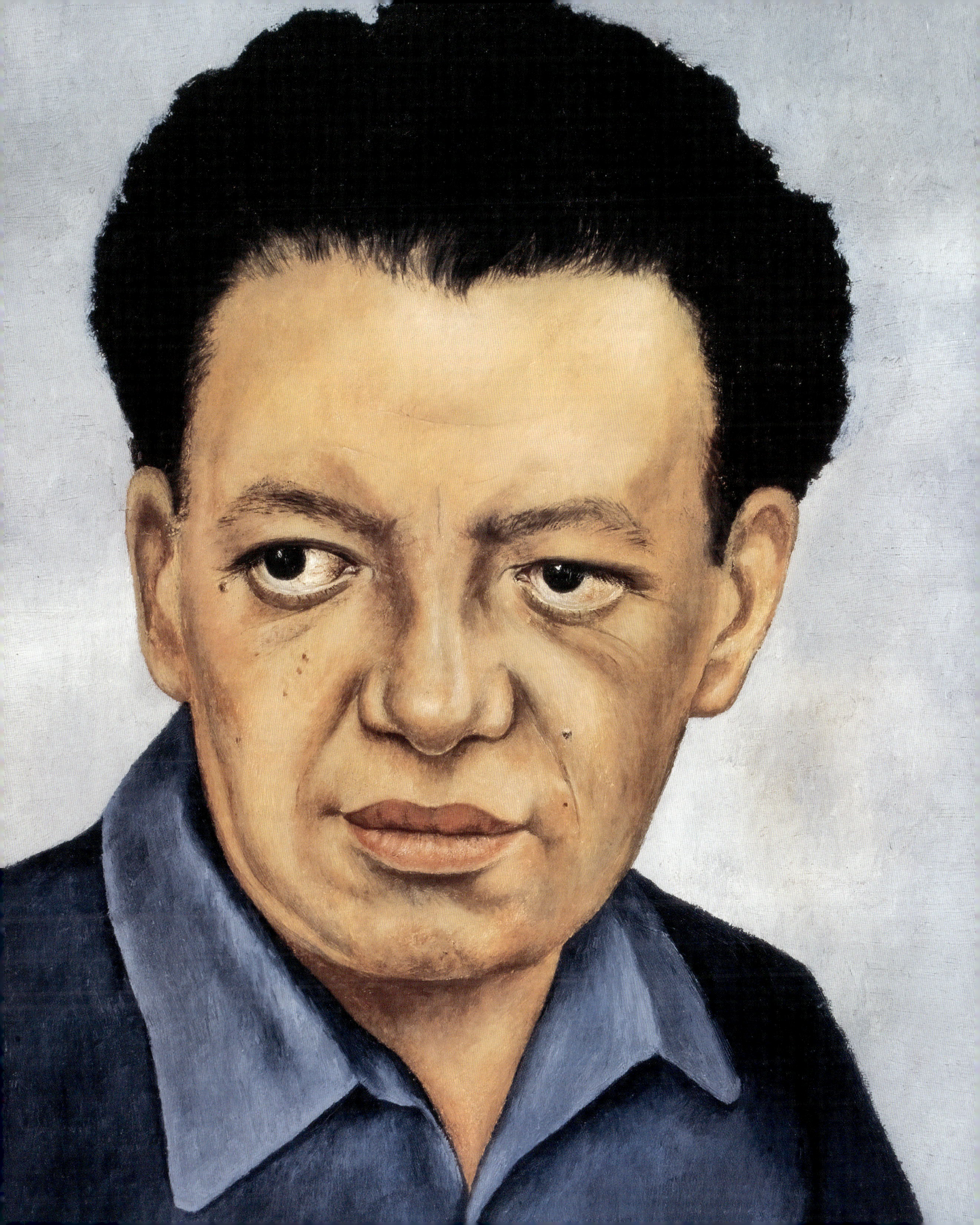

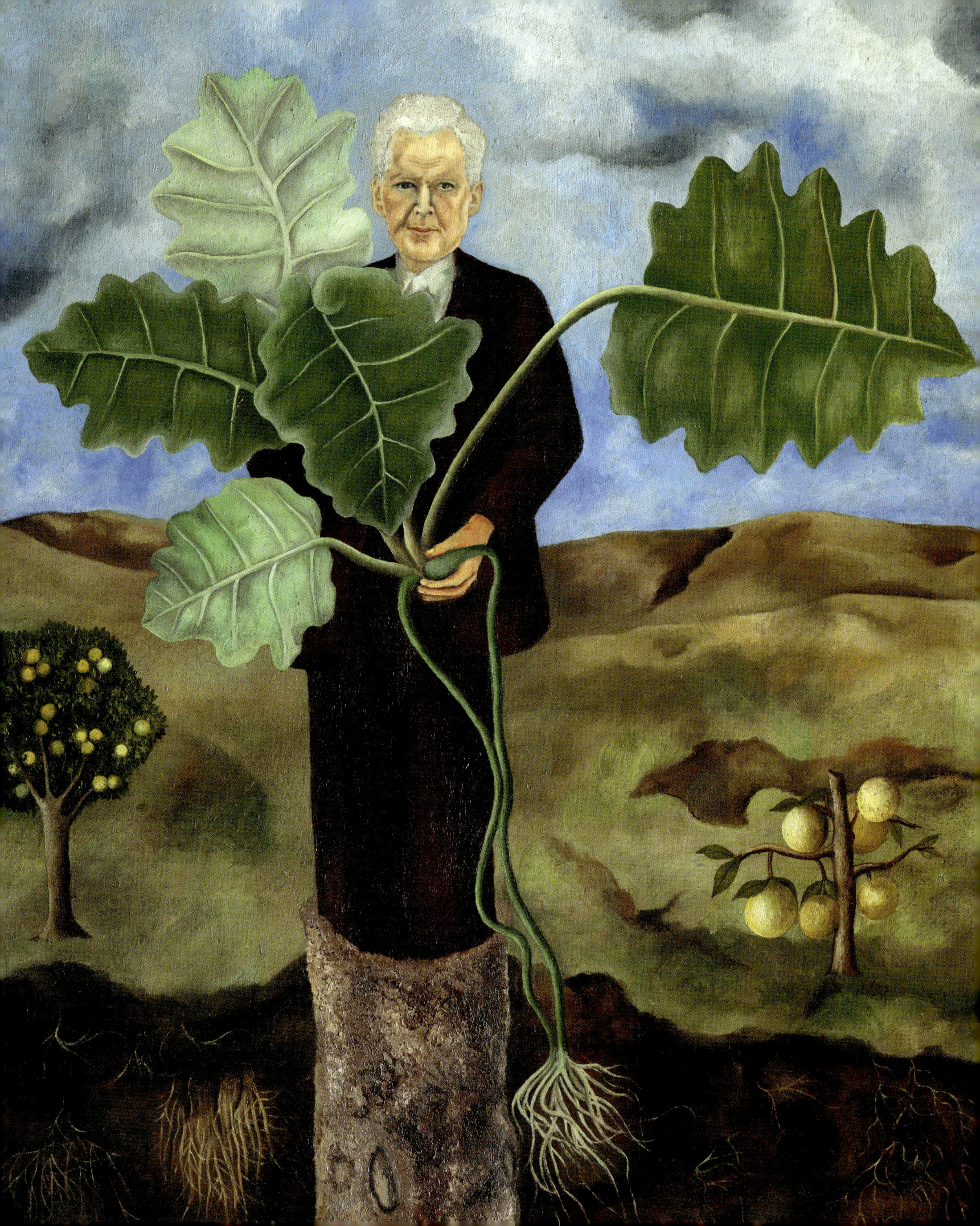

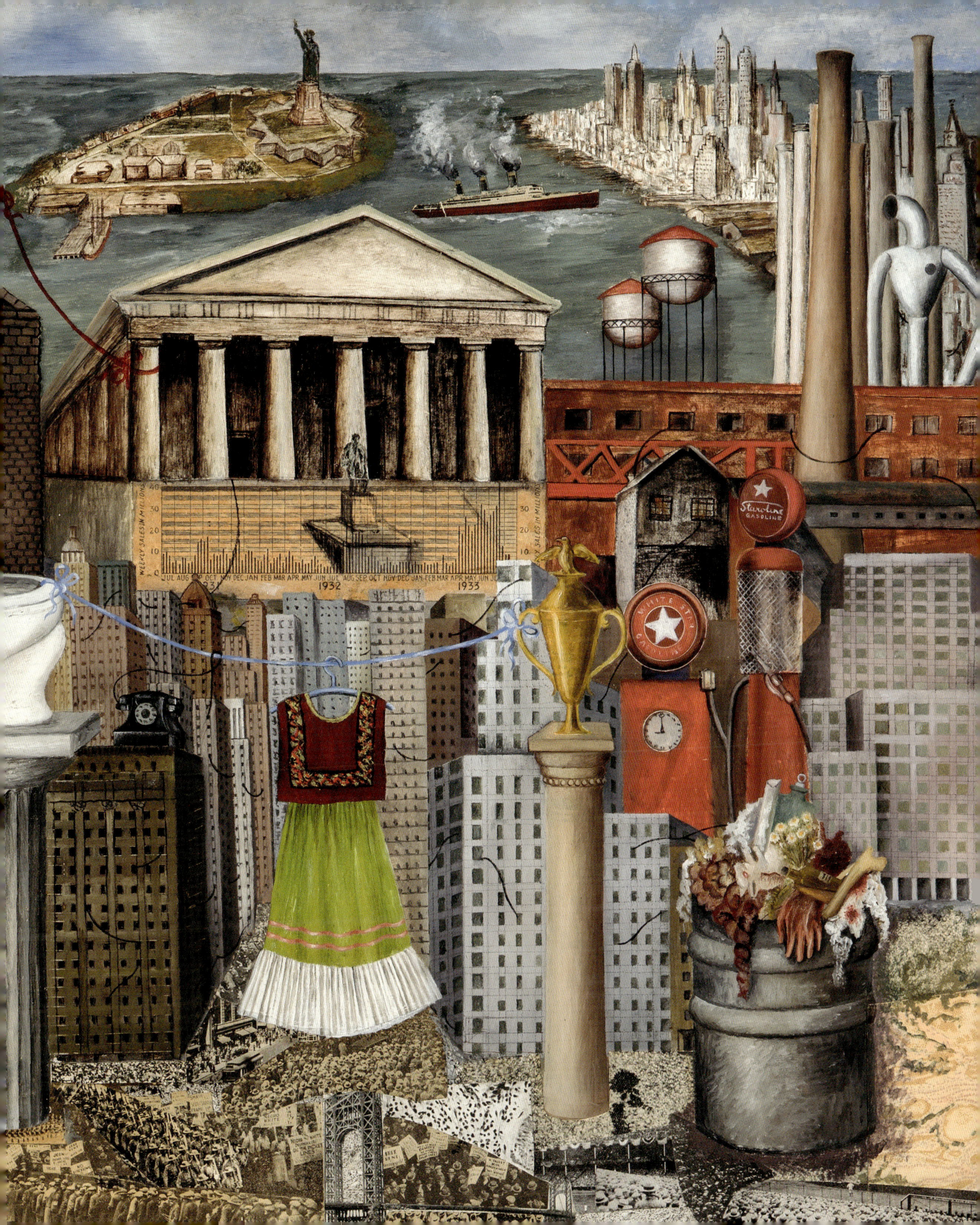
1932
1933

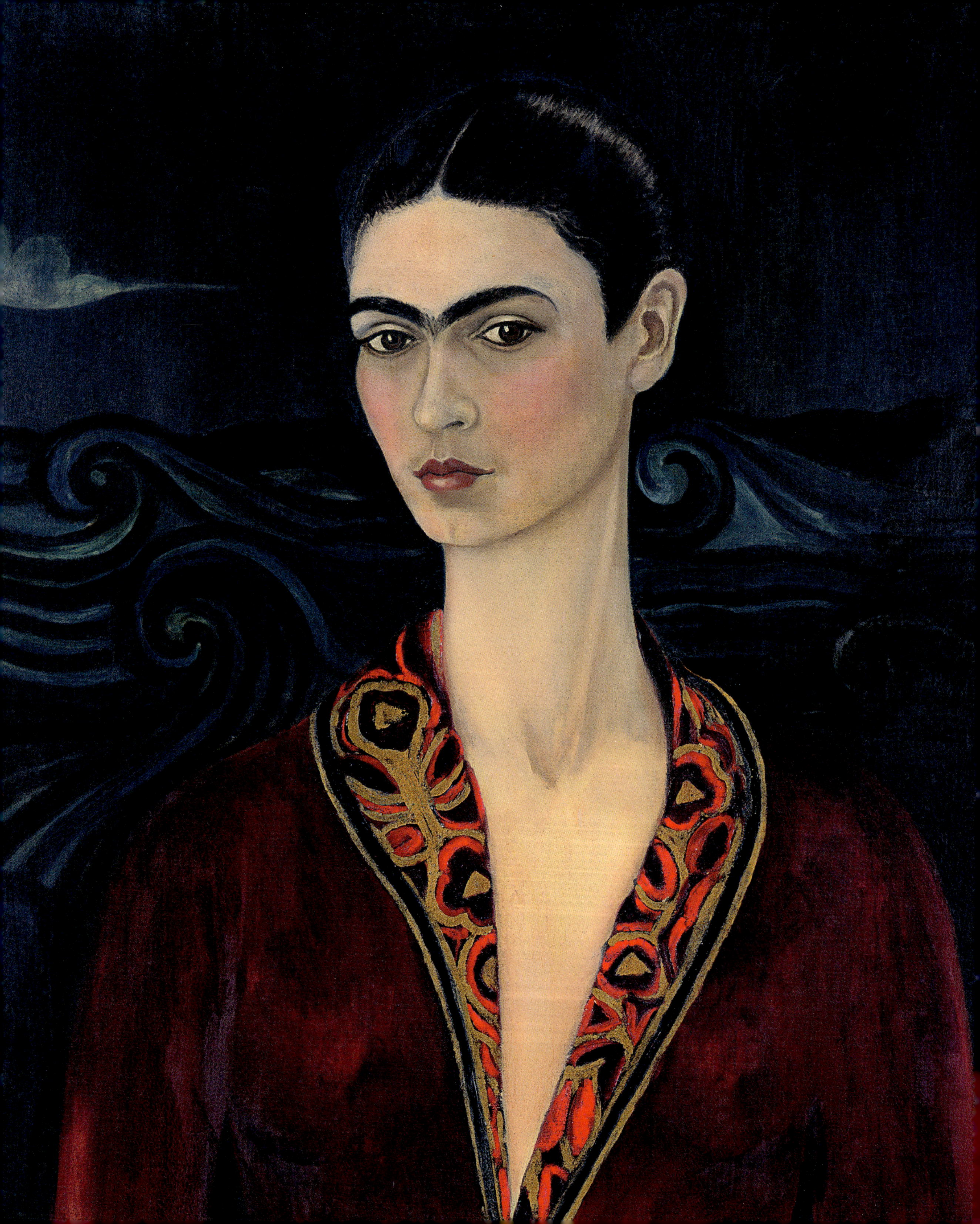

Frida Kahlo
THE MASTERWORKS

Héctor Tajonar
Roxana Velásquez

Rizzoli Electa

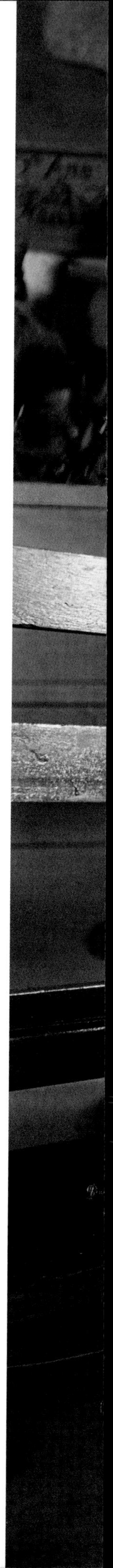

Frida Kahlo painting a portrait of her father, Guillermo Kahlo, 1951. Photograph by Gisèle Freund. Saint-Germain-la-Blanche-Herbe, IMEC-Institut Mémoires de l'édition contemporaine

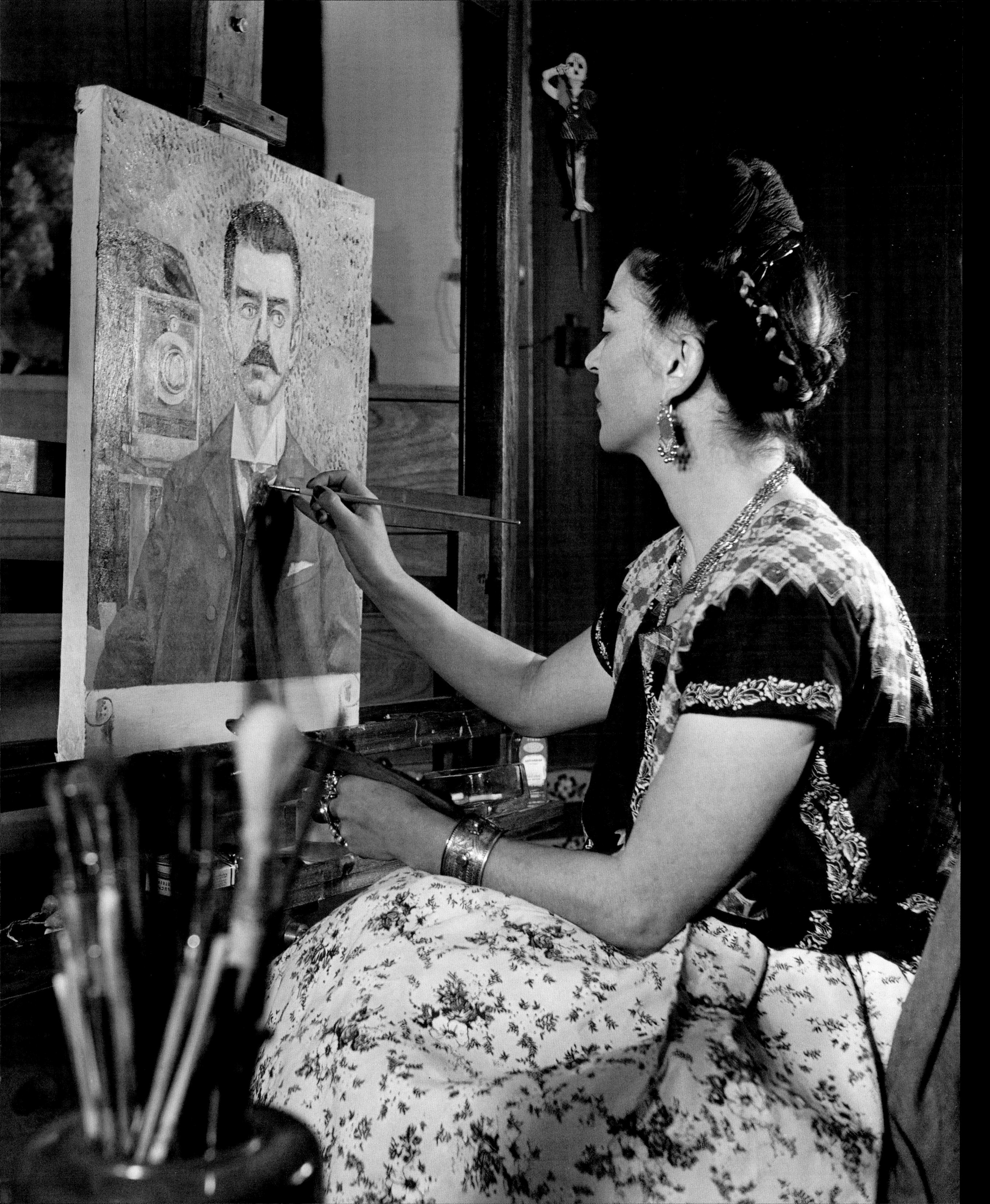

Contents

Introduction

Frida Kahlo (1907–1954) was a force of nature, and she knew it. An extraordinary woman and artist, she consciously created her own persona through her painting, her writings, her clothing, and her appearance. This not only afforded her a way of expressing her many talents, but also provided a distraction from the physical pain that accompanied her throughout her life. From a very early age, she realized that she was more intelligent than her sisters and her mother. She began using that intellect to distinguish herself from them in a bid to win her father's attention, and she succeeded, just as years later she would succeed in winning the love of Diego Rivera (1886–1957). Propelled by intelligence and ambition, she became one of the foremost women painters in the history of art, an international celebrity, and a feminist icon who inspired a phenomenon known as "Fridamania." Most admirably, she achieved all this despite the adversity of the poliomyelitis she contracted as a child and the accident at the age of eighteen that left her physically disabled and unable to bear children. Not only was Kahlo a unique and essential artist who created original work of stunning expressive force, but she also set an example of fortitude, perseverance, and love of life.

Indeed, Kahlo made her life into a work of art. Her biography and her artistic creation are inseparable and complementary, and one cannot be understood without the other. The poetic intensity of Kahlo's work was inspired in part by Walt Whitman's "Song of Myself." The poem appears in her favorite book, *Leaves of Grass*, a copy of which she kept under her pillow. Drawing deeply on her own existence and powered by her prodigious imagination, the artist created a song to herself rendered in impeccably crafted canvases. Many of her paintings clearly depict the suffering caused by her accident, which left her immobile on a bed in tremendous pain, and it is true that the suffering that imbues Kahlo's paintings can be interpreted as an aesthetic of pain, but her work is much more than that. The richness and variety of Kahlo's creations reflect lyrical heights and human depths that are fed not only by grief but by a highly developed mind and sensibility that allowed her to admire the beauty of nature, feel the joy of tequila-warmed song and conversation with her many friends, enjoy the pleasures of eroticism, and dive passionately into labyrinths of love. That very diversity is part of Frida Kahlo's fascinating personality and is expressed with genius in her painting and writing.

Frida Kahlo: The Masterworks proposes a new way of looking at and interpreting the artist's work, revealing what lies behind the paintings through a combination of psychological and aesthetic analysis. The text links the key events in Kahlo's biography with her artistic creations in order to reveal both her exceptional personal qualities and the poetic and symbolic dimension of her pictures. Aimed at a broad readership ranging from novices in the field of art to cognoscenti, this volume concisely reviews the extraordinary personal and artistic universe of Frida Kahlo within the context of the history of world art.

Kahlo painted herself, photographed herself, invented herself, made herself up, dressed herself, and expressed herself with a narcissistic delectation unequaled in the history of Mexican art. At a time when revolutionary nationalism dominated the country's artistic expression, Kahlo made herself the central subject of her art. This makes her painting a unique contribution to the Mexican art of the first half of the twentieth century, as well as to the painting produced by women in the worldwide history of art. Expressed with sincerity and talent in Kahlo's painted autobiography are her relationship with Diego Rivera, her bisexuality, her political activism, her links with Surrealism, her physical and emotional pain, and her love of beauty. Introspection is made art.

Inserted throughout the text are excerpts from exclusive interviews with seven of the world's leading specialists on Kahlo's oeuvre (Carlos Fuentes, Raquel Tibol, Salomon Grimberg, Teresa del Conde, Helga Prignitz-Poda, Juan Coronel Rivera, and Elena Poniatowska) conducted for the documentary *Yo soy Frida* (2007), written, directed, and produced by Héctor Tajonar, an author of this publication. This helps to provide a broader range of interpretations for a better understanding of Frida Kahlo's personal and artistic complexity.

Roxana Velásquez Martínez del Campo, the coauthor of this book, was the director of the Museo del Palacio de Bellas Artes in Mexico City in 2007, when that institution played host to a major international exhibition to commemorate Frida Kahlo's centenary. Roxana Velásquez acted as general coordinator of that exhibition and a member of its curatorial committee, also made up of Juan Coronel Rivera, Salomon Grimberg, Cristina Kahlo Alcalá, and Américo Sánchez.

With this book, we hope to establish a relationship of empathy between the reader and the work of Frida Kahlo. The goal is being to capture what Erwin Panofsky calls the "expressive meaning" of each piece through its iconographic characteristics and then use that to access the "intrinsic meaning" or content of the works of this groundbreaking Mexican painter. This involves revealing and interpreting the "symbolic values" of her work, as well as its deeper dimension, sometimes unknown even to the artist herself, all of which constitute the object of what Panofsky, a celebrated art historian and theorist, calls "iconology." While iconography deals with the description or formal or documentary analysis of the work, iconology denotes reasoning and interpretation and proceeds from a lively and fertile synthesis in which art illuminates ideas and is illuminated by them. According to Panofsky:

> We need a mental faculty comparable to that of a diagnostician—a faculty which I cannot describe better than by the rather discredited term "synthetic intuition," and which may be better developed in a talented layman than in an erudite scholar.[1]

Eyes on the work.

1 Erwin Panofsky, *Meaning in the Visual Arts* (New York: Doubleday Anchor Books, 1955), 38.

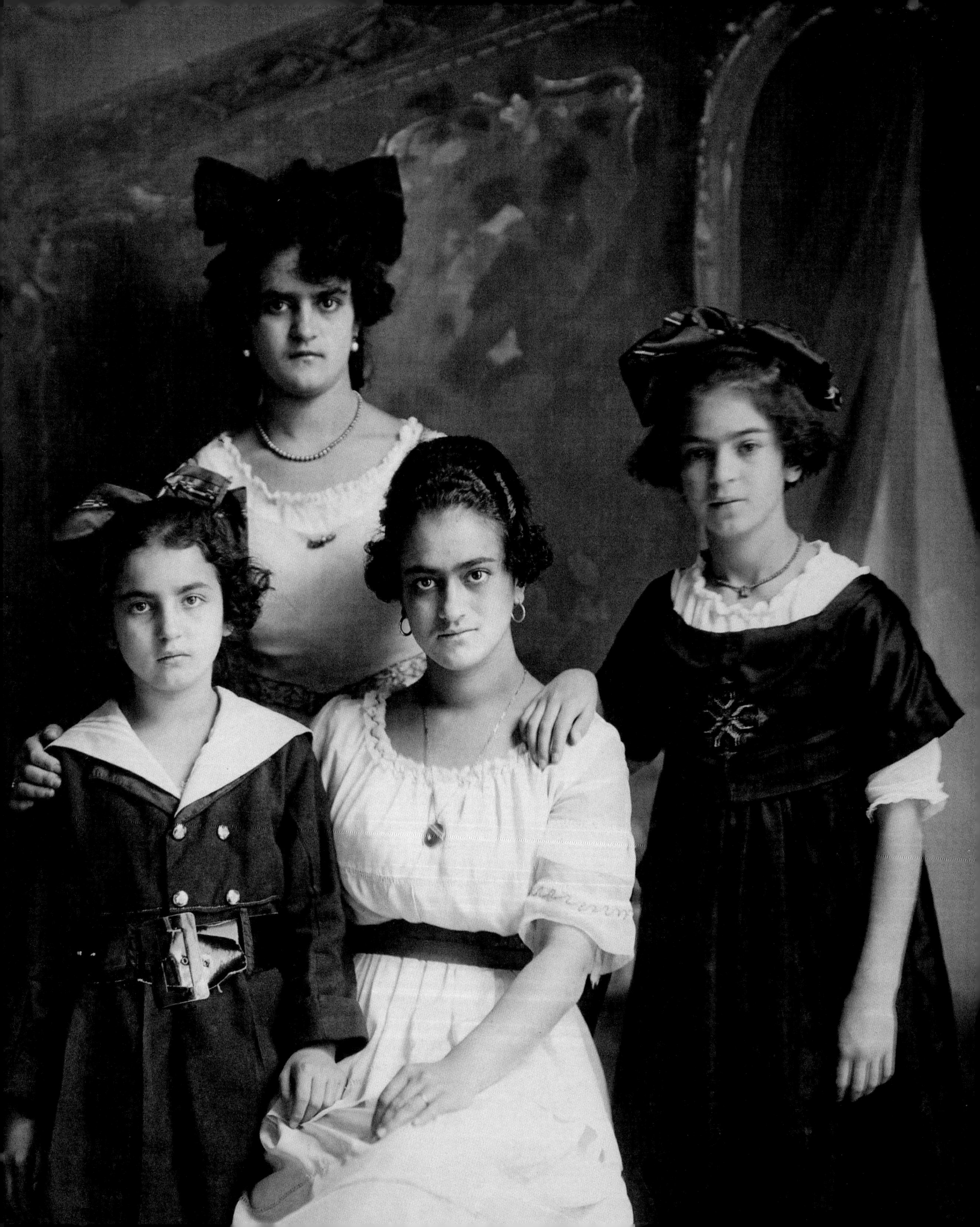

A Life Made Art

I do not pretend that Joy cannot associate with Beauty, but merely that Joy is only one of its most vulgar ornaments, whereas Melancholy is, as it were, its most esteemed companion, to such a degree that I can scarcely conceive of . . . a type of Beauty in which there is not Woe.

Charles Baudelaire[1]

Only beauty has the privilege of looking at the soul without being blinded. Frida Kahlo achieved that miracle of seeing her soul through grief and turning it into painting.

Carlos Fuentes[2]

The Kahlo-Calderón sisters (left to right): Cristina, Adriana, Matilde, and Frida, 1919. Photograph by Guillermo Kahlo. Coyoacán (Mexico City), Museo Frida Kahlo

Frida Kahlo was a daughter of the Mexican Revolution. She was born on July 6, 1907, in Coyoacán, which was then a suburb of Mexico City, but she used to say she was born in 1910 so as to make the date coincide with the armed uprising that overthrew the dictatorship of Porfirio Díaz. Besides being a political and social movement, the Mexican Revolution was also a cultural phenomenon that detonated a wave of creativity unparalleled in Mexican history in the fields of painting, poetry, the novel, the essay, music, and film. The great inspirer of cultural nationalism was the secretary of public education during the presidency of General Álvaro Obregón, the thinker and writer José Vasconcelos, who had the vision to invite artists, artisans, and teachers to collaborate in the mission of remaking Mexico, retrieving its ancient culture and traditions, while stimulating the reading of classical authors like Plato, Dante, and Goethe by distributing their books for free and editing an anthology of classical texts for children. Vasconcelos offered painters the walls of the most important buildings in Mexico City so that they could display their concept of the world and Mexican culture. The great figures of Mexican muralism, as is well known, were José Clemente Orozco (1883–1949), David Alfaro Siqueiros (1896–1974), and Diego Rivera (1886–1957). Outstanding in the field of literature were the prose of Alfonso Reyes, the poetry of Ramón López Velarde and of Los Contemporáneos (Carlos Pellicer, Xavier Villaurrutia, José Gorostiza, Jorge Cuesta, and Salvador Novo, among

Guillermo Kahlo and Matilde Calderón, the parents of Frida Kahlo, February 21, 1898. Private collection

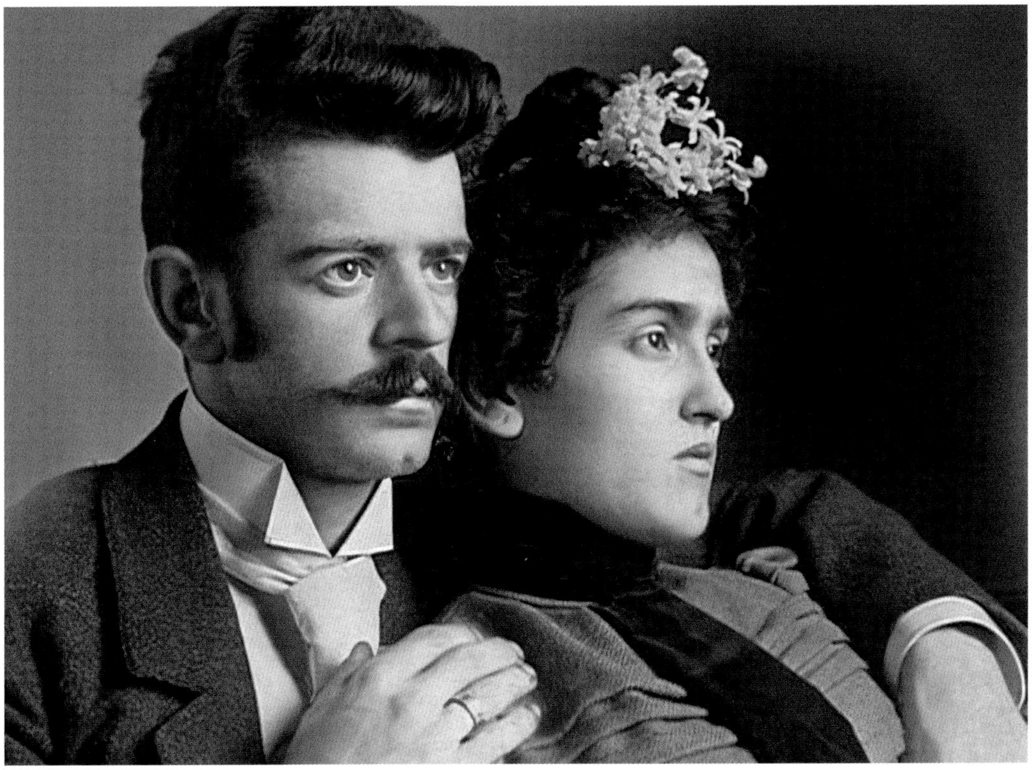

others), and the novels of Mariano Azuela, Martín Luis Guzmán, José Revueltas, Agustín Yáñez, and Juan Rulfo. Musical compositions of note were produced by Carlos Chávez, Silvestre Revueltas, and José Pablo Moncayo.

Frida Kahlo was one of the great beneficiaries and creators of the Mexican cultural renaissance during the first half of the twentieth century, since she grew up and was formed in that atmosphere of cultural ebullience to which she was both heir and protagonist. Her artistic vocation grew and developed under the influence of Mexican muralism, and especially of her mentor and greatest love, Diego Rivera. In 1922, she started attending the National Preparatory School, housed in the beautiful colonial building that had belonged to the former College of San Ildefonso, the cradle of Mexican muralism. There she met Rivera while he was painting the mural *Creation* in the Preparatory School's auditorium, the Simón Bolívar Amphitheater. That same year, Ramón Alva de la Canal (1892–1985), Fermín Revueltas (1901–1935), and Fernando Leal (1896–1964) painted scenes of feasts and religious rites on the walls and staircase of this palatial building, where the Frenchman Jean Charlot (1898–1979) also left his masterly *The Massacre in the Main Temple* or *The Conquest of Tenochtitlan* (1922–1923). In what was known as the Patio Chico (Small Court) of San Ildefonso, Siqueiros painted two murals, *Call to Liberty* or *Angels of Liberation* (1923) and *The Burial of the Sacrificed Worker* (1924). From 1923 to 1926, Orozco created magnificent works on the three floors of the main wall and staircase of the central court of San Ildefonso, including the outstanding *Maternity, The Trench, Cortés and La Malinche,* and *The Franciscans.* In the nearby church of San Pedro y San Pablo, Roberto Montenegro (1885–1968) had painted the first postrevolutionary mural, *The Feast of the Holy Cross,* in 1921. Living alongside these masterpieces of mural painting from the age of fourteen left an indelible imprint on Frida Kahlo's artistic sensibility.

Frida was the third of the four daughters of Guillermo Kahlo (1871–1941) and Matilde Calderón (1874–1932). In the picture *My Grandparents, My Parents, and I (Family Tree)* (1936) [fig. 1], the portrait of her parents is a faithful reproduction of their wedding photograph. On the bride's dress, painted in painstaking detail, there appears a fetus, which may represent the artist in her mother's womb or may symbolize a possible premarital pregnancy. Beneath the embryo is a sperm entering an egg, while alongside is an eroticized prickly pear flower, open for its fertilization by pollen. Matilde Calderón de Kahlo was of mixed blood, the daughter of an indigenous father and a Spanish mother. Meanwhile, the parents of Guillermo Kahlo, who appears in a frock coat with a somewhat nostalgic gaze, were Hungarian Jews who emigrated to Germany. Frida painted herself in the center of the composition as a nude child of two or three holding a red ribbon that joins her to her family tree. She is standing in the main courtyard of the famous Casa Azul (Blue House) in Coyoacán, where she was born and died, and which now houses the Museo Frida Kahlo. The background of the picture is a barren landscape with a few cacti and a hut. The four grandparents are suspended on clouds in the sky. Beneath the busts of the maternal grandparents is a landscape of mountains with ravines, while painted beneath that of the paternal grandparents is an ocean. Here, as in many of her works, Frida's realism is shot through with symbols, secret allusions, and a sense of humor.

Wilhelm Kahlo changed his name to Guillermo upon his arrival in Mexico in 1891 and came to be the first official photographer of Mexican cultural heritage. Between 1904 and 1908, he was commissioned by José Yves Limantour, Porfirio Díaz's finance secretary, to make a record of the pre-Hispanic, colonial, and nineteenth-century architectural heritage of Mexico with a view to the centenary celebrations of the country's independence. He carried out the task with technical precision and professionalism, using German cameras. This work allowed him to attain a comfortable financial position, build the Casa Azul, and give his daughters a good education, although the family finances were diminished by the outbreak of the Mexican Revolution. Frida Kahlo was very close to her father, who regarded her as the most like himself and the most intelligent of his daughters. Guillermo was a reserved man, a reader of Schiller, Goethe, and Schopenhauer, a lover of the music of Beethoven, and an amateur artist who painted watercolors. He taught Frida to take, develop, and tint photographs and used his own photos to share his knowledge of the art and archeology of Mexico with her. Guillermo Kahlo suffered epileptic seizures, which generally occurred during the night. In her diary, Frida wrote this reminiscence of Herr Kahlo, as she affectionately called him:

> My childhood was wonderful even though my father was a sick man (he suffered from vertigo every month and a half). He was the best example for me of tenderness and workmanship (also a photographer and painter) but above all of understanding for all my problems.[3]

In 1952, eleven years after the death of her father and two years before her own, Frida painted *Portrait of My Father Wilhelm Kahlo,* based on a photograph taken by himself, where he is seen wearing a dark brown suit with a vest and tie [fig. 3]. The melancholy and slightly lost gaze of his large green eyes, looking sideways beneath a knitted brow, denotes his introverted and perhaps anxiety-ridden personality. Behind him is a camera. The ocher background of the canvas is full of microscopic creatures: hundreds of sperm are competing to reach a few floating eggs. The obsession with masculinity and procreation is a constant in the artist's work. On the lower part of the picture, she wrote:

Guillermo Kahlo, *Self-portrait,* 1920. Coyoacán (Mexico City), Museo Frida Kahlo

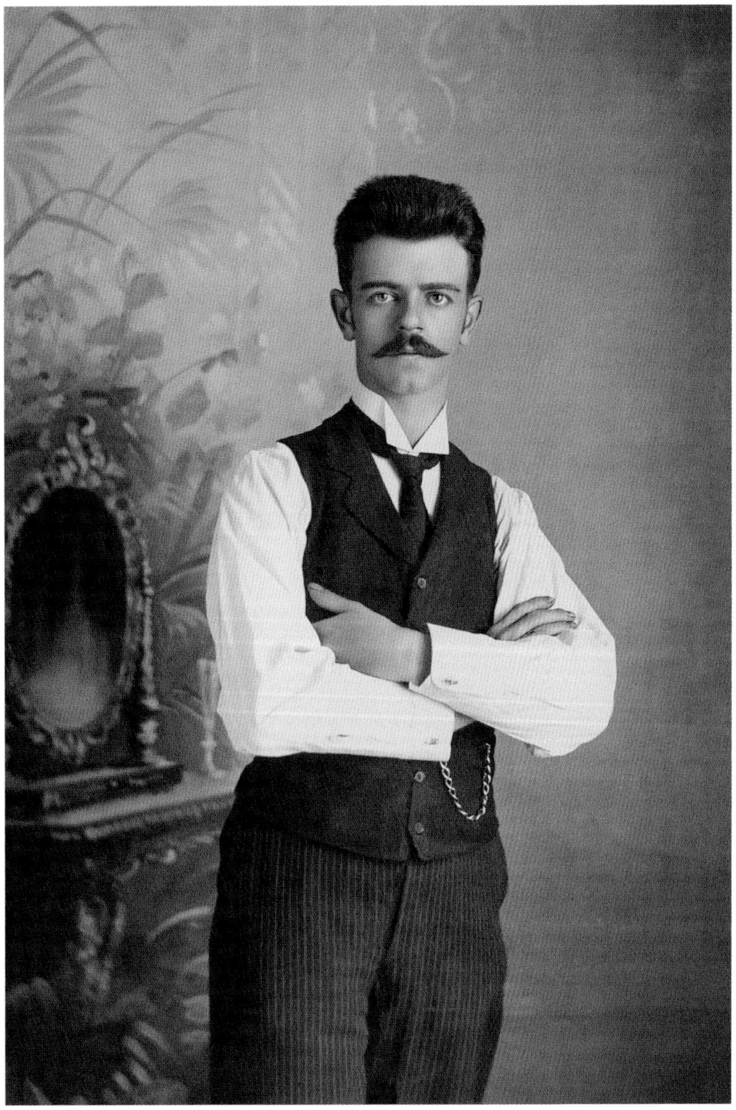

> I painted my father, Wilhelm Kahlo, of Hungarian-German origin, artist-photographer by profession, in character generous, intelligent, and fine, valiant because he suffered for sixty years with epilepsy, but never stopped working and fought against Hitler, with adoration, his daughter Frida Kahlo.

Frida's mother was a handsome, active, and largely uneducated woman, extremely religious and devoted to housework. She taught her daughters to cook, clean the house, sew, and embroider and made them attend mass every day. "My mother was hysterical about religion," Frida complained.[4] Frida's relationship with her mother was more distant, but she loved her deeply and cried incessantly when she died. In the painting *My Birth* (1932), she depicts herself emerging from the womb of her mother, whose face is covered by a sheet because she had just died when the picture was painted [fig. 2]. The room is empty save for a bed and a picture of Our Lady of Sorrows, weeping, bleeding, and

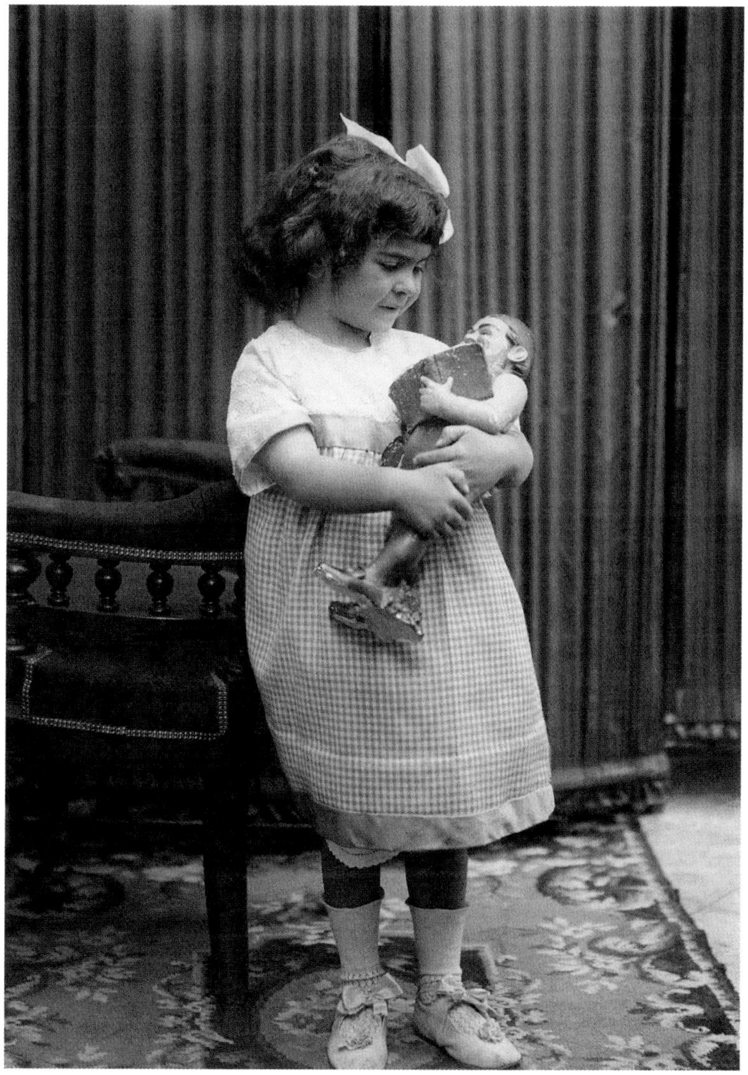

Frida Kahlo at the Casa Azul (Blue House) in Coyoacán (Mexico City), 1913

pierced by knives. According to Salomon Grimberg, a psychiatrist who has specialized in the life and work of Kahlo, Frida was trying in this painting to express the loneliness and abandonment she had felt since her birth. "If that picture were the only painting by Frida that existed, she would have done enough to produce a sublime oeuvre," Grimberg remarked in an interview we held with him.[5] Frida was in Detroit with Diego Rivera when she was told her mother was very ill. She returned to Mexico, but she never saw her mother in the hospital, and neither would she see her after she was dead.

Frida was a playful, mischievous, and athletic little girl. Her expression in the photographs taken of her by her father when she was four years old clearly reveals the intelligence she demonstrated from an early age. The attack of polio she suffered at the age of six was a terrible blow, but she managed to overcome it thanks to the strength of character she showed throughout her life and the affectionate support of her father, who encouraged her to practice sports with dedication and discipline. She played soccer, took up boxing and wrestling, and became a swimming champion. She skated and raced along on her bicycle, and she liked to climb trees and go rowing on Chapultepec Lake. She never allowed her physical handicap to interfere with her sporting activity. Besides agility and coordination, she was endowed with extraordinary grace, and as she walked, she would hop along in a way that made her appear to float like a bird in flight.

However, the child prodigy was unable to avoid the childish cruelty of her schoolmates, who called her "Frida Kahlo, *pata de palo* (wooden leg)." Obviously she was greatly affected by this and became withdrawn and introspective, but at the same time she gradually developed a solid awareness of her exceptional nature, and this allowed her to assimilate her troubles and look for a way to bring them under control. Adversity forges the character of those who refuse to be defeated, and Frida belonged to this class of individuals. A strong temperament thus emerged, consolidating itself over the years into a forceful and indomitable personality that managed to turn her misfortune into a lifelong challenge and source of artistic creation.

Frida finished her primary education at a German school and entered the National Preparatory School with a well-proportioned adolescent body, a mind open to knowledge, and a desire to experience life to the fullest. She was one of thirty-three girls among a total of two thousand students in an atmosphere of academic excellence, with first-class teachers in every specialty: Antonio Caso and Samuel Ramos (philosophy), Jaime Torres Bodet and Narciso Bassols (literature), Daniel Cosío Villegas (history), Isaac Ochoterena (biology), and many others. The first headmaster of the school, founded in 1868, was Gabino Barreda, who introduced the positivism of Auguste Comte to Mexico and authored the institution's motto, "Liberty, order, and progress: liberty as medium, order as base, and progress as goal." Positivist philosophy predominated among "the scientists," as the ministers of Porfirio Díaz's government were known. By contrast, both Vasconcelos and Antonio Caso introduced an idealist vision of this philosophy linked to the thought of Henri Bergson, the winner of the Nobel Prize for Literature in 1927, who proposed intuition, conscience, and spiritual energy rather than the empirical materialism of positivism. At the preparatory school, there prevailed an interesting mixture of intellectual debate, artistic creativity, and juvenile rebellion.

Frida's closest companions belonged to the group of "Los Cachuchas," known for the intelligence of some of its members, their interest in books and knowledge, and their fondness for conversation and debate on their many literary and philosophical readings of Mexican, Spanish, French, German, and Russian authors. All were voracious readers. Frida read books in Spanish, German, and English. Los Cachuchas also became famous for their audacious pranks, such as setting off a rocket inside "El Generalito," the ceremonial assembly hall at San Ildefonso decorated with the choir stalls from the former convent of Saint Augustine, while philosopher Caso was delivering a professorial lecture. Although glass was broken and rubble fell from the ceiling, Caso reacted with remarkable aplomb and continued his lecture as though nothing had happened. Those responsible escaped sanctions because they were never identified. Some of those cultured rogues became respectable and noted professionals.

One of them was to become a recognized poet, and Kahlo painted his portrait. *Portrait of Miguel N. Lira* (1927) is influenced by Stridentist art, current in Mexico at that time. It is one of the finest portraits she painted of a figure other than herself [fig. 4]. Shown in profile, the poet's face denotes considerable command of academic style and technique. By contrast, the elements surrounding the writer are painted somewhat naively in order to give the work the "modernist" tone requested by the sitter. Among the objects included by Kahlo are an effigy of Saint Michael the archangel, a reference to the poet's first name; a lyre, the symbol of poetry, which also corresponds to the writer's surname; a hobbyhorse, *dada* in French; a rag doll; and a skull. There are also two erotic allegories introduced with an exquisite sense of humor:

a three-colored pinwheel and a half-open yellow fruit alluding to a volume of poetry by Lira entitled *La guayaba* (*The Guava*, 1927), both visual metaphors for female sexuality. This small picture prefigures the style of Kahlo's self-portraits, where she combines academic skill with a great symbolic wealth of animals, vegetables, fruits, and other objects. That same year, Kahlo also painted the *Portrait of Alicia Galant* [fig. 5].

Another member of Los Cachuchas was Alejandro Gómez Arias, a brilliant orator, lawyer, columnist, and political essayist, who was also Kahlo's first great love. He regularly traveled with her on the bus on which she suffered the tragic accident of September 17, 1925, when it crashed into a streetcar. Miraculously Kahlo did not die, but her body was destroyed:

> Her spinal column was broken in three places in the lumbar region. Her collarbone was broken, and her third and fourth ribs. Her right leg had eleven fractures and her right foot was dislocated and crushed. Her left shoulder was out of joint, her pelvis broken in three places. The steel handrail had literally skewered her body at the level of the abdomen; entering on the left side, it had come out through the vagina.[6]

Kahlo spent a month in the Red Cross Hospital, where her body was literally reassembled, and she remained immobile at her home for another two months.

The most dramatic pictorial testimony to the accident is *The Broken Column* (1944), a startling work that makes an immediate and unforgettable impact on the viewer [fig. 7]. Quoted here is an edited extract from the text written about this painting by the prestigious art historian Teresa del Conde:

> Subtle as she was, exercised in the metaphorical methods practiced by the Surrealists, . . . Frida preferred not to eliminate the corset in this painting, which displays her body from just above the knees, opened in the middle from the neck down to reveal the slender Ionic column broken at several points . . . crowned by a capital with volutes which seems to be supporting her chin. Since the body is perforated, as if it were of cardboard or ceramic, the bands, belts, and braces attached to it . . . seem to be holding it together in "realistic" fashion. The position of the column also suggests a penetration of a phallic type, from below to above, especially if one considers that in the original version of this painting, the body is said to have been naked, with the mons veneris visible. The question arises of why Frida modified it. . . . It could be assumed that Frida wrapped her hips in a loincloth similar to ones used to cover the groin area of Christ figures on crucifixes . . . either to allude indirectly to Christian iconography, or to conceal the mons veneris, pubic hair and all. . . .
>
> It is possible the proportions of the painted body—virtually perfect—in *The Broken Column* correspond to Frida's own: a small waist, perfect, well-placed breasts, separated but not deformed. . . .

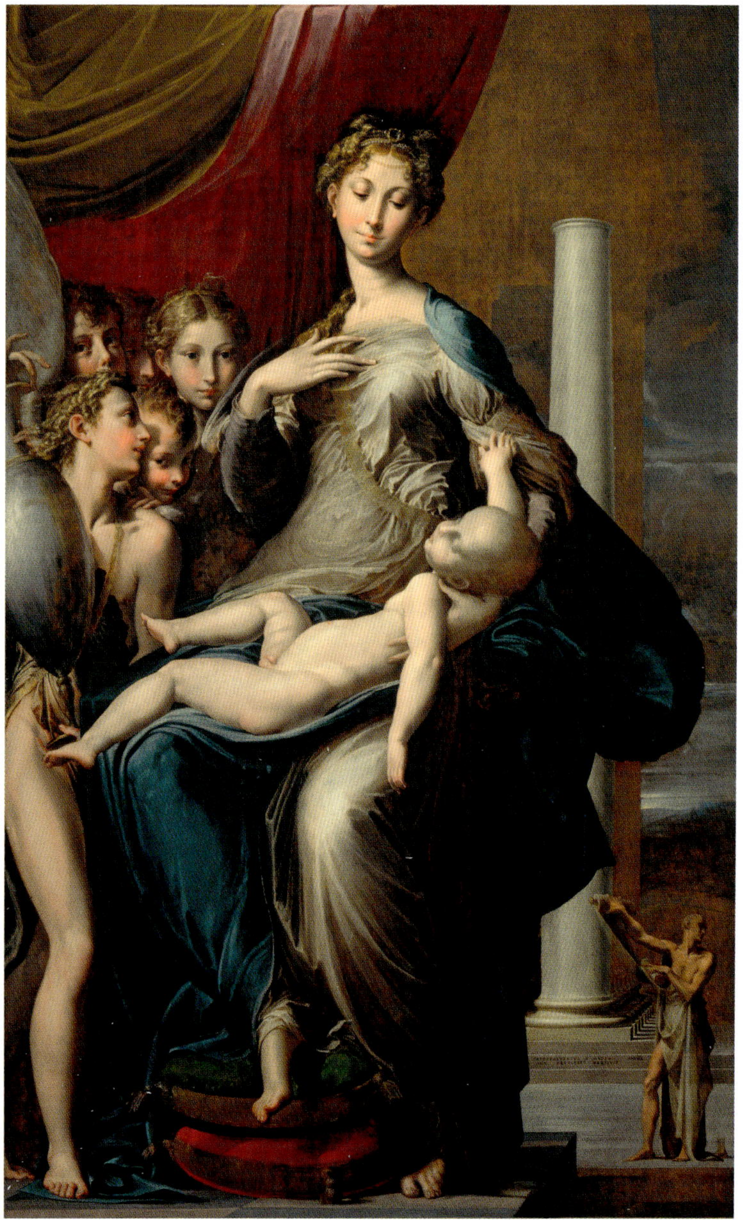

Girolamo Francesco Maria Mazzola, known as Parmigianino, *Madonna with the Long Neck*, 1534–40, oil on panel, 85¼ x 52⅛ in. (216.5 x 132.5 cm). Florence, Gallerie degli Uffizi, Palatina no. 230

> In *The Broken Column* her expression is more vacant and self-absorbed, owing in part to the white tears, which give light to the crystalline ones. . . . The loosened hair softens the contours of the face, framing it and rendering it less severe. . . .
>
> *The Broken Column* is one of the most emblematic autobiographical testimonies in all of Frida's work.[7]

We should like to add a reflection. *The Broken Column* accomplishes the feat of reconciling three concepts that tend to be regarded as incompatible from an aesthetic point of view: horror, beauty, and eroticism. At first sight, we are horrified and even repelled by the image of the woman split down the middle and pierced by a column. In addition to our first impression of the painting's iconography, however, a close observation of its pictorial quality—its composition, line, proportions, color, texture, volume, perspective, depth, and expressive power—allows us to appreciate the picture as a notable technical and artistic achievement. If we further add an iconological analysis of the work, we shall discover the symbolic dimension and the erotic elements of the piece, and so the keys to its beauty.

Although Frida Kahlo never received formal training, much of her work surprises us with an extraordinary technical quality and a fascinating symbolic complexity.

> I never thought about painting until 1926, when I was bedridden because of a traffice accident. I was very bored lying there in bed . . . so I decided to do something. I stole some oils from my father and my mother had a special easel made, since I couldn't sit up. That's how I began to paint.[8]

And that, too, is how she started to create the character of Frida Kahlo, the reinvention of herself. That was the start of the gestation of the artist and the writer, the myth and the legend, the irresistible seductress whose presence captivated everyone who met her, both in her own country and abroad, and whose personality and talent lit up the Mexican cultural panorama of the first half of the twentieth century with the unmistakable expressive force of her work and the passionate authenticity of her life.

Kahlo's first great painting is the exceptional *Self-portrait in a Velvet Dress* (1926), painted only seven months after the accident that left her semiparalyzed in an attempt to win back the love of Alejandro Gómez Arias [fig. 6]. It is considered one of the artist's most beautiful works. The perfect oval of the face is turned a little to the sitter's right, and the profound almond-shaped eyes gaze enigmatically at the viewer. The expression blends self-assurance and seduction with a certain melancholy. The sensuality of the lips prefigures a kiss. The verticality of the slender figure heightens the charm and distinction of Kahlo, here elegantly attired in a carmine dress adorned with gold and black brocade and a V-shaped neckline that accentuates her breasts and the length of her neck, imbuing the picture with a delightful erotic refinement. The influence of Italian Mannerism is clear, especially that of *Madonna with the Long Neck* by Girolamo Francesco Maria Mazzola, called Parmigianino (1503–1540), and so, too, that of Amedeo Modigliani (1884–1920).

Kahlo manages to express *grazia*, that peculiar mixture of elegance and sweetness with a touch of distortion associated with Mannerism, modernized here by Expressionism and the elongation of faces and figures typical of Modigliani. Correct proportion produces beauty but not *grazia*. To achieve the casual virtuosity of grace requires skill and spontaneity, both amply demonstrated in this small and captivating masterpiece. Kahlo gave the picture to Gómez Arias, who was extremely moved. They were reconciled, but did not ultimately marry. In the copious correspondence they kept up during and after their relationship, Kahlo referred to her self-portrait as "your Botticelli," alluding to the Renaissance master's *Birth of Venus*. Gómez Arias kept it hanging in a prominent place in the hall of his house until his death in 1990. The fruit of tragedy and lovelessness, *Self-portrait in a Velvet Dress* marked an early climax in the fascinating development of Frida Kahlo's life and art.

1 Charles Baudelaire. *Oeuvres completes*, ed. Claude Pichois (Paris: Gallimard, 1975), 1: 657.
2 Carlos Fuentes, "Introduction," in Frida Kahlo, *The Diary of Frida Kahlo: An Intimate Self-portrait* (New York: Harry N. Abrams, 1995), 16; and "Entrevista con Carlos Fuentes. Frida amada," in *Yo soy Frida*, ed. Héctor Tajonar (Mexico City: Milenio Diario, 2007), 14.
3 Kahlo, *Diary*, 282.
4 Hayden Herrera, *Frida: The Biography of Frida Kahlo* (London: Bloomsbury, 2018), 12.
5 "Entrevista con Salomon Grimberg. Frida inventada," in *Yo soy Frida*, ed. Héctor Tajonar (Mexico City: Milenio Diario, 2007), 14.
6 Herrera, *Frida*, 49.
7 Teresa del Conde, "The Broken Column," in *Frida Kahlo: National Homage, 1907–2007* (Mexico City: Instituto Nacional de Bellas Artes, 2008), 242–47.
8 Kahlo to Julien Levy, 1938, *Frida by Frida*, ed. Raquel Tibol and trans. Gregory Dechant (Mexico City: Editorial RM, 2006), 191.

1

My Grandparents, My Parents, and I (Family Tree)

1936
Oil and tempera on zinc,
12⅛ x 13⅝ in. (30.7 x 34.5 cm)
New York, Museum of Modern Art,
Gift of Allan Roows, M.D., and B. Mathieu Roos, 102.1976

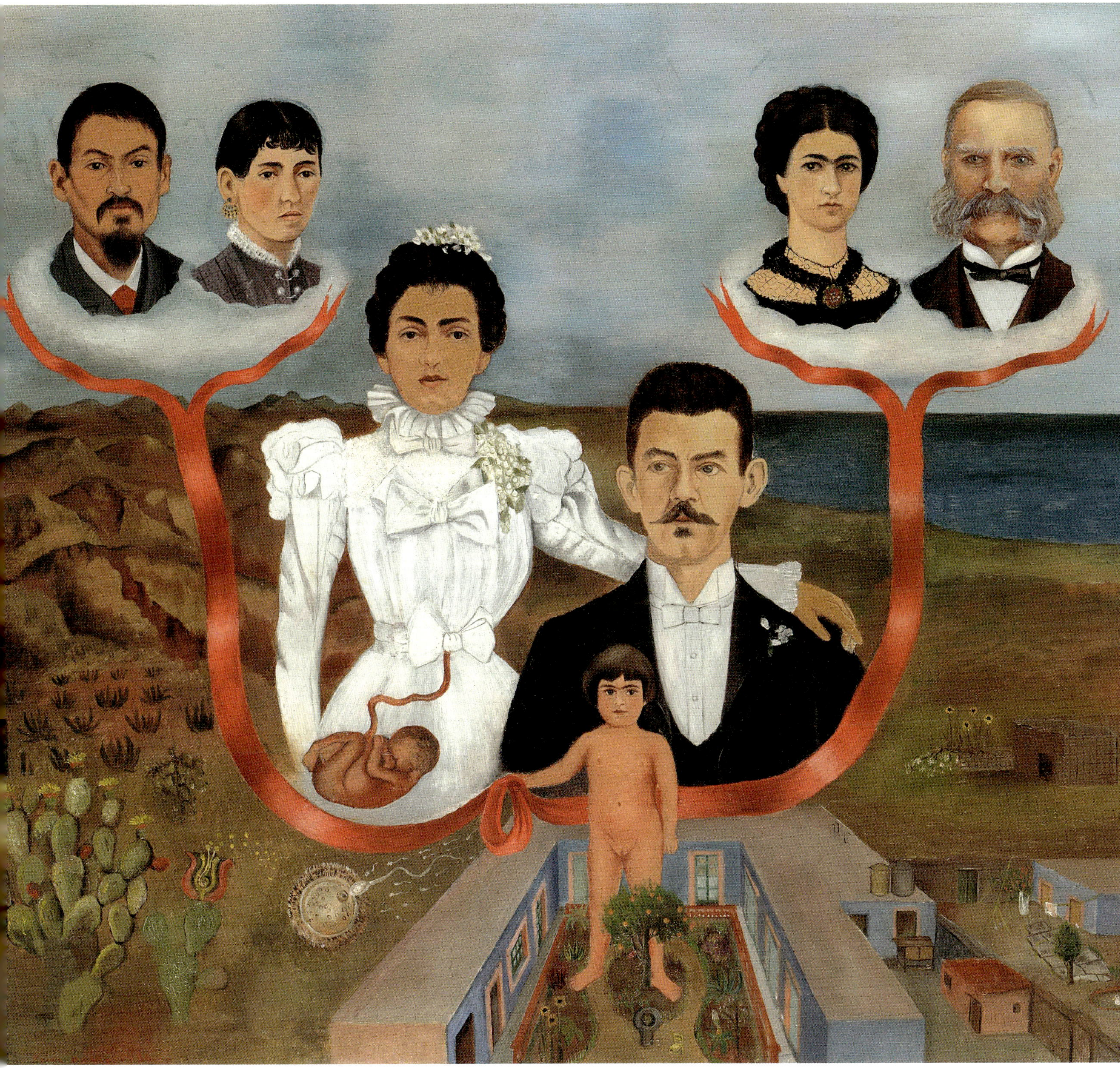

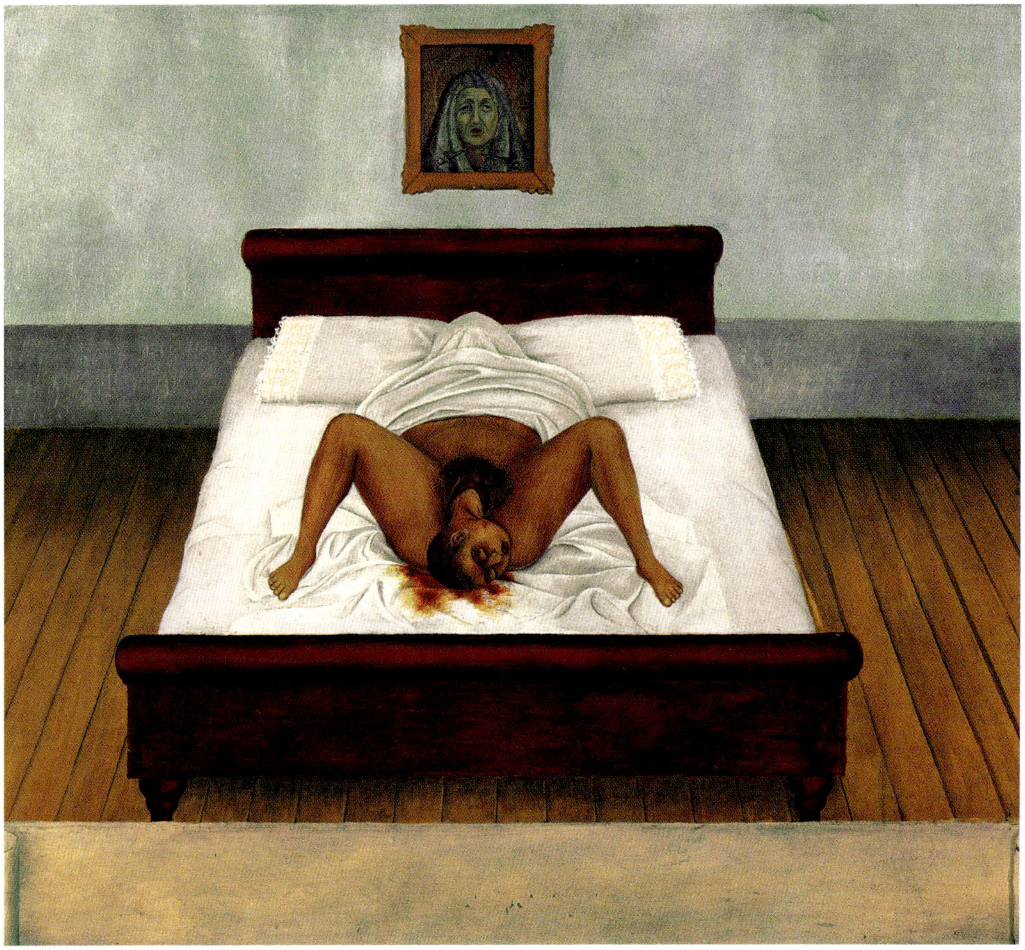

2

My Birth

1932
Oil on metal, 12 x 20⅞ in. (30.5 x 53 cm)
Private collection

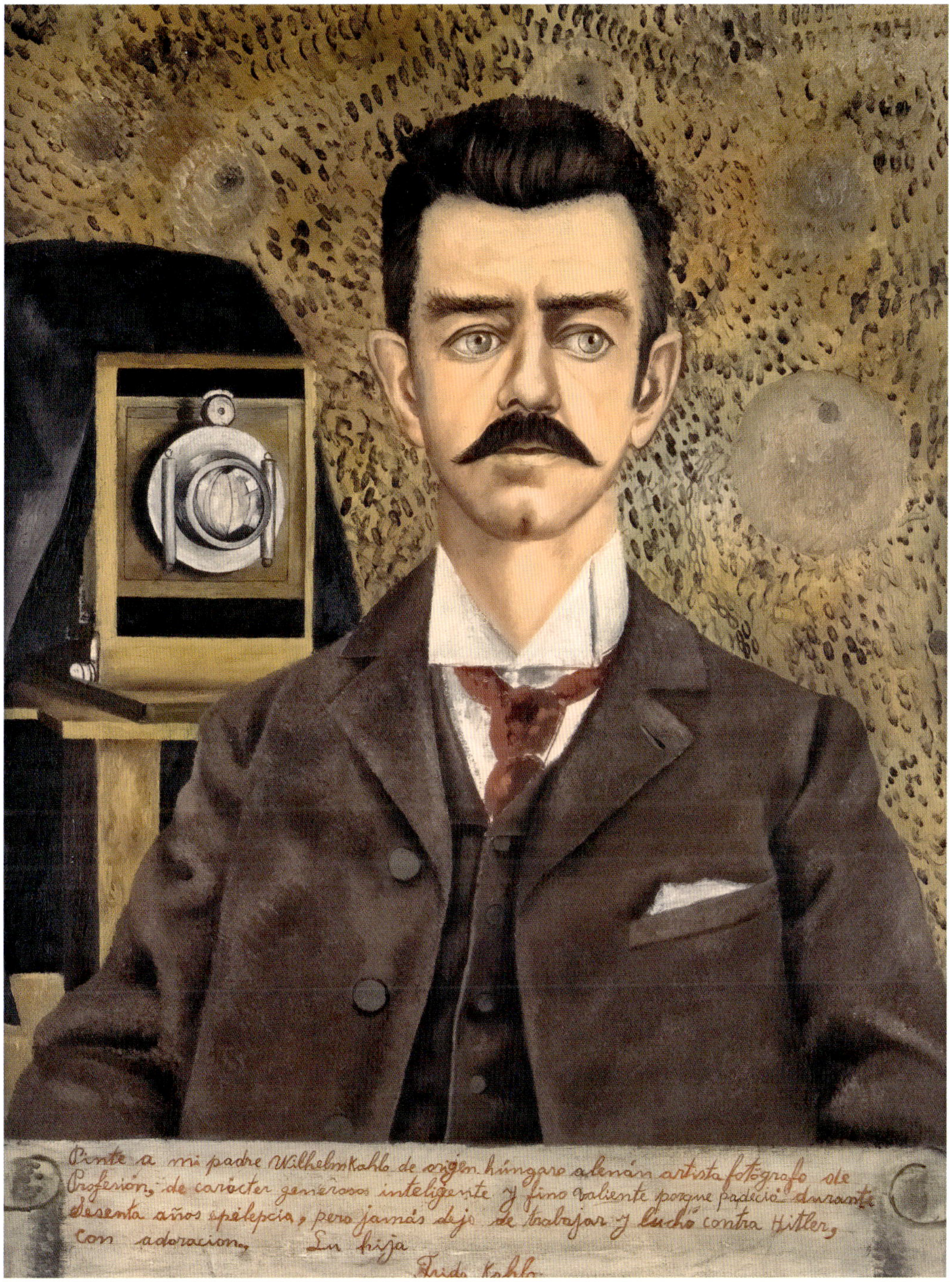

3

Portrait of My Father Wilhelm Kahlo

1952
Oil on canvas, 24 x 18½ in. (61 x 47 cm)
Coyoacán (Mexico City), Museo Frida Kahlo

4

Portrait of Miguel N. Lira

1927
Oil on canvas, 37¾ x 25⅝ in. (96 x 65 cm)
Tlaxcala de Xicohténcatl, Gobierno del Estado de Tlaxcala, Instituto Tlaxcalteca de Cultura, Museo de Arte de Tlaxcala

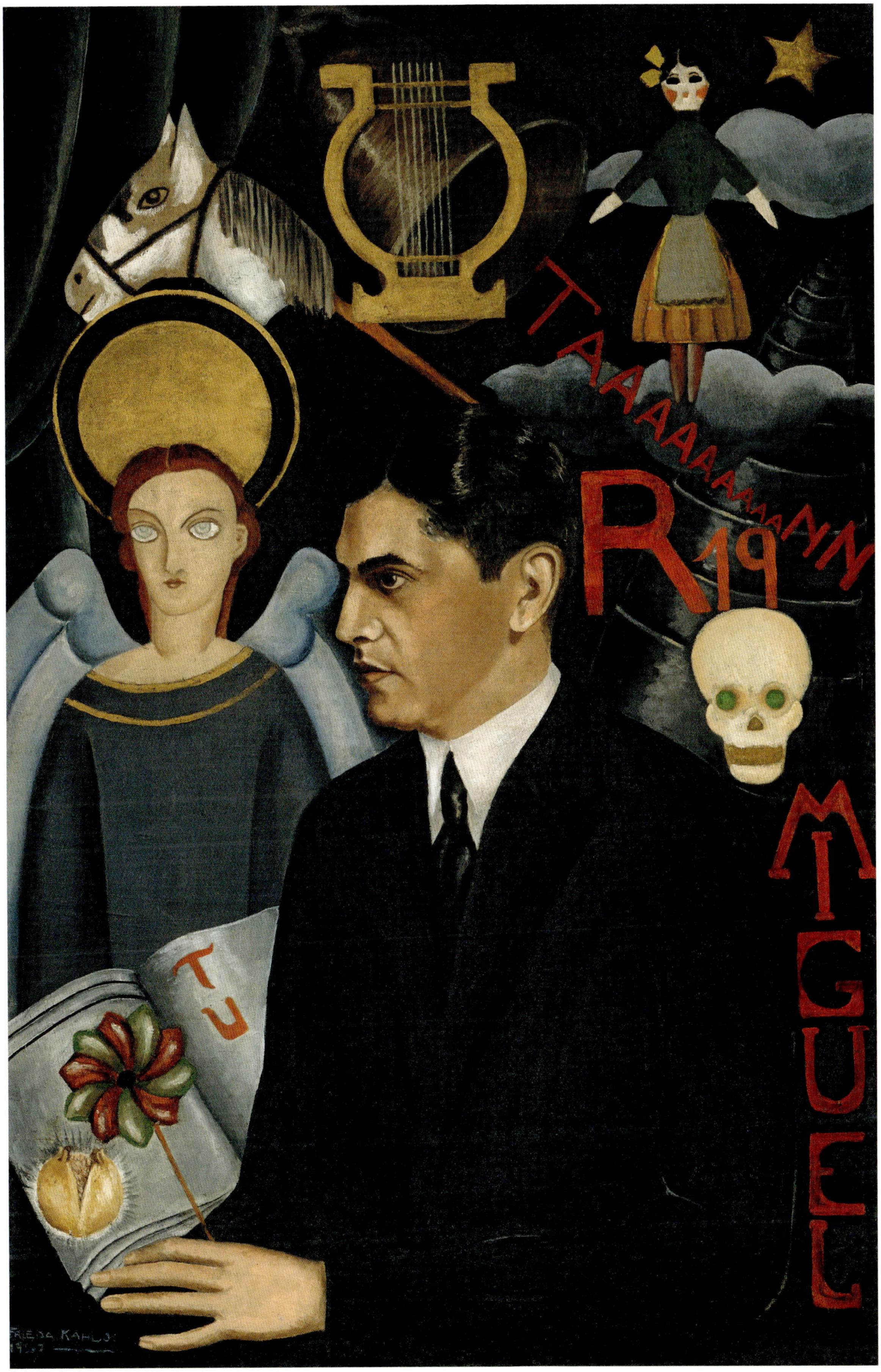
TAAAAAAAAAANN
R19
MIGUEL
TU
FRIEDA KAHLO

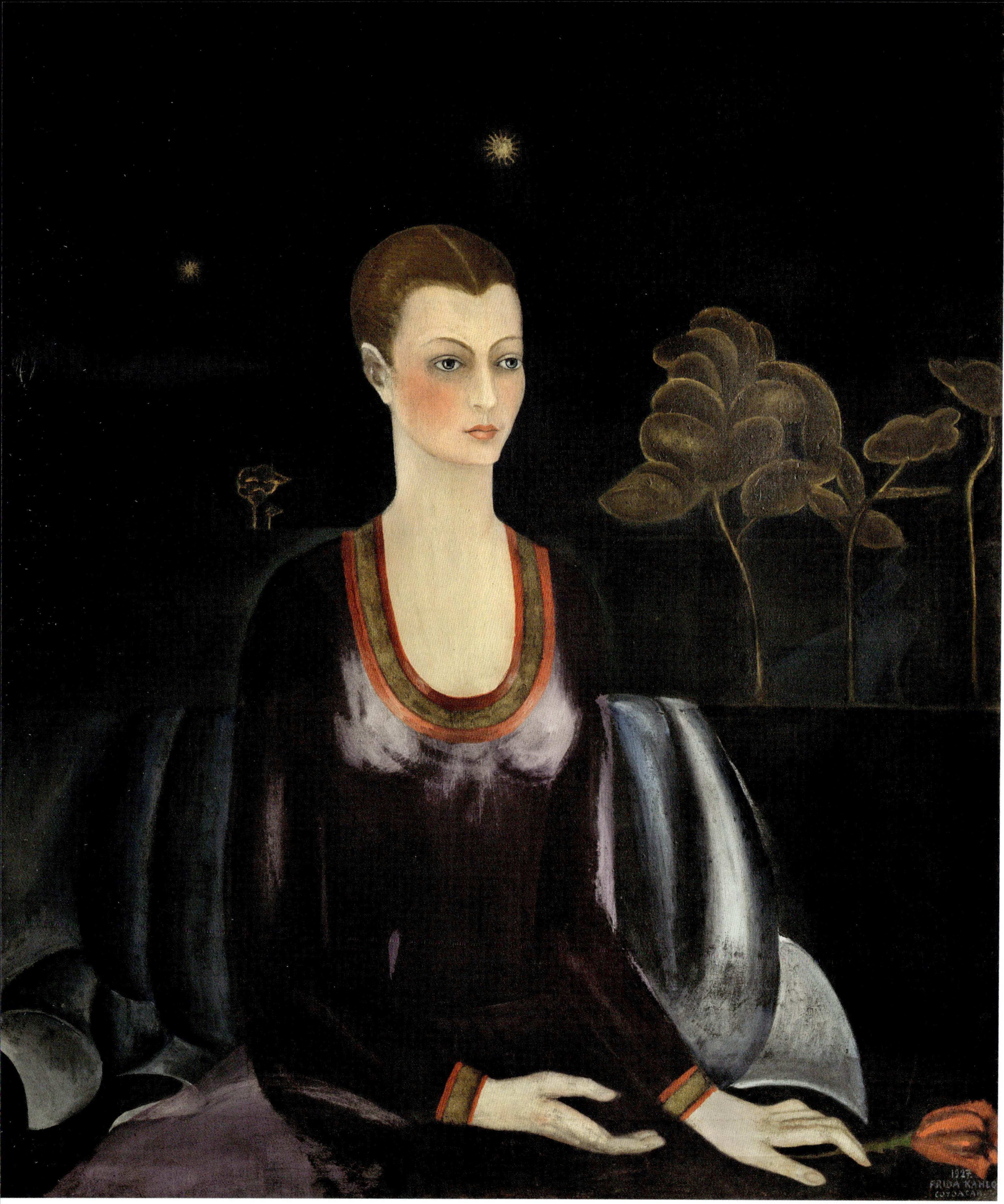
1927

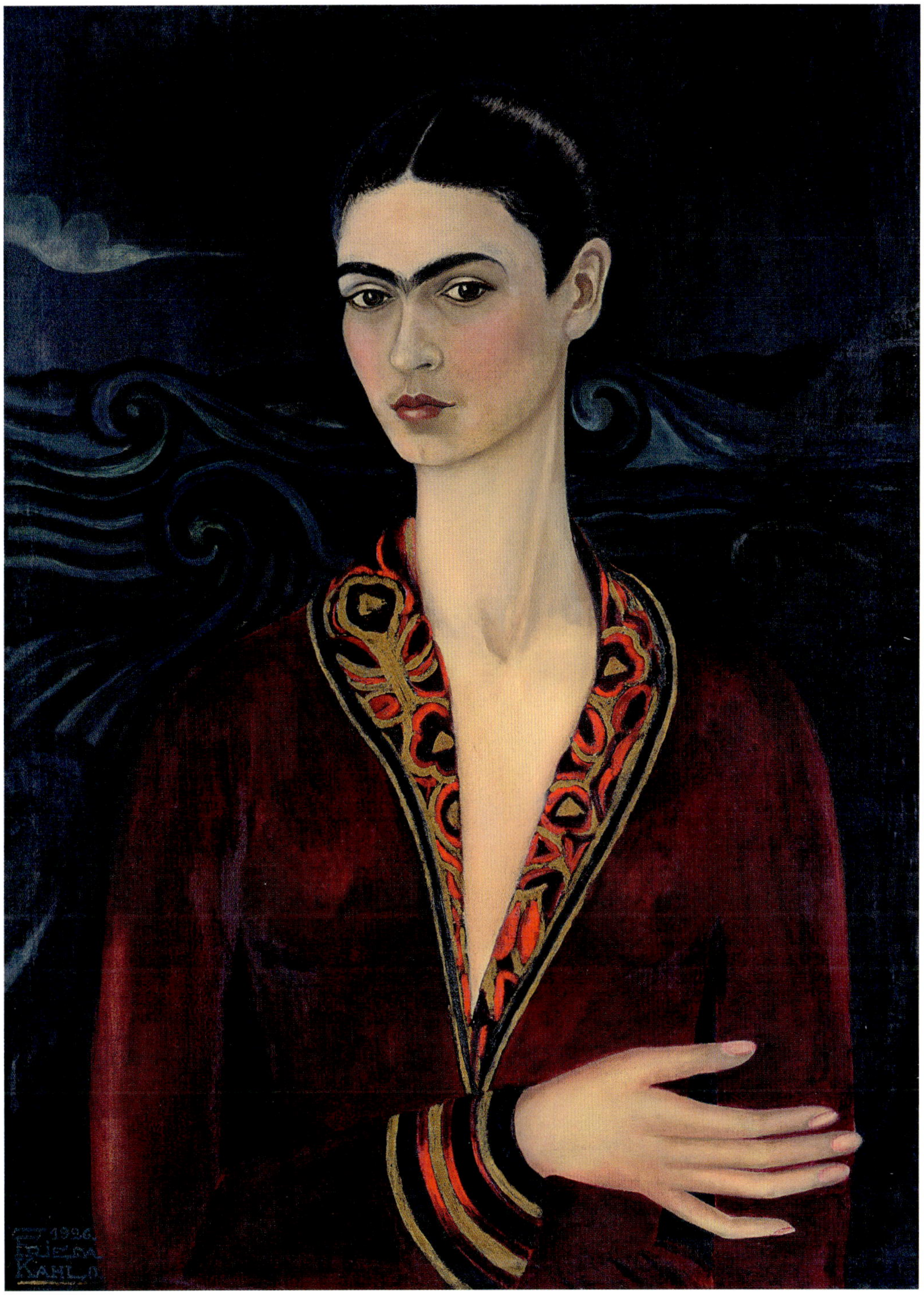

5
Portrait of Alicia Galant

1927
Oil on canvas,
42½ x 36¾ in. (108 x 93.5 cm)
Xochimilco (Mexico City),
Collection Museo Dolores Olmedo

6
Self-portrait in a Velvet Dress

1926
Oil on canvas, 31 x 23 in. (78.7 x 58.4 cm)
Mexico City, private collection

7

The Broken Column

1944
Oil on canvas on Masonite,
15⅔ x 12 in. (39.8 x 30.5 cm)
Xochimilco (Mexico City), Collection
Museo Dolores Olmedo

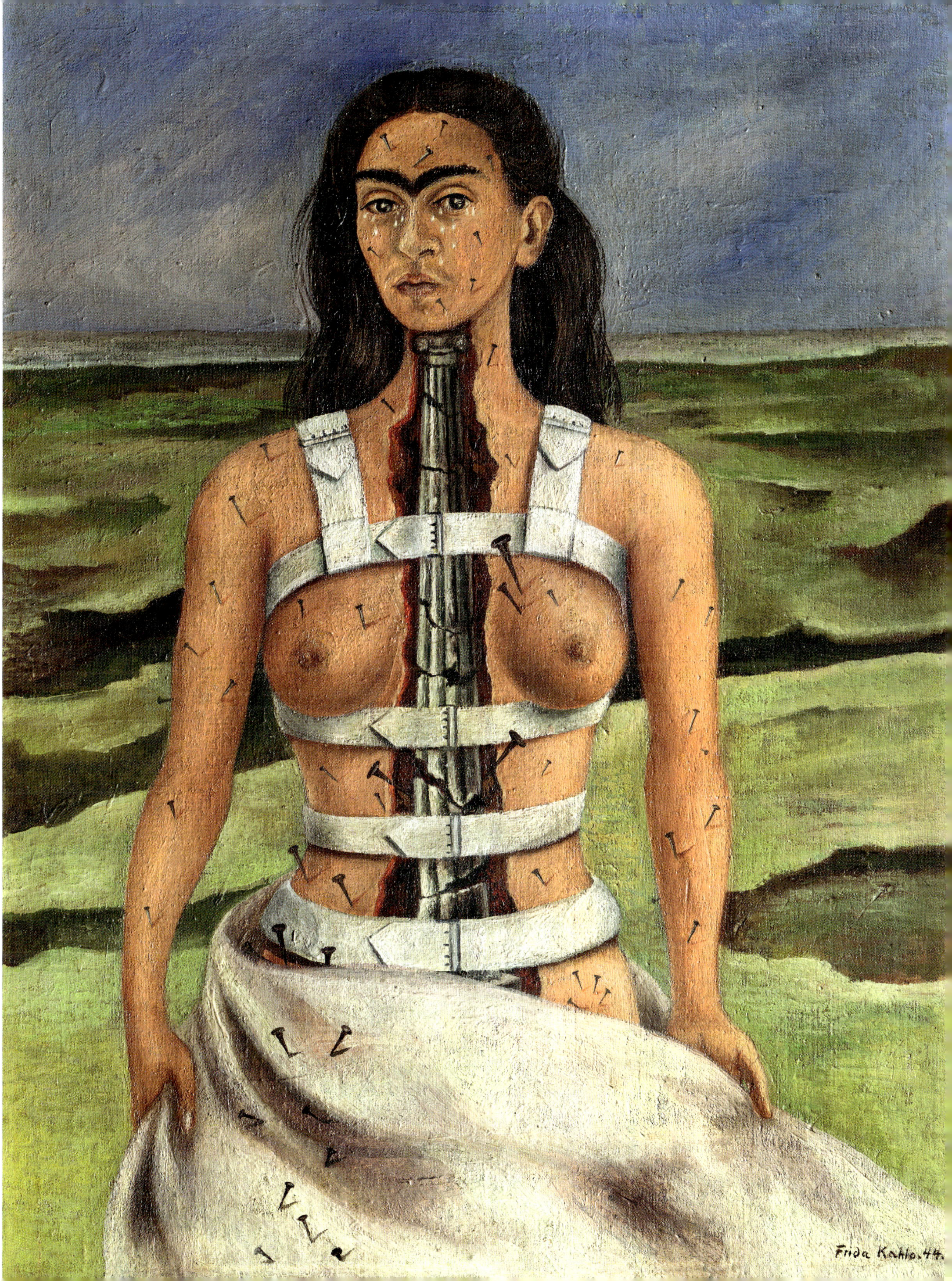
Frida Kahlo.44.

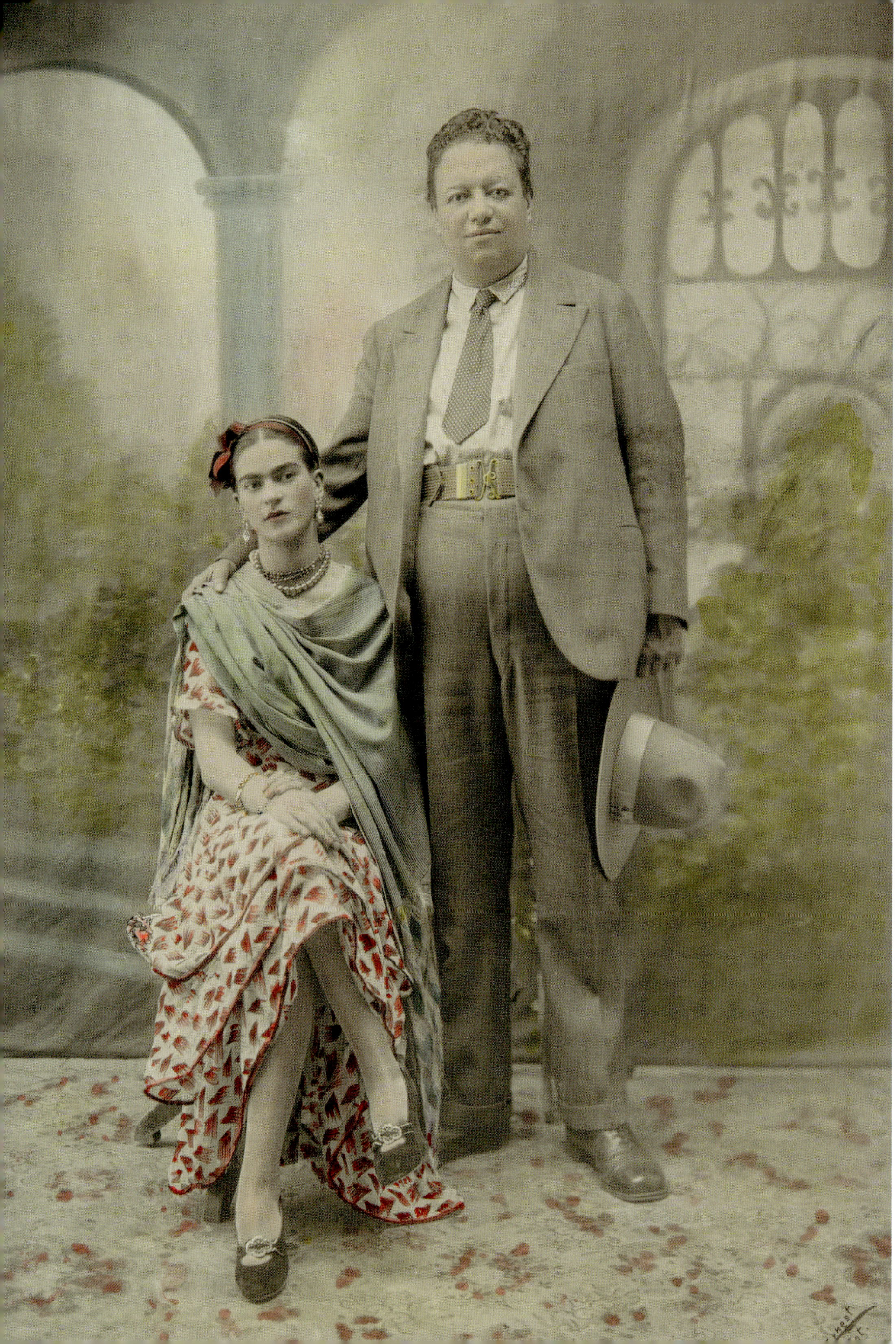

Perennial Love

Because, basically, that is what love is: a declaration of eternity to be fulfilled or unfurled as best it can be within time: eternity descending into time.

Alain Badiou[1]

Love may be best approached as a subspecies of the imagination. . . . When the amorous imagination ricochets back and forth—each person seeing himself as both lover and beloved—a new totality results, an interacting oneness.

Irving Singer[2]

Frida Kahlo and Diego Rivera shared an unbreakable bond that will endure forever. Their passionate love for each other could easily be the stuff of the great romantic literature of the West, with its combination of lyricism, joy, anguish, and grief, as well as betrayal and mutual infidelities. Visually, these two great Mexican artists formed a dissimilar couple. He was twenty years older and as many centimeters (eight inches) taller and weighed seventy kilos (155 pounds) more than she did. However, their souls were truly fused into one. Despite numerous obstacles and the opposition of the bride's mother, who did not attend the ceremony, they were married. This is how Kahlo relates it:

> At seventeen [twenty] I fell in love with Diego, and my [parents] did not like this because Diego was a Communist and because they said he looked like a fat, fat, fat Brueghel. They said that it was like marriage between an elephant and a dove.
>
> Nevertheless, I arranged everything in the court of Coyoacán so that we could be married the 21st of August, 1929. I asked the maid for skirts, the blouse and *rebozo* were also borrowed from the maid. I arranged my foot with the apparatus so that it couldn't be noticed and we got married.

Wedding portrait of Diego Rivera and Frida Kahlo, August 21, 1929. Photograph by Victor Reyes. Boston, Museum of Fine Arts, 2016.112

> No one went to the wedding, only my father, who said to Diego, "Notice that my daughter is a sick person and all her life she will be sick; she is intelligent, but not pretty. Think it over if you want, and if you wish to get married, I give you my permission."[3]

By then, Diego Rivera was already a major personality. He had painted more walls than any of his colleagues and was the most famous and controversial artist in Mexico, not only because of his work but also owing to the legend he built around himself. He described himself as not only an artist but "a man who performs his biological function of producing paintings in the same way a tree produces flowers and fruits."[4] When he painted his murals, he was always surrounded by friends and spectators, whom he would entertain by telling made-up anecdotes. For example, he once said he had experimented with a diet of human meat, particularly the flesh of young girls, which he supposedly ate in tacos. "It's like the tenderest young pig," he said.[5] Some laughed, others doubted the truth of the story, and his detractors, who were fairly numerous, spread the word that Rivera was a cannibal.

The first time that Kahlo approached Rivera was when he was painting the mural *Creation* in the Simón Bolívar Amphitheater, the auditorium at San Ildefonso. Lupe Marín, Rivera's corpulent and temperamental wife (represented as Mother Earth on the main wall of the Rivera Chapel at the Autonomous University of Chapingo), hurled abuse at Kahlo, but she was not intimidated, surprising both Marín and Rivera. Rivera related the incident in his autobiography:

> One night, as I was painting high on the scaffold and Lupe was sitting and weaving down below, there was a loud hubbub. It came from a group of young students shouting and pushing against the auditorium door. All at once the door flew open, and a girl who seemed to be no more than ten or twelve was propelled inside.
>
> She was dressed like any other high school student but her manner immediately set her apart. She had unusual dignity and self-assurance, and there was a strange fire in her eyes. Her beauty was that of a child, yet her breasts were well developed.
>
> She looked straight up at me. "Would it cause you any annoyance if I watched you at work?" she asked.
>
> "No, young lady, I'd be charmed," I said.
>
> She sat down and watched me silently, her eyes riveted on every move of my paint brush. After a few hours, Lupe's jealousy was aroused, and she began to insult the girl. But the girl paid no attention to her. This, of course, enraged Lupe the more. Hands on hips, Lupe walked toward the girl and confronted her belligerently. The girl merely stiffened and returned Lupe's stare without a word.

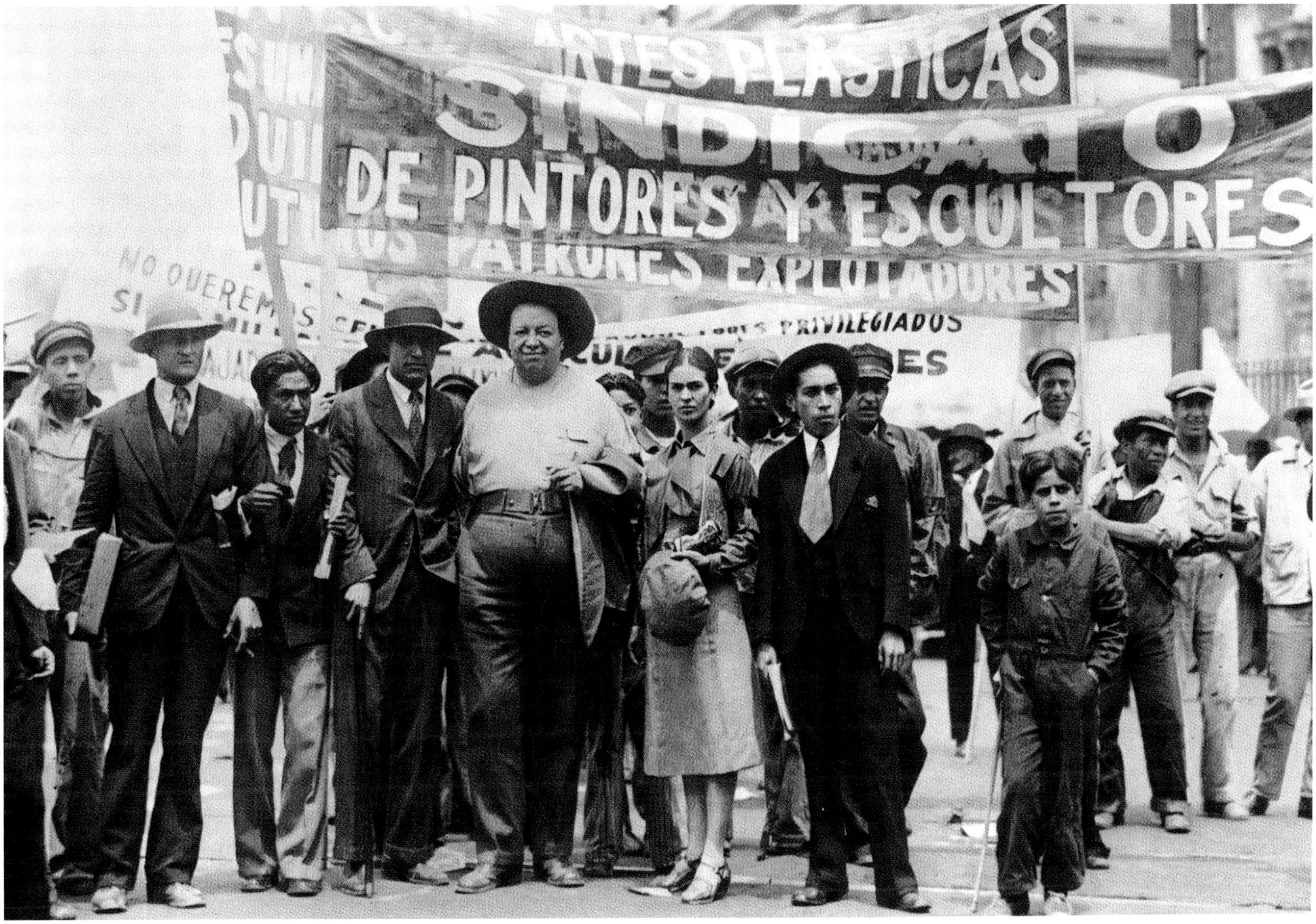

Diego Rivera and Frida Kahlo leading a delegation of the Union of Revolutionary Painters, Sculptors, and Engravers on a Labor Day march, Mexico City, May 1, 1929. Photograph by Tina Modotti

> Visibly amazed, Lupe glared at her a long time, then smiled, and in a tone of grudging admiration, said to me, "Look at the girl! Small as she is, she does not fear a tall, strong woman like me. I really like her."
>
> The girl stayed about three hours. When she left, she said only, "Good night." A year later I learned . . . that her name was Frida Kahlo. But I had no idea that she would one day be my wife.[6]

Kahlo joined the Communist Party at the instigation of Tina Modotti (1896–1942), assistant to the photographer Edward Weston (1886–1958) and lover of exiled Cuban communist revolutionary Julio Antonio Mella. At party headquarters she saw Diego Rivera again, and gradually she gained the master's confidence until they became close

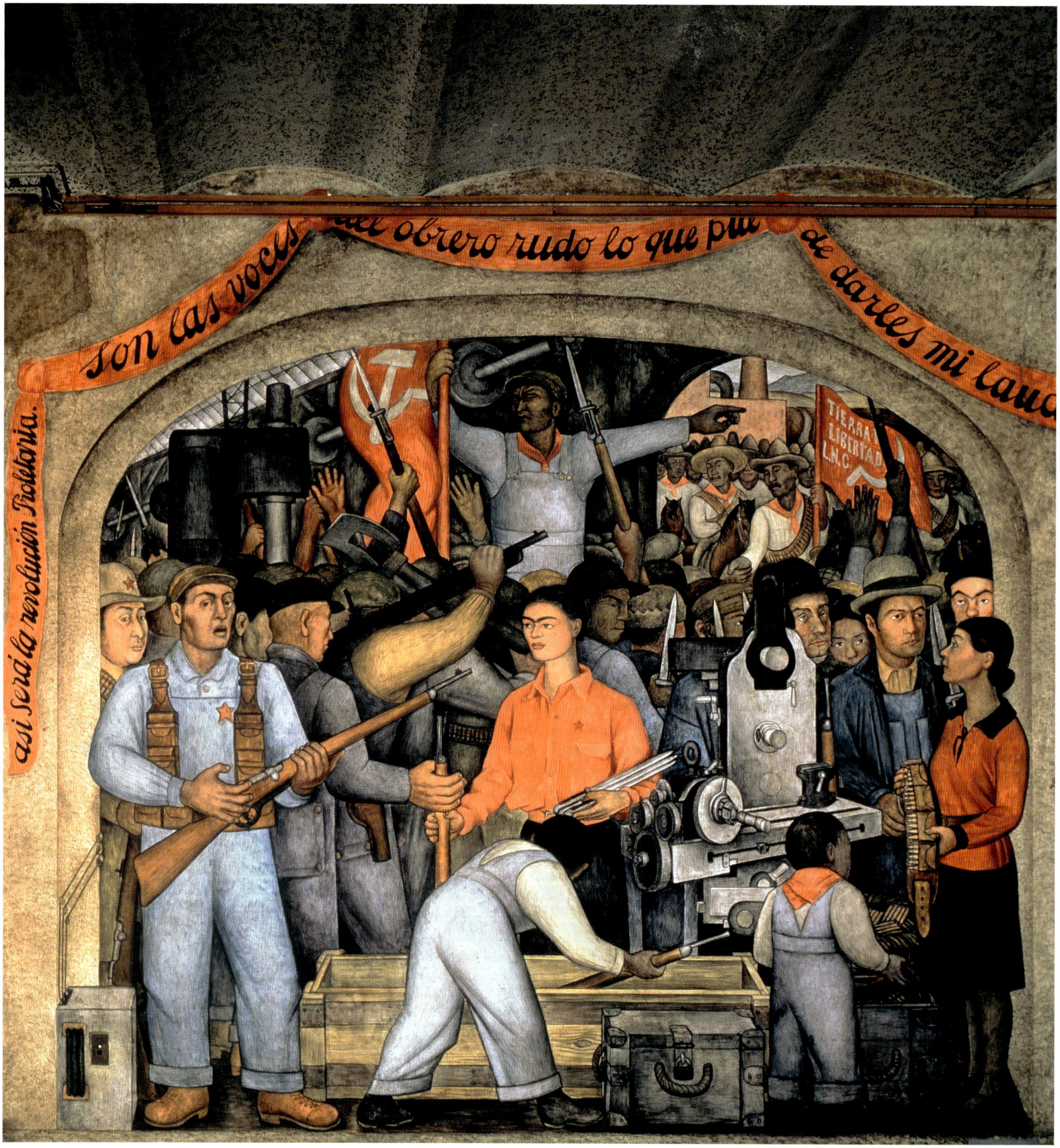
Son las voc
obrero rudo lo que pu
de darles mi lau
así será la revolución Proletaria.
TIERRA
LIBERTAD
L.N.C.

Diego Rivera, *The Arsenal* (from *Corrido of the Revolution*), 1928, fresco, 80 x 156⅔ in. (203 x 398 cm). Mexico City, Public Education Secretariat, south wall of the third floor of the Patio de las Fiestas

associates. The attraction the muralist felt for Kahlo increased until her boldness and peculiar femininity finally seduced him. In 1928, one year before their marriage, Rivera painted Frida Kahlo as the central figure of the mural *The Arsenal*, located on the upper floor of the Patio de las Fiestas (Court of the Feasts) in the Public Education Secretariat. The painting shows the beginning of the workers' struggle, which the peasants join to fight for their rights. In the center of the composition, Kahlo, wearing a red shirt and with a star, the symbol of the revolution, painted on her chest, is supplying the insurrectionists with arms. David Alfaro Siqueiros, Julio Antonio Mella, and Tina Modotti also appear in the mural. From then on, Kahlo embraced communism as an ideology and as a link with Rivera.

The great poet and art historian Luis Cardoza y Aragón spent a week at Kahlo and Rivera's house when Rivera was painting the mural at the Palace of Cortés in Cuernavaca. His fascination with the couple is eloquently expressed in this short statement:

> Frida . . . was grace, energy, and talent united in one of the beings who has most stirred my imagination to enthusiasm. Diego and Frida were part of the spiritual landscape of Mexico, like Popocatepetl and Iztaccihuatl in the valley of Anahuac.[7]

As Kahlo's mentor, Rivera was shrewd enough to encourage and advise her without forcing anything on her, so as not to condition or ruin the artist's innate talent. "Your will must bring you to your own expression," he would say to her.[8] However, it cannot have been easy to rise above the great artistic presence of her husband. She always recognized that Rivera had taught her the revolutionary sense of life and the true meaning of color, among other things. While Kahlo did find her own pictorial style, the influence of Rivera's personality on her concept of life and art is undeniable, particularly the profound sense of Mexican national identity professed by the great muralist. This was immediately reflected in Kahlo's second self-portrait, entitled *Time Flies*, and in *The Bus* (both 1929) [figs. 8 and 9], as well as in *Frieda and Diego Rivera* (1931) [fig. 11].

The contrast between the *Self-portrait in a Velvet Dress* [fig. 6] and *Time Flies* illustrates a drastic shift in Kahlo's manner of painting. The Mannerist and Modiglianiesque features of the first self-portrait completely disappear to make way for a deliberately naive pictorial Mexicanism reminiscent of the votive offerings known as *milagritos* (small miracles) or other manifestations of popular art. In her second self-portrait, Kahlo painted herself frontally with a challenging gaze in her deep black eyes, rouged cheeks, a simple short-sleeved white blouse with lace trimmings, colonial-style Mexican earrings, and an eye-catching pre-Hispanic necklace of green jade. It is a painted self-affirmation of her new identity as a mixed-blood mestiza, Mexican to the core, probably adopted to please Rivera both artistically and personally. There is even a patent innocence in the supposedly symbolic title of the work, with time represented by an alarm clock and flight illustrated by an airplane above the painter's head. Her *Self Portrait* of the following year also presents similar characteristics of sober exoticism [fig. 10].

In *The Bus*, also painted in 1929 in the same intentionally naive style, Kahlo depicted herself as a self-absorbed figure on the far right of the canvas, on board the vehicle she was riding with Alejandro Gómez Arias on the fateful day of September 17, 1925. Her fellow passengers represent emblematic social types sharing the same means of city transport: a housewife, a worker, a peasant woman with a child in her arms, and her other child, with holes in his shoes, seen from behind as he looks out at the city landscape. Kahlo's boyfriend is there, too, wearing a suit, hat, waistcoat, and bowtie and holding a bag that seems to contain coins. Before the accident, she was an ordinary girl with no greater ambition than to win Gómez Arias's love, and she wanted to leave testimony to that nostalgic past that would never return. The new Kahlo had reinvented herself as woman and artist.

Based on a photograph of her wedding, *Frieda and Diego Rivera* reaffirms the artist's decision to adopt an ironclad Mexican persona, here emulating the naive quality of popular art. She replaced the religiosity of small painted votive offerings with the only subject of devotion that marked her life and work, Diego Rivera. The heaviness of the groom, who serenely holds a palette and brushes in his right hand, contrasts with the smallness of the bride, who looks out at the viewer with an expression of pleasure and self-assurance, as if she knew she was going to bring the monster under control. The display of conjugal love is emphasized by a handwritten message on a scroll held by a bird in static flight: "Here you see us, me, Frieda Kahlo, together with my beloved husband, Diego Rivera." She might have added that they would love each other all their lives. This turned out to be true, although their intense, passionate, and profoundly human love had its share not only of great joys but also of suffering and mutual infidelities.

In the midst of this process of artistic transition in search of her own style, it is admirable that Kahlo should have painted the exceptional *Portrait of Luther Burbank* (1931), where her command of line, color, and composition unites with her portentous imagination [fig. 12]. Burbank was an eminent American botanist known as the "Wizard of Horticulture" who grew more than eight hundred enriched varieties of fruits, flowers, and vegetables (with pride of place going to the russet Burbank potato) by means of natural genetic variation of the plants based on the discoveries of Charles Darwin. He is remembered for his generosity and love of nature. Kahlo did not know him personally, but she was moved by the botanist's legacy and his wish to be buried after his death with no coffin beneath a cedar in the garden of his Santa Barbara, California, home. She therefore chose to depict him emerging from the earth, fused with the trunk of the tree whose roots are fed by his own buried corpse. It is a way of representing

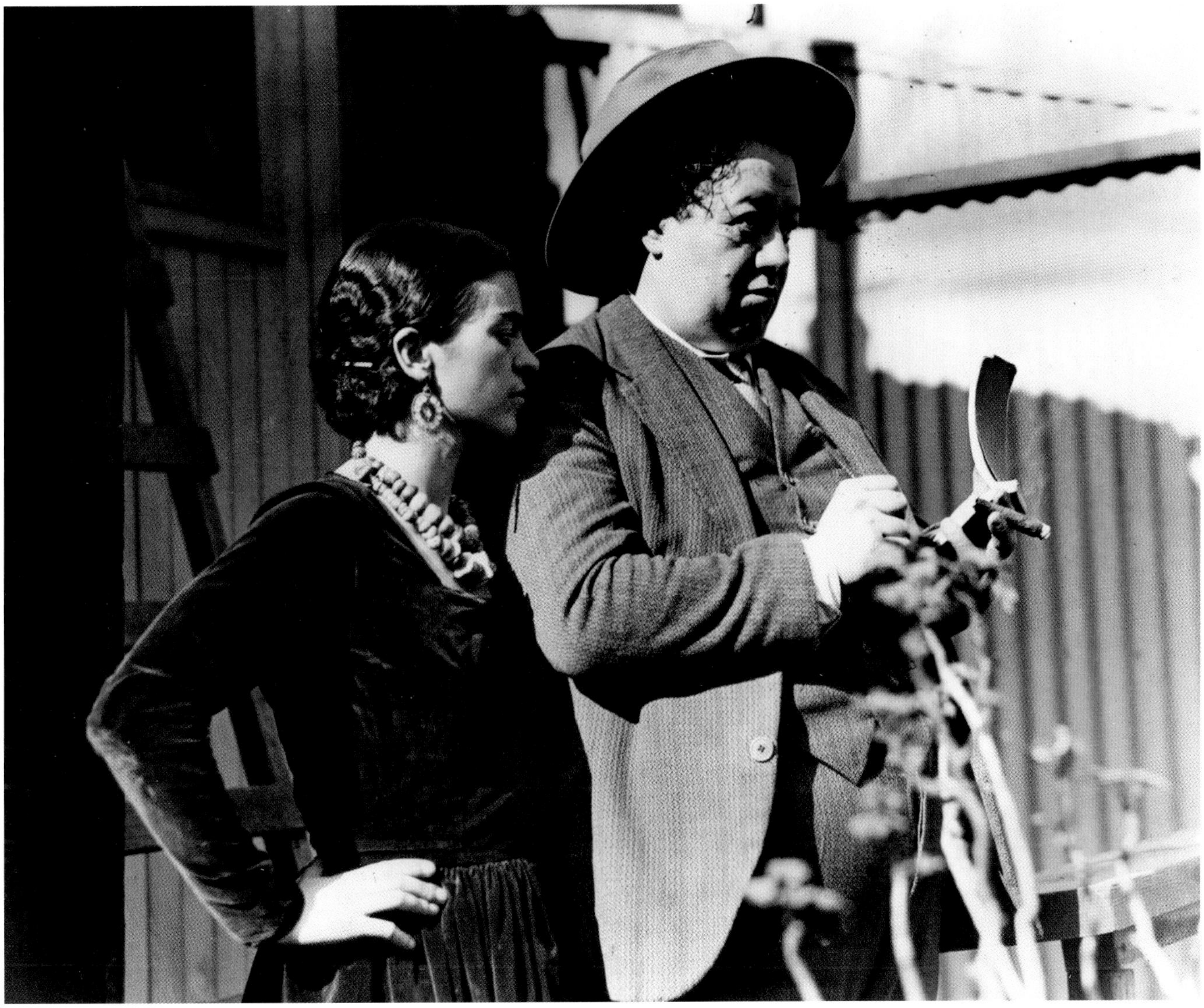

Diego Rivera records his first impressions of San Francisco, 1930. New York, Museum of Modern Art, The New York Times Collection, 2148.2001

the life cycle while symbolizing the cyclical concept of the universe, as found in pre-Hispanic myths and those of many other ancient cultures, in which life and death are part of an uninterrupted process of creation and destruction. This is one of the masterpieces in Kahlo's production, a fact she acknowledged by including it in the two most important exhibitions of her paintings, in New York (1938) and Paris (1939).

In November 1930, Kahlo and Rivera went to the United States so that Rivera could fulfill some commitments there. His reputation in that country was on the rise, and he was keen to take advantage of the opportunities that had opened up to him. He painted two murals in San Francisco: *Allegory of California* in the Luncheon Club of the Pacific Stock Exchange and *The Making of a Fresco Showing the Building of a City* at the California School of Fine Arts. As soon as Rivera completed the second of these works, the couple had to return to Mexico in June 1931 because President Pascual Ortiz Rubio had asked Rivera to finish the mural on the staircase of the National Palace. Their return was a short one, as the Museum of Modern Art (MoMA) in New York organized a retrospective exhibition on the work of Diego Rivera that ran from December 22, 1931, to January 27, 1932. This was a great honor for the Mexican painter, who was the second artist to have a solo exhibition at the MoMA, preceded only by Henri Matisse (1869–1954). Made up of 143 pictures, watercolors, and drawings, together with six transportable frescoes, the show was a resounding success, and was visited by 56,575 people. Rivera became a great celebrity in the United States. All this meant a radical change of lifestyle for Kahlo, who had never traveled abroad before. Lavish receptions and parties were held for the couple and attended by the country's financial and cultural elite, headed by John D. Rockefeller Jr., and by the president of the MoMA, A. Conger Goodyear, who struck up a great friendship with Kahlo. Abby Aldrich Rockefeller, John's wife, also became a friend and a patron of the muralist's work.

Kahlo also began a relationship of great affection and trust with her physician Leo Eloesser, who became her correspondent and confidant. In her peculiar style, Kahlo told him bluntly what she thought of "Gringoland":

> I don't like the *high society* here at all and I feel a bit of indignation at all these moneybags around here, as I've seen thousands of people in the most terrible poverty, without anything to eat or anywhere to sleep, it's what has struck me most here, it's frightful to see the rich throwing *parties* day and night while thousands and thousands of people are dying of hunger. . . .
>
> To tell you the truth, I'm [sic] just don't feel at home here, as the servants say, but I have to make the best of it and stay.[9]

Besides Kahlo's compassion for those affected by the social devastation caused by the economic depression of 1929, there was a conflict between Diego Rivera's communist convictions, expressed explicitly in the murals he painted in the United States, and his professional, commercial, and social dealings with the New York financial elite. These tensions eventually erupted. The murals painted at the Detroit Institute of Arts, unveiled in March 1933, had caused considerable public controversy. Nevertheless, Edsel Ford, the son and heir of Henry Ford and the sponsor of the project, came out in support of Rivera: "I really believe he was trying to express his idea of the spirit of Detroit."[10] Weeks later, the young Nelson Rockefeller, who knew the Detroit murals and the criticisms they had received, signed a contract with Rivera for the execution of a mural at Rockefeller Center, recently inaugurated on Manhattan's Fifth Avenue. It was strange that a mural for one of the emblematic buildings of American capitalism should have been commissioned from an artist known for his communist sympathies, but that is what occurred. The muralist gave his project a title: *Man at the Crossroads Looking with Hope and High Vision to the Choosing of a New and Better Future.* Both the title and the sketches presented by the artist were enthusiastically accepted by the patron of the project, and the painter started work immediately. The media began to criticize the magnate John D. Rockefeller Jr., Nelson's father, for paying Rivera's bill while the artist was spreading communist ideas, and this caused some tension at Rockefeller Center. In response, the muralist decided to depict a workers' leader with the face of Lenin. In May 1933, Nelson Rockefeller asked him to replace the image with that of an unknown person, since the portrait of the Soviet leader might "seriously offend a great many people."[11] Rivera refused, alleging that this would destroy the whole concept of the work. A few days later, an official from Rockefeller Center arrived with several bodyguards and ordered the artist to step down from the scaffolding. The official handed him a check for the remainder of the agreed upon amount, together with a letter informing him that the contract had been rescinded and work must stop immediately. Surprised, the artist had to leave the premises. The mural was sealed up and destroyed. In December 1933, Rivera and Kahlo returned to their country, and the muralist was offered a chance by the Mexican government the following year to reproduce the work demolished in New York on the west wall of the third floor of the Palacio de Bellas Artes.

For Kahlo, the time spent in the United States prompted a mixture of disparate experiences and feelings—a miscarriage, an intense social life, loneliness, confusion, nostalgia—which, as always, stimulated her artistic creativity. Among the works that came out of the terrible experience of the miscarriage, two are especially notable. In *Henry Ford Hospital* (1932), Kahlo expressed one of the saddest moments of her life with heartrending valor and aesthetic rigor [fig. 14]. The artist lies nude on the bloodstained sheet of a bed in the sanatorium. Falling from her left eye is a tear that covers nearly her whole cheek, and from her belly, still swollen from the pregnancy, there emerge veinlike strings that lead to six objects, three of them floating above the bed and three resting beneath it. In the center, suspended in the air over her wounded body, a large fetus with male sexual organs represents the longed-for "Dieguito," who would now never come. In the upper right part of the picture is a snail, a lunar symbol, protruding from its shell like a dangling penis to signify fertility and periodic regeneration in a perpetual cycle of death and rebirth. In Aztec mythology, Tecciztecatl, the moon god, is represented inside a shell. Like other mollusks, the snail is a sexual symbol related also to the vulva, flesh, movement, and slime. Most snails are hermaphrodites, and their coupling is one of the most fascinating erotic rituals in the animal kingdom. Kahlo obviously knew the symbolism of the snail and used it consciously. To the left of the fetus, a salmon-colored torso was included to visualize "my idea of explaining the insides of a woman,"[12] to use Kahlo's own expression, as though the process of conception were being viewed through X-rays. The orchid that appears in the lower center of the composition is a reference to the one given to her by Diego in the hospital, and denotes, in Kahlo's words, "a sexual thing mixed with the sentimental."[13] On the right is a female pelvis, an image of the bone that was fractured in three places by the steel handrail that pierced her and exited through her vagina during her tragic accident of 1925, occasioning her inability to give birth to a child. At the lower left edge of the picture is an iron apparatus in reference to the decomposed machinery to which her desecrated female anatomy was reduced. Glimpsed on the horizon is the industrial complex of Rouge River, as distant as Diego was when she was in the hospital. The bed floating in the air emphasizes the desolation, anguish, and despair suffered by Kahlo as a result of this devastating experience.

The following year, the artist painted *Self-portrait with Necklace* (1933), one of her most sober studies of herself [fig. 15]. Here, Kahlo is all eyes. The joined eyebrow, the down over her lip, and the black hair tied back all enhance the depth of her look of sorrow contained with resignation and fortitude and attenuated only by the red of her lips and cheeks. The plain background harmonizes with the rich color of the pre-Hispanic necklace of jade beads. Jade was the sacred stone of the Mesoamerican civilization, associated with the origin of the universe, corn, power, life, and the afterlife.

In the lithograph *Frida and the Miscarriage* (1932), the artist shows herself nude and in a standing position, as if she were a doll, to illustrate the different phases of pregnancy [fig. 13]. The left side of her body is more darkly shaded than the right, an allusion to the duality of life and death. Inside her uterus is an embryo from which there emerges a vein that coils around her right leg and connects with the umbilical cord of a more developed fetus in a vertical position; this fetus is the size of her leg and nearly identical to the one in *Henry Ford Hospital*. Shown above the fetus are two phases in the process of fertilization of an egg and formation of a zygote. Emerging from the figure's left shoulder is a third arm that holds a palette, perhaps to insinuate that owing to the impossibility of bearing a child, Kahlo will give birth to artworks instead. Overhead, a circular moon with a face drawn on it in profile sheds tears upon seeing the weeping face of the inert Kahlo. The hemorrhage produced by the miscarriage, which occurred before the twentieth week of pregnancy, is represented in the lithograph as a row of small drops running down the inside of the thigh, shin, and foot until it joins the earth, where it fertilizes three plants rooted in the ground. This is a poignant way of accentuating the unnaturalness of her inability to procreate. Like *Henry Ford Hospital*, this work is a visual metaphor of frustrated maternity. In an eloquent passage, Diego Rivera declared his recognition and admiration for the quality of Kahlo's work, and for the way she had transformed her personal tragedy into stark poetry, earning her a prominent place in the history of painting:

> [Frida] began work on a series of masterpieces which had no precedent in the history of art—paintings which exalted the feminine qualities of endurance of truth, reality, cruelty, and suffering. Never before had a woman put such agonized poetry on canvas as Frida did at this time in Detroit.[14]

Apart from the torment caused by the miscarriage, the homesickness and discomfort Kahlo felt in the United States led her along a path of reflection upon her identity as a Mexican woman. From that introspection came *Window Display in a Street in Detroit* (1931–32) [fig. 17] and two marvelous pictures, *Self-portrait on the Border Line between Mexico and the United States* and *My Dress Hangs There* [figs. 16 and 18].

In *Self-portrait on the Border Line between Mexico and the United States* (1932), Kahlo places herself in the center of the composition, standing on a pedestal that indicates the border that divides—and joins—the two nations. Dressed in an elegant pink dress and a necklace of coral and jade, she has a Mexican flag in her left hand and a cigarette in her right. On the left-hand side of the picture, Mexico is represented by a pre-Hispanic pyramid illuminated by the sun, the moon, and a lightning bolt. There is also a broken-down stone wall together with three pre-Columbian sculptures: a Colima warrior, a fertility goddess, and a fallen cranium from an ancient Mexican *tzompantli* (skull rack). By contrast, the side of the United States is represented by images of industrialization, modernity, and progress. The American flag floats above smoking factory chimneys, skyscrapers, machinery, and industrial conduits. In the lower part of the picture, the two worlds seem to merge: flowers and vegetables sprout on the Mexican side, while emerging from the right are an electric fan, lamp, and megaphone. The disparity could not be greater or more disturbing. Kahlo has no doubts about the place she prefers, but she does question herself about her location, even if temporary, on the side of civilization and the future of the world.

Kahlo's critical and pessimistic view of Mexico and its relationship with the United States is expressed in another letter to her doctor:

> Mexico is as always, disorganized and gone to the devil, it has nothing left but the great beauty of the land and of the Indians. Everyday [sic] the ugliness of the United States steals a little piece of it, it's sad, but people have to eat and there's no help for the fact that the big fish eats up the little one.[15]

My Dress Hangs There (1933–1939) is one of Frida Kahlo's most important works, owing to the originality of the composition, its technical innovations (she used collage and photomontage integrated with oil paints), and its aesthetic and political commitment laced with a sense of humor. Since the artist is absent from the picture, set in New York City, she makes evident the emotional distance she feels from the United States, creating a devastating visual critique of American capitalism. She does so with a degree of formal and conceptual complexity unseen until then and seldom equaled in the overall context of her oeuvre. She took six years to finish this small masterpiece, a unique case in her entire production. She started it during the last year of her stay in the United States, and she finished it the year of her divorce from Diego Rivera.

In spite of its small format, *My Dress Hangs There* is of an astounding iconographic and symbolic richness. In the lower center of the composition, a Tehuana dress with colors alluding to the Mexican flag hangs from a cord tied to two symbolic objects on columns that give the composition symmetry: a toilet, as a scatological joke on the "gringo" obsession with cleanliness, and a trophy, as mockery of the culture's veneration of sports. Located in the upper left corner, Trinity Church has a stained-glass window with a crucifix traversed by a red *S* to form a dollar sign, emphasizing the link between Protestantism and capitalism. Hanging in front is a huge and slightly torn poster with an effigy of Mae West, the famous actress, singer, sex symbol, and icon of American show business, whom Diego Rivera once described as "the most wonderful machine for living I have known—unfortunately on the screen only."[16] Beneath her are some buildings in flames, perhaps an allusion to the ephemeral nature of luxury, fame, and frivolity. Seen behind Kahlo's dress is a forest of impersonal buildings full of tiny windows. On one of them is a huge telephone, and on another an enormous clock. Time is money.

In the upper center of the picture, just above the hanging dress, rises Federal Hall, the first capitol of the United States, where George Washington, whose statue appears on the steps of the Neoclassical building, was sworn in as the first president of the United States in 1789. To simulate steps, Kahlo used a collage technique, sticking on graph paper with an accountant's log of million-dollar investments. At the base of the composition, she also used photomontage to represent the lonely masses lining up for food, marching as soldiers, or wandering about like ants to attend a sporting event. These masses of tiny gregarious creatures support the entire urban, industrial, and financial structure of Manhattan. Besides her satire on the dehumanization of New York, Kahlo adds a biting critique of the culture of waste, symbolized by a huge trash can brimming with garbage that conspicuously includes a heart, a hand, and some bleeding entrails. Arranged above this are buildings, factories, chimneys, and humanoid tubes in the style of Giorgio de Chirico (1888–1978). Everything is cold and inert, nothing is alive, and human beings are absent from the painting, as Kahlo is from her dress—as far away as the Statue of Liberty lost on the horizon.

The period in the United States saw a growing distance between the couple, and this was to become aggravated after their return to Mexico. Nevertheless, Rivera and Kahlo were always the apple (or "half orange," as we say in Mexico) of each other's eye. They might have been a single being, analogous to the androgyne (man-woman) described by Aristophanes in Plato's *Symposium* (ca. 385–370 B.C.E.), who was split into two different sexes by the gods in order to curb the creature's arrogance. Once divided, each half missed the other, and when they were reunited, "they threw their arms around one another and embraced, in their longing to grow together again."[17] Rivera and Kahlo, too, were inseparable and indomitable. Theirs was a love-hate relationship, painful for Kahlo, but they loved and needed each other, besides professing mutual admiration.

Kahlo was a great writer as well as a painter. She left evidence of this in her illustrated diary, in her abundant letters, and in other texts that show us her passion for language—the artist's thoughts, poems, and dreams—her lively and spontaneous talent for narrative, and her delightful sense of humor. The diary covers the decade from 1944 to 1954 and includes texts that reveal her adoration for Diego Rivera, like this one:

> *Diego* beginning
> *Diego* builder
> *Diego* my child
> *Diego* my boyfriend
> *Diego* painter
> *Diego* my lover
> *Diego* "my husband"
> *Diego* my friend
> *Diego* my mother
> *Diego* my father
> *Diego* my son
> *Diego* = *me* =
> *Diego* Universe
> *Diversity within* unity.[18]

1 Alain Badiou and Nicolas Truong, *In Praise of Love*, trans. Peter Bush (New York: The New Press, 2012), 47.
2 Irving Singer, *The Nature of Love: Plato to Luther* (Cambridge: The MIT Press, 2009), 16–22.
3 Hayden Herrera, *Frida: The Biography of Frida Kahlo* (London: Bloomsbury, 2018), 99.
4 Diego Rivera, "Detroit Dinámico, una interpretación," in Diego Rivera, *Textos de arte*, ed. Xavier Moyssén (Mexico City: Instituto de Investigaciones Estéticas (UNAM), 1986), 177–78.
5 Diego Rivera quoted in Herrera, *Frida*, 81.
6 Diego Rivera with Gladys March, *My Art, My Life: An Autobiography* (Garden City: Dover Publications, 1991), 75–76.
7 Luis Cardoza y Aragón quoted in Herrera, *Frida*, 105–6.
8 Diego Rivera quoted in Herrera, *Frida*, 95.
9 Kahlo to Leo Eloesser, November 26, 1931, and July 29, 1932, *Frida by Frida*, ed. Raquel Tibol and trans. Gregory Dechant (Mexico City: Editorial RM, 2006), 105 and 123.
10 Edsel Ford quoted in Herrera, *Frida*, 161.
11 Nelson Rockefeller quoted in Herrera, *Frida*, 165.
12 Herrera, *Frida*, 144.
13 Herrera, *Frida*, 145.
14 Rivera, *My Art, My Life*, 123–24.
15 Kahlo to Eloesser, June 14, 1931, *Frida by Frida*, 105.
16 Diego Rivera quoted in Anita Brenner, "Career of Rivera Marked by Strife; Many of His Pictures, Like That in RCA Building, Refer to Class Struggles," *The New York Times*, May 14, 1933.
17 Plato, *The Symposium*, trans. Walter Hamilton (Harmondsworth: Penguin, 1988), 61.
18 Frida Kahlo, *The Diary of Frida Kahlo: An Intimate Self-portrait* (New York: Harry N. Abrams, 1995), 235.

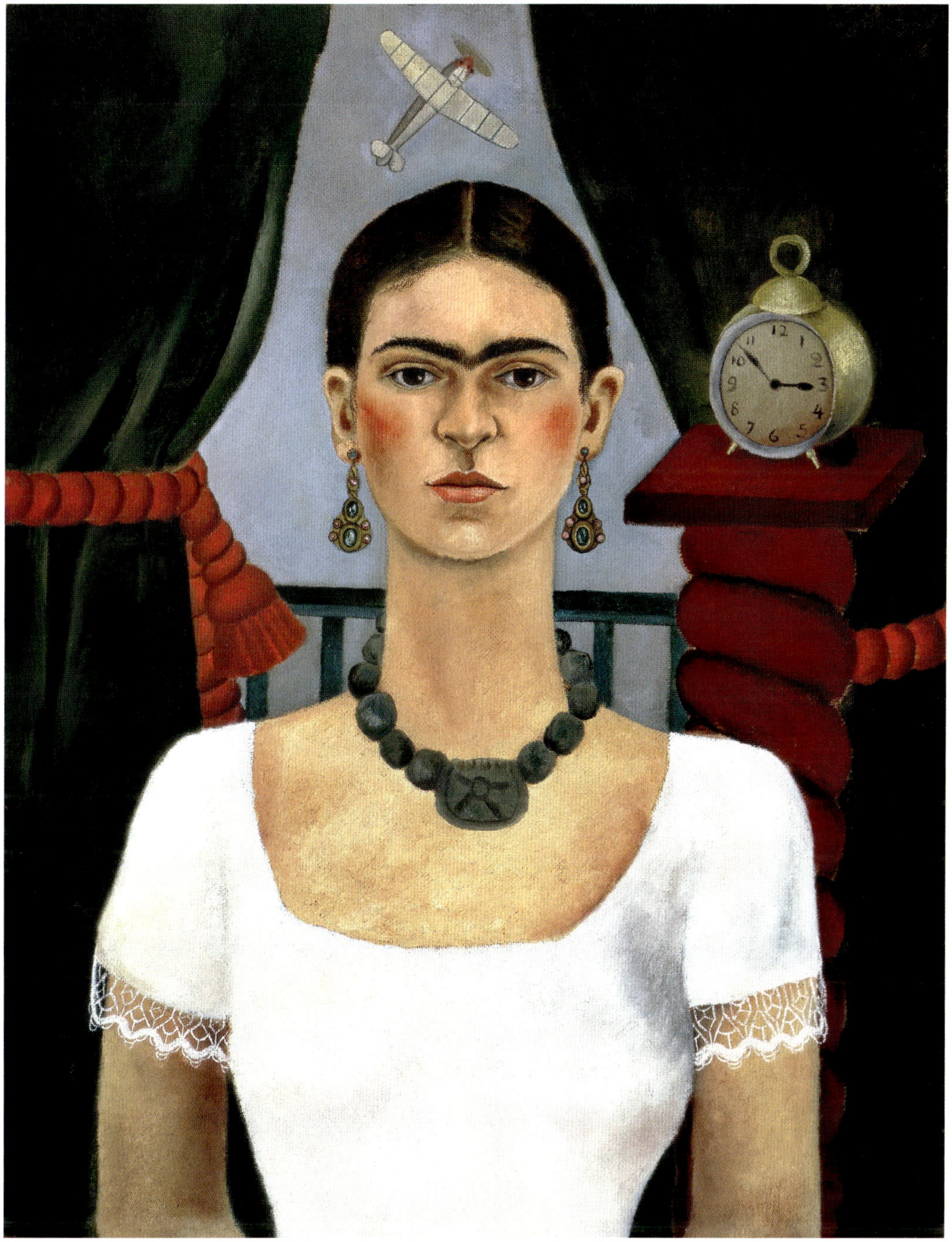

8

Time Flies

1929
Oil on Masonite,
30½ x 24 in. (77.5 x 61 cm)
Antony Bryan Collection

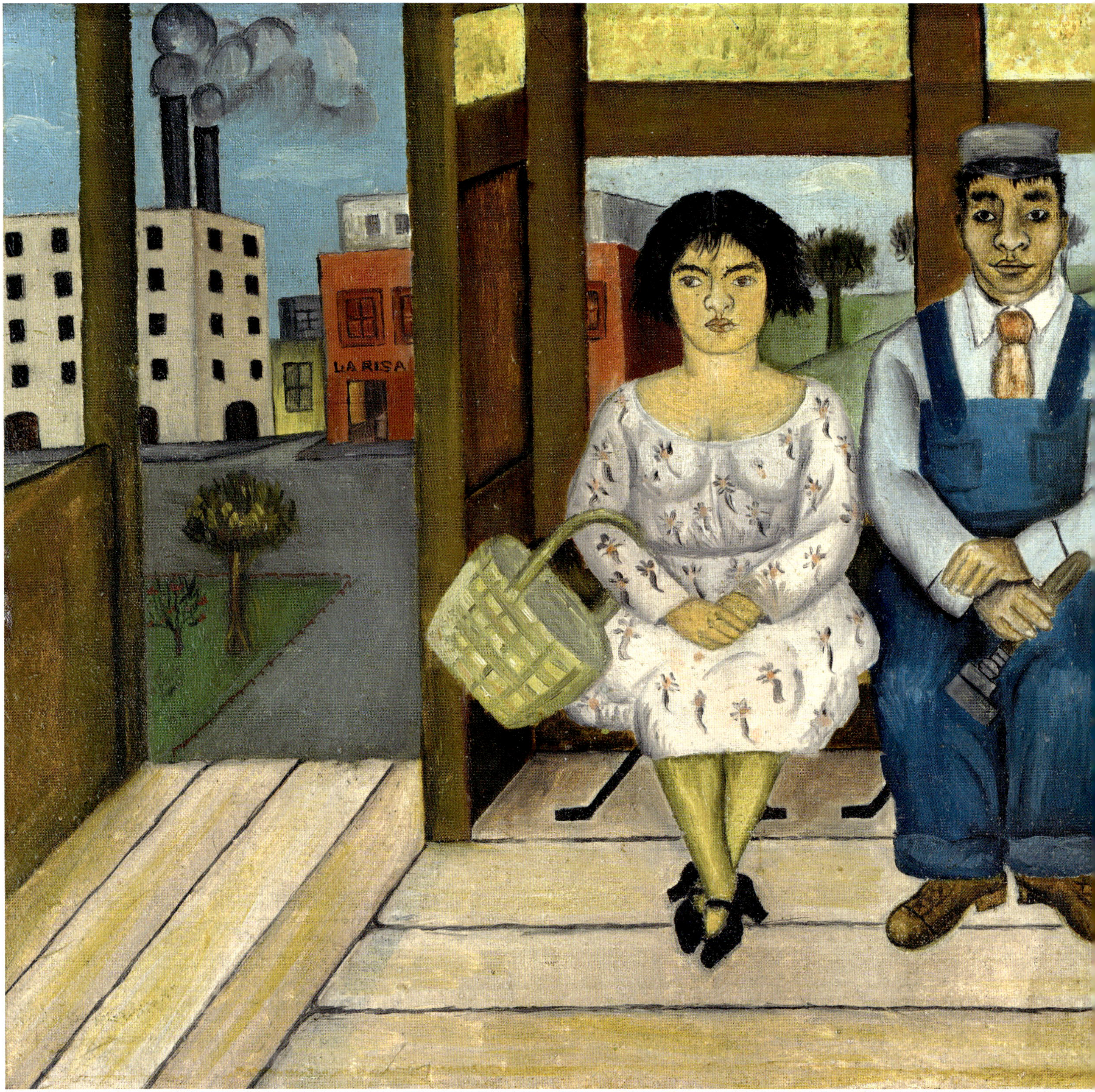

9

The Bus

1929
Oil on canvas, 10¼ x 21⅞ in. (26 x 55.5 cm)
Xochimilco (Mexico City),
Collection Museo Dolores Olmedo

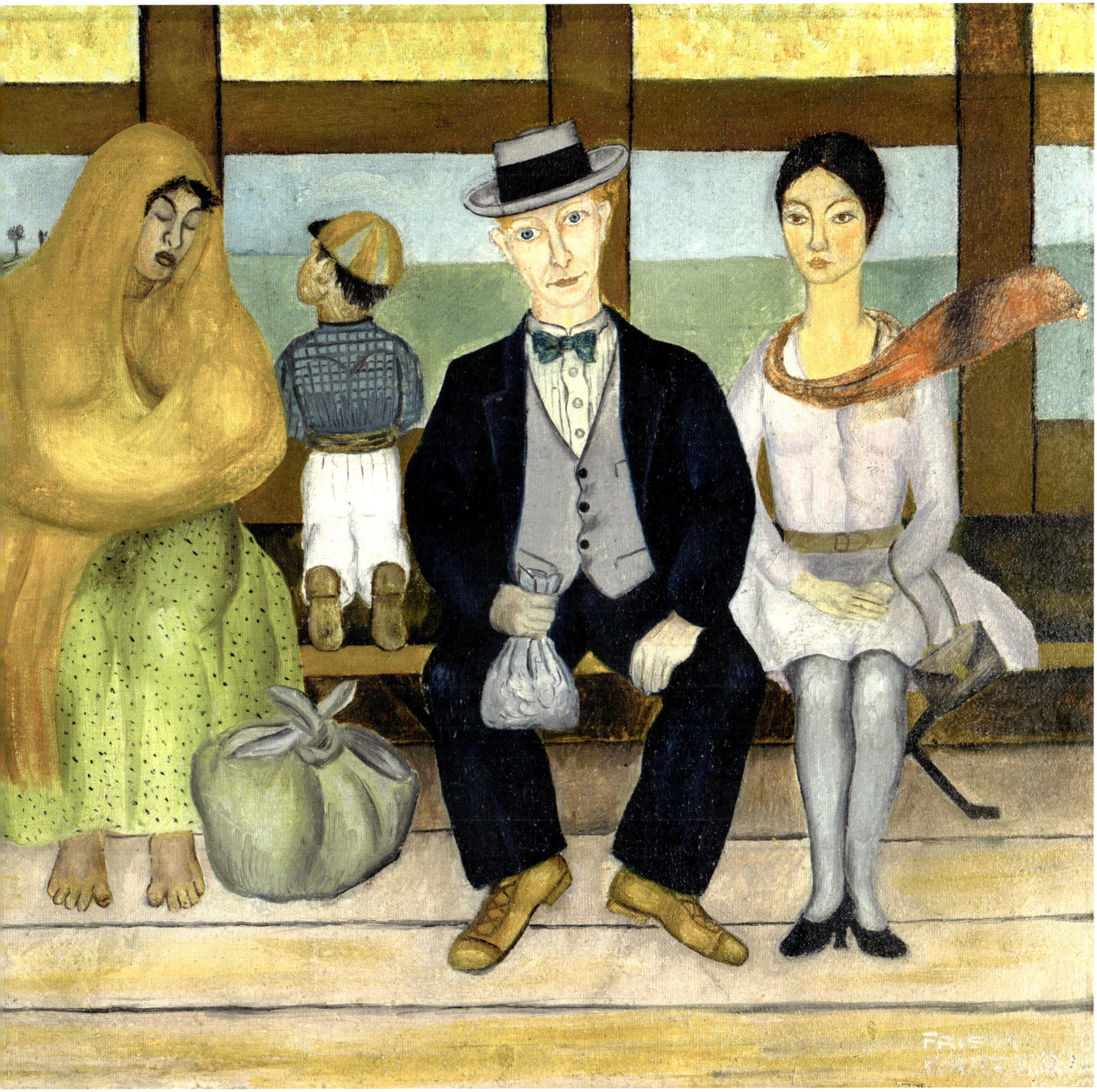

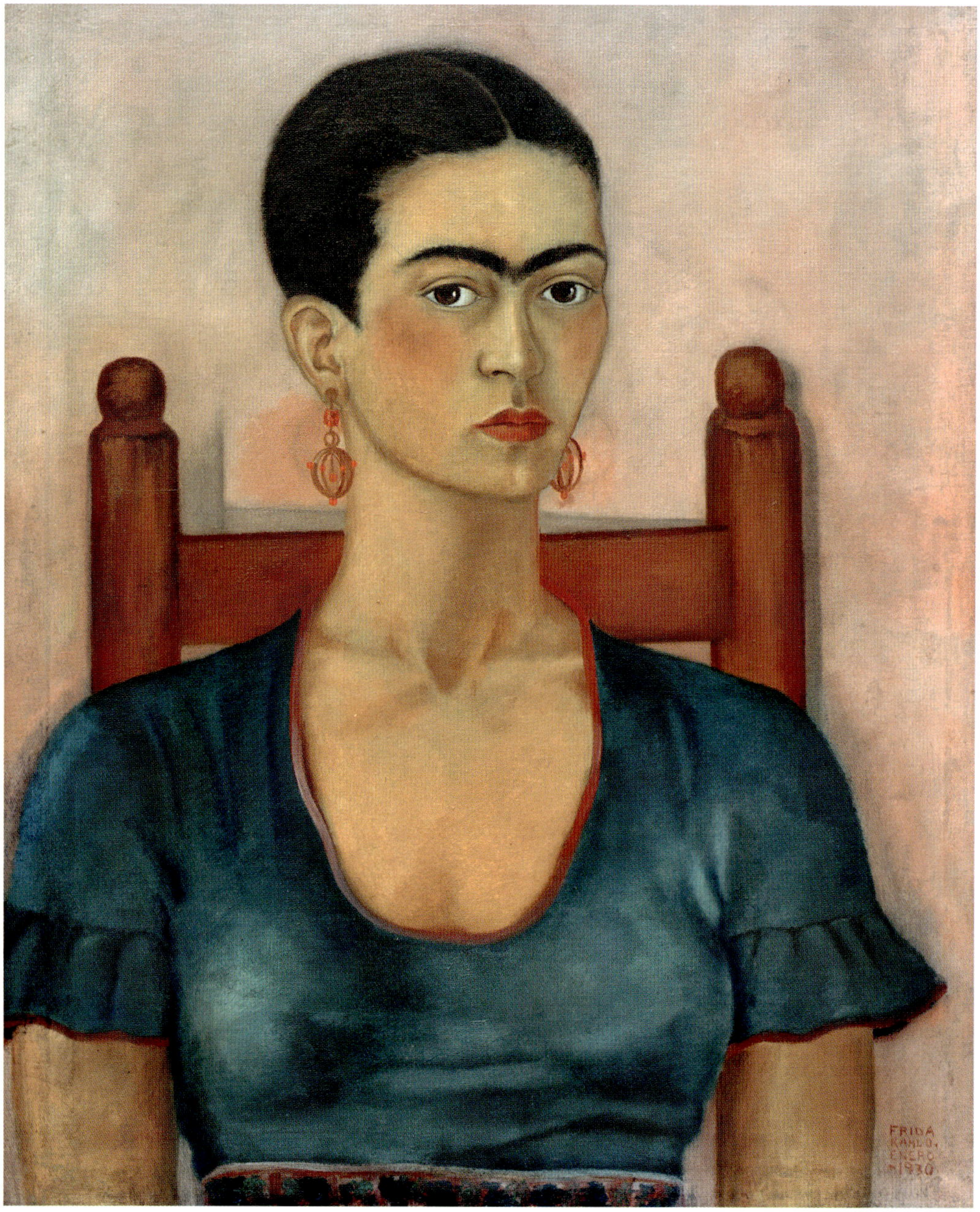

10
Self Portrait

1930
Oil on canvas, 25⅝ x 21¼ in. (65 x 54 cm)
Boston, private collection

11
Frieda and Diego Rivera

1931
Oil on canvas,
39⅜ x 31 in. (100 x 78.7 cm)
San Francisco (California), San Francisco Museum of Modern Art, Albert M. Bender Collection, gift of Albert M. Bender, 36.6061

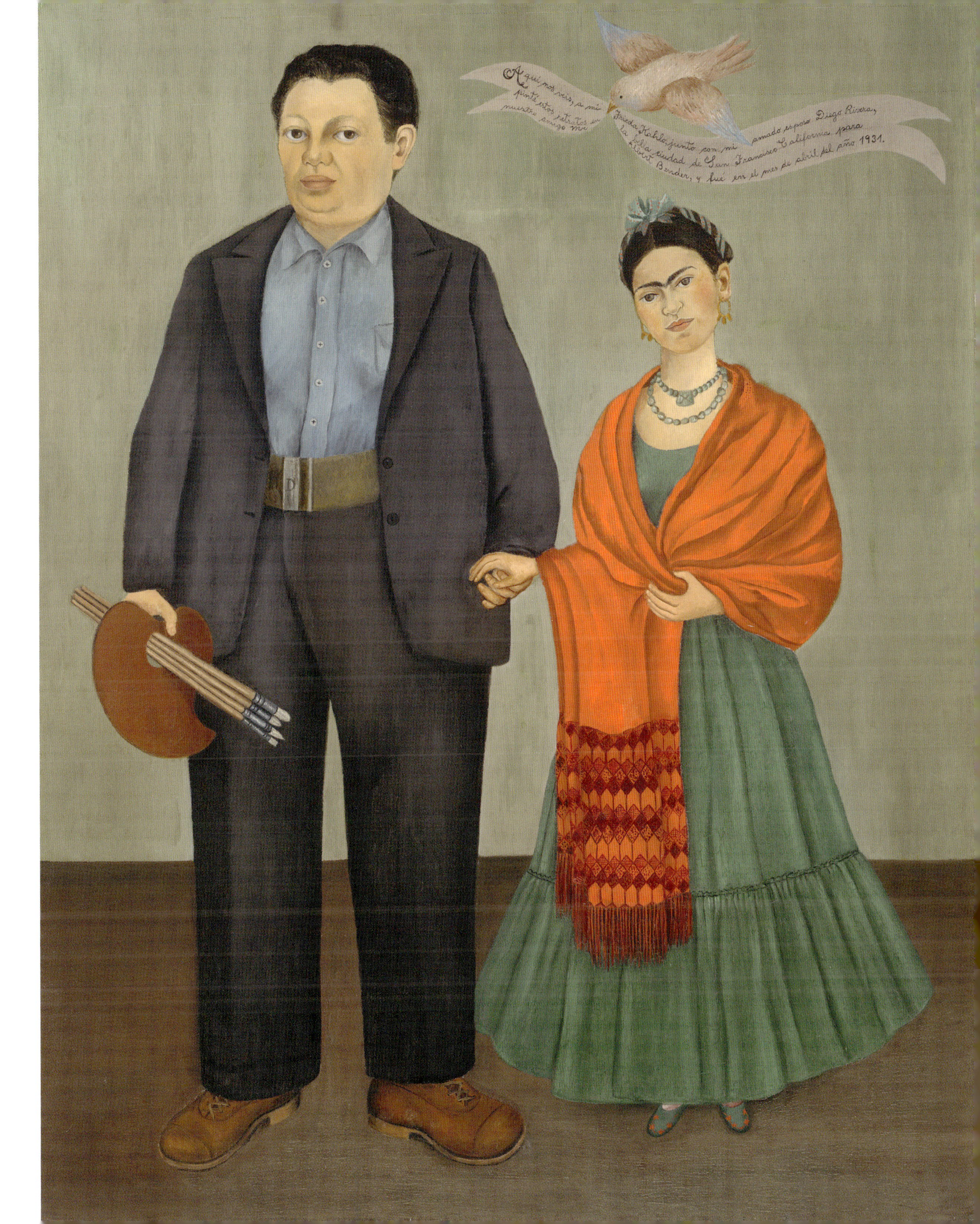
Aquí nos veis, a mí Frieda Kahlo, junto con mi amado esposo Diego Rivera,
pinté estos retratos en la bella ciudad de San Francisco California para
nuestro amigo Mr Albert Bender, y fué en el mes de abril del año 1931.

12

Portrait of Luther Burbank

1931
Oil on Masonite,
34¼ x 24⅜ in. (87 x 62 cm)
Xochimilco (Mexico City),
Collection Museo Dolores Olmedo

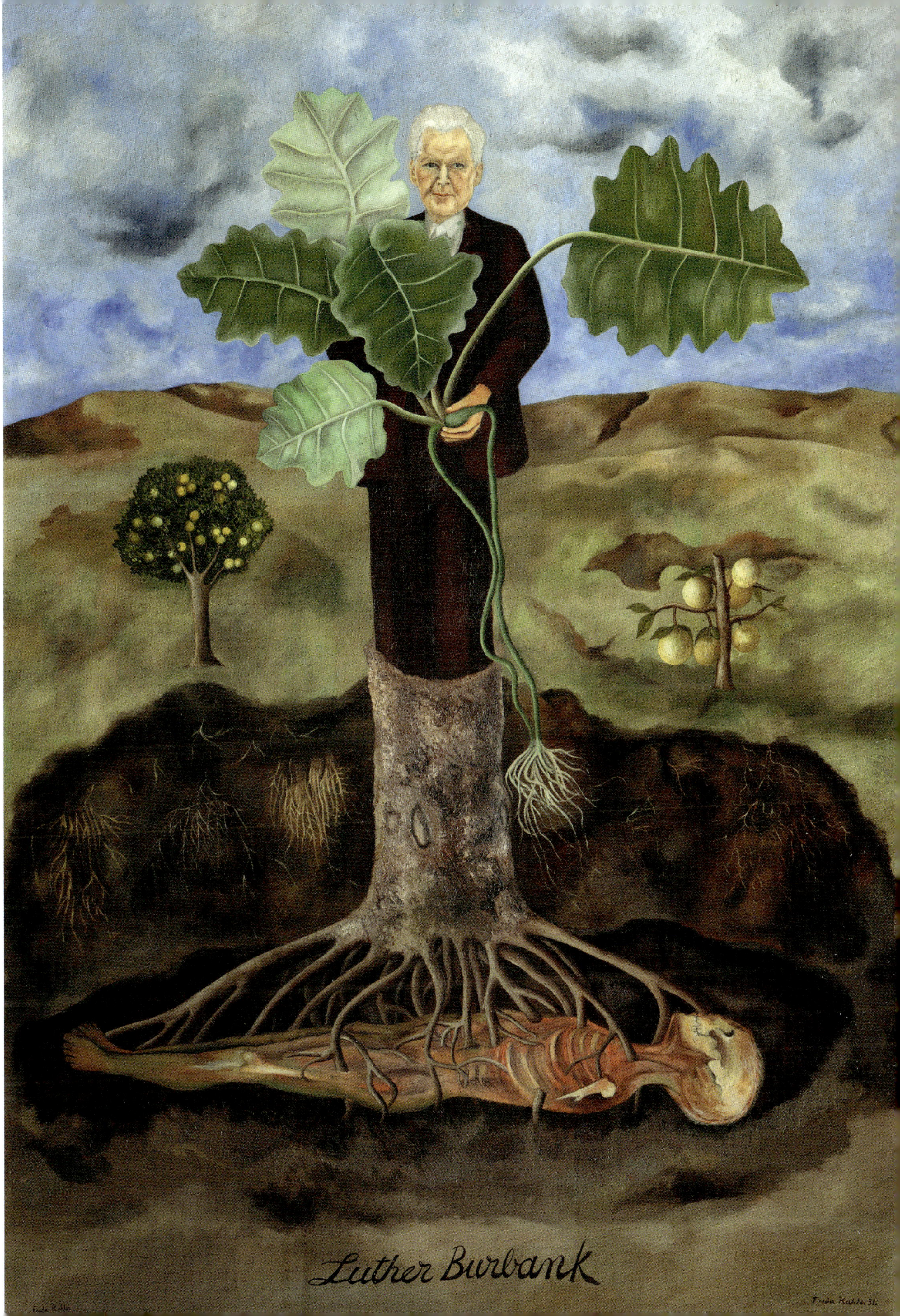
Luther Burbank
Frida Kahlo 31.

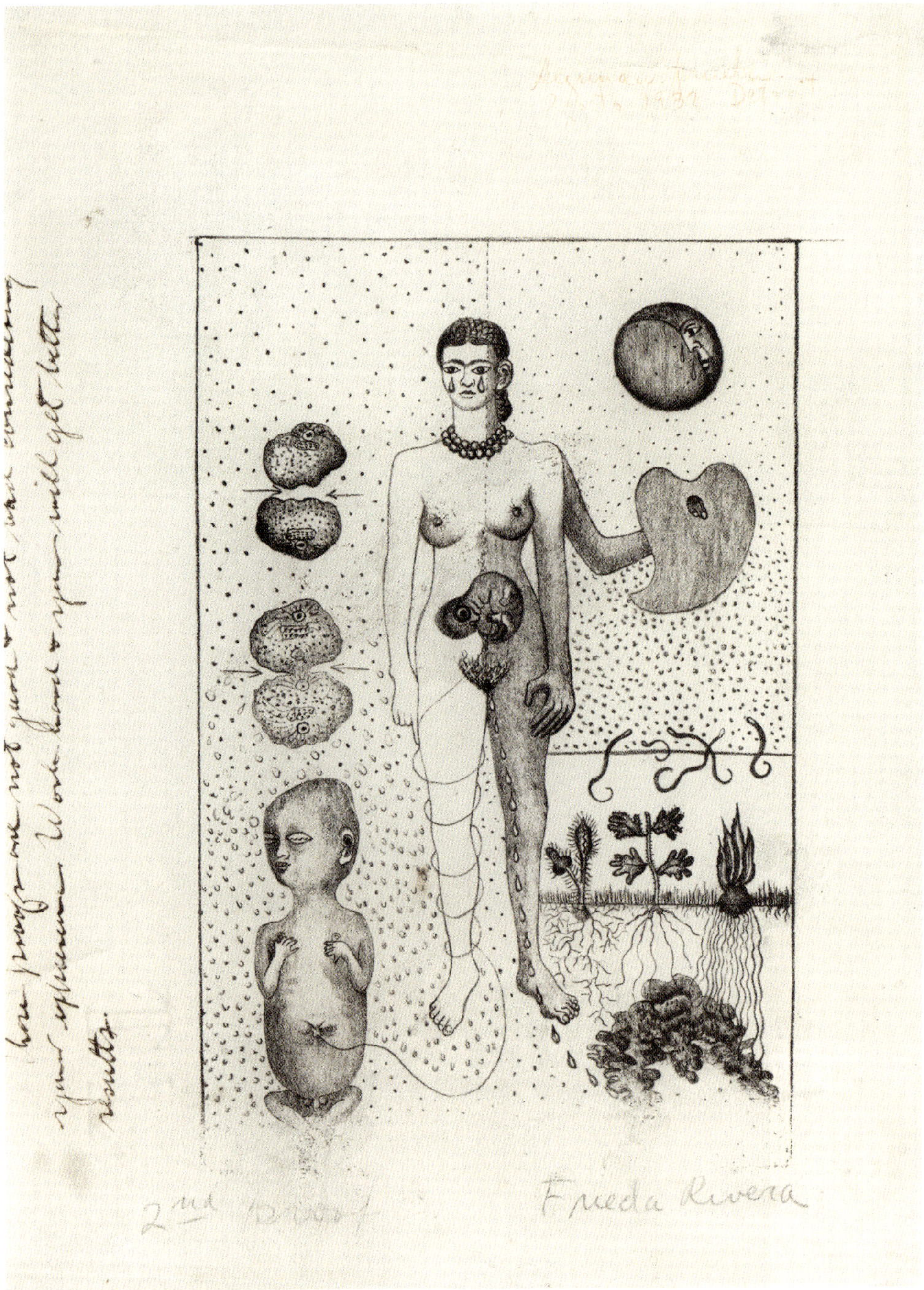

13

Frida and the Miscarriage

1932
Lithograph on paper,
12½ x 9½ in. (31.7 x 24 cm)
Xochimilco (Mexico City),
Collection Museo Dolores Olmedo

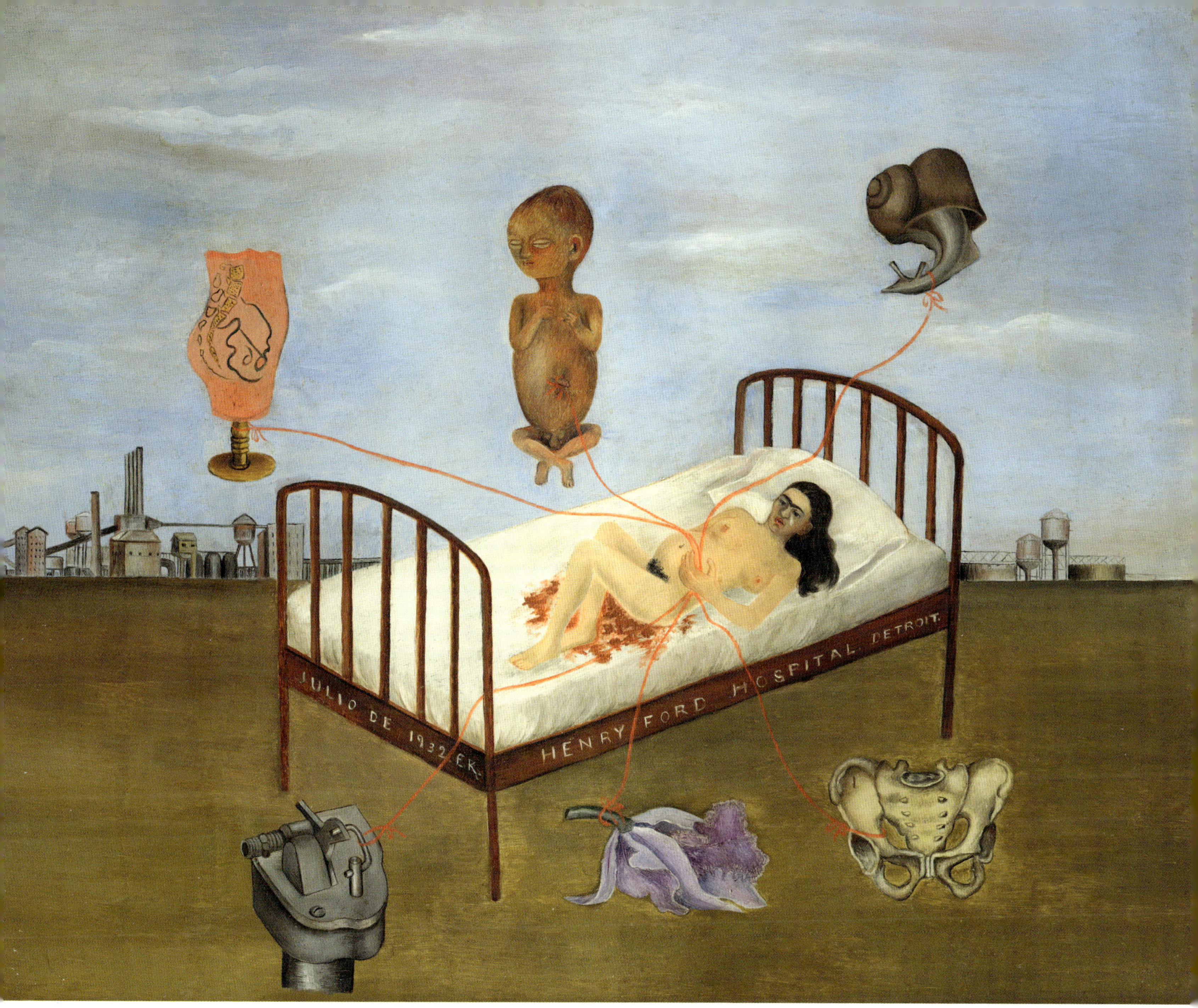

14

Henry Ford Hospital

1932
Oil on metal,
12¼ x 15⅛ in. (31 x 38.5 cm)
Xochimilco (Mexico City),
Collection Museo Dolores Olmedo

15

Self-portrait with Necklace

1933
Oil on metal,
13⅝ x 11⅔ in. (34.5 x 29.5 cm)
Gelman Collection

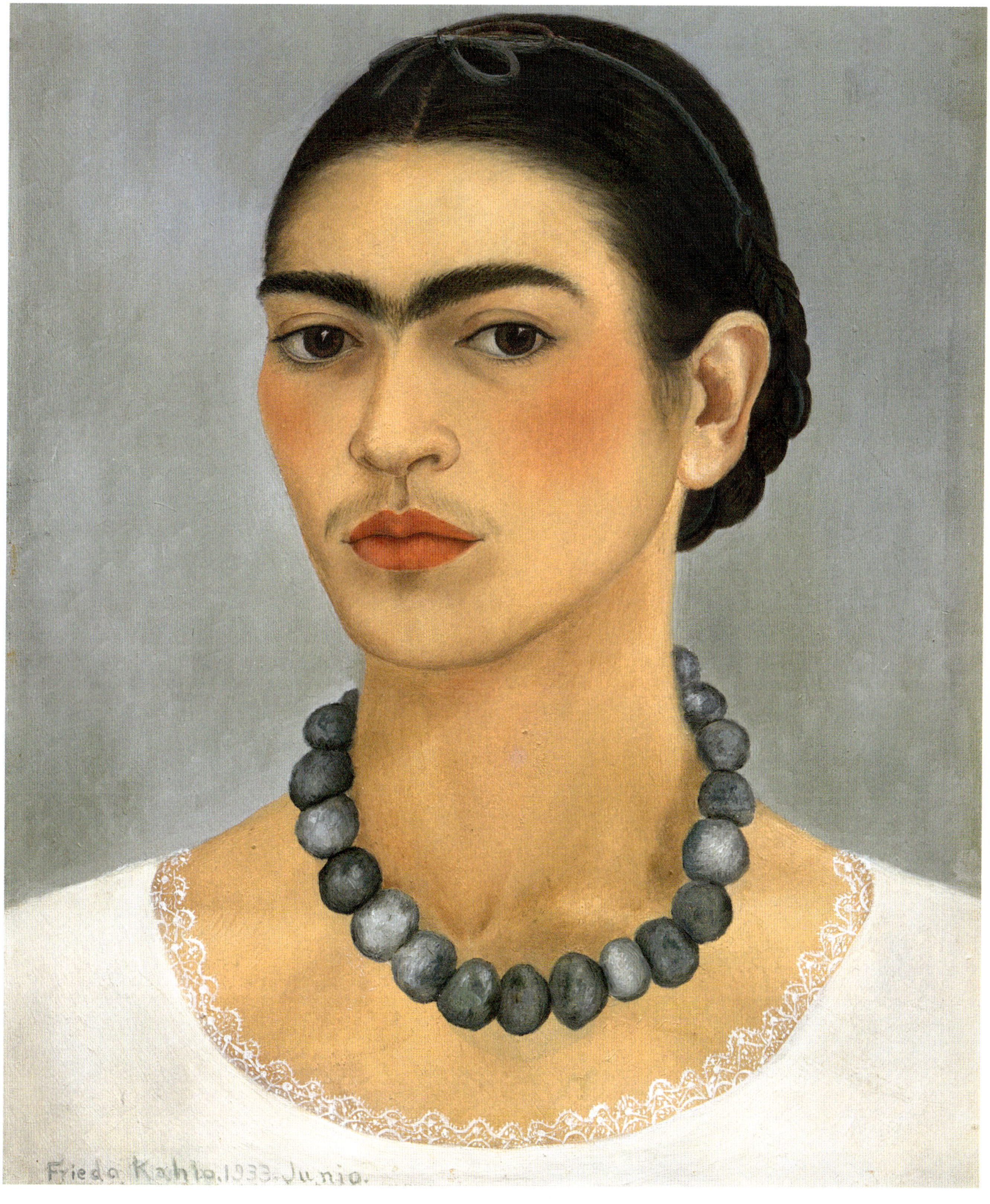
Frieda Kahlo. 1933. Junio.

16

Self-portrait on the Border Line between Mexico and the United States

1932
Oil on metal,
12¼ x 13¾ in. (31 x 35 cm)
New York, María Rodríguez de Reyero Collection

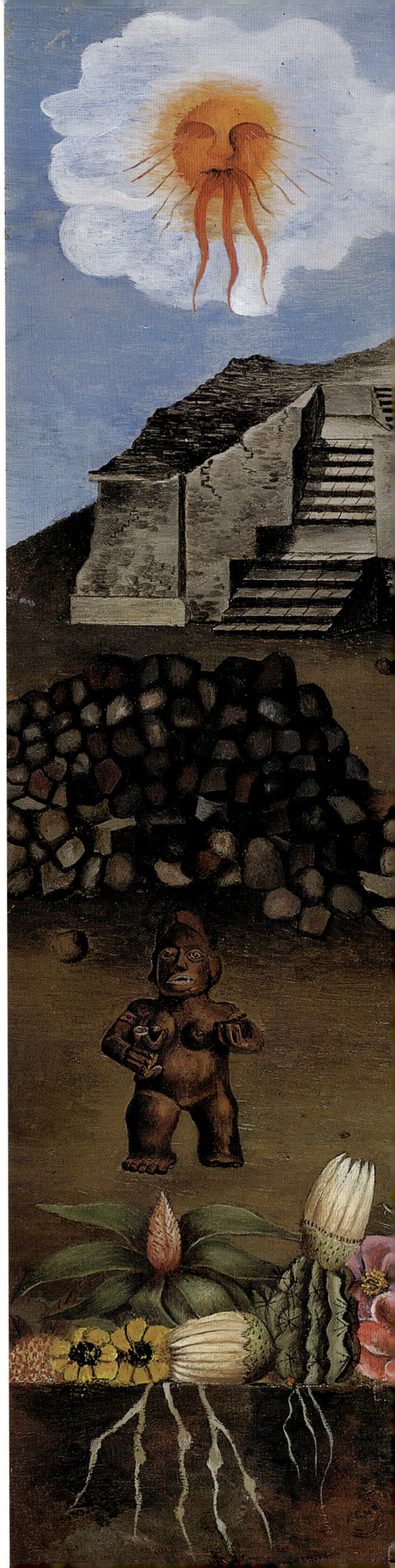

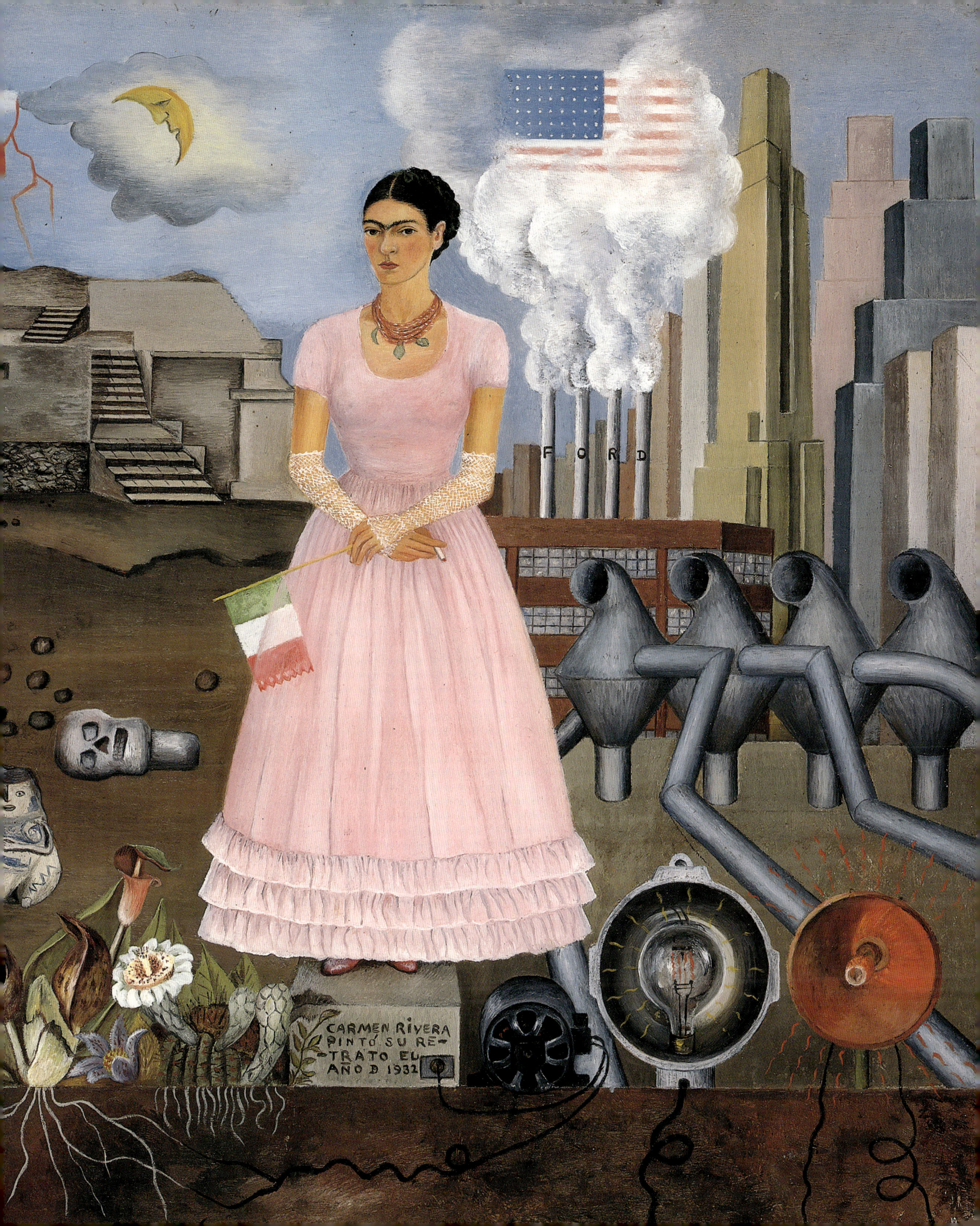
FORD
CARMEN RIVERA
PINTÓ SU RE-
TRATO EL
AÑO D 1932

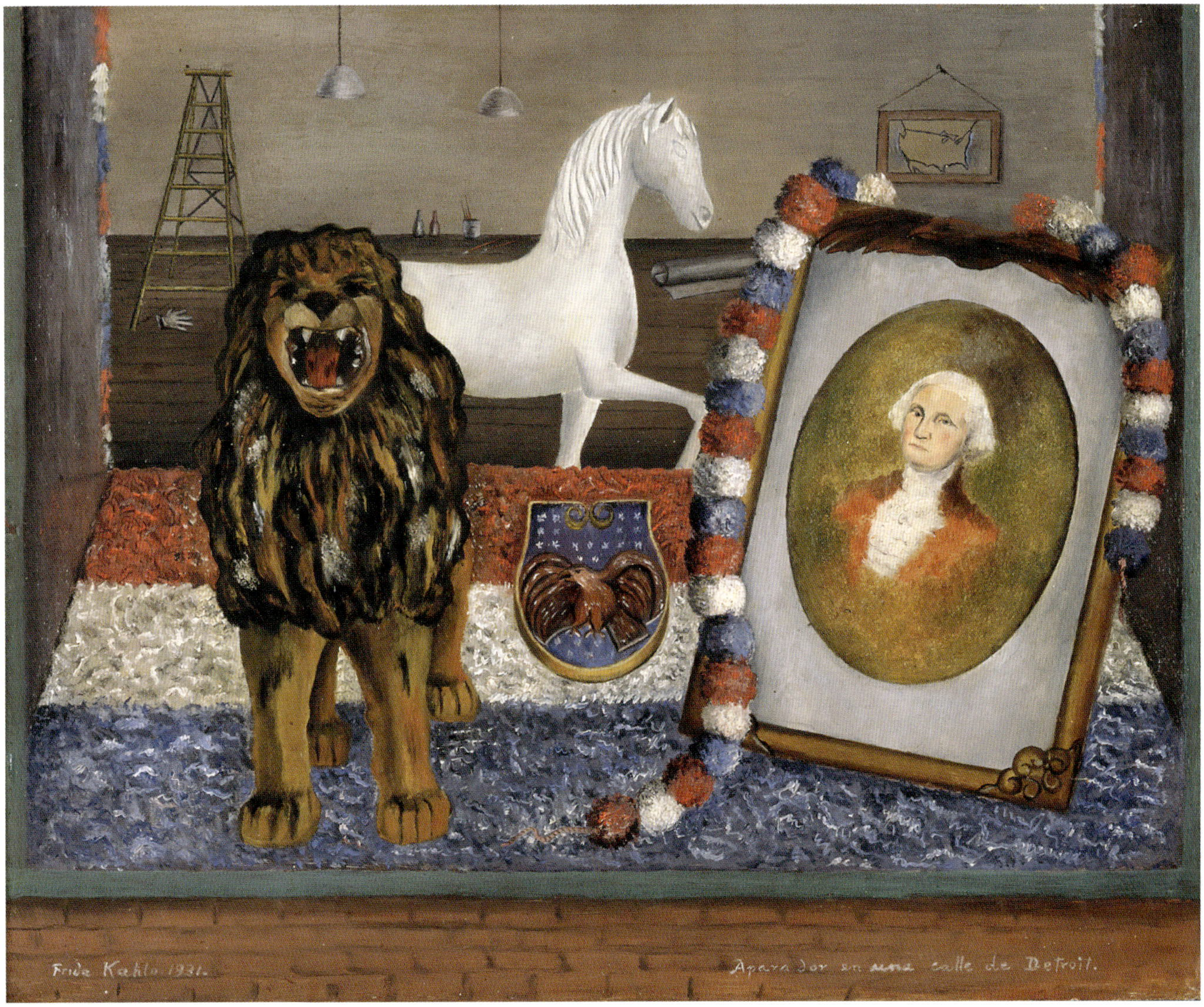

17

Window Display in a Street in Detroit

1931–32
Oil on metal, 12 x 15 in. (30.3 x 38.2 cm)
Miami (Florida), Fana Holtz Collection,
courtesy of Gary Nader Fine Art

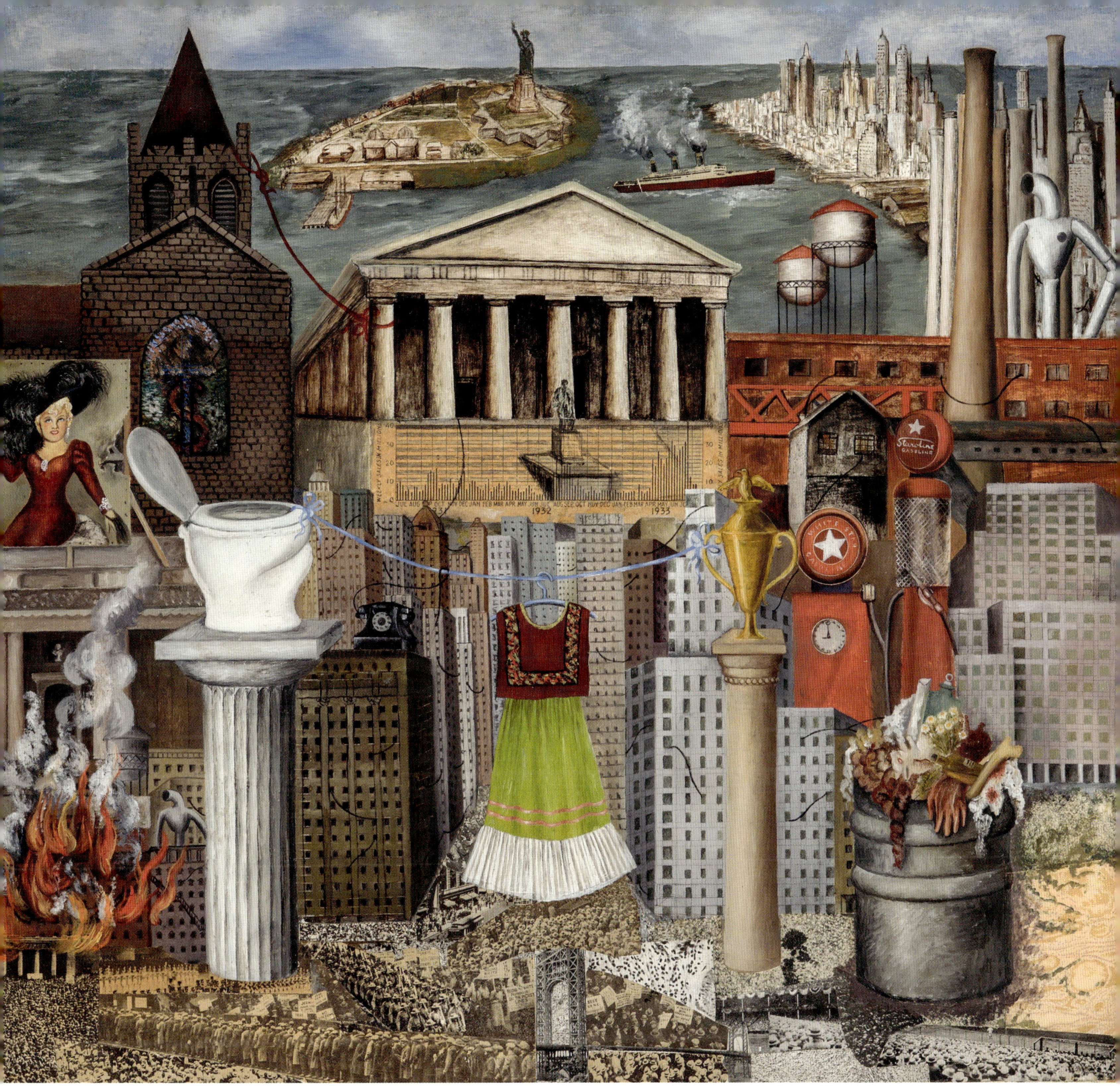

18

My Dress Hangs There

1933–39
Oil and collage on Masonite,
17⅞ x 19⅞ in. (45.5 x 50.5 cm)
Monterrey (Mexico), FEMSA Collection

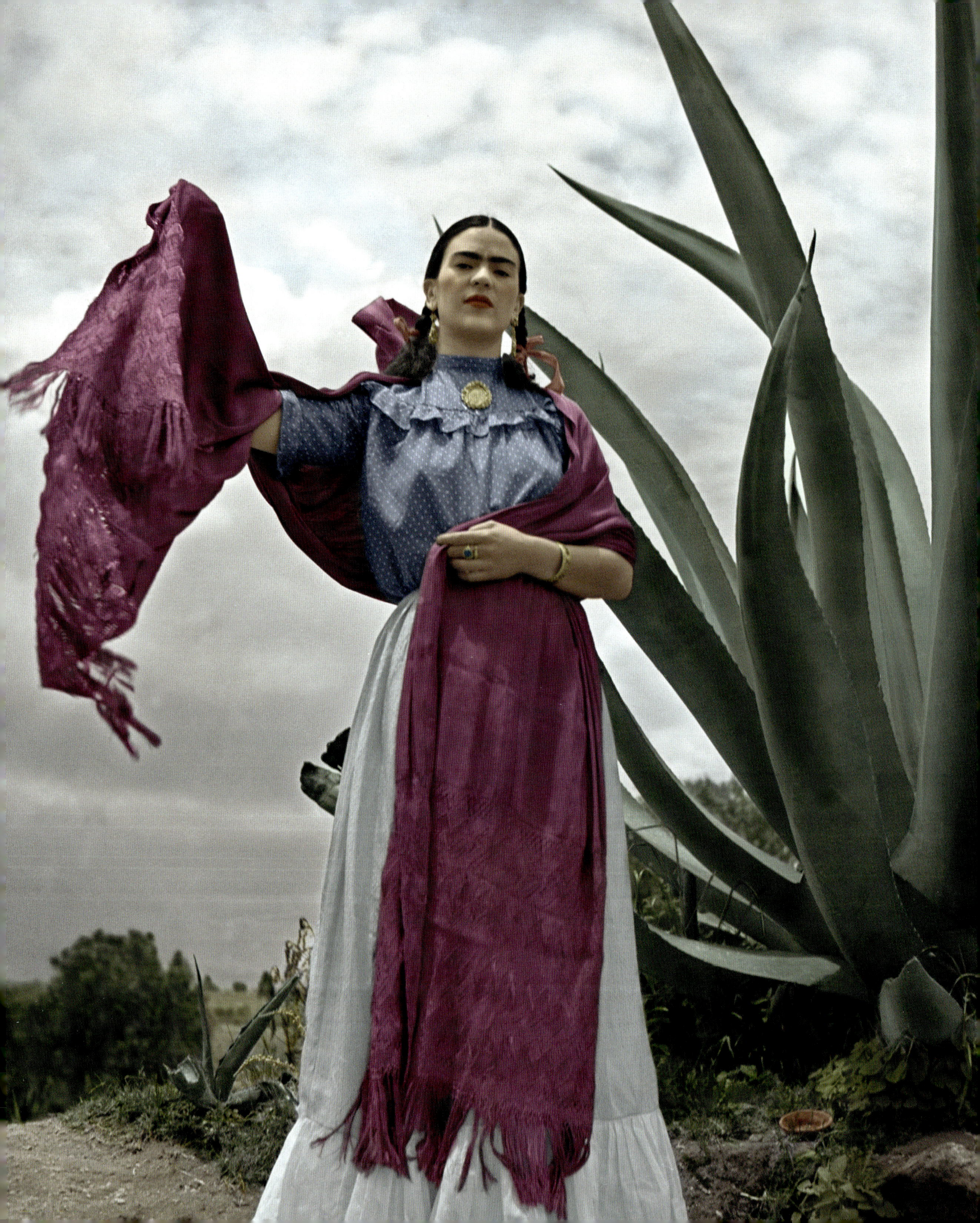

Seduction and Sublimation

Kahlo's art is at once ruthlessly self-revealing *and* profoundly theatrical, fictional accounts of a life lived.

Stine Høholt[1]

And besides—when one wakes up, the person one meets is always oneself. . . . The poem gains in greatness if we sense that it is the expression of a desire, a longing, rather than the narration of an event.

Jorge Luis Borges[2]

Of the approximately 150 works painted by Frida Kahlo in her 47-year life, 65 were self-portraits, a clear example of the overt biographical content of her oeuvre. This has given rise to a range of interpretations of the origin and nature of the link between the life and the work of the celebrated Mexican painter. The daughter of a photographer, Frida Kahlo realized from an early age that photography can capture reality as it is, but it can also modify it, as her father demonstrated when he retouched his photos. Indeed, she learned the trade herself by tinting the pictures he took. Coloring photographs is a minutely precise technique that involves painstaking attention to detail, with tiny brushstrokes on a very small scale, and Kahlo integrated this precision in her painting as a fundamental part of her style and technical refinement. At the same time, she grew aware of the power of art to transform.

Art historians and critics around the world have taken an interest in Frida Kahlo's singular creation of her life and art, establishing her importance in art history. This is confirmed by Raquel Tibol:

> In the context of women producers of art, Frida has a singularity: she treats the biology of woman, her psychology, and the immersion in individuality from

Frida Kahlo posing for a photo to accompany the article "Señoras of Mexico," *Vogue* magazine, 1937. Photograph by Toni Frissell

> the point of view of the sex; individuality with suffering and fantasy. In this sense, she is unique not only in Mexico but in the worldwide history of women's art.[3]

How much authenticity and how much artifice are there in the image Kahlo created of herself? Does the aesthetic value of her self-portraits depend on the sincerity of the pictorial version of herself, or rather on the expressive intensity and technical quality of the picture?

In Kahlo's case, it is very hard, if not impossible, to separate life from art and vice versa. It is just as complicated to ascertain the degree of truth or pretense there may have been in the creation of the image of her persona and the pictorial manifestation of that representation. The two form an indissoluble entity: her life is transformed into art in the same way that art blends into her biography. The singularity of her oeuvre lies in fusing the stark revelation of her existence with the invention of a being that is both her and someone else, as in the quotation from Borges used as an epigraph for this chapter. Kahlo never intended to offer a mere painted narrative of her life, but instead aimed to express the reinvention of herself as woman and as artist in her work. Imagination was the norm in her art. Carlos Fuentes puts it succinctly:

> Frida Kahlo is an extraordinary creature because converting the pain [of a devastated body] into art is one of the most difficult things there is. Pain is mute, pain is felt by whoever experiences it . . . it can be a scream, a howl, but it is complex to turn it into words. She transforms it into art, she makes a transmutation of pain, essentially mute, into art. . . . I think that leads us to Kahlo's great artistic ability to express beauty through pain. . . . We can see many things in the world, but not our soul, nor the souls of others. That is something that escapes us. I think Kahlo achieved the miracle of seeing her soul through pain and converting it into painting.[4]

To doubt the authenticity of a person who experienced tremendous physical pain throughout her life would mean ignoring the full scope of her bodily suffering. It must not be forgotten that Kahlo had polio at the age of six, and at eighteen had a terrible accident that left her paralytic, condemned to a sedentary life and unable to procreate. She had more than thirty-five surgical operations, seven spinal fractures, and three miscarriages, and one of her legs was amputated. Pain of such intensity can only be palliated with opiates like morphine or other drugs like alcohol or marijuana. Only the imagination can tame that anguish. Only exceptional people are able to transcend such handicaps and such indescribable bodily suffering through artistic creation. Kahlo is a paradigm of such exceptionality.

> Frida was a precocious coquette, and thanks to that she was able to cope with much of that aesthetic of pain, because there's an element of the conquest of life, of the

> beings around her, whether men, women, animals. . . . She is a multifaceted human being, polyhedric if you like. The notion of the painter does not quite cover her because she is also a human being in pain.[5]

Understanding Kahlo's coquettishness and charm, alluded to above by Raquel Tibol, is vital to understanding the artist's complex personality and assessing her ability to project it onto the canvas. From a very early age, Kahlo was conscious of her individuality and what distinguished her from others. Her character was forged by adversity, and polio did not prevent her from excelling at sports. Added to her strength was an acute intelligence that she used to get what she wanted. Being physically disabled not only made her different but also brought her taunts, like "Frida Kahlo, *pata de palo* (wooden leg)," yet she was determined to stand out and excite admiration, not pity. It was thus that she developed her desire to conquer life, with flirtation and self-assurance as her weapons. Her intelligence and charm were to fulfill the dual function of hiding and mastering her disability. Many surrendered to her. The first to do so was her father, and the most important Diego Rivera. A single commandment was to rule her attitude to life: Thou shalt captivate thy neighbor as thyself.

The combination of seduction and sublimation proved infallible. Kahlo's work and persona managed to bewitch not only men and women, but also the world and history. Of course, the process was not an easy one. Kahlo later commented that she had had two accidents in her life, the crash that injured her severely and meeting Diego Rivera. The first produced terrible bodily pain, and the second caused her deep emotional suffering combined with tremendous joy, the result of a profound, complicated, genuine, and totally unconventional love with abundant infidelities on both sides.

Teresa del Conde, a specialist in Kahlo who applied the theories of Sigmund Freud, defined the relationship between the two artists as "symbiotic by antonomasia,"[6] meaning it was codependent. Kahlo depended on Rivera, but Rivera also depended very much on Kahlo. This codependence or symbiosis persisted throughout both their lives, even during the time in 1940 when they were divorced.

> What there is in the case of Diego and Frida is an iron-clad fidelity in the manner they were able to feel it, which is what might be called *amicitia*, a Ciceronian concept that means "having admiration for the other." They certainly did, both Diego for Frida and Frida, to a greater extent, for Diego. Diego says in the biographical sketch he wrote about her that she is the only woman capable of putting her sufferings and also her physical moments, her spiritual moments, into painting. He greatly admired her, too.[7]

Indeed, their reciprocal admiration and identification went very deep. Both were exceptional in their artistic genius and irresistible personalities, with the ability to enchant anyone who stood in front of them. Both were confirmed seducers, besides having highly developed libidos that they exercised to the fullest and with absolute disdain for social conventions. In spite of his obesity and his peculiar toad-like face, Rivera was a recalcitrant and very successful Don Juan. Nearly all of his models, including Pita Amor, Tina Modotti, María Félix, and many others, were also his lovers for varying lengths of time. According to Salomon Grimberg, however, the causes of Rivera's and Kahlo's infidelity were different:

> Frida lived in despair, and one way of softening that despair was through any emotional contact. There were certain people with whom she could have contact that was not only personal but intimate and sexual, and the intensity of those relationships allowed Frida to tolerate her loneliness, her sadness, her continual sensation of being abandoned. That's why Frida had so many lovers, both men and women. I don't think she did it out of a simply sexual impulse, though that, too, is possible. Diego was promiscuous, but not Frida. She liked handsome, intelligent, creative men who treated her respectfully and affectionately and who surrendered themselves to a relationship that eventually, on many occasions, ended up being sexual.[8]

Kahlo suffered over Rivera's infidelities, but she tolerated them up to a point because she knew they were inevitable. Kahlo thought that "Diego is not anybody's husband and never will be."[9] However, what destroyed her emotionally was to learn of the intimacy between Rivera and her younger sister Cristina, whom she held in very special affection.

Kahlo and Rivera returned from the United States at the end of 1933 and started to live in a house designed especially for them by the architect Juan O'Gorman (1905–1982), with a separate studio and living area for each of them connected by a bridge and built in the functionalist style of Le Corbusier (1887–1965) with a Mexican touch. Kahlo painted no pictures in 1934 because she was fully occupied with decorating both halves of the house, and she hoped to restore some harmony to her marriage, which had deteriorated owing to Rivera's excessive work and Kahlo's consequent feeling of loneliness, together with her discomfort at living in "Gringoland" and her nostalgia for her own country. Moreover, Rivera had not wanted to return to Mexico and blamed his wife for it. It was at this stage that Frida found out about Diego's affair with Cristina, her younger and closest sister, whom she had painted in *Portrait of Cristina, My Sister* (1928) [fig. 19]. Infidelity is one thing, and disloyalty and betrayal are quite another.

Devastated, Frida painted *A Few Small Nips* or *Passionately in Love* (1935), based on a newspaper report of a drunkard who had killed his girlfriend by stabbing her twenty times [fig. 20]. Protesting at his arrest, the criminal cried out, "I just gave her a few small nips!" The painting depicts the murder with unrelenting realism, showing the victim stretched on a bed and bathed in blood. Standing, with the knife in his right hand, the drunken murderer looks wildly out at the viewer. In the upper part of the painting, two doves, one white and one black, hold a ribbon with the title of the picture. The cruelty of the scene reveals Frida's feeling of having been "murdered by life" due to her husband's deception and her sense of betrayal by him and her sister. Despite the bloody scene depicted in the work and the emotional suffering that prompted her to paint it, the artist also clearly wanted the picture to exude the macabre black humor of gore.

In his autobiography, Rivera admitted the brutality of the outrage he had committed against Frida and her sister: "If I loved a woman, the more I loved her, the more I wanted to hurt her. Frida was only the most obvious victim of this disgusting trait."[10] Frida decided to separate from Diego and went to live in a small apartment, although they still saw each other frequently. In July 1935, she wrote her husband a moving letter in which, after mentioning his many flirtations, she said to him:

> At bottom you and I love each other very much, and even if we go through countless affairs, splintered doors, insults and international claims, we shall always love each other. I think what it is, is that I'm a little stupid and just a bit of a dissembler, because all these things have happened and happened again for the seven years we've lived together and all of the rages I've gone into have only led me to understand better that I love you more than my own skin, and though you don't love me the same way, in any case you love me somewhat, no? Or if that's not true, I'll always have the hope that it may be, and that's enough for me . . . Love me just a little. I adore you, Frieda.[11]

As the Mexican writer Elena Poniatowska noted in an interview, in the bedroom of the Casa Azul, where Frida Kahlo was born and died, there is a sign between the wall and the ceiling that reads: "This room is the room of Elenita Vázquez Gómez, of Pita Amor, of Machila Armida, and of María Félix."[12] Kahlo remained very close to all the women Rivera seduced by painting them, or whom he painted and then seduced.

> She used to say that she had to let him because the edges of rivers are what let the river flow . . . he was her great love. She chose him, she wanted to marry him. . . . What Frida didn't look for was her accident, her operations, she didn't look for her broken spinal column, she didn't look for her polio as a child, she didn't look for her gangrenous leg, she didn't look for any of that. But she did look for Diego Rivera, and it was a monumental sickness.[13]

Apparently, she never wanted to be cured of that "monumental sickness." Kahlo adored Rivera until she died, despite the suffering he might have caused her. *Memory* or *The Heart* (1937) is an upsetting image of the pain caused by betrayed love [fig. 21]. In the

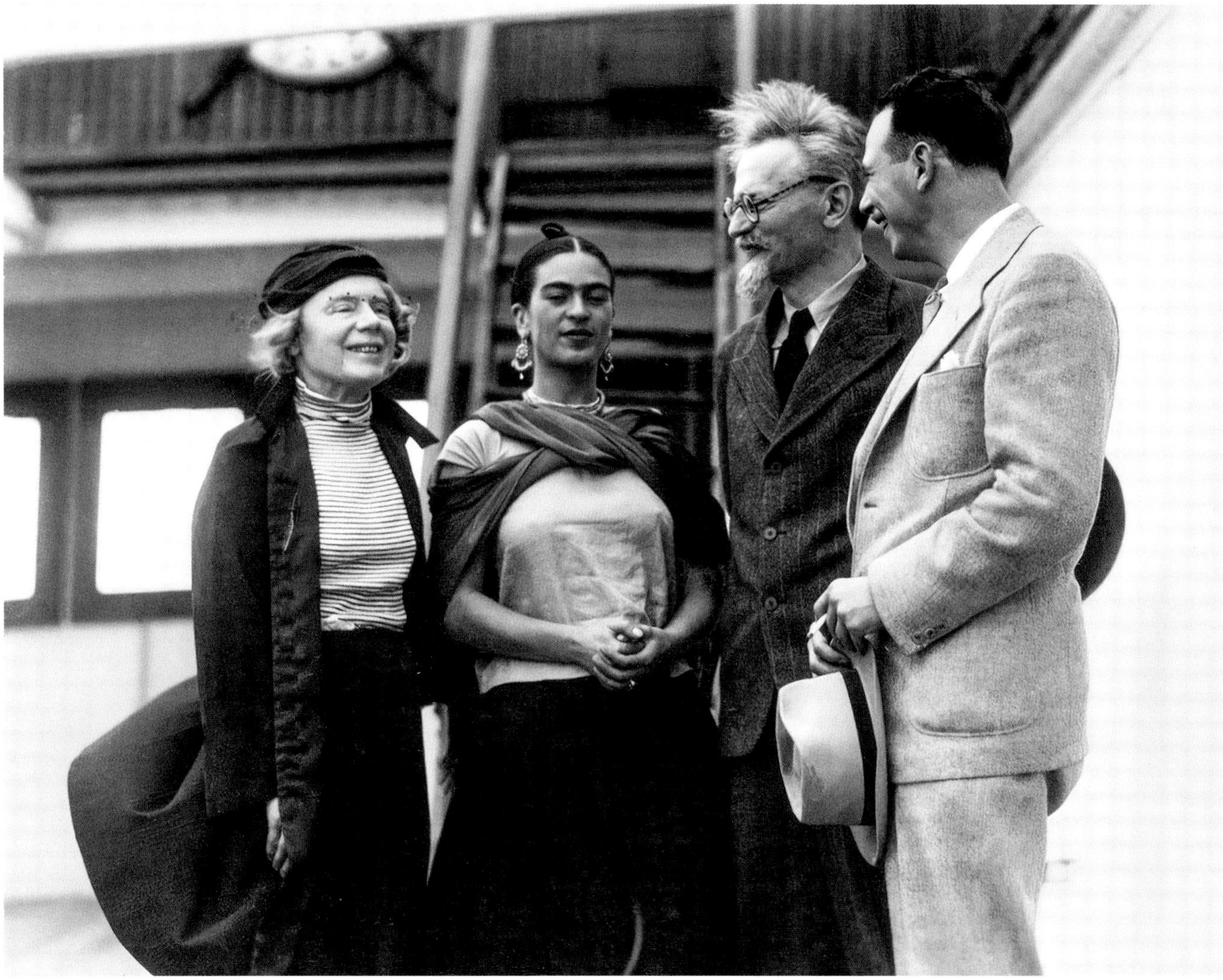

Frida Kahlo and the Marxist theorist Max Shachtman welcome Leon Trotsky and his wife, Natalia Sedova, upon their arrival in Mexico on the oil tanker *Ruth*, Tampico, January 9, 1937. Private collection

center of the picture, the artist is flanked by her school uniform and a Tehuana dress like the one in *My Dress Hangs There* [fig. 18]. She has no arms: the left one is in the uniform, and the right one emerges from the Tehuana dress. Her chest is pierced with a hole, and her immense bleeding heart lies on the ground next to a sea of tears. Even so, that same year Kahlo painted the idyllic *Portrait of Diego Rivera* (1937), in which the muralist looks like a matinee idol [fig. 23].

The years 1937 and 1938 were very productive ones for Kahlo. She painted more pictures than in the previous eight years put together. Among them were *Fulang-Chang and I* and *Me and My Doll*, both from 1937 [figs. 22 and 24], as well as *Itzcuintli Dog with Me* and *Self-portrait with Monkey*, from 1938 [figs. 26 and 36].

Leon Trotsky and his wife, Natalia Sedova, arrived in Mexico in 1937 and lived in the Casa Azul for two years. In a letter, Kahlo confided to a friend that Trotsky's arrival in Mexico had been the most important event of her life. She was greatly impressed by the intelligence and historical importance of the leader of the Fourth International, and he was fascinated by Kahlo's charm. Tibol gives an amusing account of the episode:

> Frida was tremendously coquettish. Natalia, Trotsky's wife, was not physically attractive. She was a woman in the revolutionary armor of the time, with flat shoes and no makeup, ornaments, or jewelry, dressed almost like a nun. Suddenly Frida appears in Tampico dressed in all her very peculiar finery, her hair adorned, and Trotsky must have gone cross-eyed.[14]

Taking advantage of the situation, Kahlo paved the way for an amorous encounter with Trotsky to give Rivera "a few small nips." An adventure with her husband's friend and political idol was the perfect revenge for Rivera's romance with Cristina Kahlo. Frida Kahlo unleashed her powers of seduction and succeeded in conquering the Soviet revolutionary, who had gone into exile in Mexico after his rift with Stalin. The lovers exchanged letters hidden in books and met secretly at Cristina's house to give free rein to their erotic desires. Rivera preferred to ignore their fling, but Sedova was stung by it and complained about it to her husband in writing. To leave a record of their romance and her attractions, Kahlo gave Trotsky *Self-portrait Dedicated to Leon Trotsky* on November 7, 1937, the date of the anniversary of the Russian Revolution and, coincidentally, Trotsky's birthday [fig. 25]. Kahlo appears elegantly attired in the center of the composition with a seductive and distinguished expression, flanked only by two fine white curtains to showcase the refinement of her beauty. "For Leon Trotsky with all my affection," reads the dedication. Frida Kahlo combined creative sublimation with her capacity for seduction, and that is where her greatness and originality lie.

In the political sphere, the story is darker. Kahlo, like Rivera, was first a Trotskyist and then a Stalinist. The founder of the Fourth International was able to take refuge in Mexico because Rivera petitioned President Lázaro Cárdenas to grant him asylum in the country, and Trotsky and Sedova lived in the Casa Azul for two years, but despite those events and Kahlo's dalliance with Trotsky, what finally wielded the greatest impact was Rivera's desire for readmission to the Mexican Communist Party. Trotsky therefore left the Casa Azul and went to live with his wife in a large house on nearby Calle de Viena, also in Coyoacán. There he suffered two attempts on his life, ordered by Stalin and orchestrated by the Mexican Communist Party. The first, perpetrated in the early hours of May 24, 1940, and commanded by the painter David Alfaro Siqueiros (1896–1974), was a failure. Trotsky, Sedova, and their grandson threw themselves on the floor, managing to evade gunfire and save their own lives. Siqueiros went to prison for less than a year and was granted asylum in Chile with the aid of Pablo Neruda. The leader of the Fourth International was assassinated on August 20, 1940, by the Spaniard Ramón Mercader, a Soviet agent who struck Trotsky on his head with a mountaineer's ice pick. Trotsky died the following day. Mercader spent twenty years in jail for his crime, but Stalin secretly awarded him the Hero of the Soviet Union medal, which was presented to him in Moscow in 1961 after he came out of prison the previous year. Frida Kahlo knew Mercader in Paris and met him a couple of times at the Casa Azul. This led the police to interrogate her, search her house, and imprison her for two days along with her sister Cristina. "My sister and I . . . cried for two days in jail. . . . [T]hey freed us because we were not guilty either of the assassination or of the shooting."[15] Diego Rivera was not interrogated or arrested because after divorcing Kahlo in 1940 he went to the United States and painted the mural *Pan-American Unity* in San Francisco. Rivera's political frivolity reached the point where he boasted of having won asylum for Trotsky with the intention of preparing for his murder. Kahlo was a silent accomplice to this ominous play-acting and died a Stalinist.

1 Stine Høholt, "Performing Herself Through Art," in *Frida Kahlo: A Life in Art* (Ostfildern/Copenhagen: Hatje Cantz/Arken Museum for Moderne Kunst, 2013), 12–22.
2 Jorge Luis Borges, "The Other," in *The Book of Sands and Shakespeare's Memory*, trans. Andrew Hurley (New York: Penguin Books, 2007), 5–9.
3 "Entrevista con Raquel Tibol. Frida poliédrica," in *Yo soy Frida*, ed. Héctor Tajonar (Mexico City: Milenio Diario, 2007), 6.
4 "Entrevista con Carlos Fuentes. Frida amada," in *Yo soy Frida*, 2.
5 "Entrevista con Raquel Tibol. Frida poliédrica," in *Yo soy Frida*, 6.
6 "Entrevista con Teresa del Conde. Frida pintora," in *Yo soy Frida*, 20.
7 "Entrevista con Teresa del Conde. Frida pintora," in *Yo soy Frida*, 20.
8 "Entrevista con Salomon Grimberg. Frida inventada," in *Yo soy Frida*, 16.
9 Hayden Herrera, *Frida: The Biography of Frida Kahlo* (London: Bloomsbury, 2018), 365.
10 Diego Rivera with Gladys March, *My Art, My Life: An Autobiography* (Garden City: Dover Publications, 1991), 180.
11 Kahlo to Diego Rivera, July 23, 1935, *Frida by Frida*, ed. Raquel Tibol and trans. Gregory Dechant (Mexico City: Editorial RM, 2006), 158.
12 "Entrevista con Elena Poniatowska. Frida color," in *Yo soy Frida*, 32.
13 "Entrevista con Elena Poniatowska. Frida color," in *Yo soy Frida*, 34.
14 "Entrevista con Raquel Tibol. Frida poliédrica," in *Yo soy Frida*, 11.
15 Herrera, *Frida*, 297.

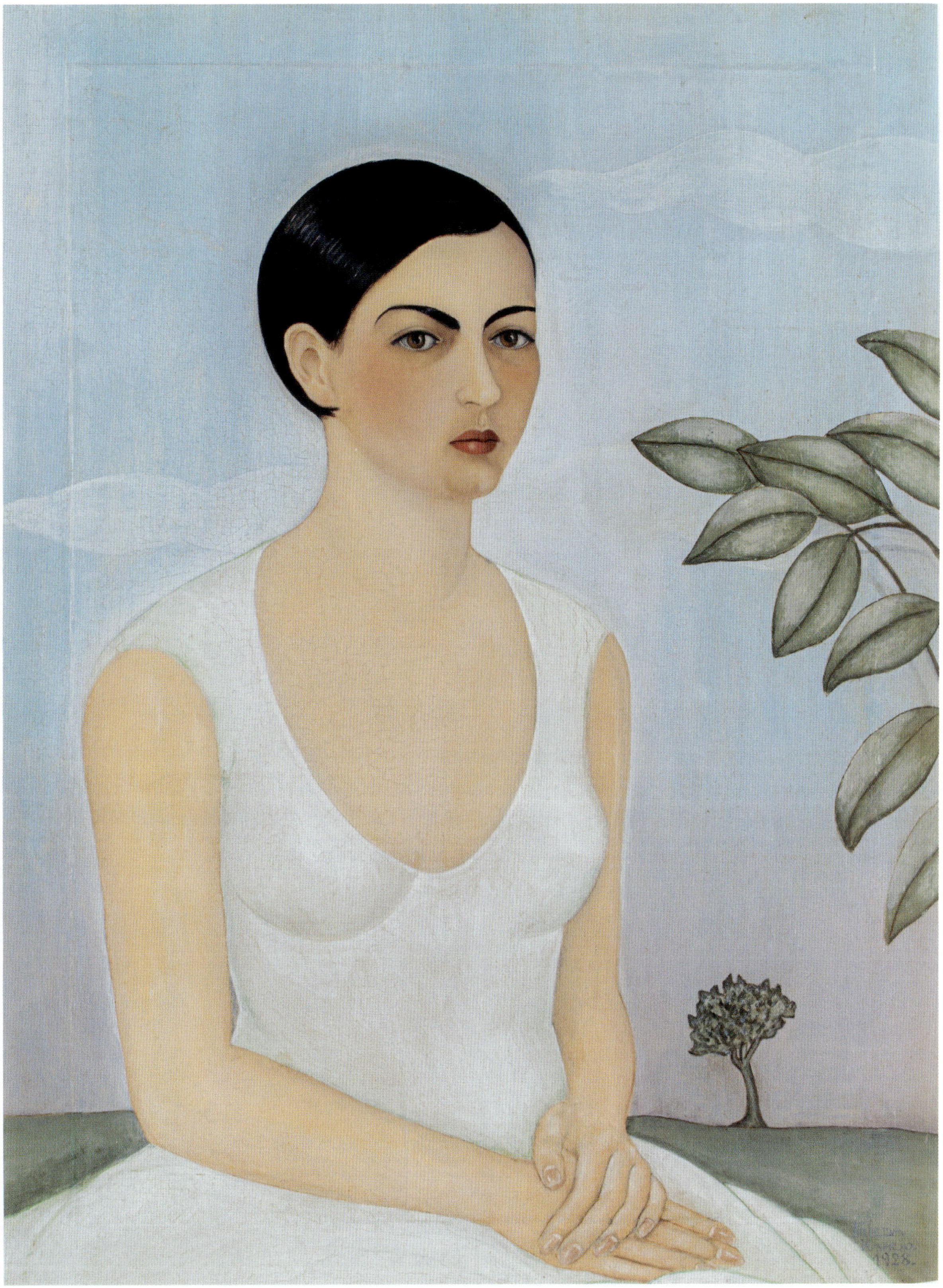

Portrait of Cristina, My Sister

1928
Oil on wood,
39 x 32 in. (99 x 81.5 cm)
Otto Atencio Collection

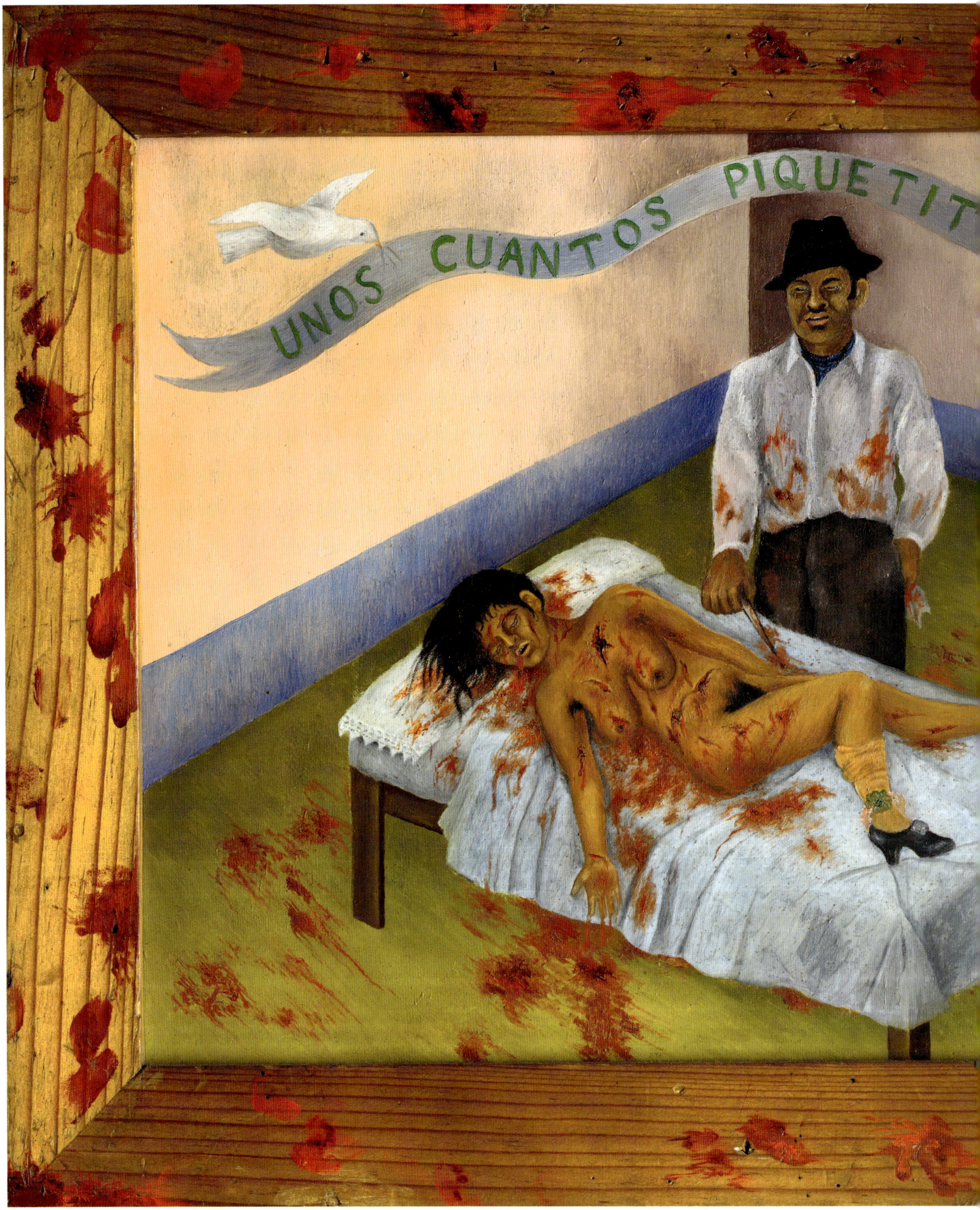
UNOS CUANTOS PIQUETIT

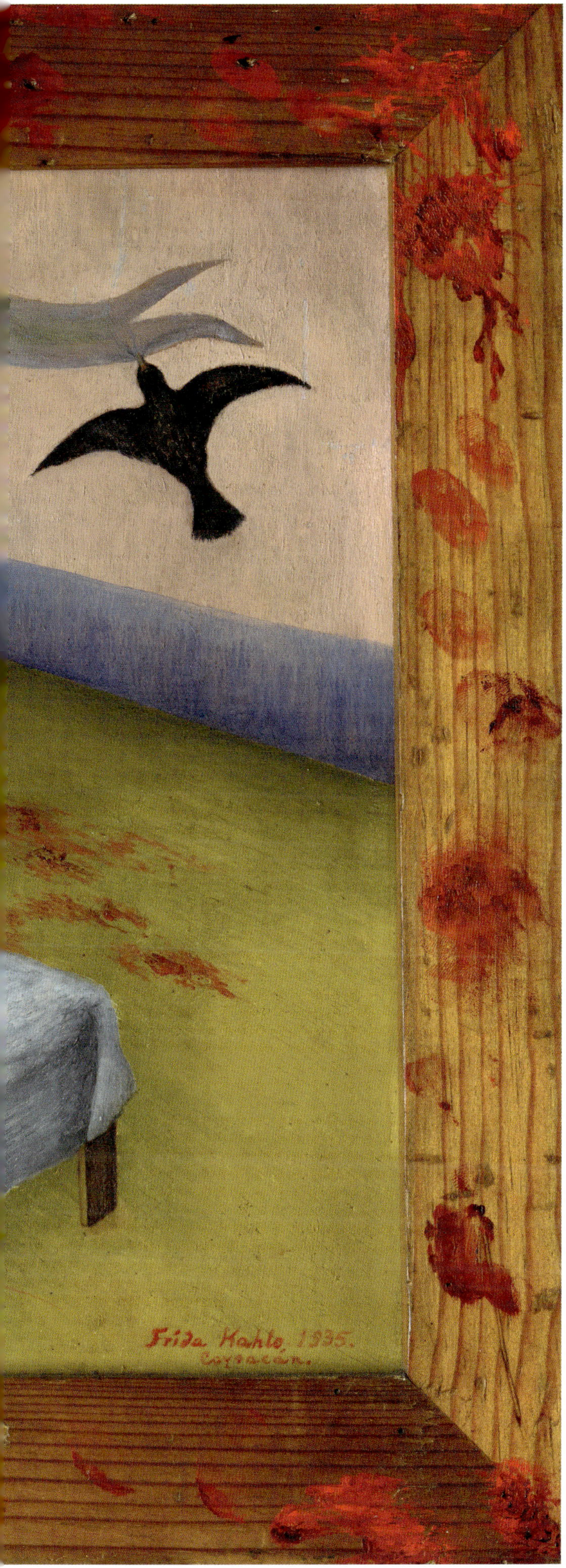

20

A Few Small Nips or
Passionately in Love

1935
Oil on metal,
15 x 19 in. (38 x 48.5 cm)
Xochimilco (Mexico City),
Collection Museo Dolores Olmedo

21

Memory or **The Heart**

1937
Oil on metal,
15¾ x 11⅛ in. (40 x 28.3 cm)
Private collection

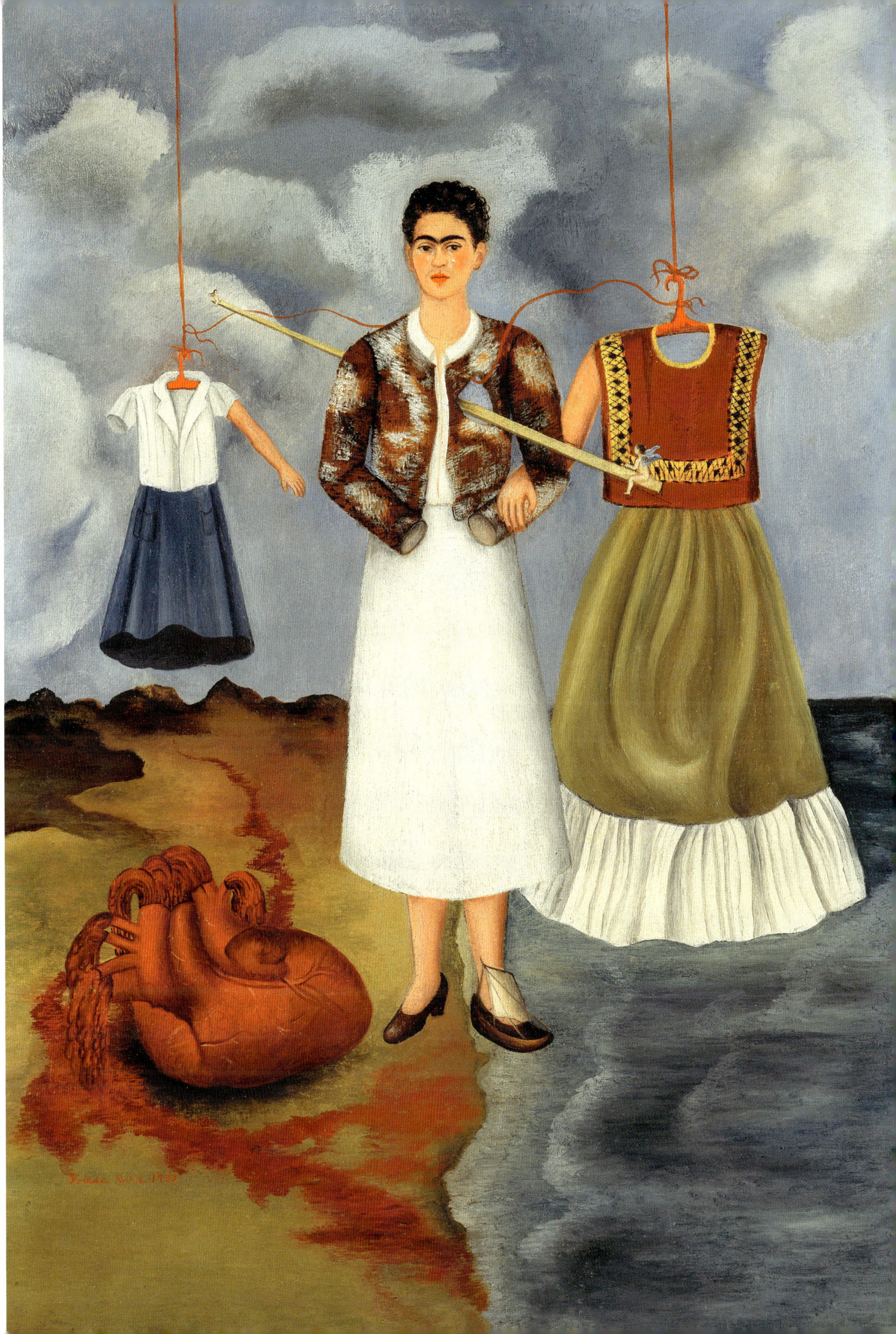
Frida Kahlo. 1937.

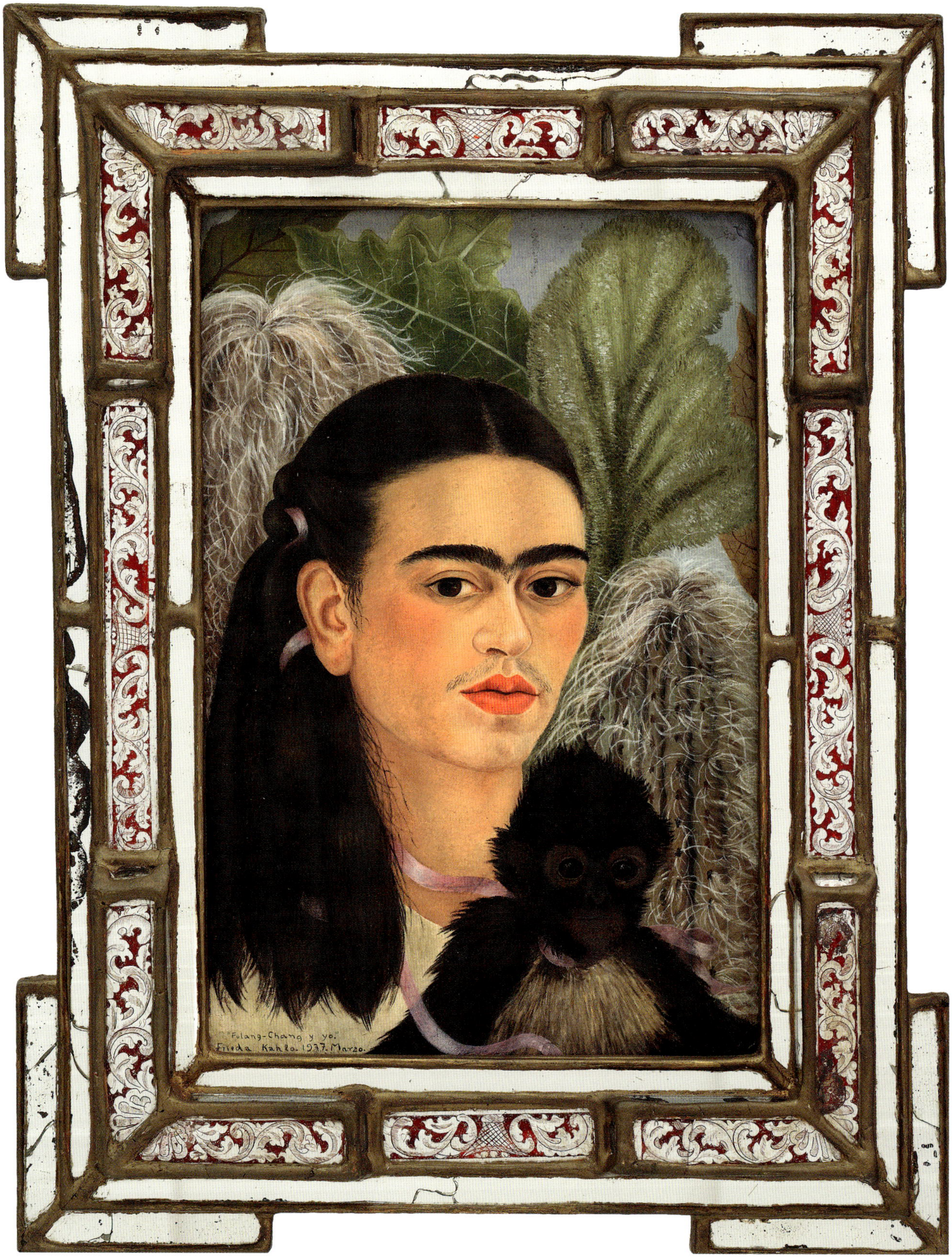
"Fulang-Chang y yo."
Frida Kahlo. 1937. Marzo.

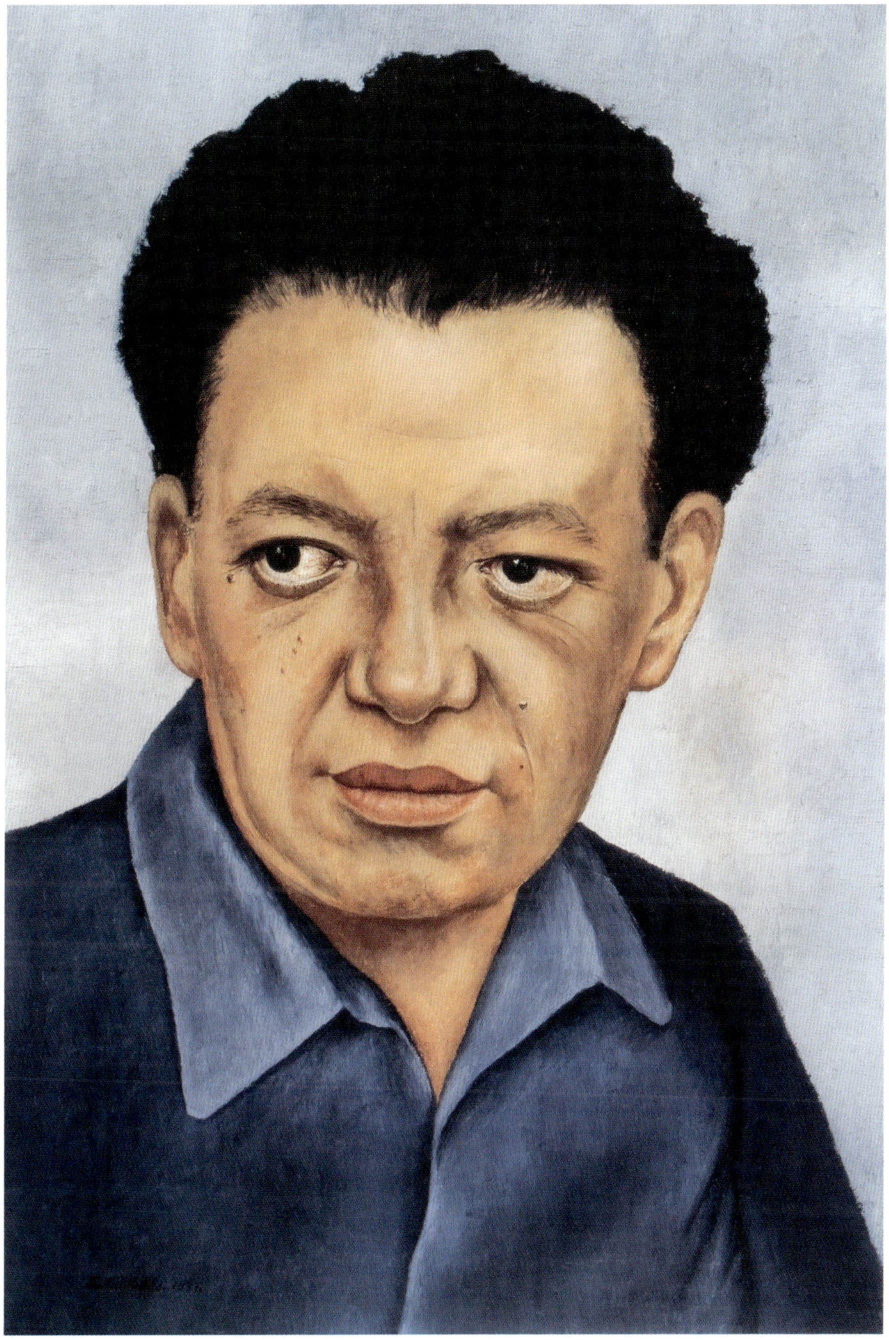

22

Fulang-Chang and I

1937 (assembled after 1939)
Oil on Masonite with painted mirror frame,
22¼ x 17⅜ x 1¾ in. (56.5 x 44.1 x 4.4 cm)
New York, Museum of Modern Art,
Mary Sklar Bequest, 277.1987.a-b

23

Portrait of Diego Rivera

1937
Oil on wood,
20⅞ x 15⅜ in. (53 x 39 cm)
Gelman Collection

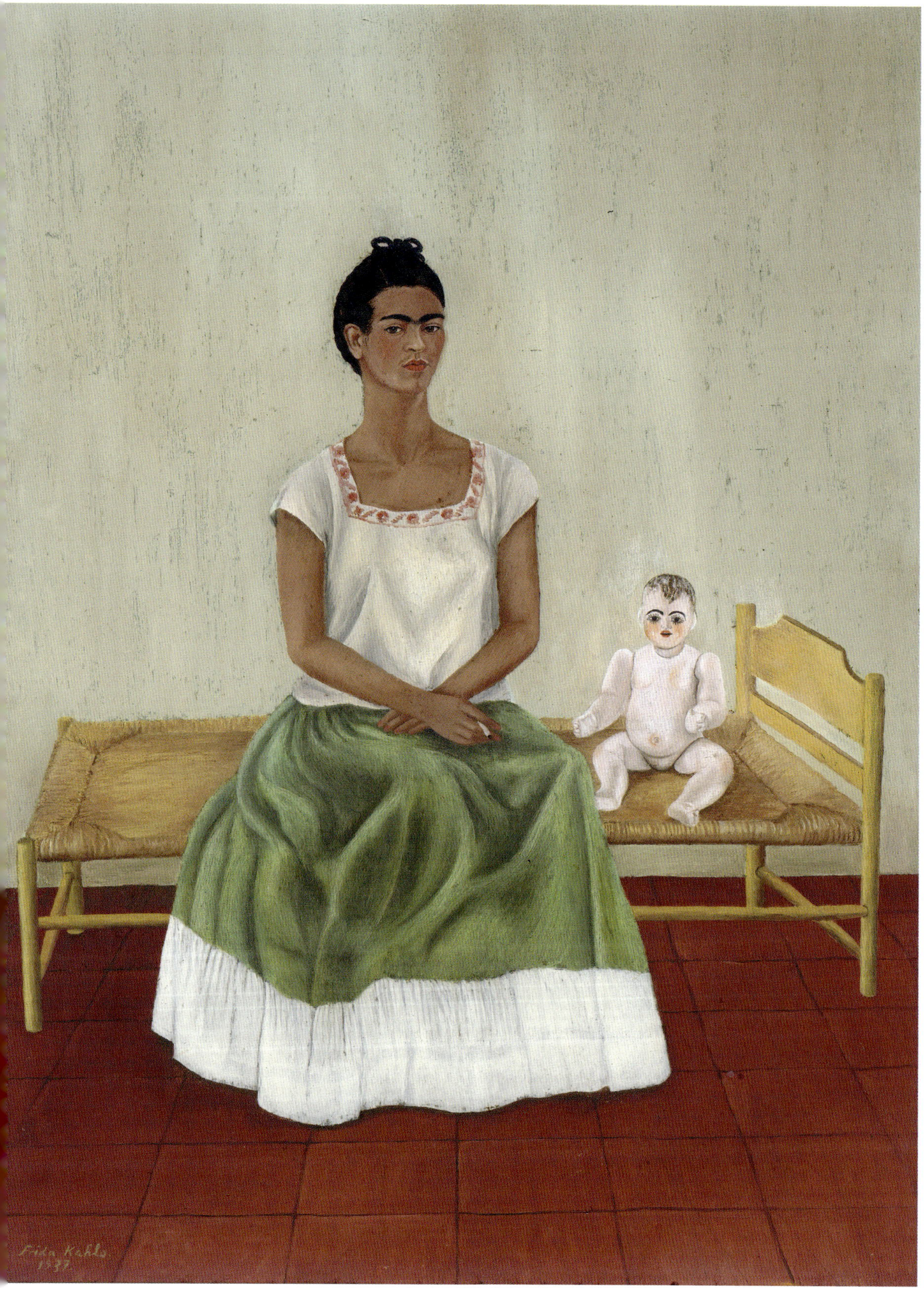

24

Me and My Doll

1937
Oil on metal,
15¾ x 12¼ in. (40 x 31 cm)
Jacques and Natasha Gelman
Collection

25

Self-portrait Dedicated to Leon Trotsky

1937
Oil on Masonite,
30 x 24 in. (76.2 x 61 cm)
Washington D.C., National
Museum of Women in the Arts,
Gift of The Honorable
Clare Boothe Luce

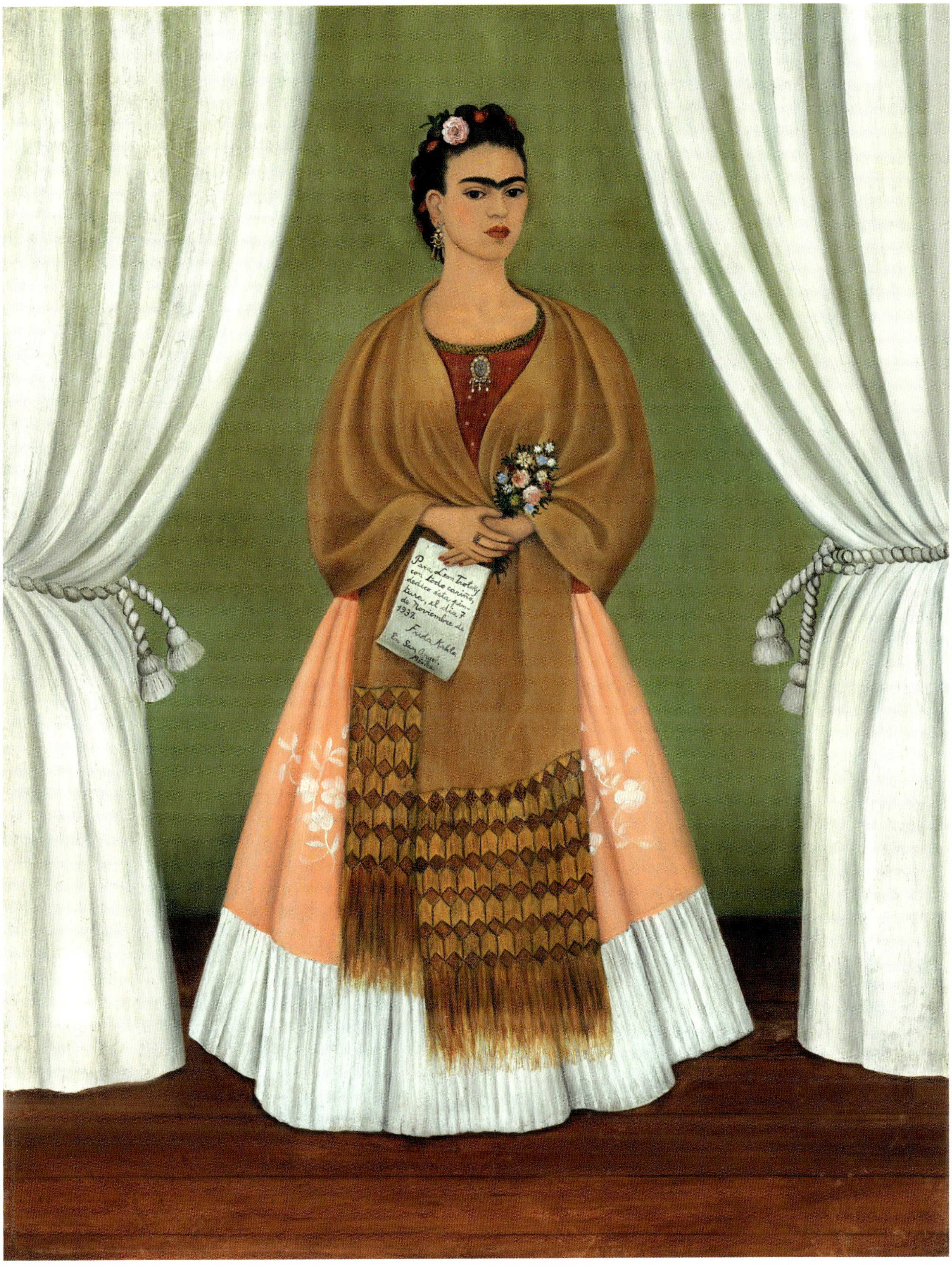
Para Leon Trotsky
con todo cariño,
dedico ésta pin-
tura, el día 7
de Noviembre de
1937.
Frida Kahlo.
En San Angel.
México.

26

Itzcuintli Dog with Me

1938
Oil on canvas,
28 x 20½ in. (71 x 52 cm)
Dallas (Texas), private collection

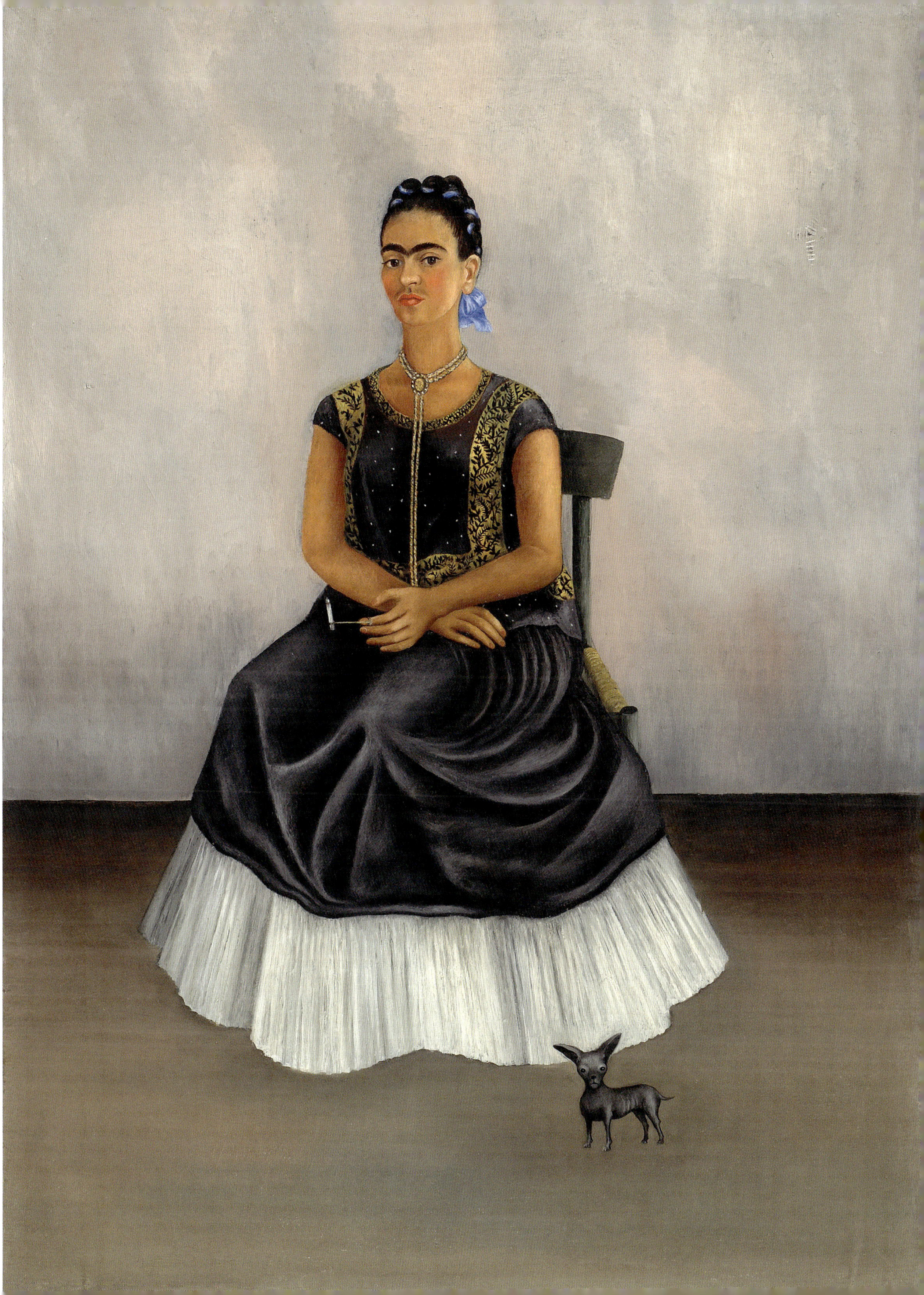

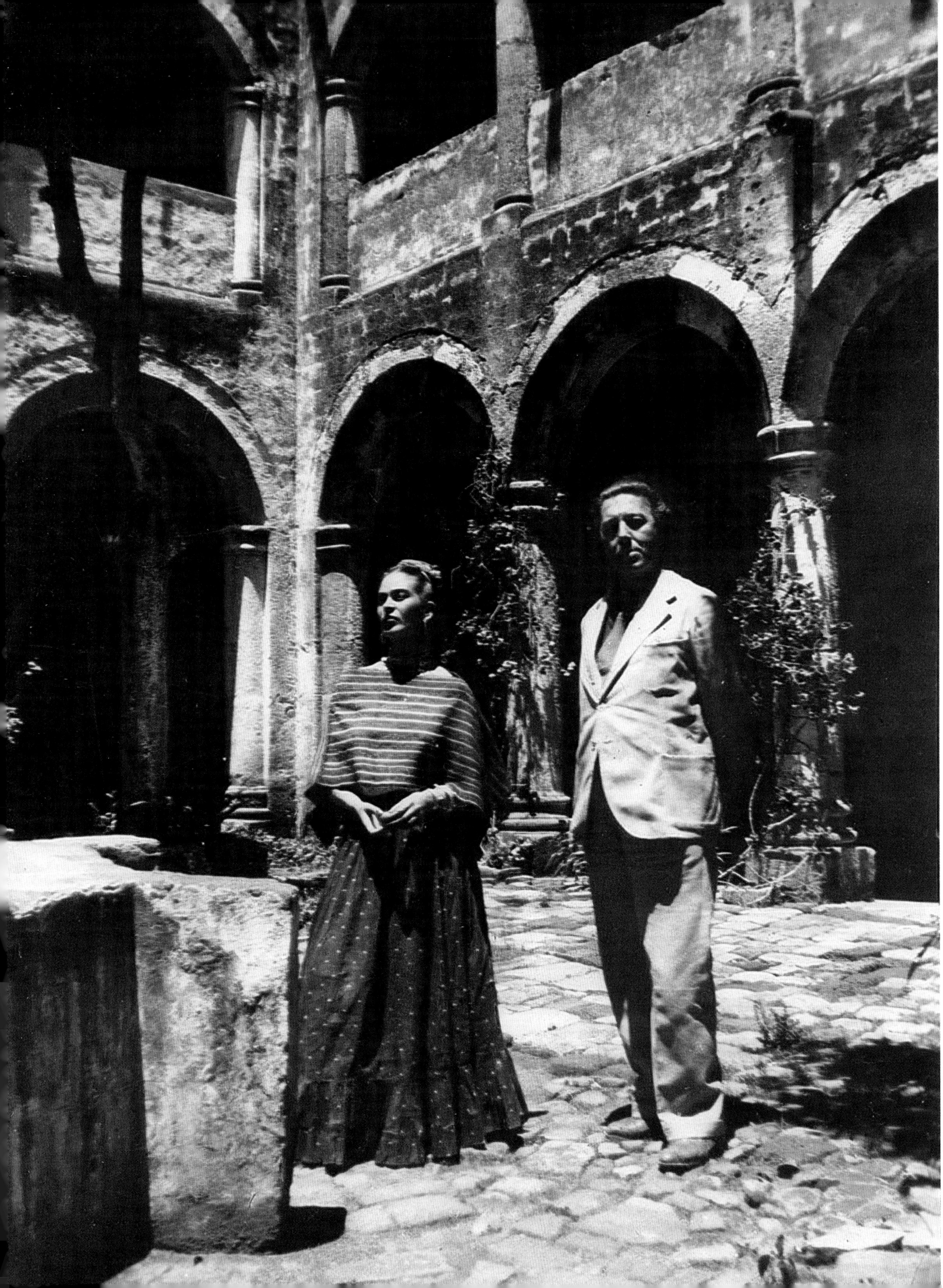

Automatic Surrealism

There is no art more exclusively feminine, in the sense that, in order to be as seductive as possible, it is only too willing to play alternately at being absolutely pure and absolutely pernicious. The art of Frida Kahlo is a ribbon about a bomb.

André Breton[1]

In 1938, the French poet André Breton (1896–1966), the founder of the Surrealist movement, traveled to Mexico with his wife, the painter Jacqueline Lamba (1910–1993), with the intention of meeting Leon Trotsky. There, he also met Frida Kahlo and Diego Rivera. He was extremely impressed by some of the works of Kahlo, whom he considered a "born Surrealist." About *Self-portrait Dedicated to Leon Trotsky* [fig. 25], he wrote:

> I have for long admired the self-portrait by Frida Kahlo de Rivera that hangs on a wall of Trotsky's study. . . . She has painted herself dressed in a robe of wings gilded with butterflies, and it is exactly in this guise that she draws aside the mental curtain. We are privileged to be present, as in the most glorious days of German romanticism, at the entry of a young woman endowed with all the gifts of seduction, one accustomed to the society of men of genius.[2]

Breton was even more impressed by Kahlo's art and personality when he saw the picture *What the Water Gave Me* (1938), a dazzling self-portrait regarded as one of the artist's greatest masterpieces, and probably the most complex and enigmatic of her works [fig. 27]. The picture shows the viewpoint of the painter as she sits with her legs stretched out in a bathtub. At the opposite end of the tub, her toes protrude above the water and are reflected to form a kind of mollusk. Seen beneath the toes are a selection of iconic objects and fragments from the artist's own paintings representing key moments in her life, both real and imaginary. Among these is the wedding portrait of her parents, while floating on a sponge are the dark Frida and the

Frida Kahlo and André Breton in Pátzcuaro (Michoacán), May 27, 1938. Photograph by Fritz Bach. Paris, Association Atelier André Breton

light Frida, as seen in the picture *Two Nudes in the Forest* or *The Earth Itself* (1939), the pictorial testimony of her lesbianism [fig. 66]. Also seen floating are the Tehuana dress from *My Dress Hangs There* [fig. 18] and an image of herself hanged and nude. The Empire State Building emerges from an erupting volcano as an allegory for the bitter memory of her time in the United States, while at the foot of the mountain are a skeleton and a male figure with a pre-Columbian mask. An enormous bird lies dead on a tree. There is also eroticized vegetation together with a large seashell with jets of water spouting from it as symbols of life. The work is an extraordinary visual metaphor for the tormented life of the great Mexican painter, with echoes of Bosch (c. 1450–1516), Pieter Brueghel (c. 1525–1569), and Salvador Dalí (1904–1989), all artists she admired.

Fascinated by the originality and expressive force of this painting, Breton helped to organize an exhibition of Kahlo's work that same year at the Julien Levy Gallery in New York, and wrote an essay for the catalogue in which he categorized her painting as Surrealist:

> My surprise and joy were unbounded when I discovered, on my arrival in Mexico, that her work had blossomed forth in her latest paintings, into pure surreality. . . . I was witnessing here, at the other end of the earth, a spontaneous outpouring of our own questioning spirit. . . .
>
> This art even contains that drop of cruelty and humor . . . [Frida] displays them proudly with a mixture of candour and insolence.[3]

Despite the recognition expressed by the founder of Surrealism, Kahlo always denied belonging to that artistic movement: "I never painted dreams. I painted my own reality."[4] There is some controversy over the question of whether Kahlo was or was not influenced by Surrealism. On the one hand, it is true that the subjects of Kahlo's work are related to her own life, enriched by an abundance of symbolic elements originating in the mythologies of many cultures, though mainly in that of Mexico, with its pre-Hispanic and Spanish roots. On the other hand, Surrealism, which appeared in 1924 with Breton's first manifesto, could not have been unknown to Kahlo. Juan Coronel Rivera, grandson of Diego Rivera, an art critic and writer who specializes in the work of Frida Kahlo and Rivera explains it as follows:

> By 1930, when Frida had this opening to the world, Surrealism was the dominant movement. It was virtually impossible not to know what Surrealism was. She was certainly very aware of the whole Surrealist aesthetic. Now we have the other part of Frida, which drew inspiration from the popular Mexican aesthetic . . . of certain artists . . . like José Guadalupe Posada or Hermenegildo Bustos, painters of the second half of the nineteenth century. Frida used to say she wasn't a Surrealist, and

she said so on several occasions. But I think there's a little of the artist's vanity in this. On a personal level, I think Frida did have Surrealist features, she did know about Surrealism, and she did use Surrealism. Although it suited her for nationalist purposes to say she wasn't a Surrealist, she does have very clear links with Surrealism.[5]

Definitions and affiliations aside, what is certain is that the meeting with Breton led to the international recognition of Frida Kahlo. Her exhibition at the Julien Levy Gallery, the epicenter of New York Surrealism, was a success in terms of both sales and the number of visitors, many of them celebrities, as well as favorable reviews in the American press. The actor Edward G. Robinson purchased four works, and the photographer Nickolas Muray (1892–1965), one of Kahlo's lovers, bought *What the Water Gave Me*. The celebrated painter Georgia O'Keeffe (1887–1986) and the great sculptor Isamu Noguchi (1904–1988) were also at the show's opening. Both also belong to the list of Kahlo's lovers, as does Jacqueline Lamba, Breton's wife. We shall return later to the topic of Kahlo's extremely free sexuality.

The next year, 1939, another exhibition of Kahlo's work was held at the Galerie Renou et Colle in Paris, the cradle of Surrealism. This time there were organizational difficulties, as Breton washed his hands of the affair and failed to fetch the pictures from customs or confirm the gallery booking. Fortunately, Kahlo was helped by none other than Marcel Duchamp (1887–1968), one of the foremost figures of the twentieth-century artistic avant-garde. "Duchamp (a marvellous painter) who is the only one who has his feet on the earth, among all this bunch of coocoo lunatic sons of bitches of the surrealists,"[6] Kahlo wrote. Entitled *Mexique*, the show finally opened on March 10. In addition to seventeen paintings by Kahlo, it included a number of pre-Hispanic, colonial, and contemporary Mexican works, "all that junk" in Kahlo's opinion.[7] Her pictures were the main attraction of the exhibition. The opening was both well attended and very well received by the critics. The Musée du Louvre acquired the piece entitled *The Frame* (1938), an unusual small-format self-portrait in which the artist experiments with several techniques [fig. 28]. Kahlo's face and the blue background are painted on a sheet of aluminum, while the birds and flowers that surround her are painted on the glass that covers the portrait. The bright colors and the figures around the face are deliberately naive to emphasize the popular style of the painting. This work, the first by a contemporary artist to be acquired by the Louvre, is currently part of the Centre Pompidou collection.

The critic L. P. Foucaud wrote in the magazine *La Flèche* that Kahlo's works were "a door opened on the infinite and on the continuity of art."[8] He praised the purity of the colors, the perfection of the line, and the authenticity and sincerity of her painting. He also contrasted the Mexican artist's "striking probity and exactitude" with the lies and deceit then in vogue.[9] In addition, Kahlo received warm congratulations from painters of the stature of Wassily Kandinsky (1866–1944), Joan Miró (1893–1983), Yves Tanguy (1900–1955), Wolfgang Paalen (1905–1959), and Pablo Picasso (1881–1973), who gave her some earrings in the form of stylized ivory hands with gold hoops. Diego Rivera was not present at either of his wife's two exhibitions, but on another occasion Picasso did remark to Rivera: "Look at those eyes: neither you nor I are capable of anything like it."[10]

In *Self-portrait Dedicated to Dr. Eloesser* (1940), the artist wears one of the earrings given to her by Picasso [fig. 29]. In this autumnal scene dominated by shades of ocher, Kahlo, seen in three-quarter view, wears brown and is surrounded by a vegetation of dry leaves and twigs, except for three twigs with an ivory tone like that of the earring. The floral headdress of yellow and pink harmonizes with the gray, pink, and violet sky in the background. Drops of blood fall from Kahlo's neck owing to the thorn necklace she wears around it. The look on her face is hard and firm, expressive of pain stoically borne.

That same year, she painted her *Self-portrait with Thorn Necklace and Hummingbird* (1940), a masterpiece of great symbolic complexity [fig. 30]. Kahlo is shown frontally, with the thorn necklace running not only around her neck but also over her shoulders and chest. Hanging in the center of the necklace is a stuffed hummingbird. The artist's face is flanked by a spider monkey and a black cat whose green eyes are fixed on the viewer. The background of the composition is covered by exuberant foliage allusive to *Le Douanier* by the painter Henri Rousseau (1844–1910). Two butterflies rest on her purple headdress and flying next to them are two flowers transformed into dragonflies. In contrast with the previous work, Kahlo is here completely self-absorbed, deep in an introspection that is closer to Buddhist meditation than to the defiant stoicism of the canvas dedicated to her doctor. Both self-portraits reveal the artist's profound suffering caused by her divorce from Rivera. *Self-portrait with Thorn Necklace and Hummingbird* has generally been interpreted from the perspective of the Catholicism of the colonial iconography of New Spain and the popular art of Mexico. Kahlo lived with such art from an early age, and it was undoubtedly engraved on her memory and sensibility, even though she always rejected the religiosity that her mother was determined to force on her. It therefore makes sense to interpret the thorn necklace as an analogy to the suffering of Christ, crowned with thorns on his way to Calvary and his death by crucifixion. Frida Kahlo experienced her own Calvary during her life, not only because of the physical pain she suffered as a result of illness, accidents, surgical operations, miscarriages, and immobility, but also as a result of the emotional torture produced by her passionate love for Rivera and, above all, by their divorce in 1939.

The symbolism of the hummingbird comes from Aztec mythology. It was believed that the spirits of dead warriors returned to earthly life in the form of hummingbirds, in a sort of pagan resurrection. Moreover, this beautiful animal with phosphorescent blue and green plumage, which moves its wings and flies at astonishing speed but can also hover motionless to insert its pointed beak into a flower and drink its nectar, was a symbol of masculinity among the ancient Mexicans. The hummingbird sucking the flower is a metaphor for the sexual act, the petals of the flower represent the vulva, and the hummingbird's beak is a phallic symbol.[11] In popular lore, hummingbirds are also related to joy and beauty and are attributed magical powers for winning and retaining love, or for healing the pain of its absence. The allegorical complexity of the hummingbird, linked to life, sexuality, love, and even resurrection, is applicable to Kahlo's visual metaphor, above all when the hummingbird in her picture, as we can see, is dead.

Is the menacing gaze of the black cat, the popular symbol of bad luck, stalking Rivera or warning him of its curse? The spider monkey (Kahlo kept them as pets) accompanies her in this and other self-portraits as an allegory of lust. Admired for its lightness and elegance, the dragonfly refers to the untimely changes of life, while the symbolism of the butterfly is among the richest and most varied in nature owing both to the beauty of its colors and patterns and to its biological complexity. The metamorphosis of the butterfly alludes to the perpetual becoming of existence and the capacity of life for transformation, and the flying flowers are therefore a symbol of the soul surviving death. The Greek word *psyche* means both soul and butterfly. All this symbolic complexity may indicate that within the painter's melancholy, there was still hope.

Breton defined his movement as "pure psychic automatism . . . in the absence of any control exercised by reason, and beyond any esthetic or moral preoccupation."[12] We might talk of an automatic Surrealism that emerged in Kahlo purely or spontaneously. Some of her pictures can be read as personal pictorial versions of Surrealist "automatic writing." Indeed, on certain pages of her diary, Kahlo appears to have adopted the automatic writing method, which consists of spontaneously writing down the dictates of the imagination without passing them through the filter of rationality. Nevertheless, the allegorical and biographical specificities of her creative imagination place her beyond any school of painting. Rivera held that Kahlo's creative imagination allowed her to elevate reality toward "a marvelous logical fantasy."[13] He was of the opinion that "Frida Kahlo is the greatest of the Mexican painters" and her work "one of the finest and greatest plastic documents and most intense true human documents of our time."[14]

Having said all this, it should be mentioned that one of the reasons for Kahlo and Rivera's break with Surrealism was Breton's fervent Trotskyism, as they distanced themselves from the Soviet leader to seek readmission to the Mexican Communist Party in the 1940s.

1 André Breton, "Frida Kahlo" in *Surrealism and Painting*, trans. Simon Watson Taylor (New York: Harper & Row, 1972), 141–44, quoted in Hayden Herrera, *Frida: The Biography of Frida Kahlo* (London: Bloomsbury, 2018), 214.
2 Breton, *Surrealism and Painting*, 141–44, quoted in Herrera, *Frida*, 213–14.
3 Breton, *Surrealism and Painting*, 144, quoted in Herrera, *Frida*, 228.
4 Herrera, *Frida*, 266.
5 "Entrevista con Juan Coronel. Frida ícono," in *Yo soy Frida*, ed. Héctor Tajonar (Mexico City: Milenio Diario, 2007), 28.
6 Kahlo to Nickolas Muray, February 16, 1939, *Frida by Frida*, ed. Raquel Tibol and trans. Gregory Dechant (Mexico City: Editorial RM, 2006), 198.
7 Herrera, *Frida*, 250.
8 L. P. Foucaud, "L'Exposition de Frida Kahlo," *La Flèche* (March 1939), quoted in Herrera, *Frida*, 251.
9 Foucaud, quoted in Herrera, *Frida*, 251.
10 Herrera, *Frida*, 362.
11 Miriam López Hernández, "El colibrí como símbolo de la sexualidad masculina entre los mexicas," *Itinerarios* 21 (2015), 79–100.
12 William S. Rubin, *Dada and Surrealist Art* (New York: Harry N. Abrams, 1969), 121, quoted in Herrera, *Frida*, 254–55.
13 Raquel Tibol, "The Two Fridas," in *Frida Kahlo: National Homage, 1907–2007* (Mexico City: Instituto Nacional de Bellas Artes, 2008), 204.
14 Raquel Tibol, *Frida Kahlo en su luz más íntima* (Mexico City: Random House Mondadori, 2005), 164.

27

What the Water Gave Me

1938
Oil on canvas,
35⅞ x 27¾ in. (91 x 70.5 cm)
Paris, Collection of Daniel Filipacchi

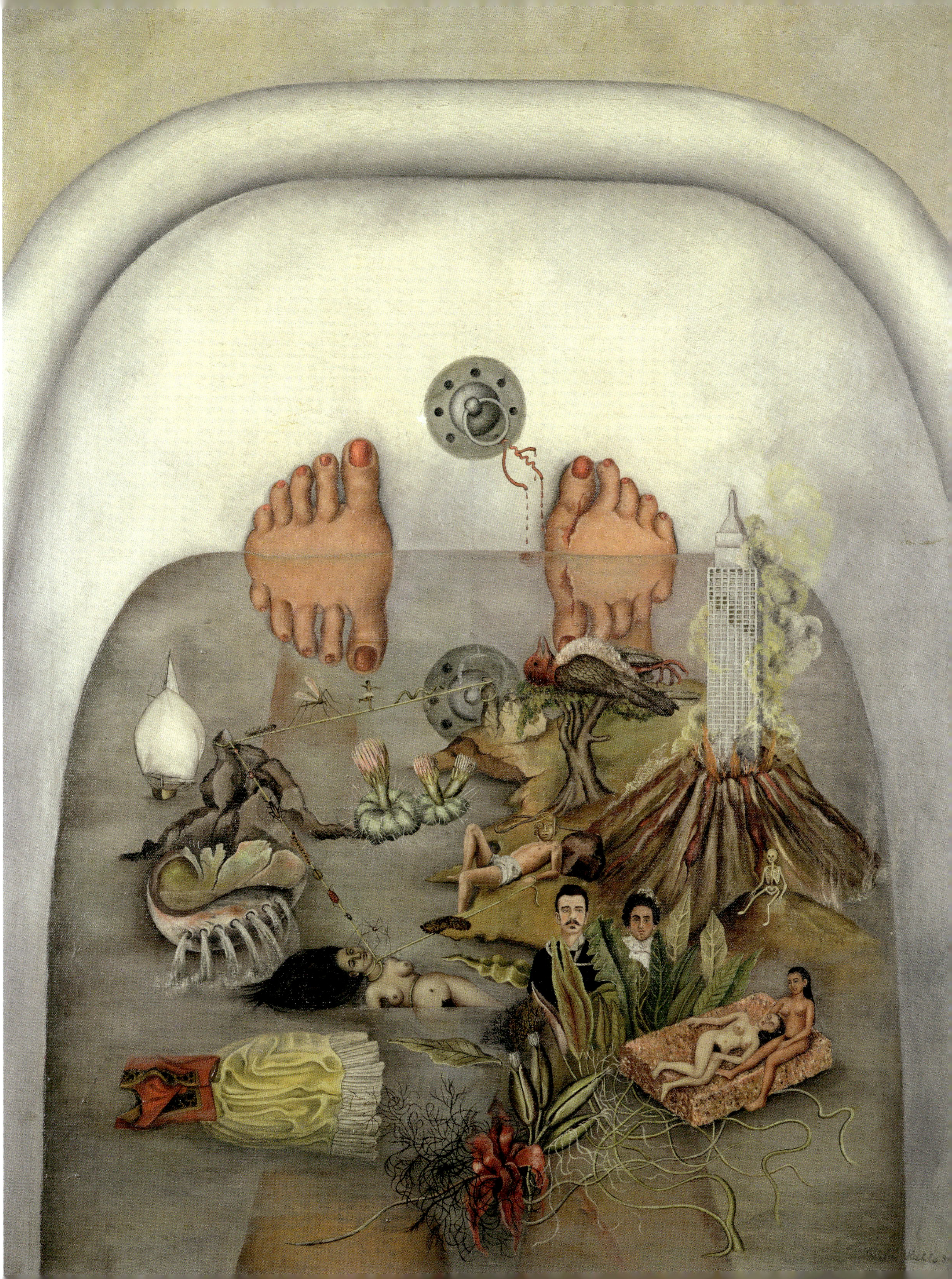

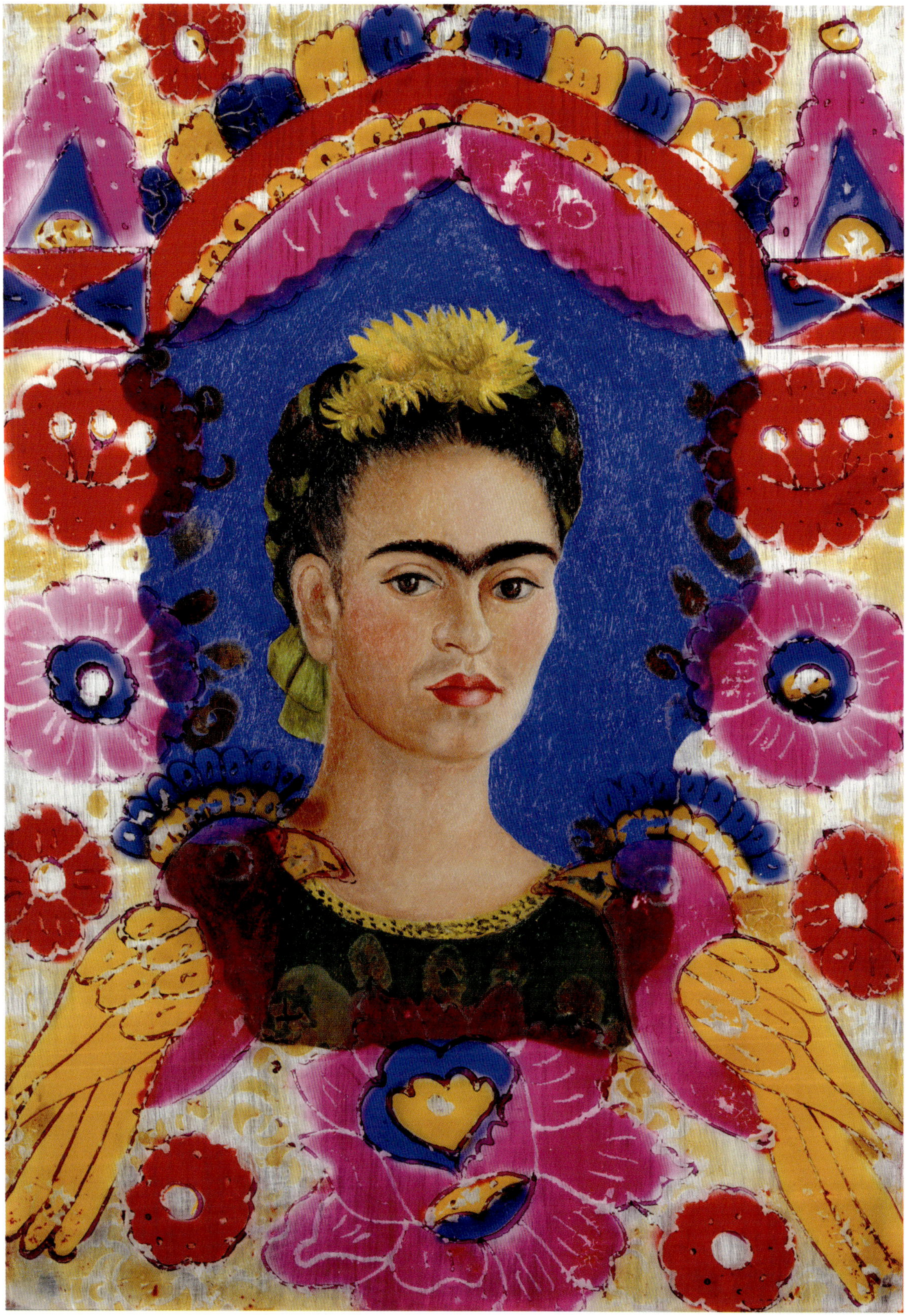

28

The Frame

1938
Oil on metal and glass,
11¼ x 8⅛ in.
(28.5 x 20.7 cm)
Paris, Centre Pompidou,
JP 929 P (1)

29

Self-portrait Dedicated to Dr. Eloesser

1940
Oil on Masonite,
23⅜ x 15¾ in. (59.5 x 40 c
Private collection

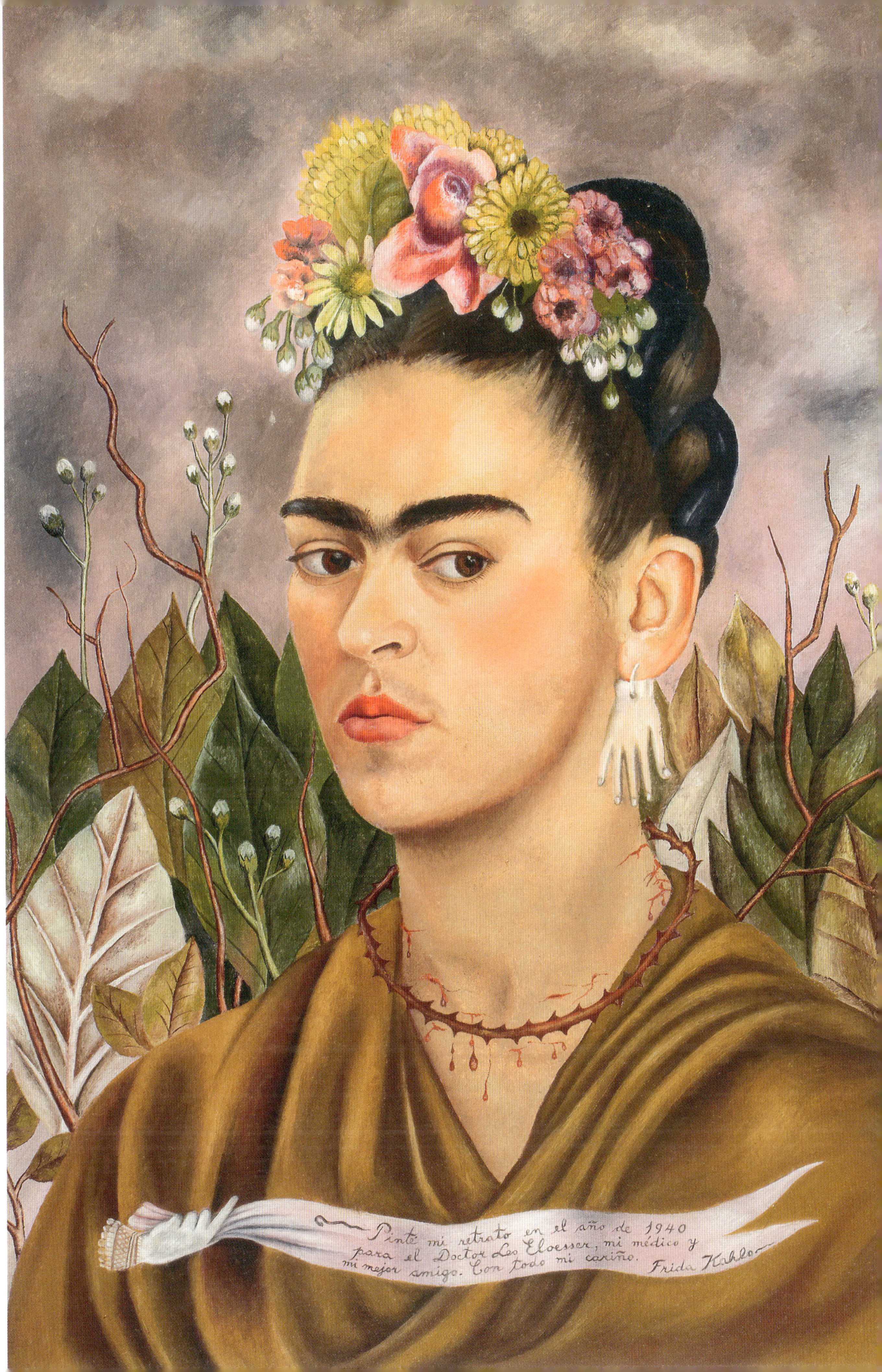
Pinté mi retrato en el año de 1940
para el Doctor Leo Eloesser, mi médico y
mi mejor amigo. Con todo mi cariño.
Frida Kahlo

30

Self-portrait with Thorn Necklace and Hummingbird

1940
Oil on canvas mounted to board,
24⅛ x 18½ in. (61.3 x 47 cm)
Austin, Harry Ransom Center,
University of Texas at Austin,
Nickolas Muray Collection of
Mexican Art, 66.6

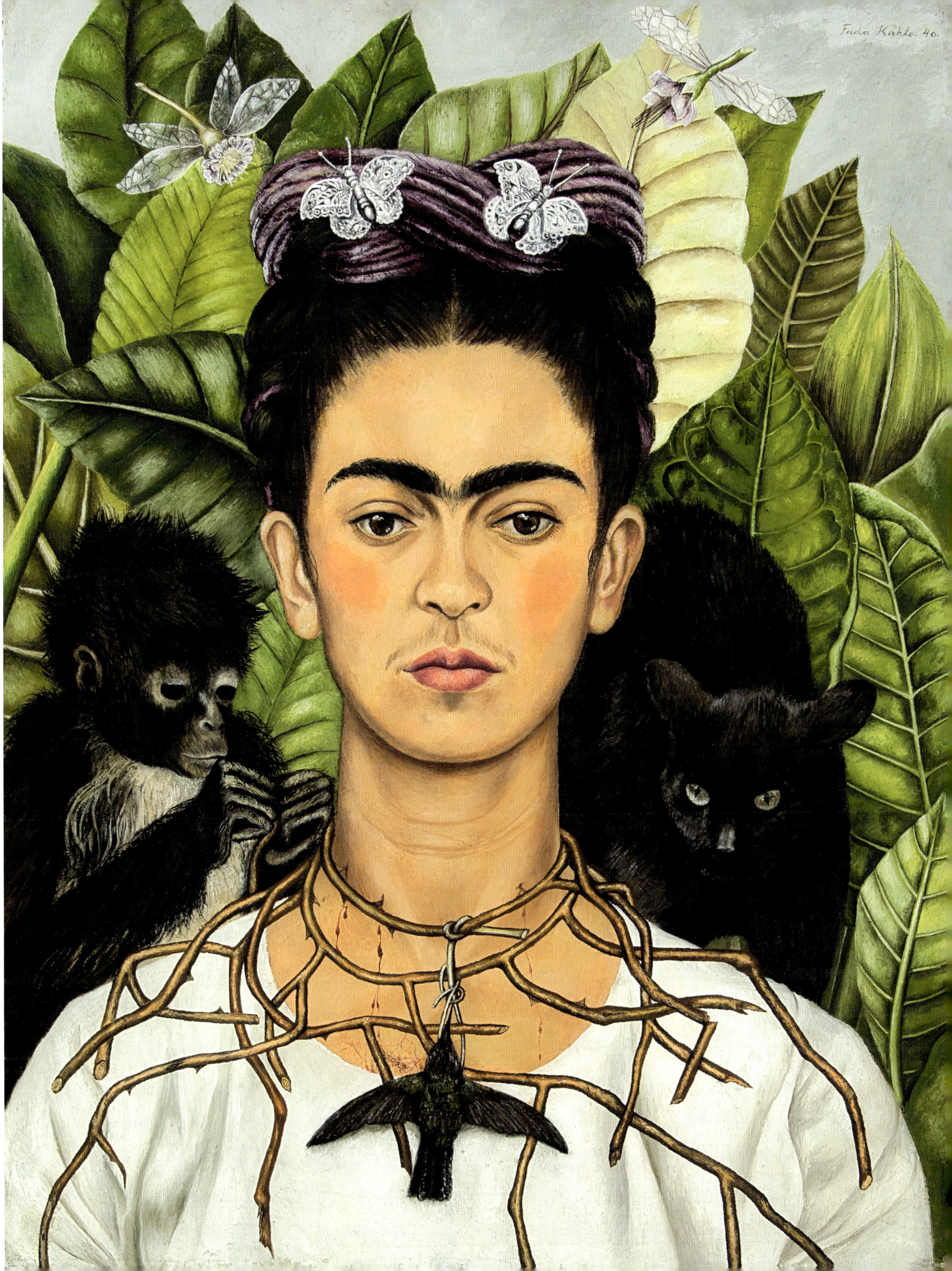
Frida Kahlo. 40.

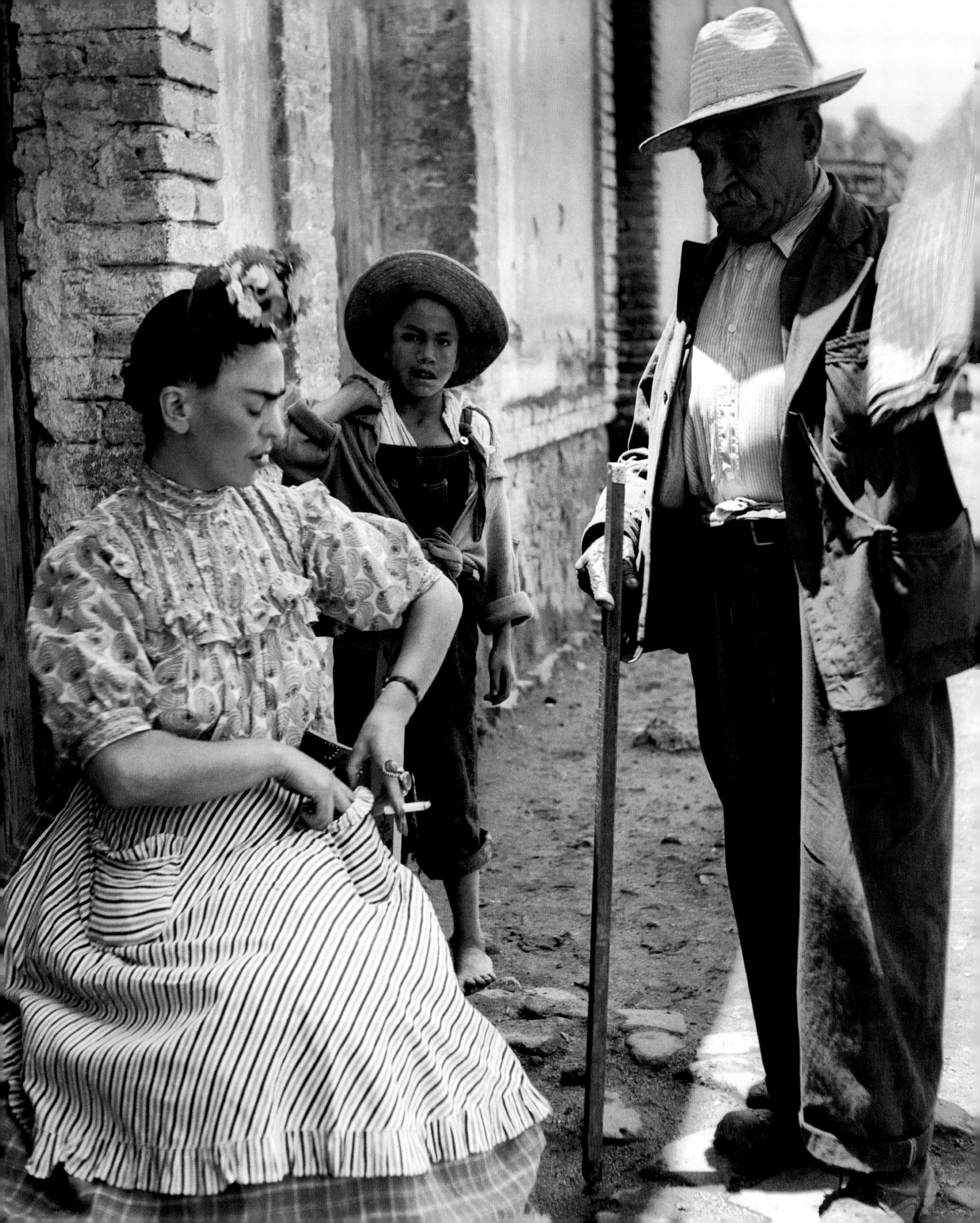

Amorous Suffering

Happy love has no history. Romance only comes into existence where love is fatal, frowned upon and doomed by life itself. What stirs lyrical poets to their finest flights is . . . not the satisfaction of love, but its *passion.* And passion means suffering. There we have the fundamental fact.

Denis de Rougemont[1]

The Two Fridas (1939) is a work painted with the heart exposed, and perhaps the work that most sincerely and dramatically bares the artist's split soul [fig. 31]. Its Spanish title is *Yo dos veces* ("Me twice"). Using the visual language of Surrealism, it makes an indelible impression on the viewer. Frida Kahlo painted it in the year when Diego Rivera asked her for a divorce, and it is considered "the sacred icon of Mexican art par excellence."[2] It was first shown at the International Surrealist Exhibition inaugurated on January 17, 1940, at Inés Amor's Galería de Arte Mexicano in Mexico City, an event organized by André Breton, Wolfgang Paalen (1905–1959), and César Moro (1903–1956). Kahlo took part with two works: *The Two Fridas* and *The Wounded Table* (1940), the only large-format pieces in the artist's production. The latter has been missing for nearly seventy years. *The Two Fridas* measures 68⅛ by 68⅛ inches (173 by 173 centimeters), and the figures are almost life-size.

In a visual metaphor for her existential duality, Kahlo depicts herself as two seated twins facing frontally and looking at the viewer, their hands joined. Both wear their hearts, connected by a vein, outside their clothing. The two facets of her personality and the two phases of her life are indissolubly fused. The Frida on the left wears a wedding dress in the style of the years of Porfirio Díaz, like the one worn by her mother when she was married. She is the old-fashioned, controlling wife who thought she would have a traditional, stable, and tranquil relationship with Diego Rivera. Although she holds forceps in her right hand to staunch a bleeding vein, she is losing blood because her husband has asked her for a divorce. The Frida on the right wears a Tehuana dress, and the blood vessel coiled around her arm ends in a miniature portrait in her left hand showing Diego at the age of four. This is the woman who adores Rivera and adopts him as her son to get the energy from him that feeds her heart and gives

Frida Kahlo and a cloth salesman, Coyoacán (Mexico City), 1945. Photograph by Leo Matiz. Mexico City, Fundación Leo Matiz

her life. *The Two Fridas* represents the dichotomy within her: the conscious and the unconscious, her bisexuality, pleasure and pain, Eros and Thanatos, body and soul. In her diary, Kahlo wrote a text entitled "Origin of the Two Fridas," in which she tells the story of her imaginary friend, the woman she had wanted to be since she was a child, had never been able to be, and upon whom she projected herself.[3] She also wrote in her diary: "Feet what do I need them for / If I have wings to fly."[4] Perhaps those wings were her imaginary friend, the doubling up of herself through the flight of the imagination. Carlos Fuentes puts it concisely: "Frida was a woman who knew herself to be double. . . . She had to think of the existence of another Frida who was the opposite of what she was and yet was also her."[5]

In his autobiography, Diego Rivera narrates the process of their divorce:

> I never was—the reader may be bored with my repeating it—a faithful husband, even with Frida. As with Angeline and Lupe, I indulged my caprices and had affairs. Now, moved by the extremity of Frida's condition, I began taking stock of myself as a marriage partner. I found very little which could be said in my favor. And yet I knew I could not change. . . .
>
> I loved her too much to want to cause her suffering, and to spare her further torments, I decided to separate from her.
>
> In the beginning, I only hinted at the idea of a divorce, but when the hints brought no response, I made the suggestion openly. Frida, who had by now recovered her health, responded calmly that she would prefer to endure anything rather than lose me completely. . . .
>
> We had been married now for thirteen years [actually ten]. We still loved each other. I simply wanted to be free to carry on with any woman who caught my fancy. . . .
>
> During the two years we lived apart, Frida turned out some of her best work, sublimating her anguish in her painting.[6]

Pleasure and pain, the opposites that Sigmund Freud saw as determining the whole of man's psychic activity, cannot be learned by hearing them described but can only be known through experience. In her self-portraits, Kahlo testified to her struggle against this existential dilemma. Suffering may have surpassed pleasure in the artist's life, but it never defeated it. Eros managed to overcome Thanatos. She wrote in her diary: "Anguish and pain—pleasure and death are no more than a process for existence . . . we foresee the death that we die every second."[7]

The Circle (c. 1954), a small work 6 inches (15 centimeters) in diameter painted in oil on a zinc plate, unsigned and undated, is a dramatic representation of the confrontation and coexistence of pleasure and death, desire and anguish: the fusion of opposites that inhabited Kahlo's damaged body [fig. 32]. Painted with brushwork close to Abstract Expressionism, it shows a nude woman in the midst of an explosion of ecstasy and disintegration. In this masterly miniature, as Raquel Tibol says, "oil paint mixes with the blood of her inner monologue."[8]

Kahlo's suffering also found expression in the work *Without Hope* (1945), where she shows herself force-fed with a funnel to make up for the enormous amount of weight she had lost [fig. 33].

Between 1940 and 1941, Kahlo painted a series of self-portraits on commission or with the intention of selling them to pay her expenses. Among the most outstanding is *Self-portrait Dedicated to Sigmund Firestone* (1940), where she is very attractive. Her gaze is severe but coquettish; she wears an elegant pink blouse that she combines with a striking necklace of pre-Columbian origin and she has her hair gathered back in a purple headwrap and a black lace mantilla [fig. 34]. In *Self-portrait with Braid* (1941), her coiffure is adorned with a skein of purple wool forming a spectacular crown-like headdress, inspired by those worn by indigenous women in Oaxaca and Puebla [fig. 35]. Instead of a dress, exotic plants cover her chest. Spider monkeys, a symbol of sexuality, were among her favorite pets and are shown accompanying her in four pictures: *Self-portrait with Monkey* (1938), *Self-portrait with Monkey* (1940), *Self-portrait with Monkeys* (1943), and *Self-portrait with Small Monkey* (1945) [figs. 36–39]. In *Me and My Parrots* (1941), Kahlo is sitting amidst four parrots, two perched on her shoulders and two on her lap, behind her forearms. She wears a white short-sleeved blouse, and in her right hand she holds a cigarette [fig. 41]. The same year, she painted the subject again in *Self-portrait with Bonito* (1941) [fig. 40].

Very different from these, *Self-portrait with Cropped Hair* (1940) represents an act of rage and rebellion on Kahlo's part: cutting off the hair that Rivera liked so much [fig. 42]. The artist, seated on a rustic chair, holds in her right hand the scissors she has just used to crop her hair, which is strewn over the ground in long tufts. She wears a very bulky gray man's suit that could well have belonged to Rivera. Written on the back wall are the lyrics and score of a song that reads, "If I loved you, it was for your hair. Now that you're cropped, I don't love you anymore." The picture, a provocative reproach to her ex-husband, shows her deprived of all her feminine attributes except the earring that hangs from her right ear.

The Dream or *The Bed* (1940) is a symbolic self-portrait that shows Kahlo fast asleep on a bed floating in a cloudy sky [fig. 43]. Resting on the canopy is a "Judas" in the form of a skeleton, its firecrackers visible and liable to go off at any moment. The Judas is a popular tradition in Mexican Catholicism: a cardboard figure in the form of a devil or other representative of evil that is burned or exploded (or both) at Easter so that good will prevail. The name is a reference to Judas Iscariot, who betrayed Jesus after the Last Supper and delivered him to his captors. The picture is an allegory of the constant presence of death, while the plants around Kahlo allude to life and resurrection: the love of Rivera, now dead, will be reborn.

In 2006, the painting entitled *Roots* (1943) was auctioned at Sotheby's for 5.6 million dollars, at that time the highest price ever fetched by a Latin American artwork at auction. Madonna was said to have been the buyer [fig. 44]. The work is a hymn to life as it emerges from Kahlo herself, represented here as a germinator of vital energy. Sprouting from her open chest are leafy vines that combine with her own veins to feed the barren surrounding landscape. By means of a visual metaphor, the woman who is unable to bear children is transformed into a source of life.

The self-portrait *My Nurse and I* (1937) was one of Kahlo and Rivera's favorites, and it was included in the exhibition at the Julien Levy Gallery in New York in 1938 [fig. 45]. The face of a wet nurse is covered by a Teotihuacan mask, a sign of the painter's pride in her indigenous heritage through her maternal grandfather and of her admiration for the legacy of pre-Hispanic culture.

> My mother was not able to breastfeed me because eleven months after my birth, my sister Cristina was born. I was fed by a nurse whose breasts they washed every time I was going to suck them. In one of my pictures, you see me, with the face of a grown woman and the body of a little girl, in the arms of my nurse, while the milk drips from her nipples as though falling from the sky.[9]

While Kahlo feeds from an indigenous breast in *My Nurse and I*, in *Roots* it is she who fertilizes the Mexican earth.

In *Girl with Death Mask* (1938), the masks depicting a skull and a fierce humanized feline relate to the tradition of masks as a fundamental part of popular festivities in the indigenous and peasant communities of Mexico [fig. 46]. At the same time, the mask covering the face of the little girl (Frida?) is related to Xipe Totec, the god of death and resurrection in Mexican mythology, also known as the "flayed god" because the skins of those sacrificed by flaying were then used to cover the bodies and faces of Xipe Totec's priests in his honor. In this picture, the cyclical duality of pre-Hispanic cosmology—life-death, creation-destruction—is symbolically adopted by the artist, who was aware of it from her earliest childhood.

Kahlo's attraction to the concept of duality in Mesoamerican mythology appears again in *Girl from Tehuacán, Lucha María* or *Sun and Moon* (1942) [fig. 47], where an indigenous adolescent sitting on a rock is flanked by the pyramids of the moon and the sun of Teotihuacán, the city of the gods, where the Nahua people situated the legend of the birth of the fifth sun, or of the creation of the era of man, in the ancient Mexican cosmogony. The myth, recorded by friar Bernardino de Sahagún in the sixteenth century, relates that two gods, Nanahuatzin and Tecciztecatl, sacrificed themselves by throwing themselves into a fire and were transformed into the gods of the sun and the moon, thereby giving rise to dawn, dusk, night, and day. The pyramids of the sun and the moon in Teotihuacán were built in commemoration of that sacrifice.

By contrast with this creation myth, Lucha María holds a fighter aircraft in her hands, an allusion to the destruction caused by World War II.

One of Kahlo's most celebrated visual allegories of herself is *Little Deer* (1946), a masterpiece that expresses her physical and emotional wounds. Here she represents herself as a deer wounded by arrows that is fleeing through a forest [fig. 48]. The deer has Kahlo's face, antlers sprout from her head, and emerging from her human ears are those of the animal, which appears from the position of the legs to be running with nine arrows still embedded in its bleeding body. The deer is surrounded by tree trunks, and in the foreground is a branch lying on the ground. Seen in the background of the composition is a horizon with water and a cloudy sky.

> A portrait of my sadness
> on the entire canvas,
> but that is my condition
> and I've no modesty.[10]

At first sight, this picture might arouse a certain amount of sympathy in some viewers, perhaps influenced by Walt Disney's film *Bambi*, released in 1942. The deer is generally considered a mild and inoffensive animal that provokes compassion when it is hunted by felines or humans. Kahlo herself had a small pet deer called Granizo. Nevertheless, an iconological analysis of the work reveals symbolic complexity originating in the artist's intellectual education, which allowed her to feed her imagination with ancient myths from all over the world, and in this case from Roman mythology and Buddhism. Helga Prignitz-Poda, the author of the catalogue raisonné of Frida Kahlo's oeuvre, shares her interpretation of *Little Deer* with us:

> For many years I tried to find another interpretation, until I came across the story of Dido and Aeneas [narrated in Book IV of Virgil's *Aeneid*]. Dido, the Queen of Carthage, had fallen in love with Aeneas. The god of love [Venus, goddess of love and mother of Aeneas] had cast a spell to make her fall into this mad amorous adventure. After initially accepting her love, Aeneas then had to reject it, which prompted the lovestruck Dido to flee like a wounded deer into the forest. This is the source and meaning of the wounded deer in Frida's work. Virgil relates that Dido finally committed suicide and went to the underworld, where she continued to run like a wounded deer. Aeneas went to the underworld to visit his father and had to take with him a branch given to him by Juno [goddess of marriage] to enable him to leave the underworld. And that branch is also in Frida's painting, and it wasn't until I found the reference to the branch in the story of Dido and Aeneas that I really became convinced that this painting is alluding to that story and nothing else. It is a very sad story and a unique painting,

> in which Frida manages to blend ancient myths with her own painful experience of lost love.[11]

Kahlo identifies in this work with Dido, whose ill-fated love drove her to suicide. It should be added to this interpretation that written in the lower left corner of the painting, beside the artist's signature and the date, is the word *carma* (karma), which is a cosmic law of retribution in Buddhism and other Eastern doctrines whereby the actions of individuals have an effect within the life cycle and successive reincarnations. In this small oil, Kahlo showed us that her karma was amorous suffering.

Melancholy, a frequent presence in her work, is expressed with special subtlety in *Self-portrait with Medallion* (1948), where Kahlo achieves prodigious delicacy through a combination of technical mastery and the exquisite minuteness and precision with which she paints the beautiful halo of spun and embroidered cloth that surrounds her tearstained face [fig. 49]. The aureola extends to the blouse; a delicate pendant rests on the blouse, while a pink lining heightens the charm of the face. The piece was commissioned by Samuel Fastlicht and was the only one Kahlo painted that year.

There are four emblematic self-portraits that give masterly expression to the indelible presence of Rivera in the mind, imagination, and heart of the artist. We shall present them in chronological order.

Self-portrait as a Tehuana, Diego in My Thoughts, and *Thinking of Diego* (1943) are the three names given to a magnificent oil painting that shows Kahlo wearing a spectacular white Tehuana dress with pink trim that covers her shoulders and neck and frames the perfect oval of her face in a dazzling gleam of starched white frills. This is crowned by a delicate floral arrangement on her hair from which numerous roots emerge and spread through the whole composition like solar rays, or perhaps like a spider's web to trap Rivera, whose face is painted—and engraved—on the artist's forehead and, presumably, in her wounded heart [fig. 50].

Double Portrait of Diego and I (1929–44) is almost a miniature painted in oil on Masonite with the faces of the two artists split in two and fitted together, Rivera on the left and Kahlo on the right [fig. 51]. The common neck and cranium spring from an imaginary figure, a mixture of a tree and a heart, whose veins, arteries, and branches invade the rest of the allegorical elements of the composition. The features of the two faces split down the middle coincide almost perfectly, but not their size, since Kahlo's face is a little smaller. The double gaze of the characters produces an enigmatic and fascinating sensation in its fusion of the smiling male expression of Rivera with the melancholy female gaze of Kahlo, evoking the androgyne mentioned in Plato's *Symposium.* The duality of the masculine and the feminine is reinforced by the symbolic presence of the sun and the moon on the right-hand side of the composition, and of a seashell and a snail in the lower part of the picture, allusions to the female

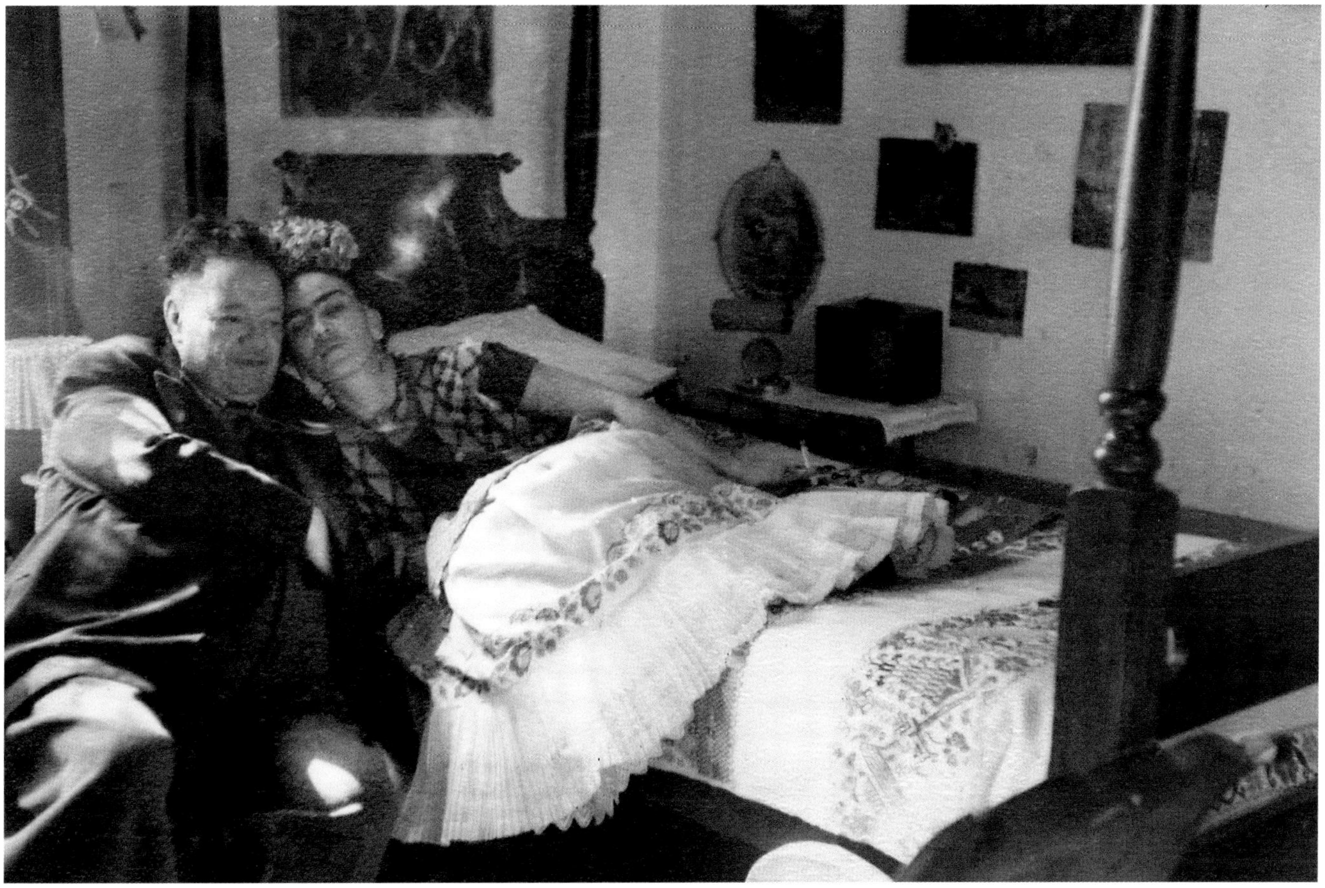

Diego Rivera and Frida Kahlo in Kahlo's bedroom in the Casa Azul, Coyoacán (Mexico City), c. 1942. Photograph by Chester Dale. Smithsonian Institution, Archives of American Art, Chester Dale papers, circa 1883–2003

and male sexual organs. The red background of the painting highlights the complicated mixture of love, passion, suffering, and pleasure that characterized the couple's relationship. The painting was a gift from Kahlo to Rivera to celebrate fifteen years of marriage (from 1929 to 1944, without counting the year they were divorced, from 1939 to 1940).

Diego and I (1949) starkly and openly reveals the artist's despair at Rivera's romance with the actress María Félix, a close friend of Kahlo's [fig. 52]. The affair became a public scandal. Apparently, the muralist fell in love with the star and was thinking of asking Kahlo for another divorce so as to be able to marry Félix. However, Félix rejected him and remained friends with Kahlo as though nothing had happened. In this painting, however, Kahlo sheds tears and has an expression of profound anguish emphasized by the loose hair that surrounds her neck as if she were going to strangle herself with it. She also has Rivera's face painted on her forehead in this self-portrait, with a third eye alluding to Rivera's mental agility. Around that time, Kahlo wrote a moving passage that confirms the deep love she felt for her husband:

> Diego: Nothing compares to your hands nothing like the green-gold of your eyes. My body is filled with you for days and days. You are the mirror of the night. The violent flash of lightning. The dampness of the earth. The hollow of your armpits is my shelter. My fingertips touch your blood. All my joy is to feel life spring from your flower-fountain that mine keeps to fill all the paths of my nerves which are yours.[12]

That same year, Kahlo painted the oil entitled *The Love Embrace of the Universe, My Earth (Mexico), Diego, Myself and Señor Xólotl* (1949), an outstanding symbolic self-portrait of her existential anguish, her cosmovision, and her longing to possess Diego Rivera as if he were her son [fig. 53]. Kahlo felt "miserable and hurt"[13] at Rivera's infidelity with her close friend, although the two painters ultimately reconciled. "Frida was happy to have me back, and I was grateful to be married to her still," Rivera remarked.[14] It was at the moment of reconciliation that Kahlo painted *The Love Embrace of the Universe*. In Tehuana dress, Kahlo is in the arms of Mother Earth, or Mexico, represented by a pre-Hispanic sculpture with its chest fractured and a drop of milk falling from its breast, while around it are eroticized cactus plants. This figure is embraced in turn by the universe, represented by a figure, half day and half night, accompanied in each part respectively by the sun and the moon. One of the artist's Xoloitzcuintli dogs sleeps on the nocturnal forearm of the universe. In her arms, Kahlo holds a robust baby with Diego Rivera's face that is endowed with a third eye, a symbol of wisdom in Eastern mythology, while its hands hold a flame, an allegory of love. Kahlo depicts Rivera as her son, as he "is not anybody's husband and never will be."[15] A jet of blood, not milk, spurts from the breast of a self-absorbed Kahlo, whose throat is cut. The work is a superb metaphor for Kahlo's melancholy and her amorous suffering for Rivera within the context of the eternal flow of the universe.

At the same time as she was producing these pictorial masterpieces, Kahlo wrote a splendid text for the catalogue of the tribute paid to Diego Rivera in 1949 by the Instituto Nacional de Bellas Artes to mark his fiftieth year of artistic activity. According to Raquel Tibol, it was so well written that it was rumored to have been done for her by Alfonso Reyes. In the opinion of this eminent art historian, it is one of the finest pieces written in the twentieth century on a Mexican artist. Here is an excerpt:

> I must warn that this portrait of Diego will be painted in colors I am unfamiliar with: in words. . . . This will not be a biographical account: . . . I will not speak of Diego as "my husband," because that would be ridiculous; Diego has never been, nor will be ever be, anyone's "husband." Nor as my lover, for he embraces much beyond sexual limitations. . . . I will try to speak the only truth: my own. . . .
>
> HIS FORM: with his Asiatic head and dark hair, so thin and fine that it seems to float in the air, Diego is an immense, enormous child, with a friendly face

> and a rather sad gaze. His large protuberant eyes, dark and extremely intelligent, are barely restrained—almost leaping from their orbits—by the swollen, bulging batrachian eyelids, and are set far apart from one another. . . . Seeing him nude one thinks immediately of a frog child. . . . His narrow, rounded, infantile shoulders continue down without angles into feminine arms and end in marvelous, small, finely-drawn hands, sensitive and subtle as antennas that communicate with the entire universe. . . . His belly, enormous, smooth and tender as a sphere, rests on strong legs, as beautiful as columns.[16]

Like herself, Kahlo's relationship with her adored "frog-toad" was the antithesis of the conventional, and it flouted the behavioral norms accepted and imposed by the society of the time, based as they were on traditions, customs, and prejudices. Kahlo was never a defeated or complaisant woman. If she had been, she would not have been able to reconstruct her image completely, as she did. She was exceptional for, among many other things, her power of recovery. And just as she recovered herself, she was also capable of recovering her marriage and preserving her love for Diego Rivera. "In spite of everything," Juan Coronel Rivera remarks, "she managed to have a successful marriage because whatever happened, whether she divorced Diego or not, and whether they had extramarital relationships or not, they were married from 1929 to 1954. That, in itself, is a successful marriage."[17] Or, at least, a lasting one. Love is perseverance.

1 Denis de Rougemont, *Love in the Western World*, trans. Montgomery Belgion (Princeton: Princeton University Press, 1983), 15.
2 "Entrevista con Teresa del Conde. Frida pintora," in *Yo soy Frida*, ed. Héctor Tajonar (Mexico City: Milenio Diario, 2007), 18.
3 Frida Kahlo, *The Diary of Frida Kahlo: An Intimate Self-portrait* (New York: Harry N. Abrams, 1995), 245–47.
4 Kahlo, *Diary*, 274.
5 "Entrevista con Carlos Fuentes. Frida amada," in *Yo soy Frida*, 5.
6 Diego Rivera with Gladys March, *My Art, My Life: An Autobiography* (Garden City: Dover Publications, 1991), 138–39.
7 Kahlo, *Diary*, 243 and 248.
8 Raquel Tibol, *Frida Kahlo: An Open Life*, trans. Elinor Randall (Albuquerque: University of New Mexico Press, 2000), 3.
9 Raquel Tibol, *Frida Kahlo en su luz más íntima* (Mexico City: Random House Mondadori, 2005), 47.
10 Tibol, *An Open Life*, 76.
11 "Entrevista con Helga Prignitz-Poda. Frida compleja," in *Yo soy Frida*, 25–26.
12 Kahlo, *Diary*, 213.
13 Rivera, *My Art, My Life*, 165.
14 Rivera, *My Art, My Life*, 165.
15 Hayden Herrera, *Frida: The Biography of Frida Kahlo* (London: Bloomsbury, 2018), 365.
16 Frida Kahlo, "Portrait of Diego," in *Frida by Frida*, ed. Raquel Tibol and trans. Gregory Dechant (Mexico City: Editorial RM, 2006), 344–45.
17 "Entrevista con Juan Coronel. Frida ícono," in *Yo soy Frida*, 29.

31

The Two Fridas

1939
Oil on canvas,
68⅛ x 68⅛ in. (173 x 173 cm)
Mexico City, Museo de Arte
Moderno, INBA

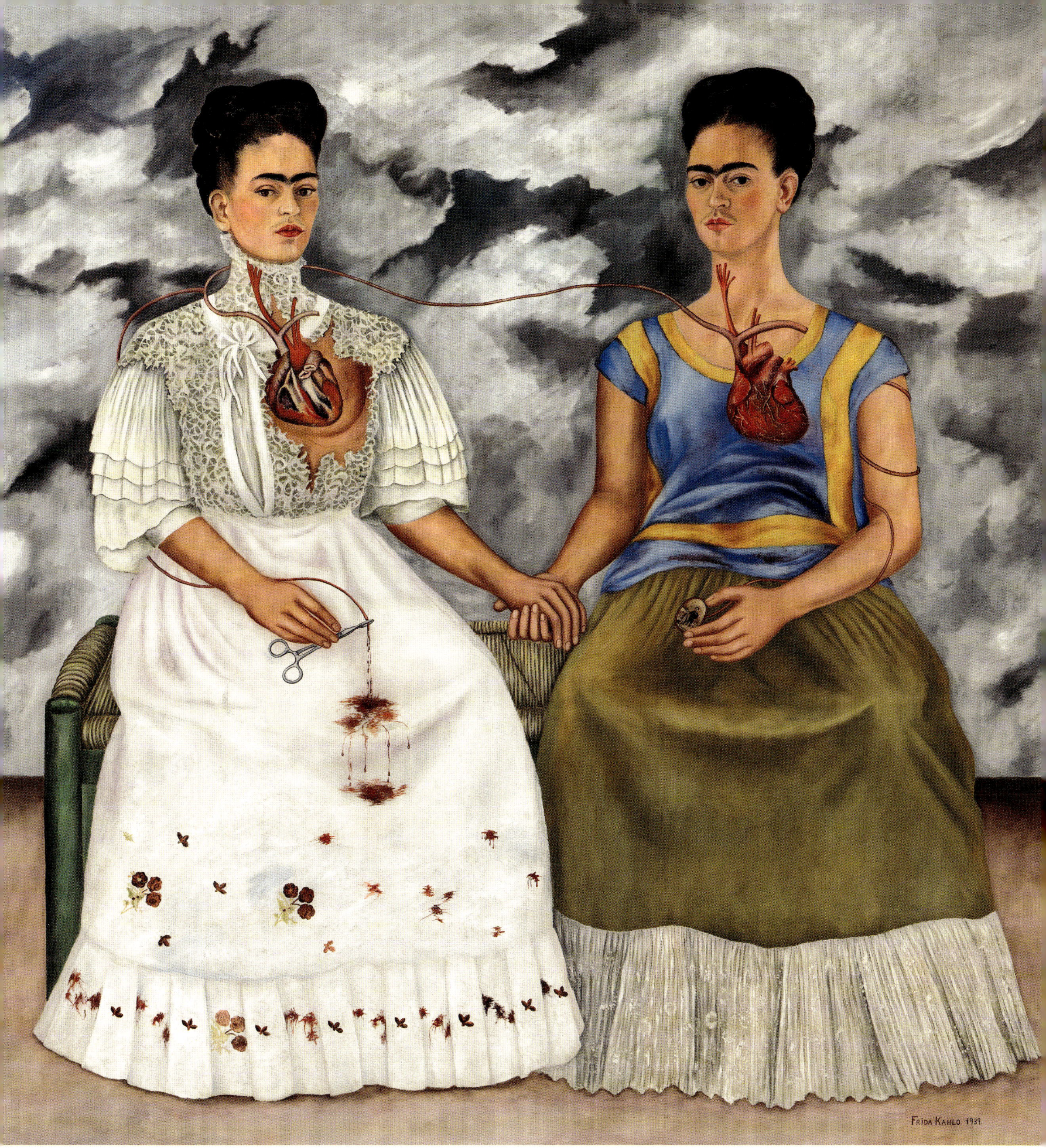
FRIDA KAHLO. 1939.

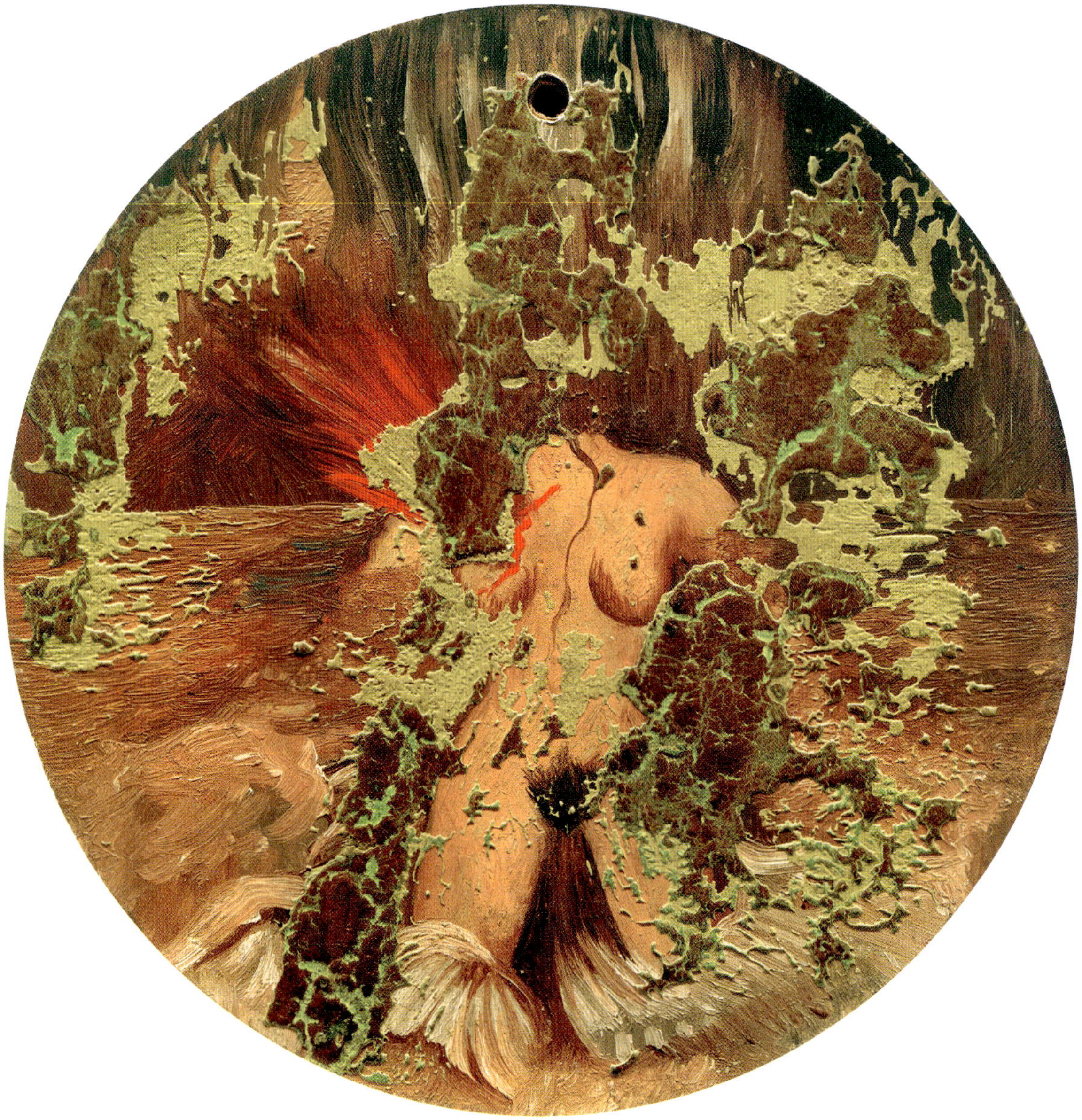

32

The Circle

c. 1954
Oil on metal, 6 in. diameter (15 cm diameter)
Xochimilco (Mexico City), Collection Museo
Dolores Olmedo

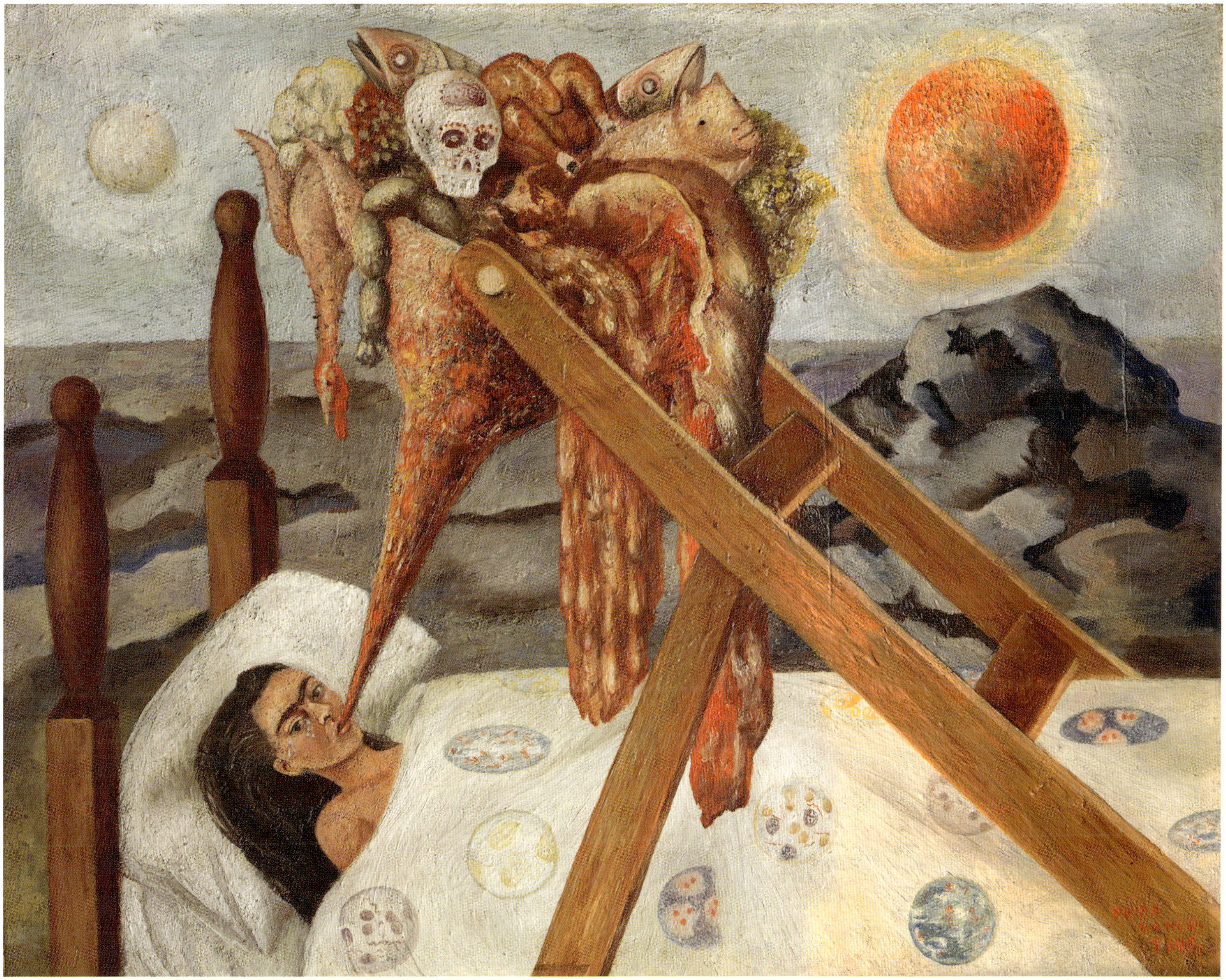

33

Without Hope

1945
Oil on canvas on Masonite,
11 x 14⅛ in. (28 x 36 cm)
Xochimilco (Mexico City),
Collection Museo Dolores Olmedo

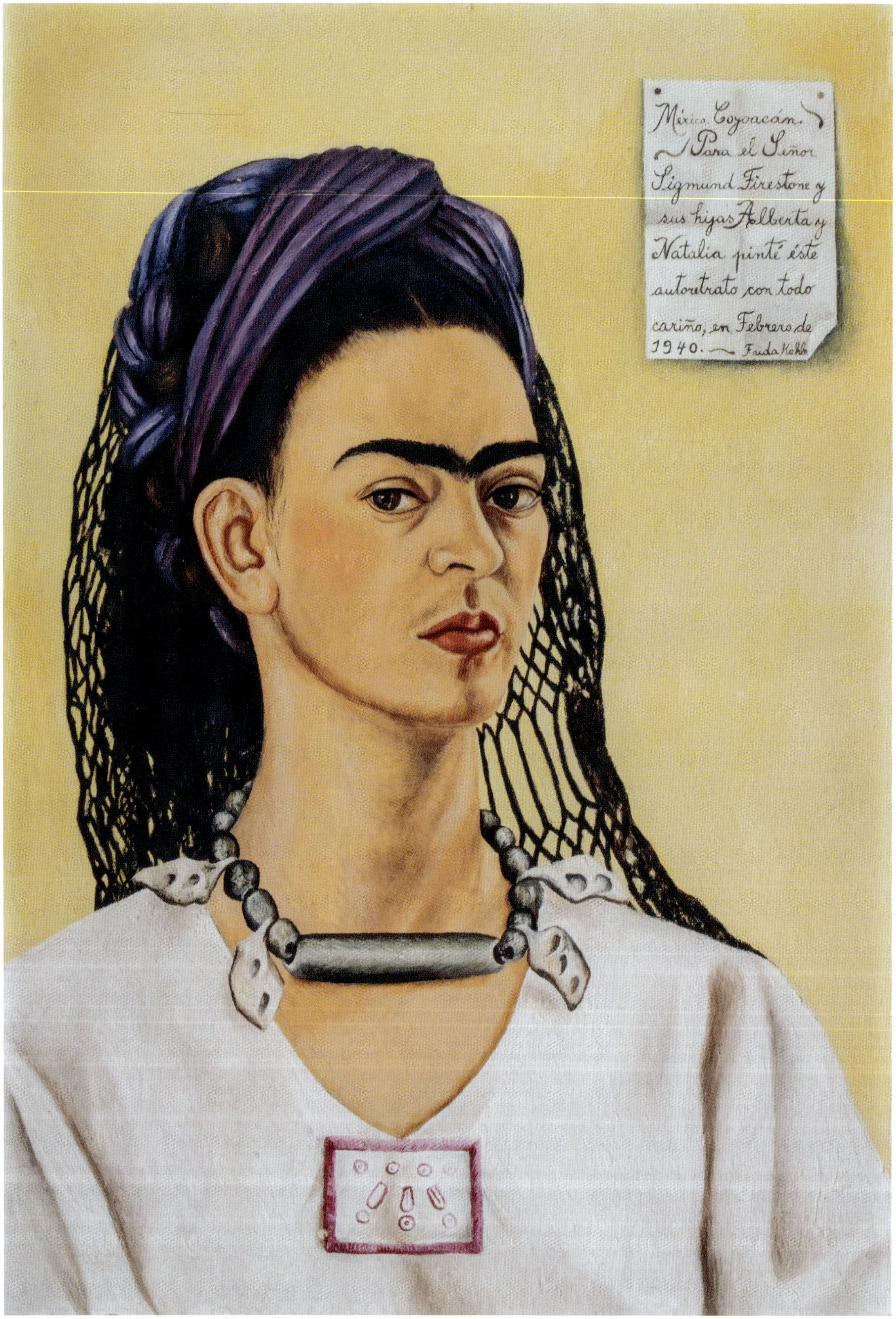

34
Self-portrait Dedicated to Sigmund Firestone

1940
Oil on Masonite,
24 x 17 in. (61 x 43 cm)
Violet Gershenson Collection

35
Self-portrait with Bra

1941
Oil on Masonite,
$23\frac{3}{8}$ x $15\frac{3}{4}$ in. (59.5 x 40 cm)
Private collection

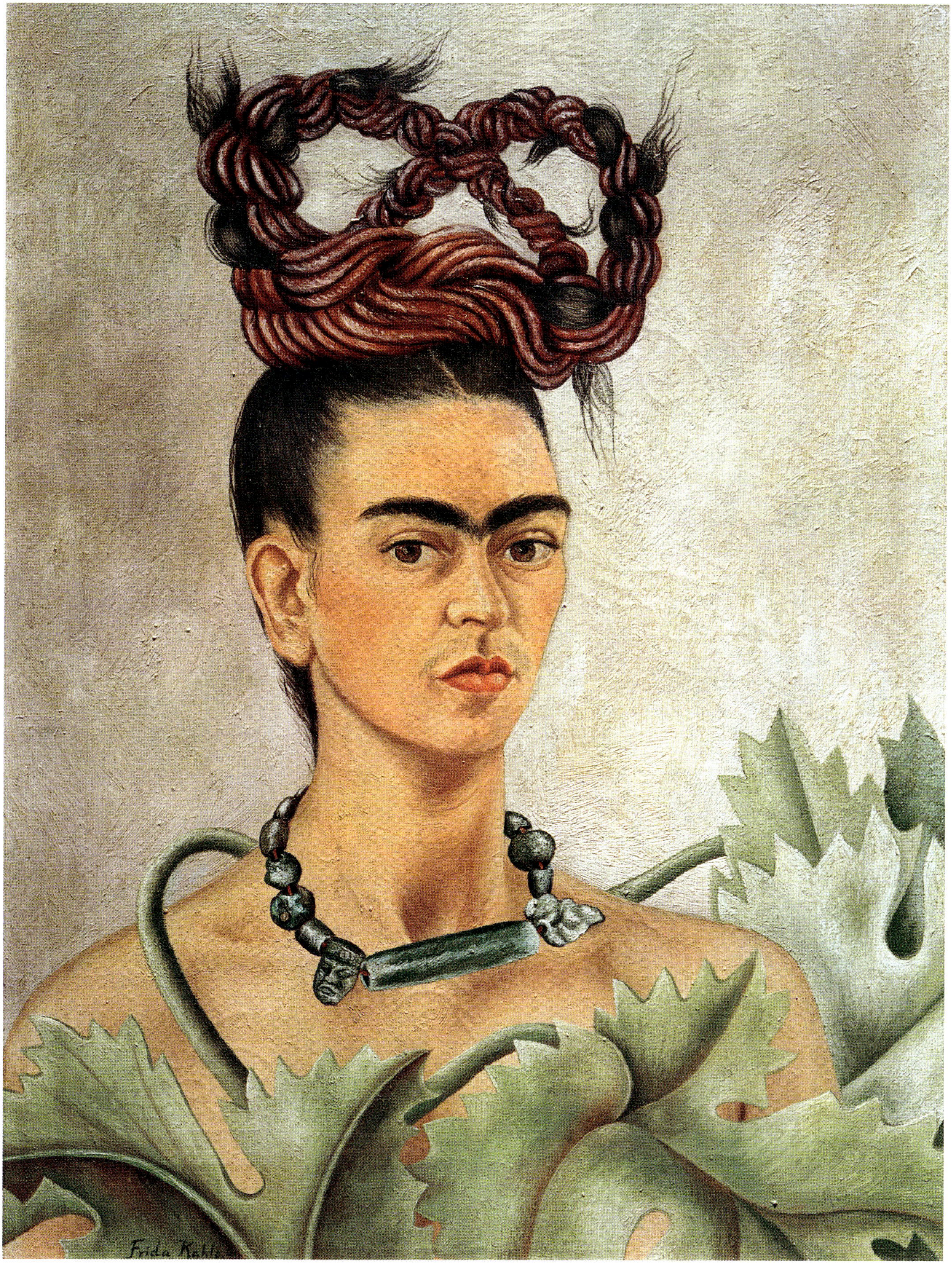
Frida Kahlo

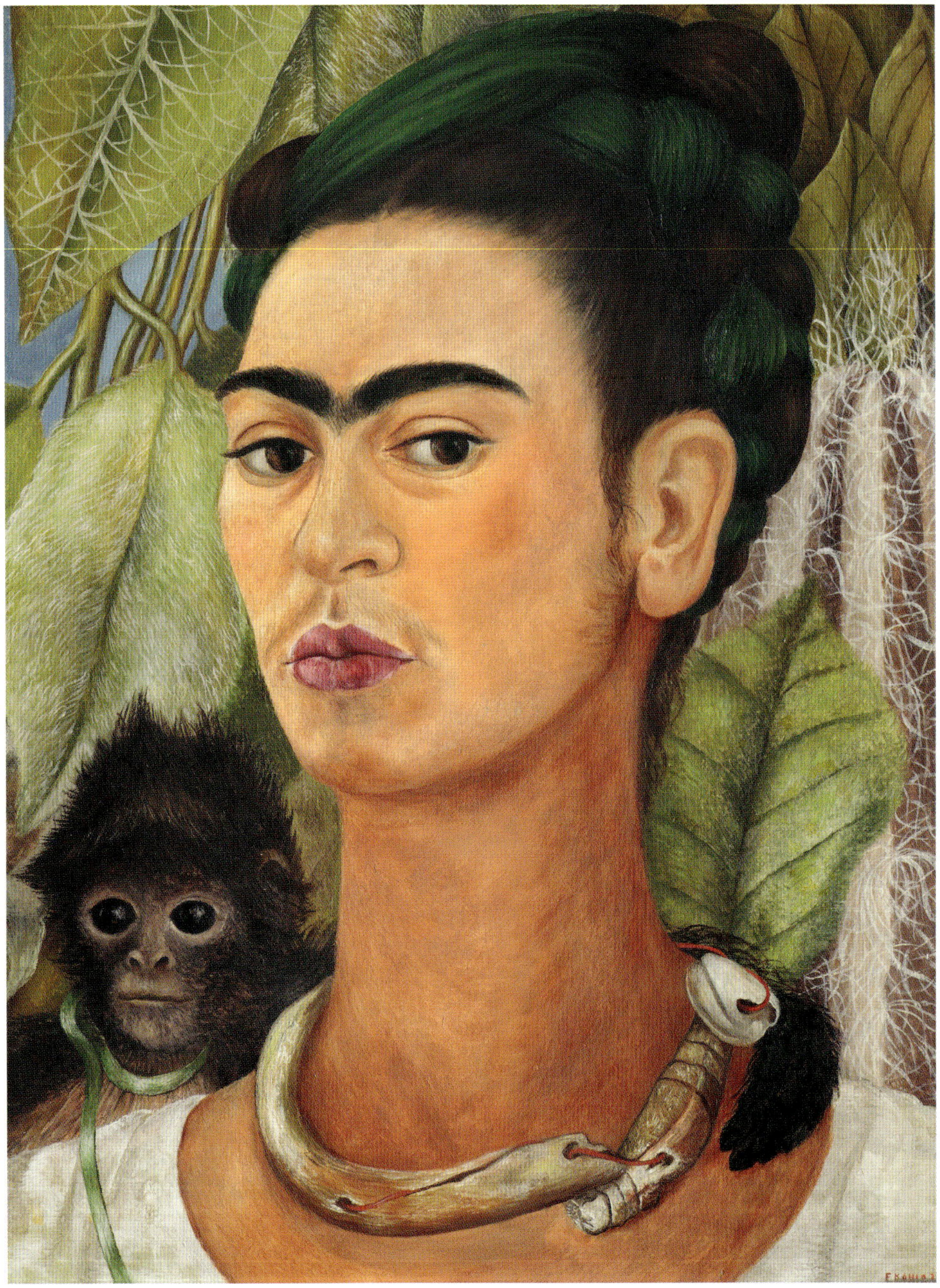

36

Self-portrait with Monkey

1938
Oil on Masonite, 16 x 12 in. (40.6 x 30.5 cm)
Buffalo (New York), Collection Albright-Knox
Gallery, Bequest of A. Conger Goodyear, 1966,
1966:9.10

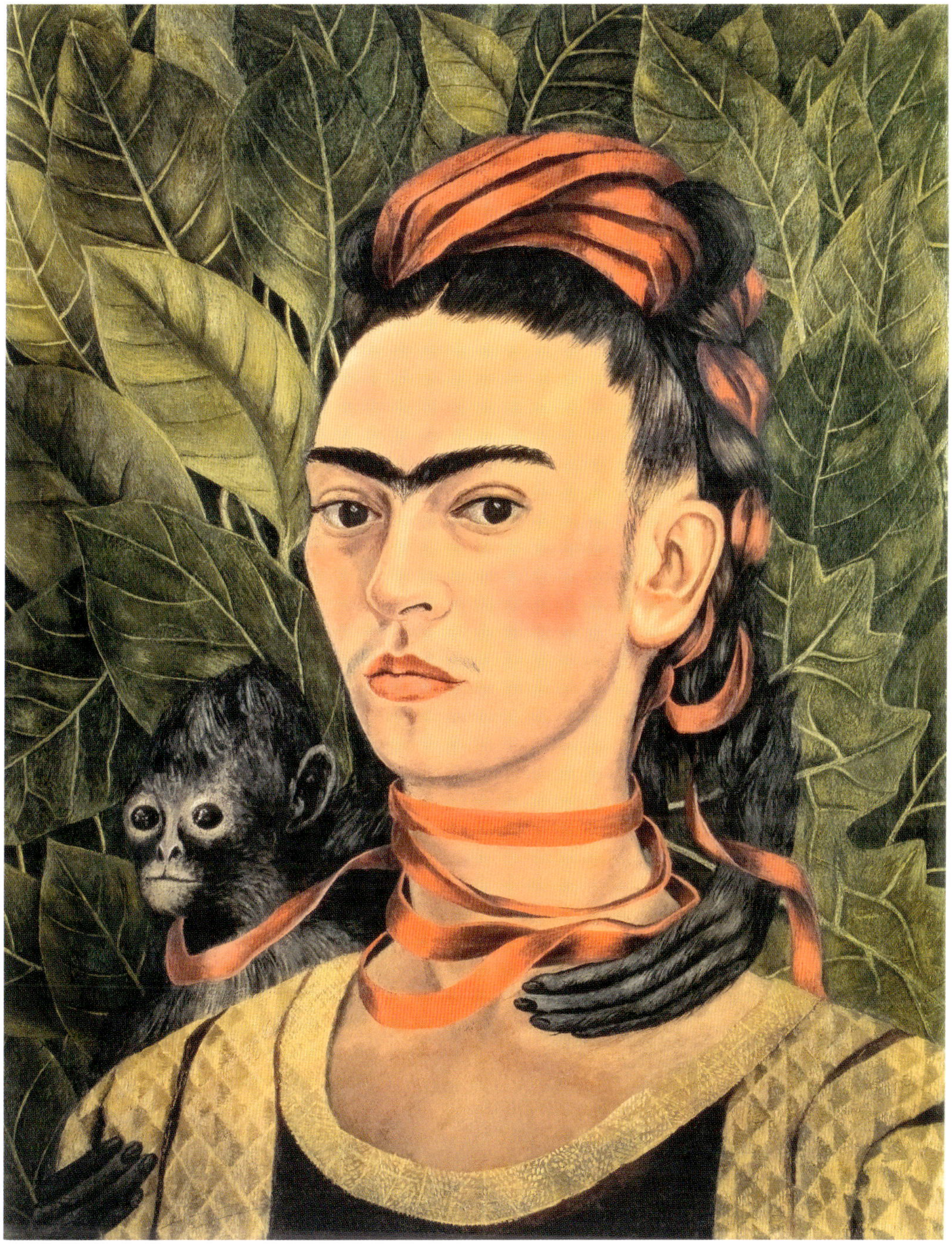

37

Self-portrait with Monkey

1940
Oil on Masonite,
21¾ x 17⅛ in. (55.2 x 43.5 cm)
Private collection

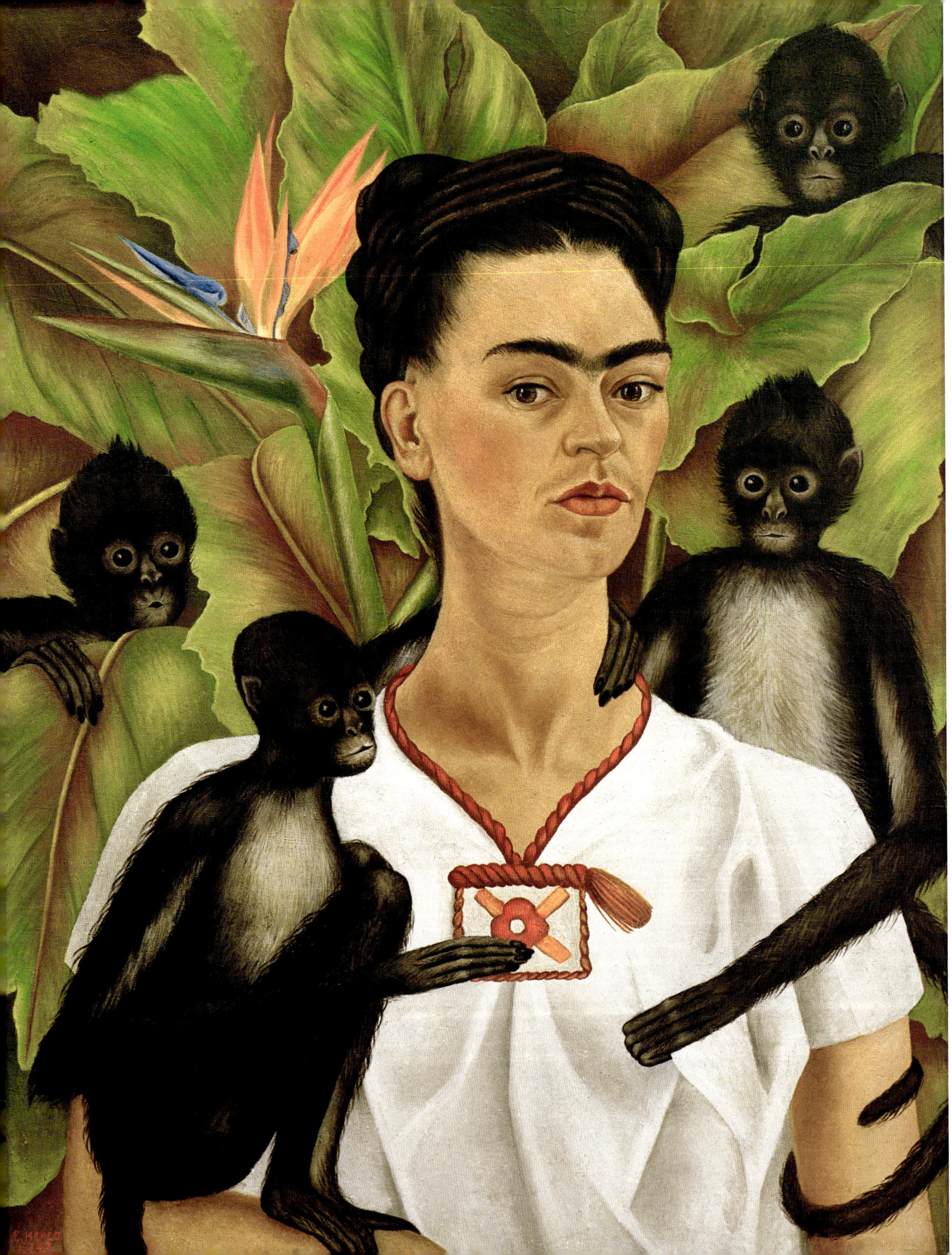

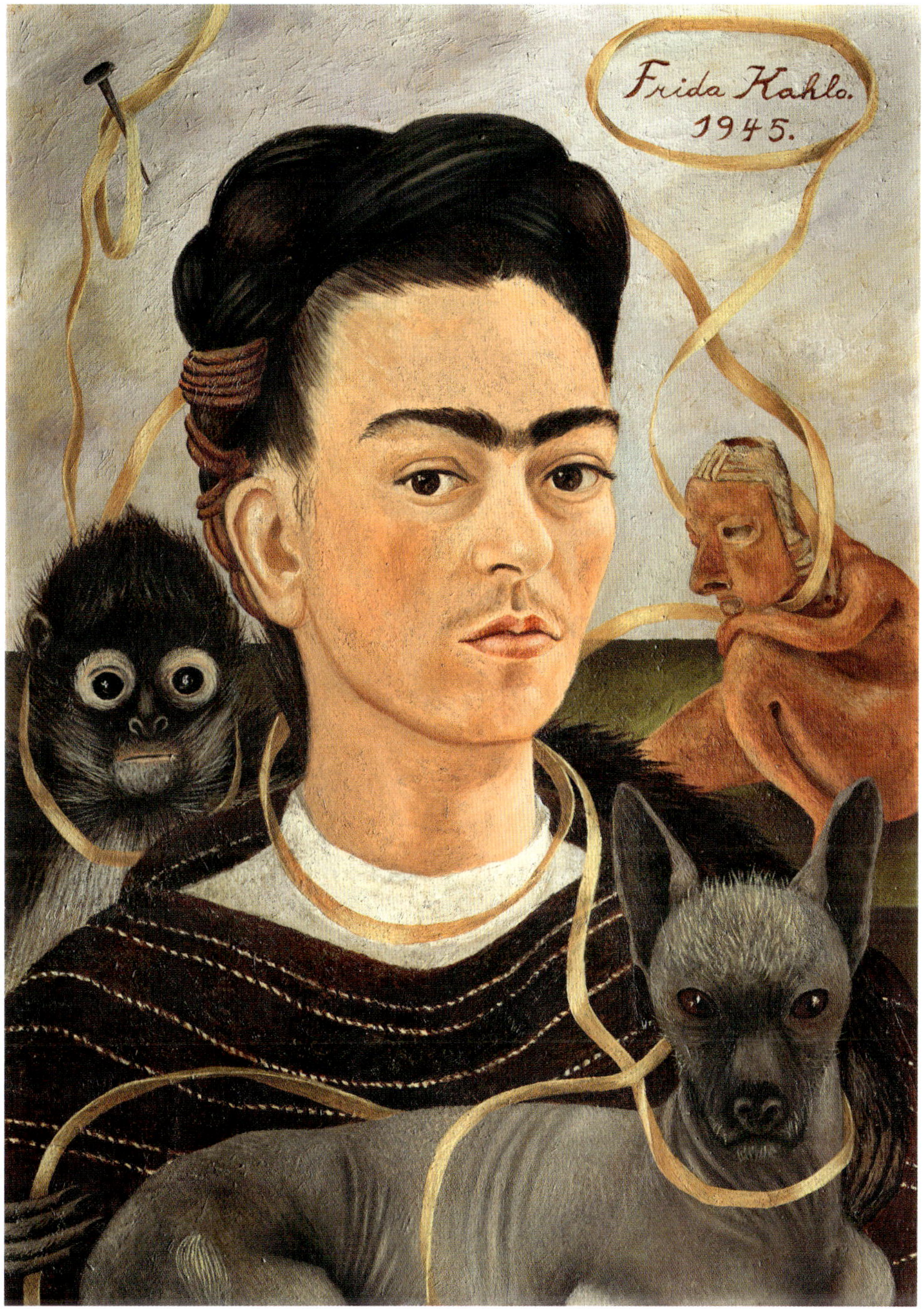

38
Self-portrait with Monkeys

1943
Oil on canvas,
32 x 24¾ in. (81.5 x 63 cm)
Gelman Collection

39
Self-portrait with Small Monkey

1945
Oil on Masonite, 22 x 16⅓ in. (56 x 41.5 cm)
Xochimilco (Mexico City), Collection Museo Dolores Olmedo

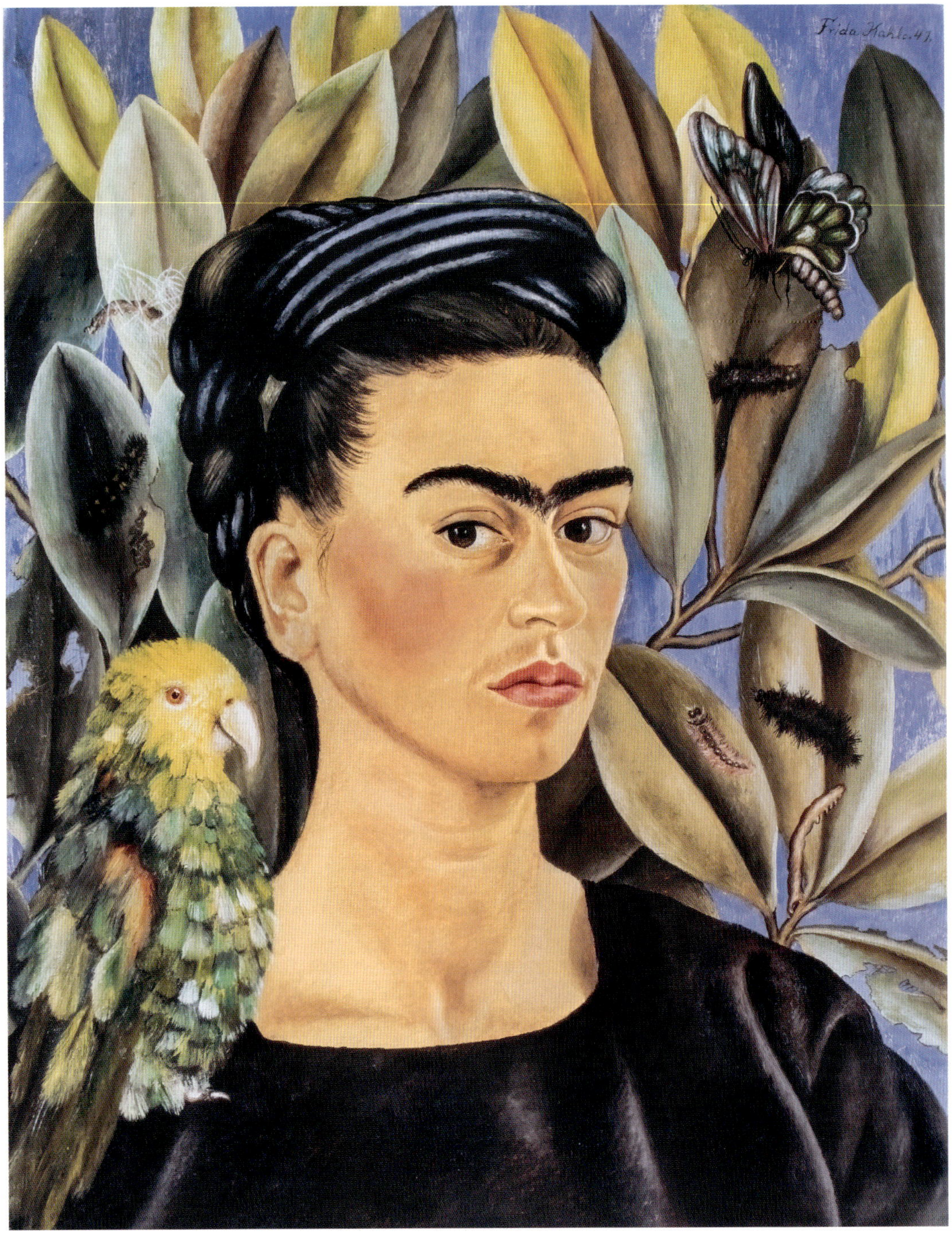

40

Self-portrait with Bonito

1941
Oil on canvas,
21⅔ x 17 in. (55 x 43.4 cm)
United States, private collection

41

Me and My Parrots

1941
Oil on canvas,
32¼ x 24¼ in. (82 x 62.8 cm
New Orleans (Louisiana),
Harold H. Stream

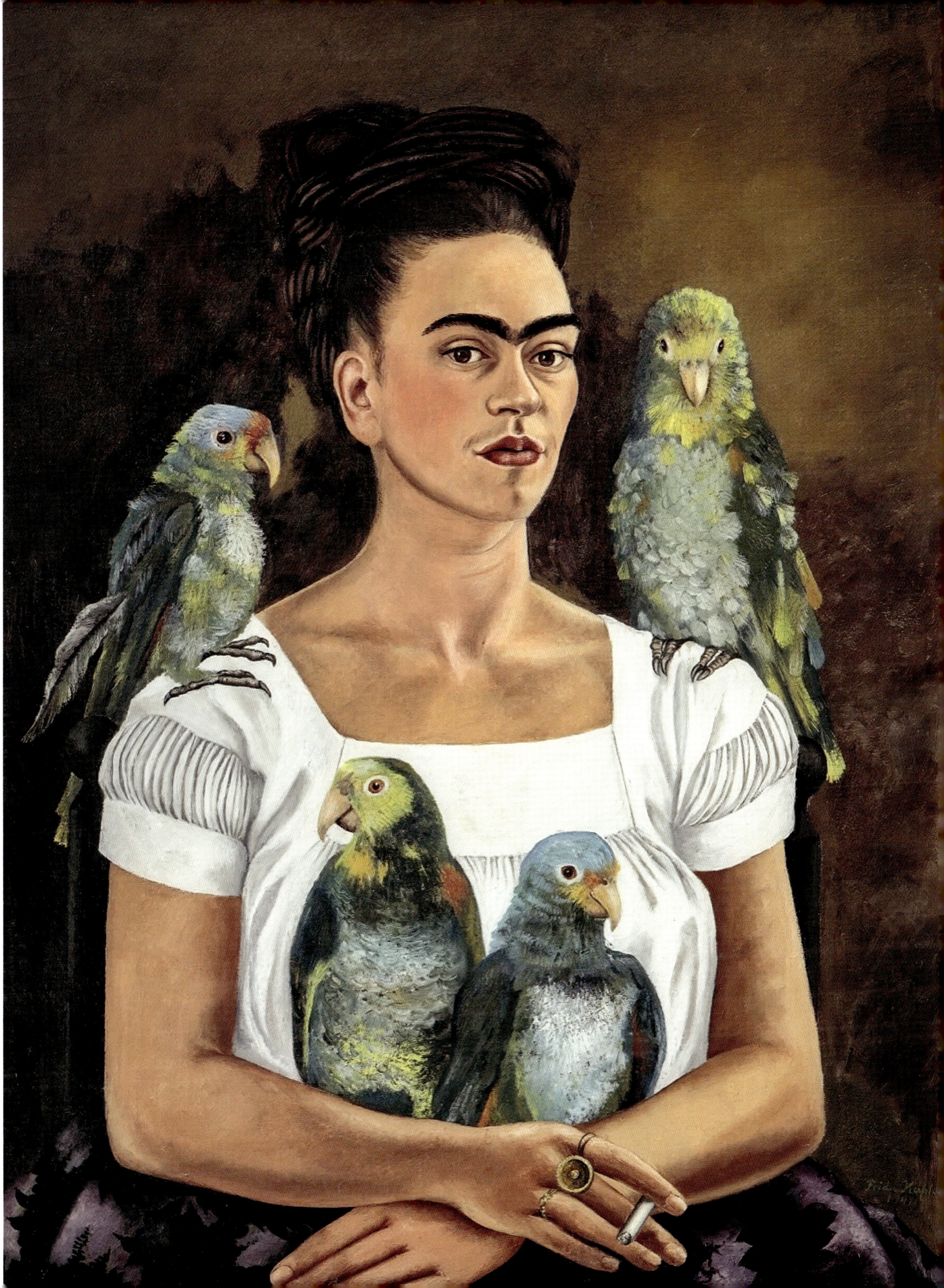

42

Self-portrait with Cropped Hair

1940
Oil on canvas, 15¾ x 11 in. (40 x 27.9 cm)
New York, Museum of Modern Art, Gift of Edgar Kaufmann, Jr., 3.1943

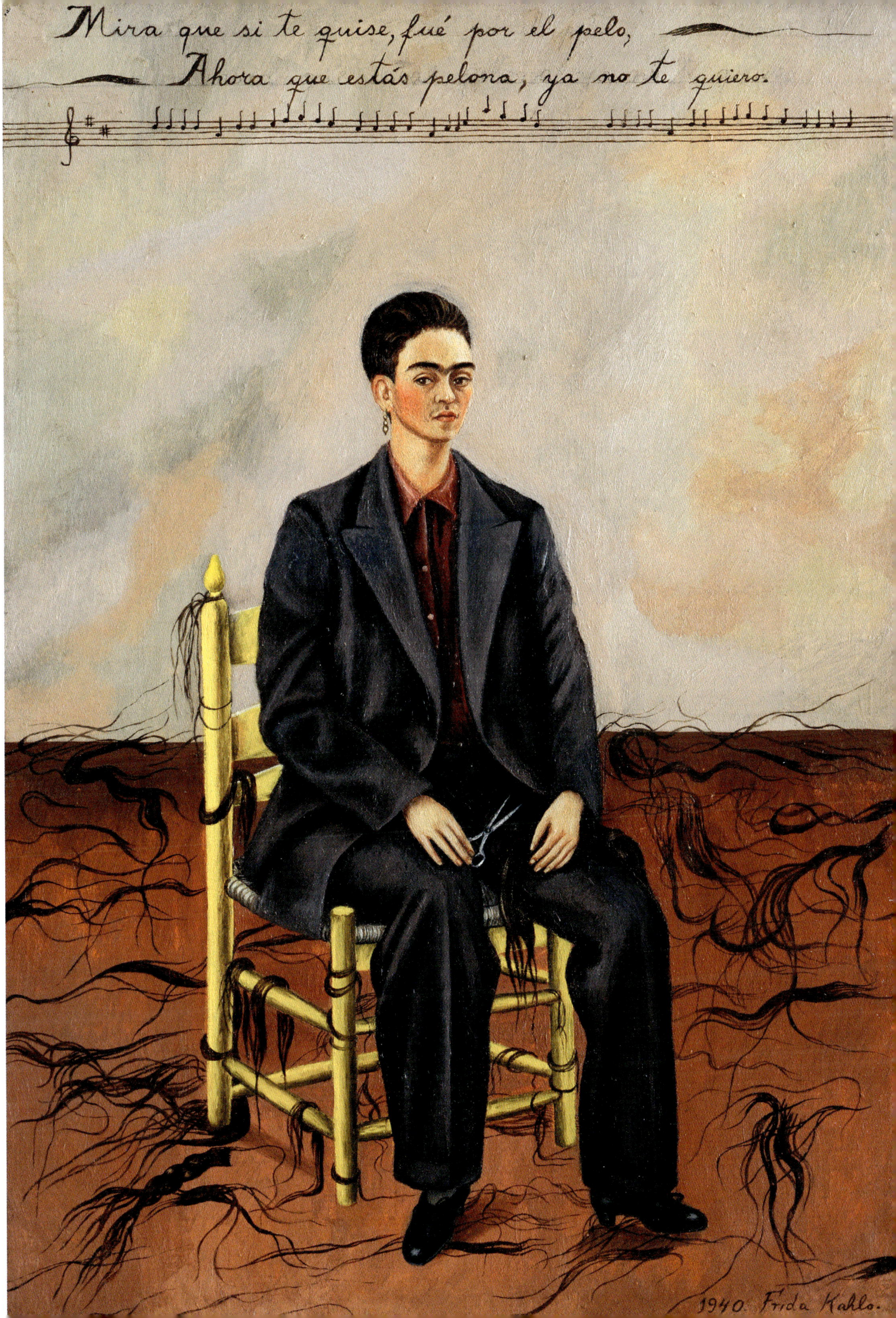
Mira que si te quise, fué por el pelo,
Ahora que estás pelona, ya no te quiero.
1940. Frida Kahlo.

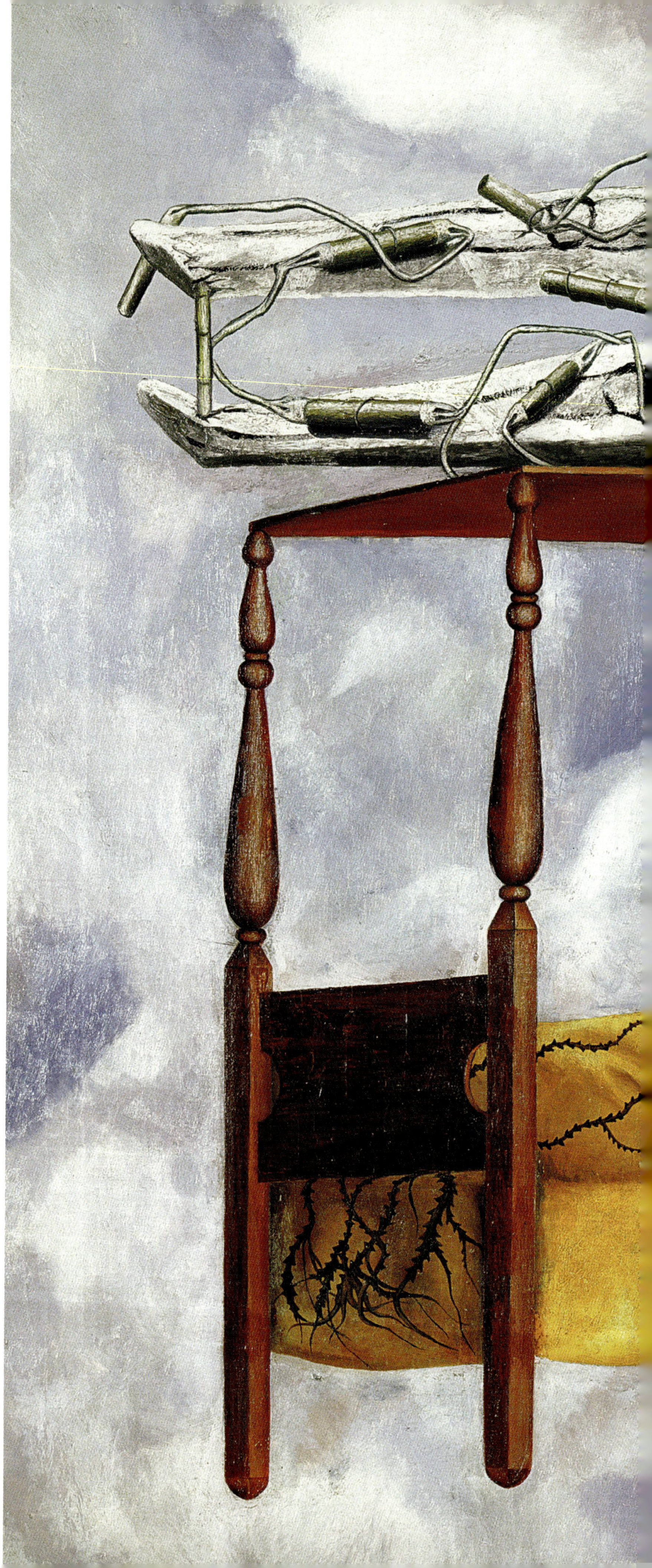

43

The Dream or **The Bed**

1940
Oil on canvas,
29⅛ x 38¾ in. (74 x 98.5 cm)
Ner York, Selma and Negushi
Ertegun Collection

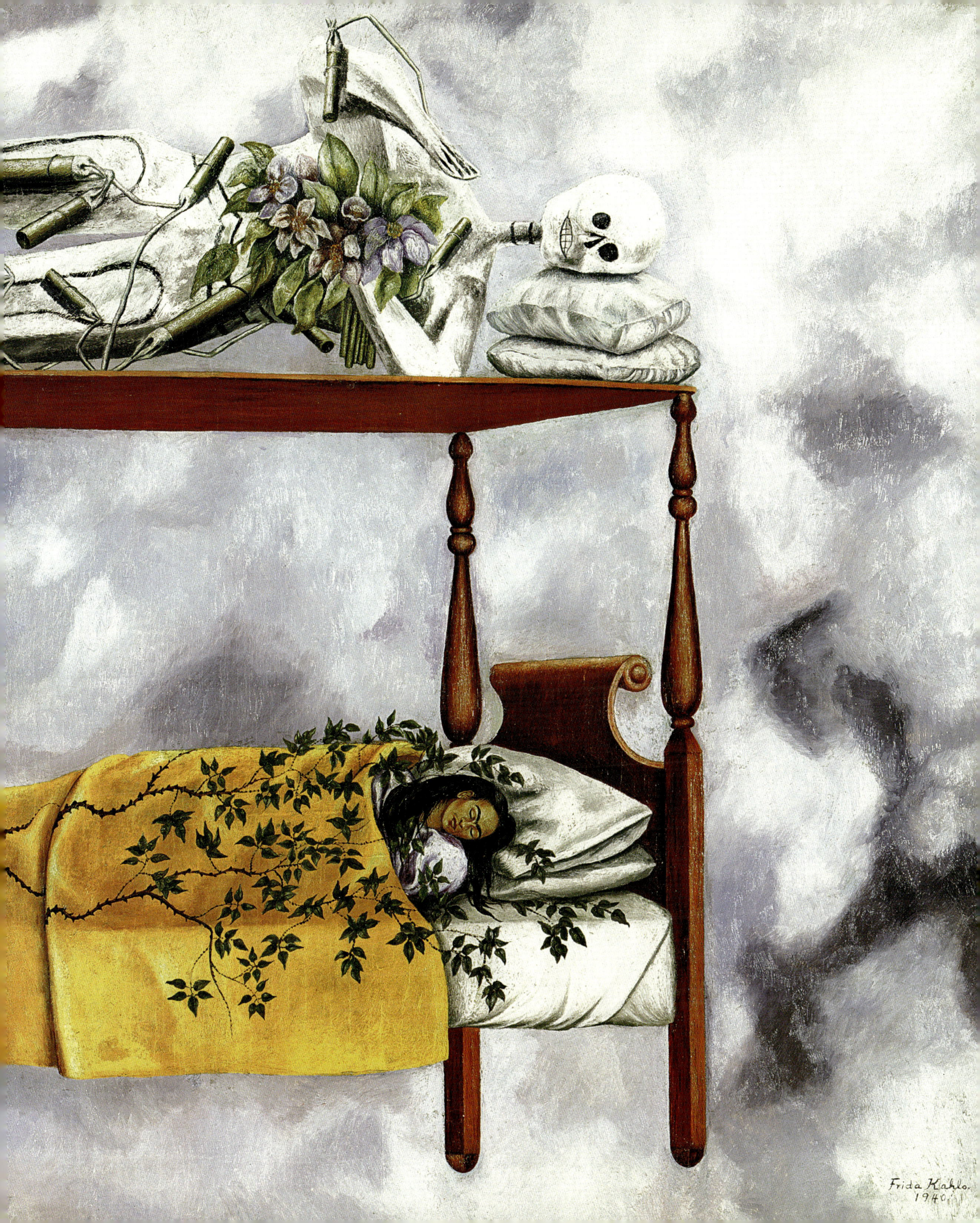
Frida Kahlo.
1940.

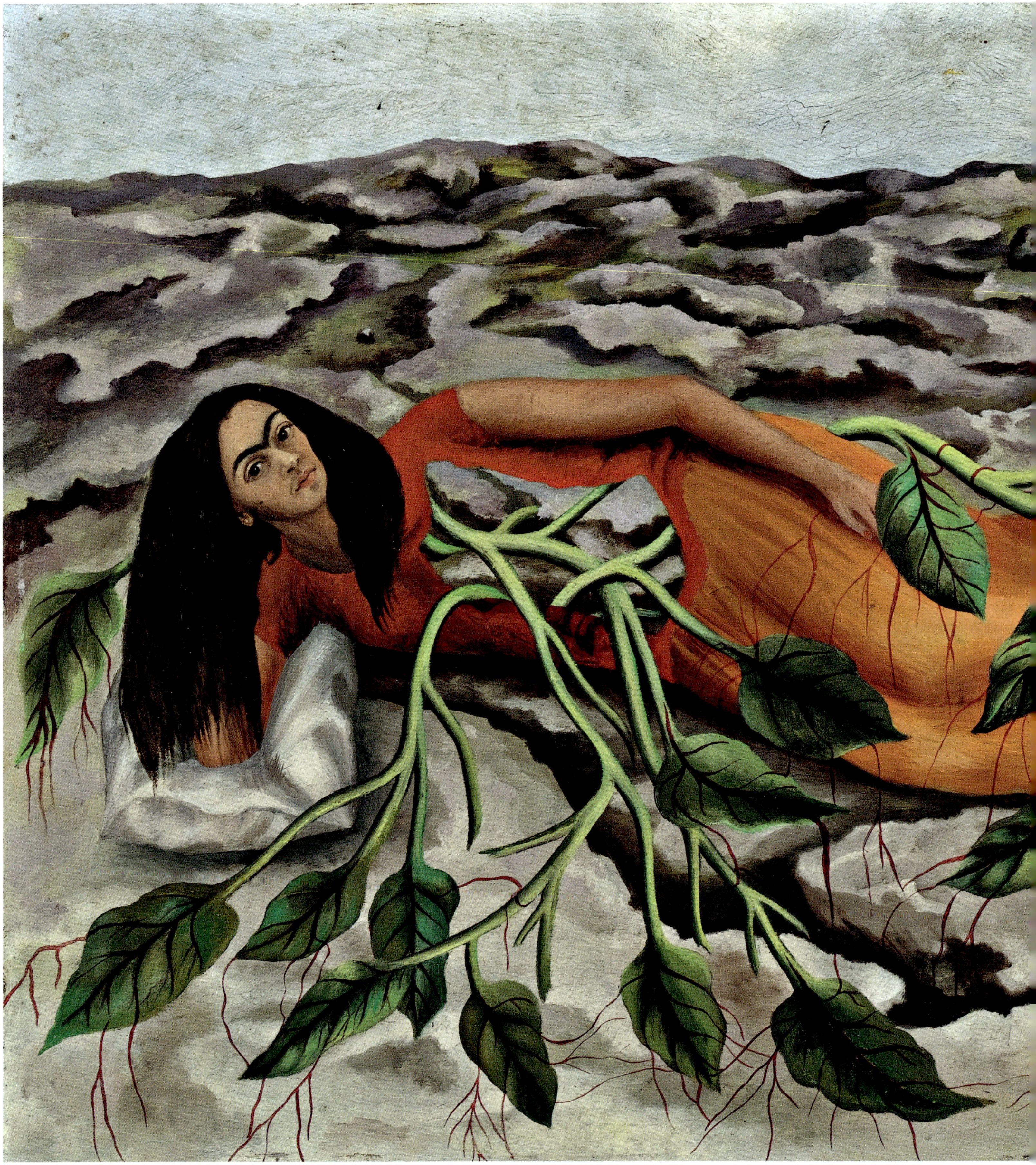

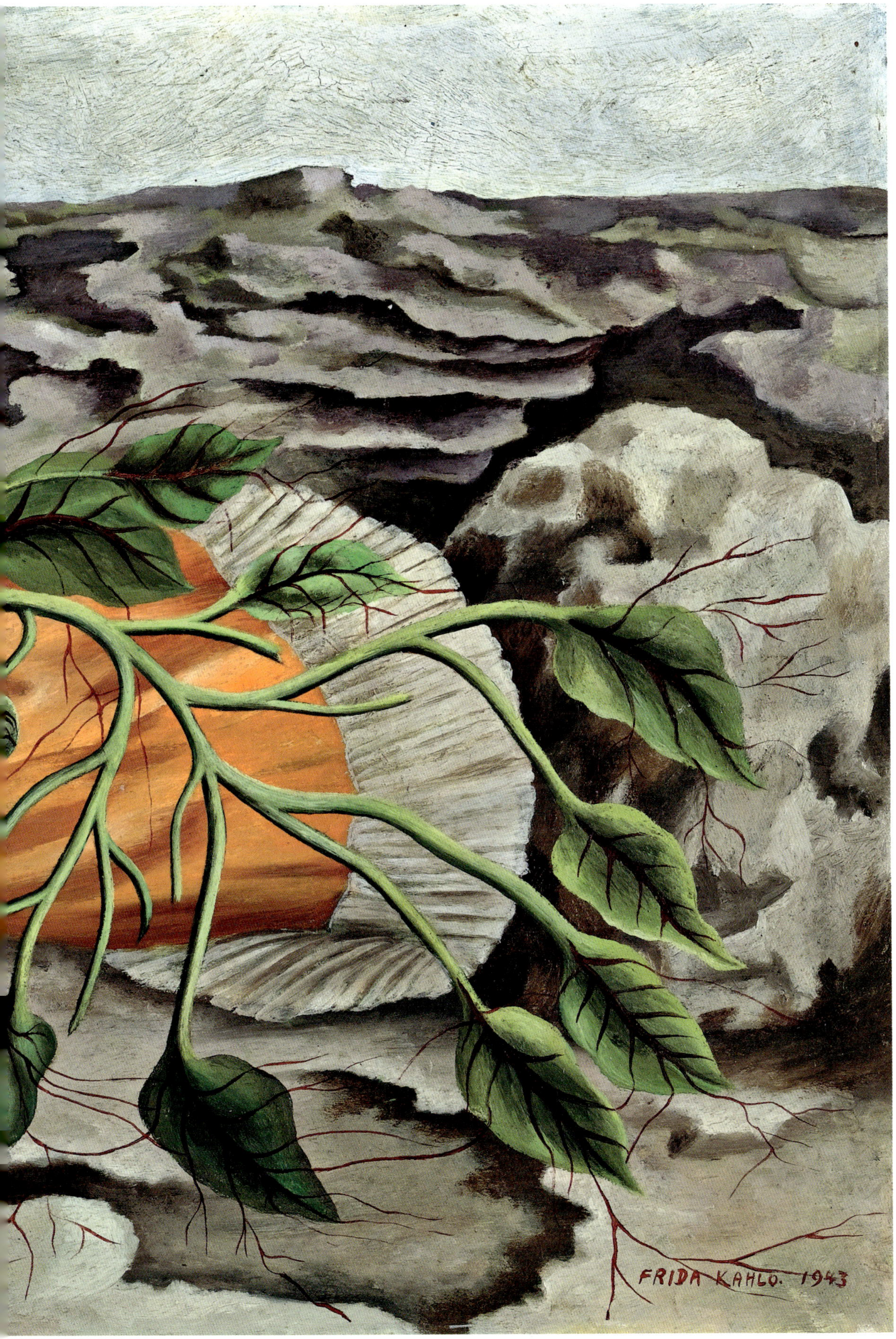

44

Roots

1943
Oil on metal,
12 x 19⅔ in.
(30.5 x 49.9 cm)
Private collection

45

My Nurse and I

1937
Oil on metal,
12 x 13¾ in. (30.5 x 35 cm)
Xochimilco (Mexico City),
Collection Museo Dolores Olmedo

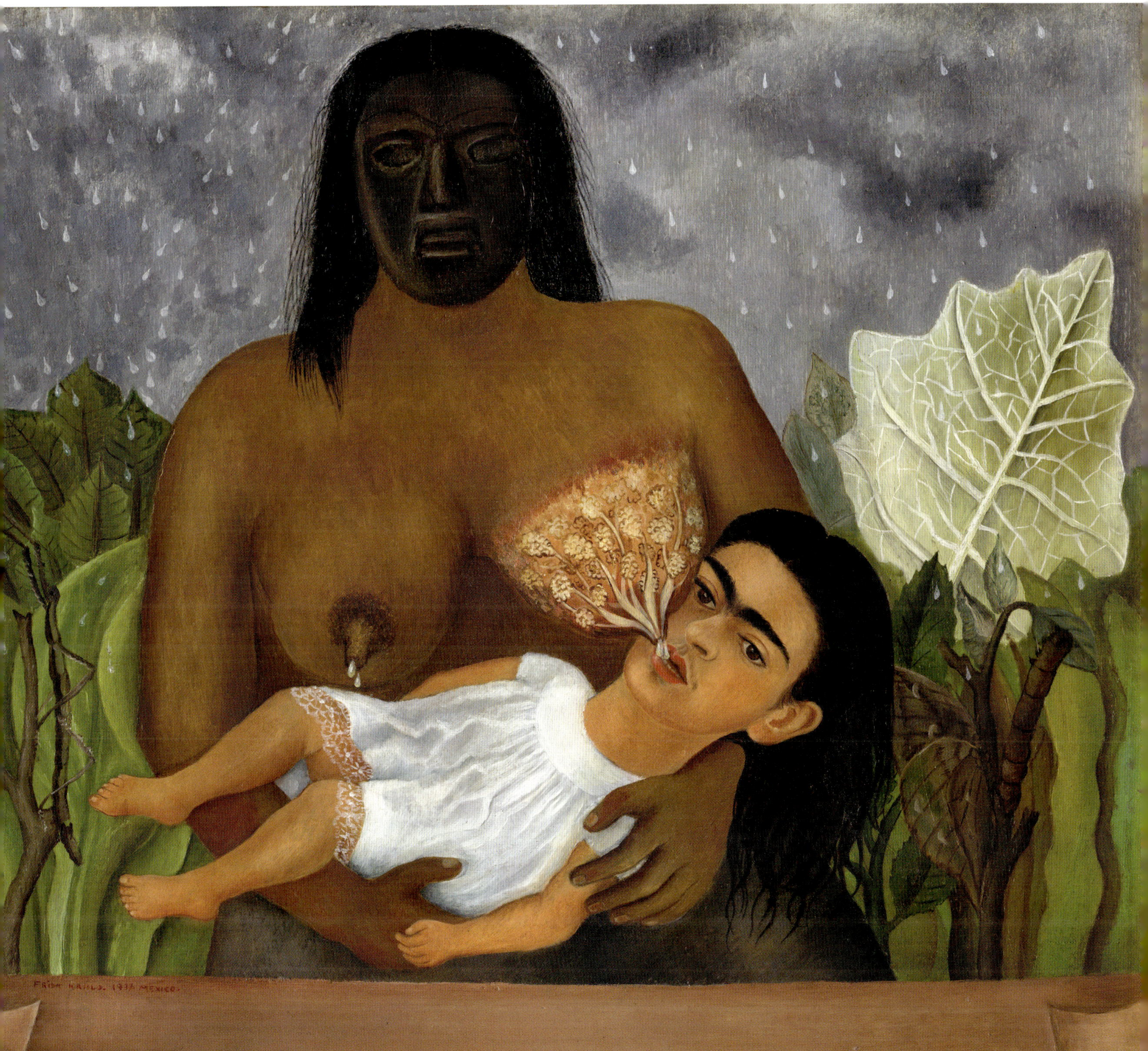

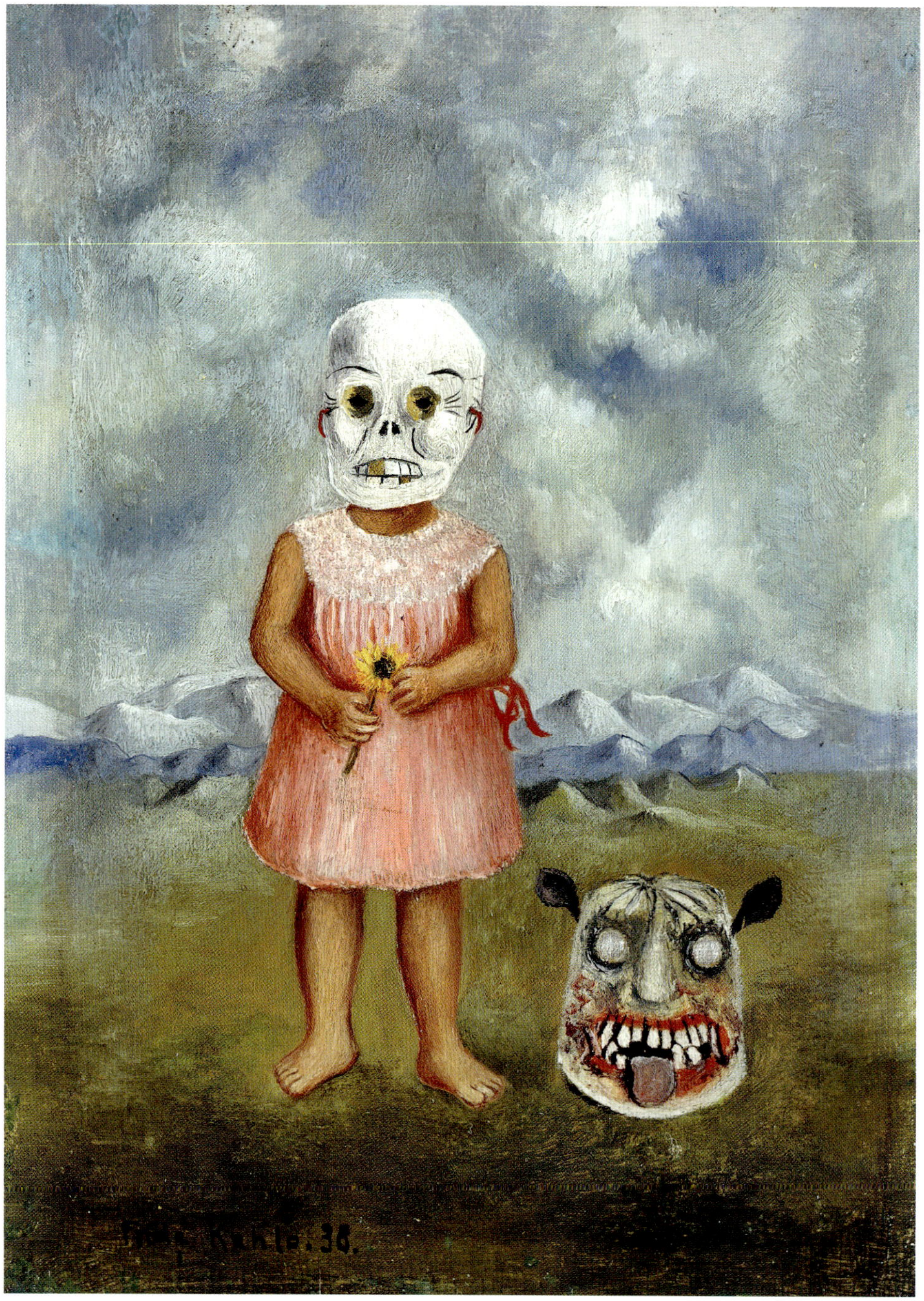

46

Girl with Death Mask

1938
Oil on metal, 5⅞ x 4⅓ in. (14.9 x 11 cm)
Nagoya City Art Museum

47

Girl from Tehuacán,
Lucha María or **Sun and Moon**

1942
Oil on Masonite,
21½ x 17 in. (54.5 x 43.3 cm)
Mexico, Pérez Simón Collection

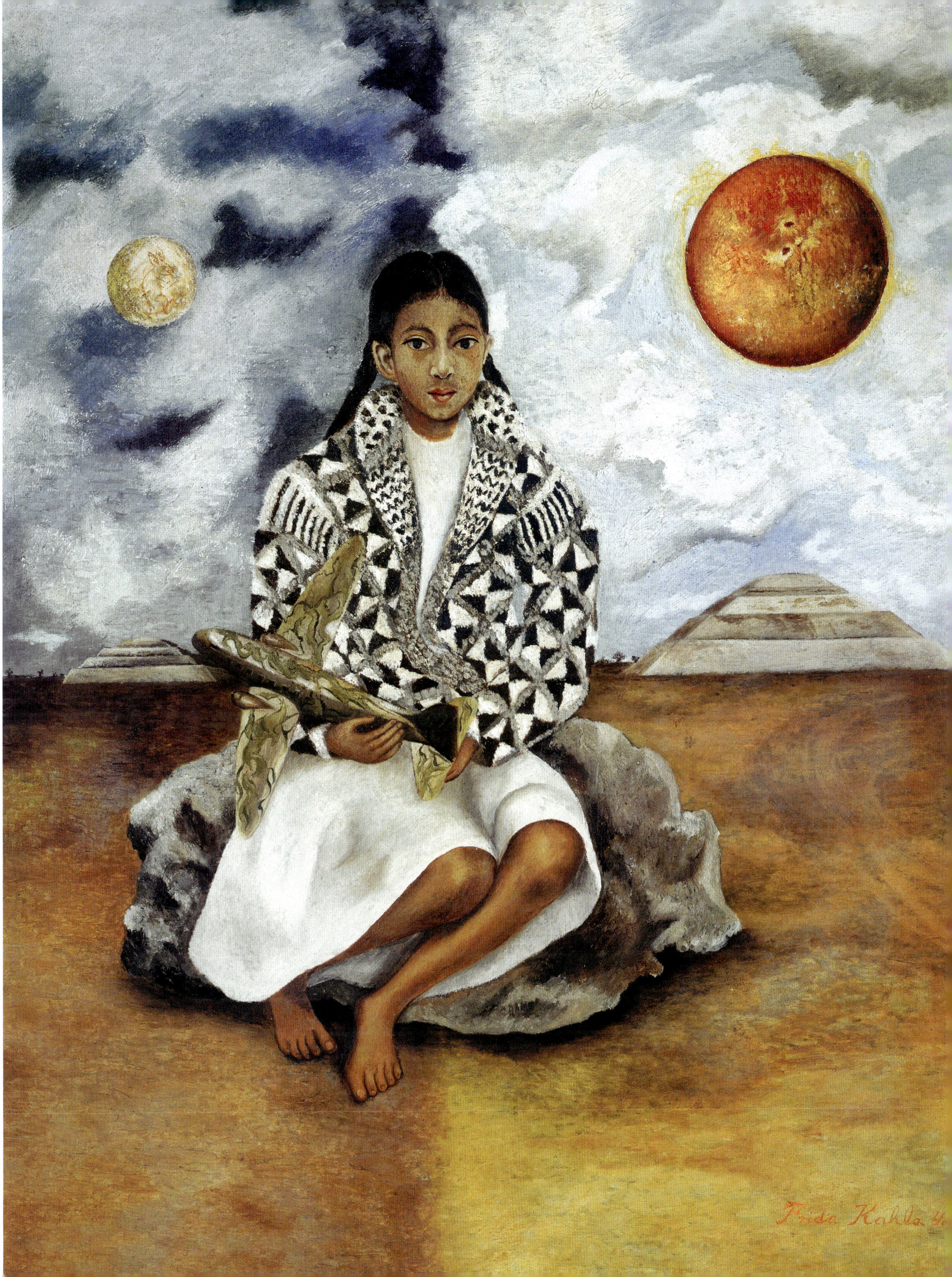
Frida Kahlo

48

Little Deer

1946
Oil on Masonite,
8¾ x 11¾ in. (22.4 x 30 cm)
Houston (Texas), Carolyn Farb

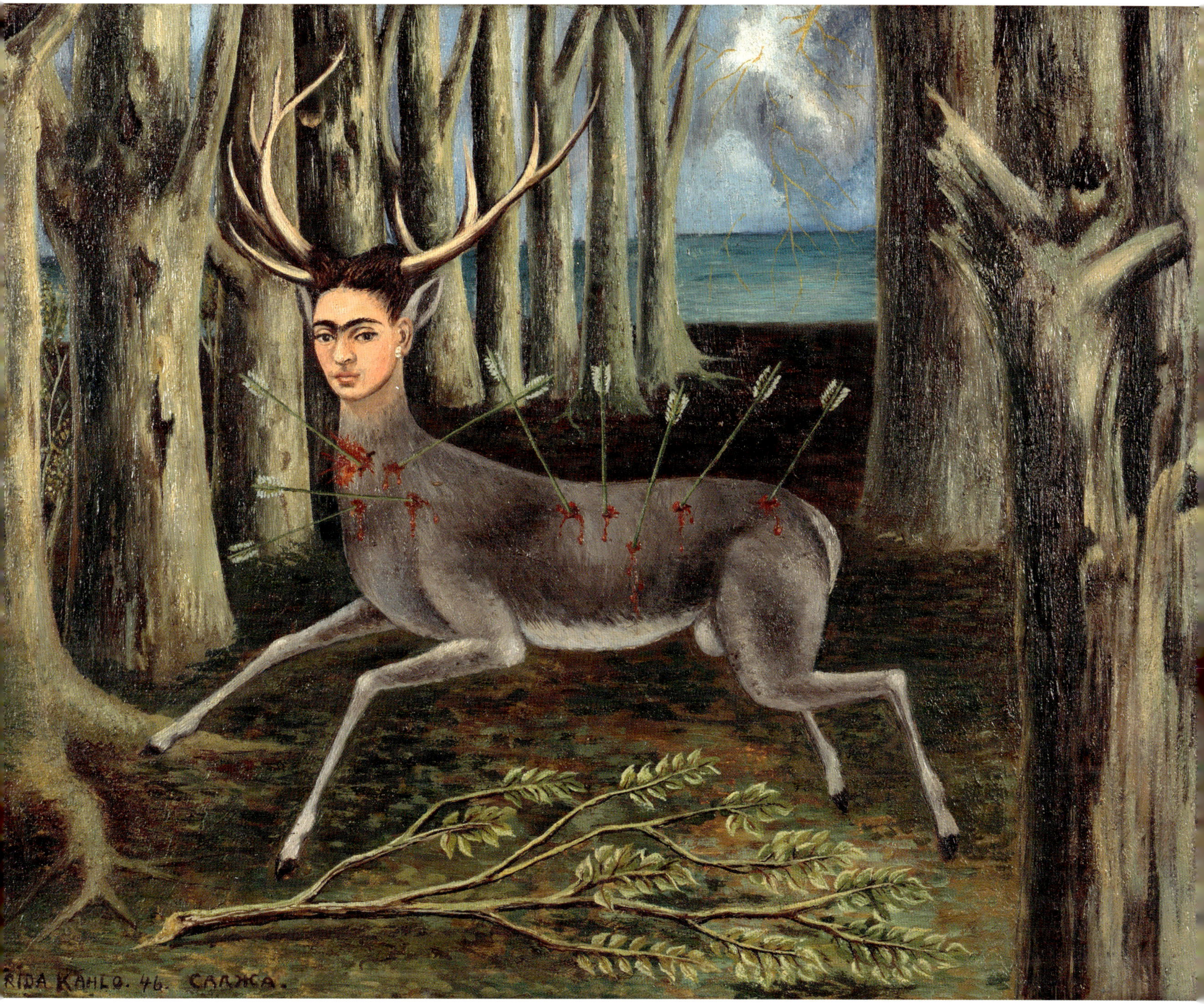
RIDA KAHLO. 46.

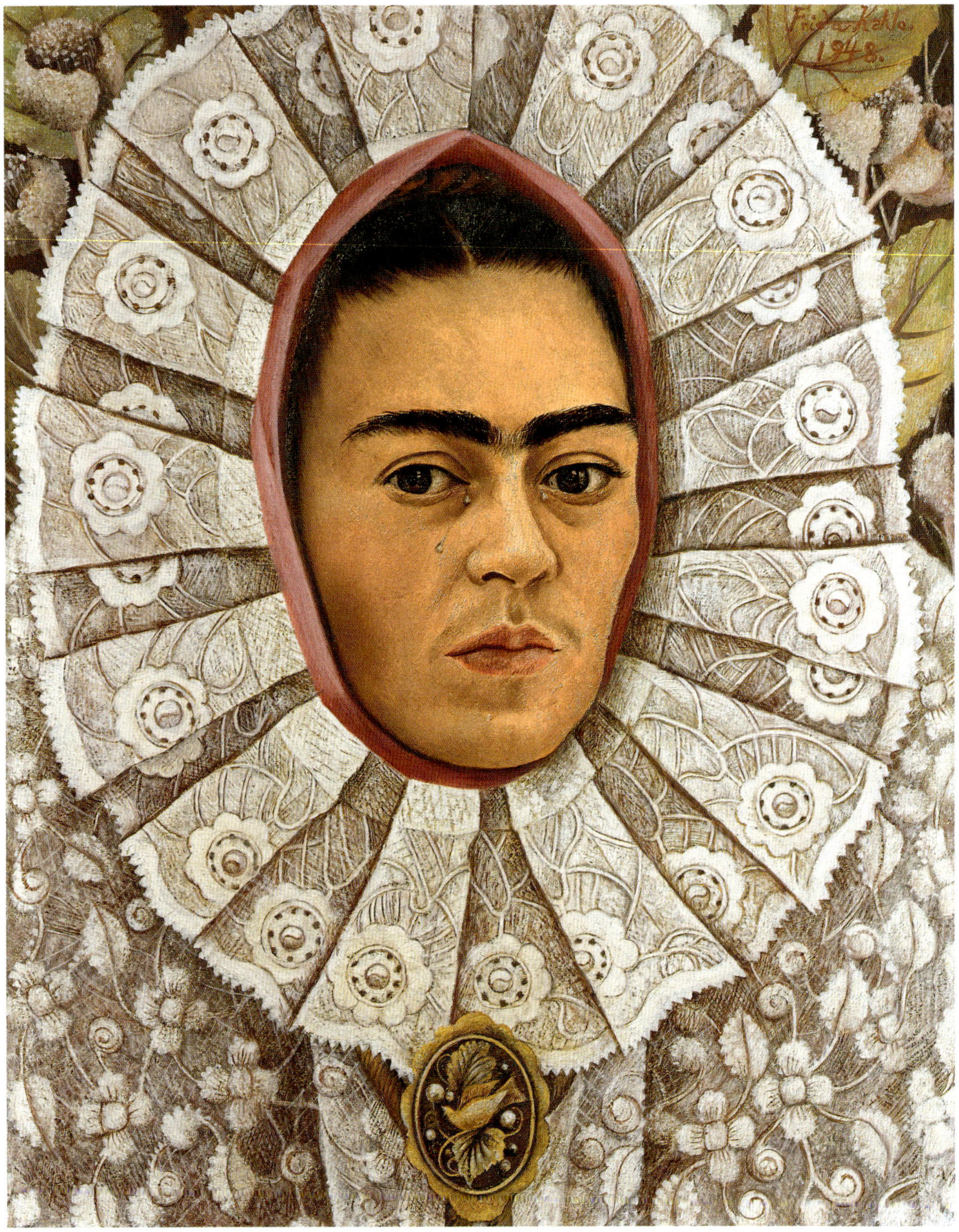

49 **Self-portrait with Medallion**

1948
Oil on Masonite,
19⅔ x 15½ in. (50 x 39.5 cm)
Private collection

50 **Self-portrait as a Tehuana, Diego in My Thoughts,** or **Thinking of Diego**

1943
Oil on Masonite,
30 x 24 in. (76 x 61 cm)
Gelman Collection

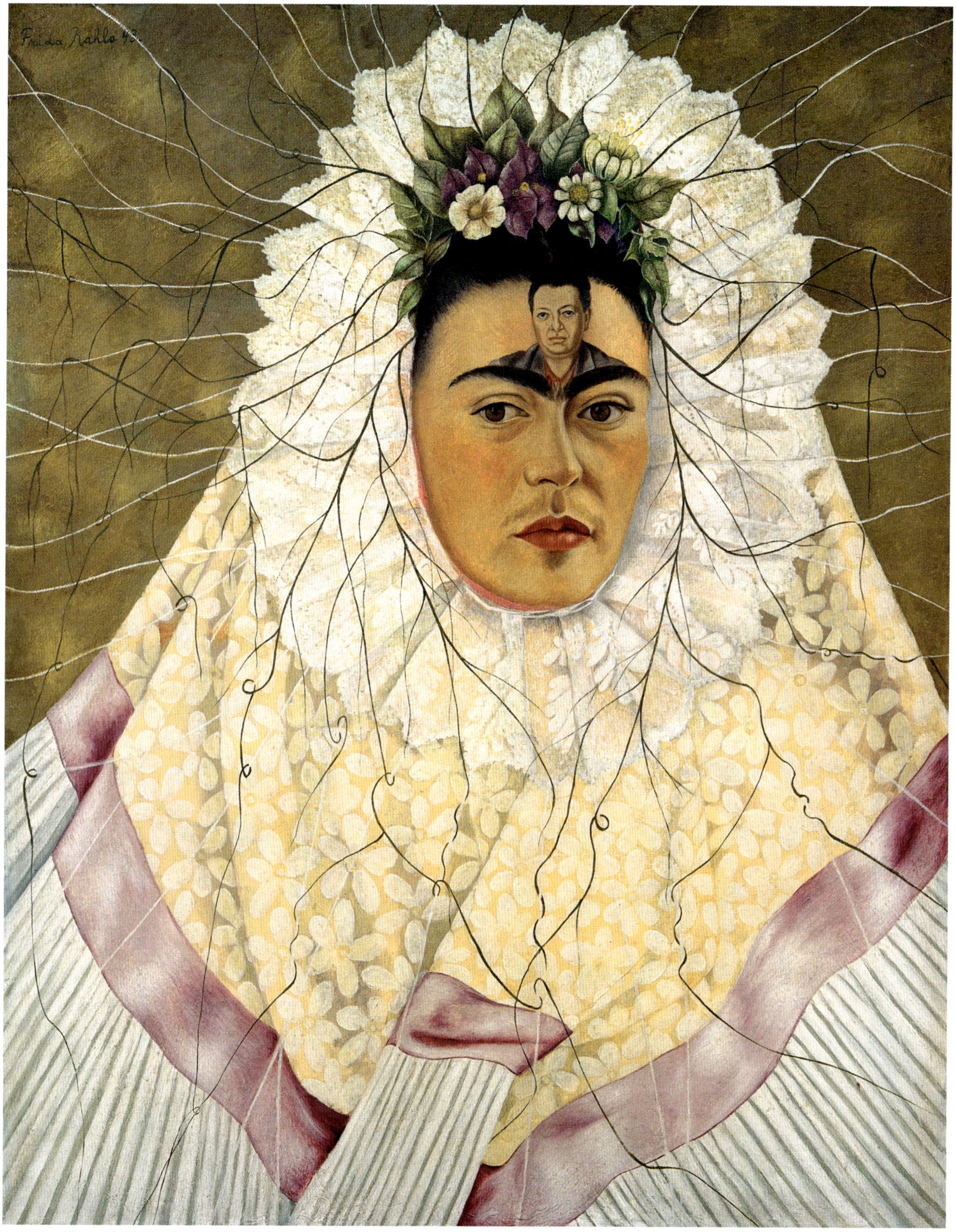
Frida Kahlo 43

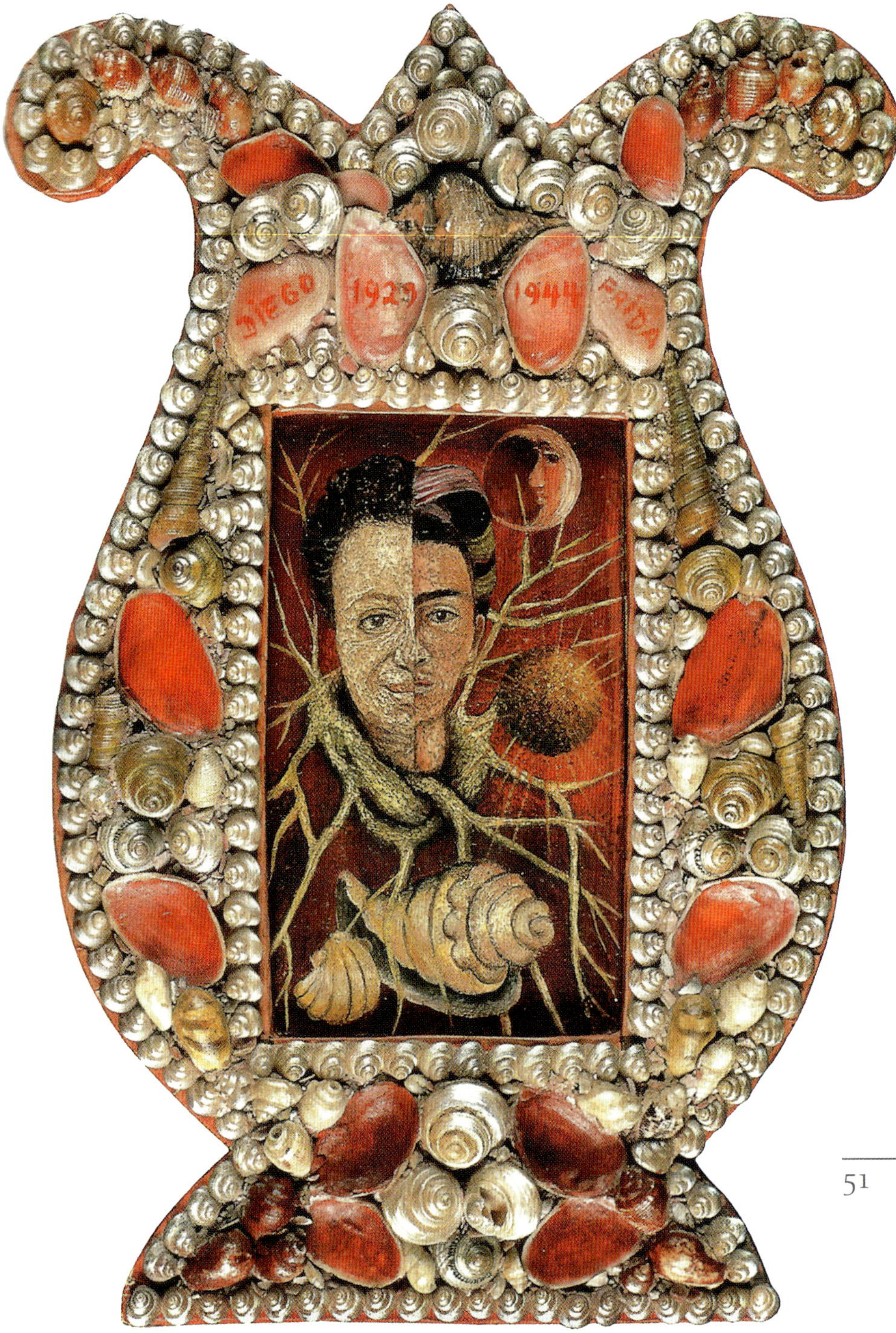

51

Double Portrait of Diego and I

1929–44
Oil on Masonite, 4⅞ x 3 in. (12.3 x 7.4 cm)
Mexico City, Galería Arvil Collection

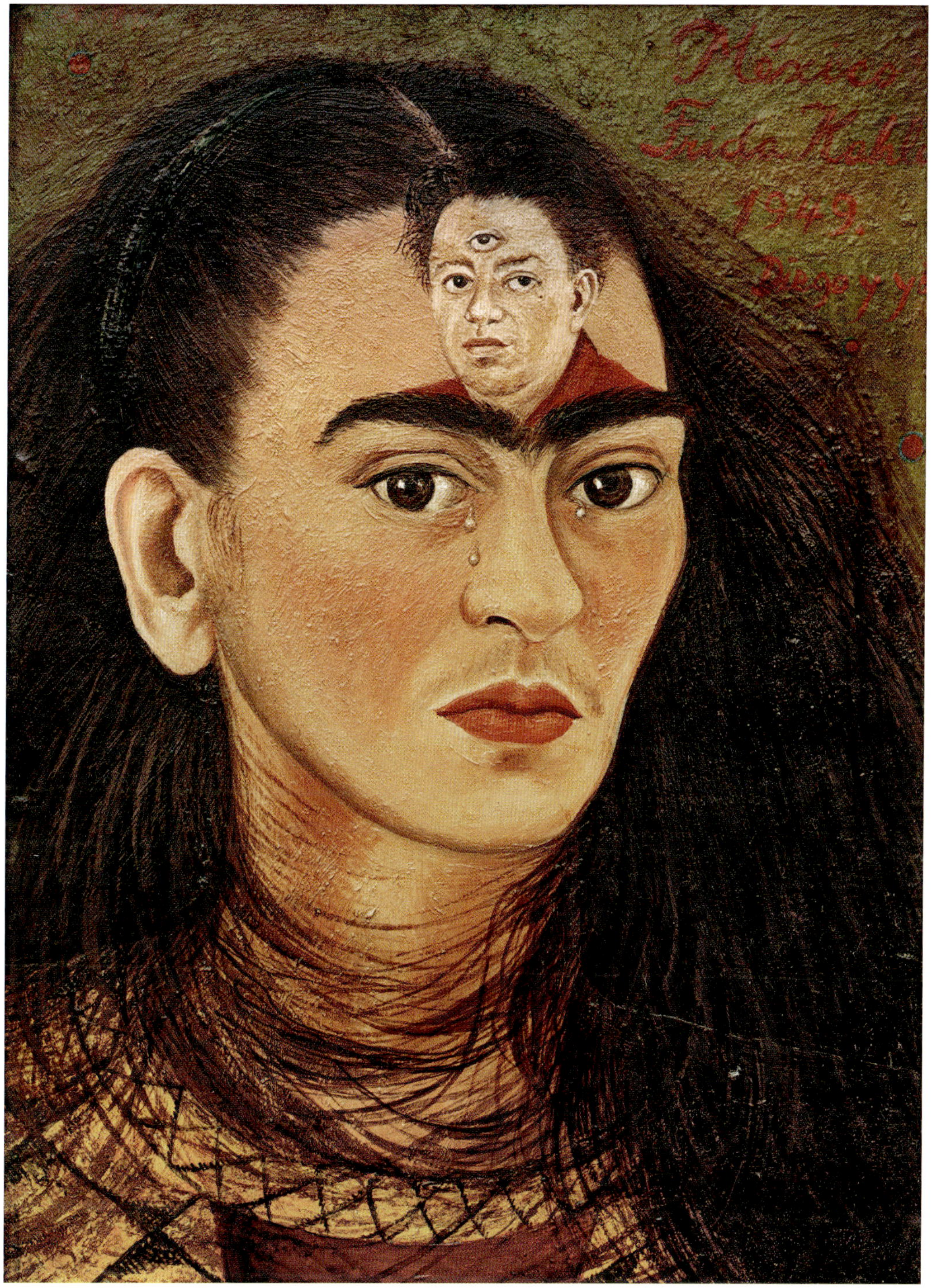

52
Diego and I

1949
Oil on canvas mounted on Masonite,
11⅔ x 8¾ in. (29.5 x 22.4 cm)
New York, private collection

53

The Love Embrace of the Universe, My Earth (Mexico), Diego, Myself and Señor Xólotl

1949
Oil on Masonite,
27½ x 23⅞ in. (70 x 60.5 cm)
Gelman Collection

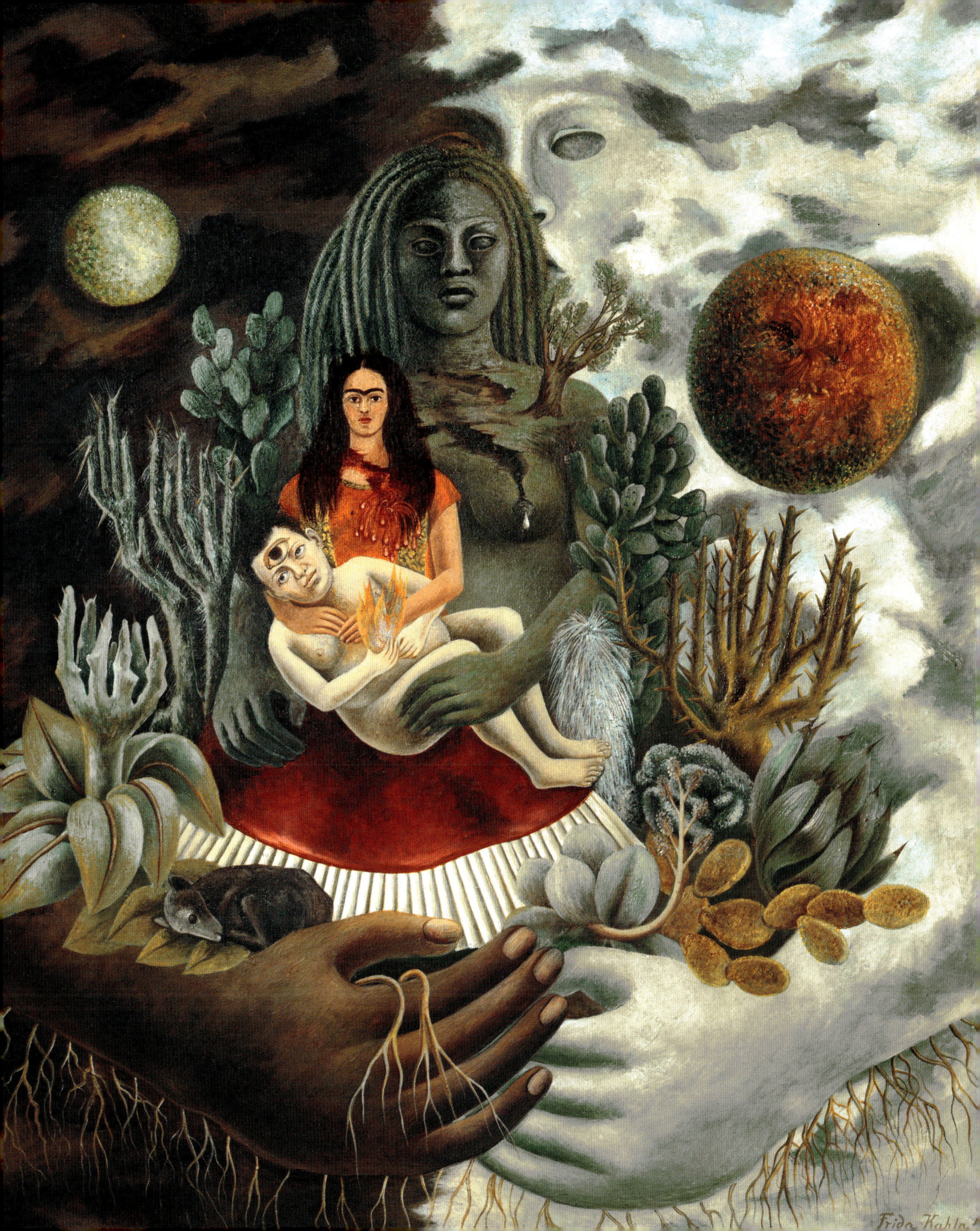
Frida Kahlo

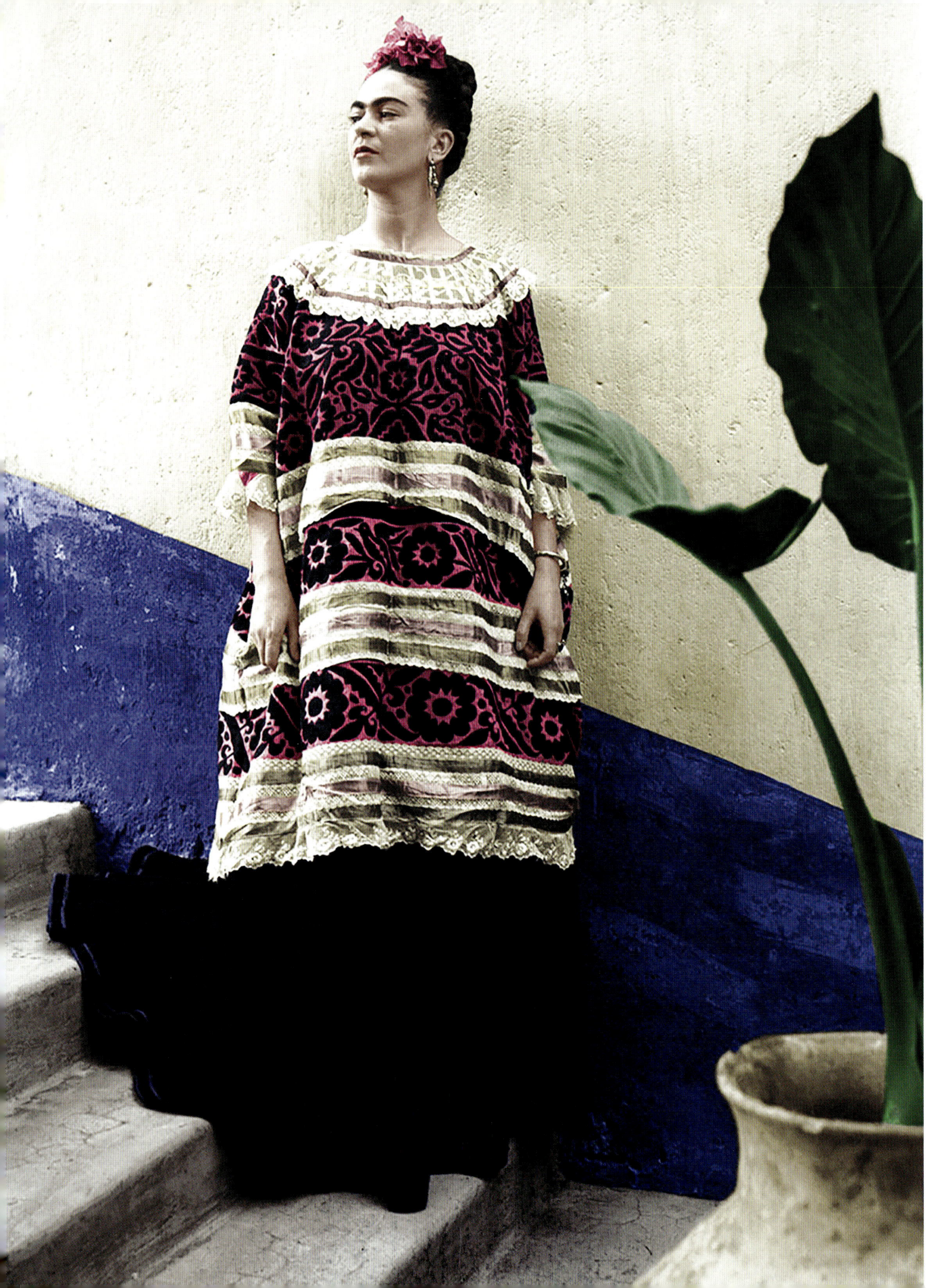

Eroticized Nature

[Eroticism] is sexuality transfigured, a metaphor. The agent that provokes both the erotic act and the poetic act is imagination.

Octavio Paz[1]

He who ungratefully leaves me, I love;
He who lovingly pursues me, I leave ungratefully;
I am constantly adoring the one who mistreats my love;
I mistreat the one who constantly seeks my love.

Sor Juana Inés de la Cruz[2]

Love, and do what you will.

Saint Augustine of Hippo[3]

Both the persona and the oeuvre of Frida Kahlo are imbued with eroticism. In her life, Eros manifested itself in an intense libido and extremely free sexuality. In her painting, the sex drive found expression in the joyful eroticism of her still lifes. Suffering and joie de vivre lived side by side in Kahlo's biography and art with as much intensity as she brought to her love for Diego Rivera, and as much spontaneity as both displayed in violating conjugal fidelity. They were ludic creatures, as Carlos Fuentes remarks:

> I think there was an agreement between them to love each other dearly—and indeed, they loved each other very much—as well as to cheat on each other without consequences. Frida Kahlo had a homosexual, lesbian side. She certainly liked men very much, but she was attracted to women, too. Diego only liked women, but they greatly loved each other. I believe there was an agreement to taste many dishes, many different dinners, but always to return to the common breakfast that was Frida Kahlo in her relationship with Diego Rivera, and Diego Rivera with Frida Kahlo.[4]

Frida Kahlo on steps in the garden of the Casa Azul, 1943. Photograph by Leo Matiz. Mexico City, Fundación Leo Matiz

There is a family photograph taken by Guillermo Kahlo in which the adolescent Frida is dressed as a man. She wears a suit with a vest, shirt, and tie, her brilliantined hair is combed back and parted in the middle, and she holds a cane while looking challengingly at the camera. She clearly intended to differentiate herself from her mother and sisters, and even flattened her breasts to look more like a man. Teresa del Conde points out an important precedent that may help us to understand Kahlo's attitude:

> She had a baby brother, but he died a few days after birth. Her mother, Matilde Calderón, quickly became pregnant again . . . with the hope she would have another boy. Well, Frida was a woman, and all her sisters were women. . . . Frida was the last but one, and I think she wished she had been a strong man, thoughtful and capable, to compensate for all the women her father was surrounded by.[5]

Moreover, she liked children's games and activities, she used coarse language, and she related to boys as though she were one of them. We know of at least one lesbian incursion during her early adolescence. She apparently fell in love with a gym teacher named Sara Senil, as she informed one of her school friends in a letter. There were other amorous brushes with women throughout her life, as well as numerous male lovers. Far from being ashamed of her bisexuality or trying to hide it, Kahlo flaunted it. She was attracted to both men and women, she seduced both with equal enthusiasm, and she also allowed herself to be enamored by both. She practiced her homosexuality and heterosexuality as naturally as the nearly 450 animal species, ranging from primates to parasites and including pygmy chimpanzees, dolphins, bison, ducks, black swans, elephants, lions, giraffes, spiders, and dragonflies, that do the same.

The pleasure afforded by her sexuality was subject to no limitations or prejudices, and so naturally included the autoerotic activity in which she engaged assiduously during her long hours in bed, alone, in pain, and immobilized by orthopedic corsets. The 1983 film *Frida, naturaleza viva* (released as *Frida Still Life* in English), starring Ofelia Medina, opens with a scene of the painter masturbating on her bed. Autoeroticism is a leitmotif of the film, directed by Paul Leduc, as it was in the artist's life. The *petite mort*, whether with men, with women, or self-inflicted, became her most effective antidote to despair. The orgasm was the only way to kill the pain, if only for an instant. It was through her alliance with Eros that Kahlo succeeded in defeating Thanatos.

Eros, like other cosmological divinities, such as Jehovah, Zeus, and Shiva, is conceived as an original unity of the male and female principles, or androgyne. Such was the human condition in Genesis before the creation of Eve from one of Adam's ribs. In *The Symposium*, Plato narrates the myth of the androgyne: human beings

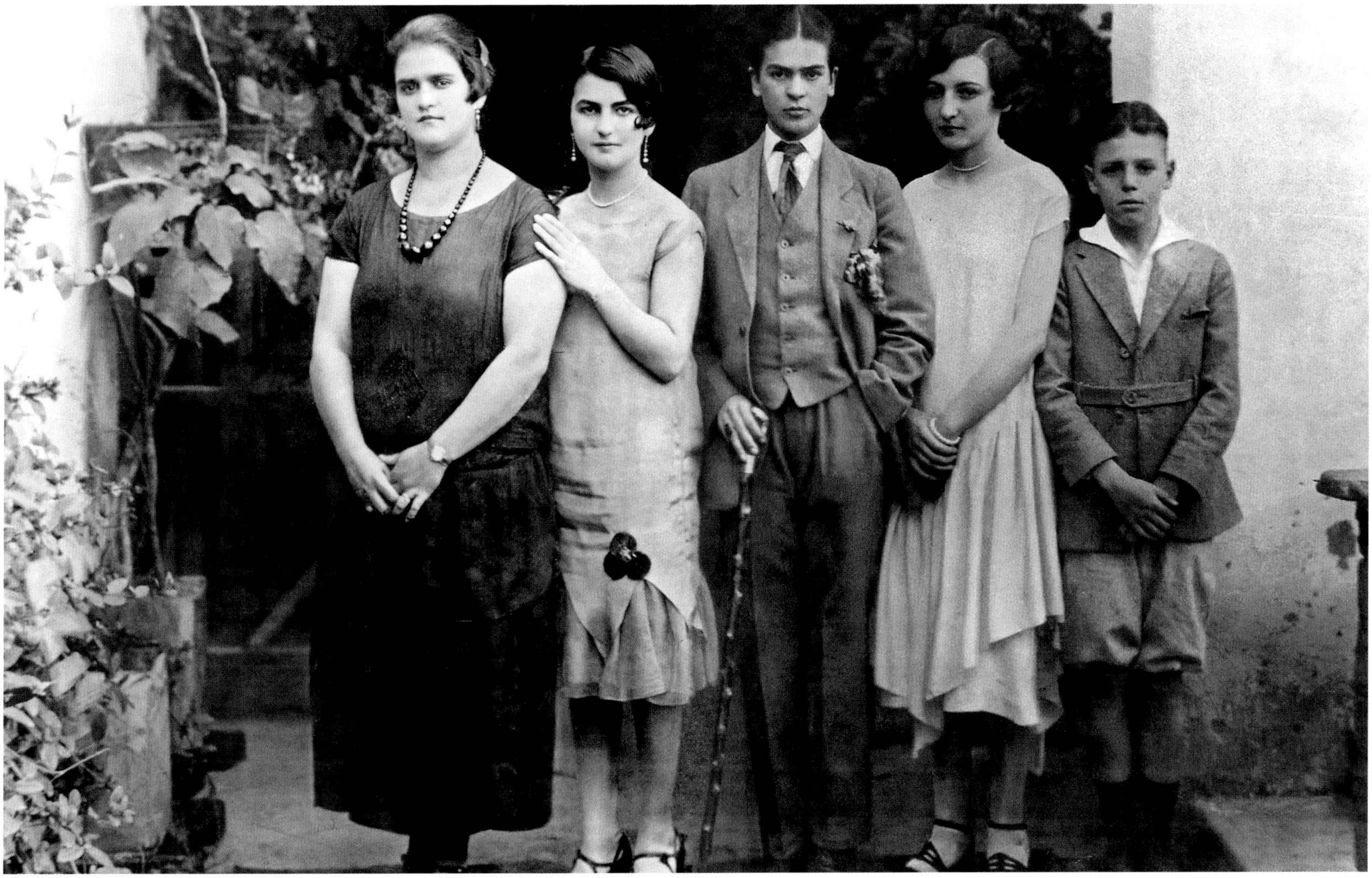

Frida Kahlo dressed as a man with her sisters Adriana and Cristina and her cousins Carmen Romero and Carlos Veraza, Coyoacán (Mexico City), February 7, 1926. Photograph by Guillermo Kahlo

originally had two bodies, two heads, and four legs and were hermaphrodites. As they were arrogant and posed a risk to the gods, Zeus decided to divide each into two halves, but when he saw them dying of longing for their lost halves, he granted them the system of procreation by placing genital organs on the front of their bodies, thereby permitting the subsistence of the human race. Each half is therefore in search of its other half, and when the two halves meet, what emerges is the plenitude of love. This allegory of love is one of the central ideas on the essence of Eros in the Platonic dialogue. Eros denotes the desire and pursuit of the original wholeness of human beings.

Diotima, the only female character whose opinions, through Socrates's narrative, are expressed in the dialogue, argues that Eros is not a god but a great daemon, an intermediary between gods and men who is the child of Penia, the representation of poverty, and Poros, the personification of abundance. This implies a mysterious duality.

Through his maternal origin, Eros is the inseparable companion of the destitute. Owing to the nature of his father, he is permanently on the lookout for the beautiful and the good; he is valiant, active, and brave, also he is avid for wisdom, and he has gifts as a magician, sorcerer, and sophist. If that is the dual nature of Eros, what function does he fulfill for mankind? Eros, Plato tells us through Diotima, represents the creative impulse, the desire to reproduce, and the longing for immortality, either through procreation or by artistic creation. The object of love is not beauty but "to procreate and bring forth in beauty."[6] Kahlo was invaded by Eros in both senses, mythological and sexual.

Kahlo's sexuality is complex. There are several documentary records of her lesbianism. One is the film made by the photographer Lola Álvarez Bravo (1907–1933), where the painter is seen on her bedroom balcony with a much younger girl. She embraces her, looks at the viewer with a rascally expression, and closes the door, making it clear she is heading for a lesbian encounter. Another document is a letter from Kahlo, written in New York in 1933, in which she mentions Georgia O'Keeffe (1887–1986), the famous American artist: "Georgia O'Keeffe has been ill, she's going to Bermuda, she's been three months in hospital, she won't be able to make love to me."[7] It could not be more crystal clear, as Raquel Tibol puts it.

Besides the intimate relationship between Kahlo and O'Keeffe, there is also a profound aesthetic affinity between O'Keeffe's work and Kahlo's still lifes. The dialogue between the two oeuvres was shown in the exhibition *En esto ver aquello. Octavio Paz y el arte* (Seeing This in That: Octavio Paz and Art), presented at the Palacio de Bellas Artes in 2014 to commemorate the centenary of the Mexican poet. We cite part of the text written by the curator of that show:

> The forms, textures, and hollows of flowers and fruits produce visual analogies with the anatomical characteristics of female sexuality that have been used symbolically throughout the history of painting. In the twentieth century, there were two outstanding representatives of that tradition: Georgia O'Keeffe, who can be considered a paradigm of the genre with paintings like *Blue Line* (1919), *Series I, White & Blue Flower Shapes* (1919), and *Series I, No. 12* (1920); and Frida Kahlo, whose still lifes, notable for their magnificent execution and sense of humor, include the outstanding *The Flower of Life* (1944), *Sun and Life* (1947), and *Still Life with Parrot and Flag* (1951). It is a pleasant discovery to observe the pictorial dialogue between these two great artists, who were also bonded by an intense friendship.[8]

Let us linger over these three paintings by Kahlo. In *The Flower of Life*, Kahlo produced an anatomically exact representation, both realistic and metaphorical, of the internal genital organs of a woman during copulation [fig. 54]. It might look at first

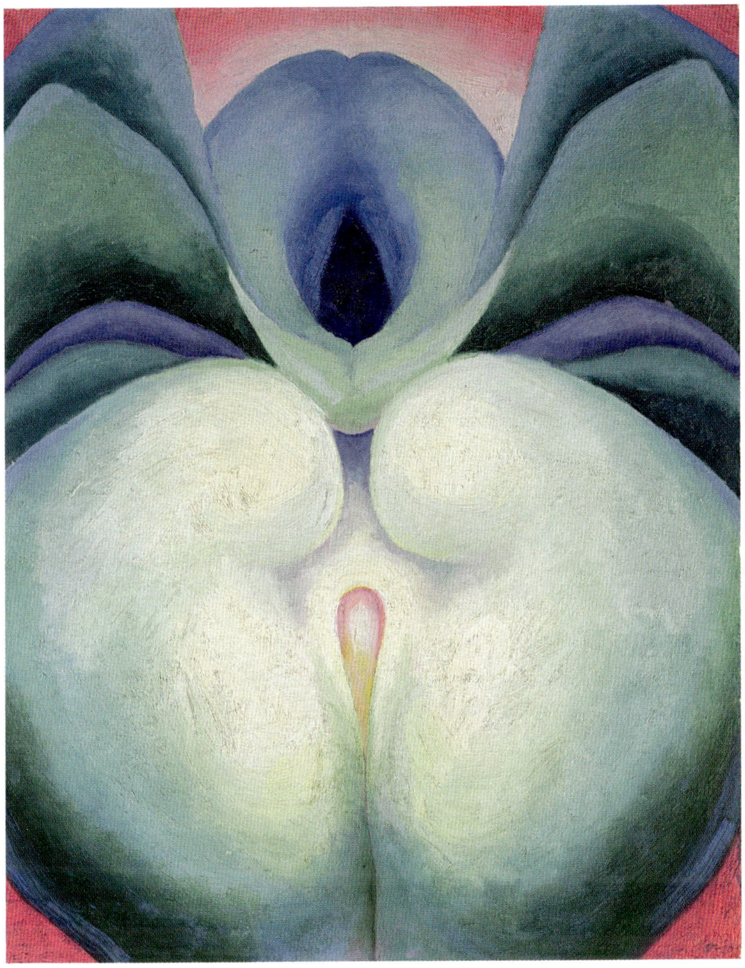

Georgia O'Keeffe, *Series I White & Blue Flower Shapes*, 1919, oil on board, 19⅞ x 15¾ in. (50.5 x 40 cm). Santa Fe, Georgia O'Keeffe Museum, Gift of The Georgia O'Keeffe Foundation, 2006.5.87

glance like a humanoid vegetable figure, but it is not. In the lower part of the work, a bush of profuse carmine foliage covers part of the vagina, which has been penetrated from beneath. On the vaginal cylinder are strokes of scarlet to heighten the texture of the veins of the erect phallus and the cellular tissue. The upper part of the uterus opens forward like the petals of a flower, while the fallopian tubes emerge from the sides like two hollow arms and hands with a somewhat menacing appearance. The ovaries are not shown. What might be confused with the head of the humanoid vegetable, surmounted by a golden star like the pistil of a flower, is in fact the gland or tip of the penis, while the shining rays emerging from it symbolize ejaculation, represented as a glittering burst aimed at the egg floating in the upper right corner. *The Flower of Life* is a prodigious symbolic exaltation of sexuality and fertilization, two decisive facets of the artist's life: the first as a source of pleasure, and the second as a motive of profound frustration and sadness owing to her failure to produce a child. A small masterpiece, it reveals the influence of Surrealist language.

In *Sun and Life*, Kahlo's pictorial poetry reaches a new dimension by almost completely eliminating the realism of the still life to create a fantastical landscape where the plants are vaginas and the pistils—the female organs of flowers—are transformed into drops of sperm that fertilize the gynoecium [fig. 55]. A red solar flower with a human face and a weeping third eye accentuates the melancholy character of this organic jungle, vegetable and animal. A human fetus also sheds tears as if foreseeing the impossibility of its birth. Despair becomes erotic art.

In Kahlo's still lifes, disillusionment lives alongside humor and the joy of living. This is the case of *Still Life with Parrot and Flag*, one of the finest and most representative examples of the painter's jubilant eroticism [fig. 56]. This harmonious and impeccably executed composition reproduces the forms, colors, and textures of the delicious fruits of Mexico, to which the artist added a touch of piquancy by emphasizing the similarity of the sliced fruit to the organs of the female reproductive apparatus. On the left of the picture, a melon split down the middle embodies the anatomical characteristics of the vulva, with the outer and inner labia and the clitoris shown in detail. In the center of the composition, an open mammee wittily evokes female sexuality and is stalked by a male banana that protrudes from testicular lemons in the direction of the desired treasure. There is plenty of life in this still life.

Apparently, Kahlo also had intimate relations with Jacqueline Lamba, the wife of André Breton, as Salomon Grimberg remarks:

> The only woman with whom I think she had a sexual relationship—not erotic, but erotic and sexual—is Jacqueline, André Breton's wife, because there's a love letter in which she writes to her, "your child is our child," and when Jacqueline decided to leave Breton, Frida wrote a very beautiful love letter in her diary, which is the letter that appears at the beginning with some things crossed out. . . . It says, more or less: "The nights are long, I miss you, the nights are long, and I remember that time you left me. You understood I had to go back to Diego and so you never wanted to say goodbye to me, but you looked at me in that round window until I disappeared." This isn't the tone of a woman writing to a friend.[9]

Grimberg is the author of several books on Frida Kahlo, one of which deals with her still lifes. His description of *Xóchitl Flower of Life* (1938)[10] is well worth quoting:

> A small but powerful image of a flower made up of two opposite but well-integrated parts: a red bell-like vagina, and a penis received from above. *Xóchitl* is Nahuatl for "flower," but it also means "something precious, delicate," . . . The image also seems influenced by the Mexican colloquialism *coger flores*, which literally means to deflower, but metaphorically to ask for sexual favors.[11]

This painting has evident similarities to *The Flower of Life*, described above, since both refer to the anatomy of the female sexual organs.

Another outstanding work in this genre is *Fruits of the Earth* (1938), a worthy successor to the still lifes of José Agustín Arrieta (1802–1879) and Hermenegildo Bustos (1832–1907), two major nineteenth-century Mexican artists [fig. 57], with clear references to Bustos in this case. It is the largest still life painted by Kahlo, and its angle of vision produces the impression that the items are going to slip off the table they rest upon. Three ears of corn, the sacred plant of Mesoamerica, frame the composition, establishing a diagonal. In the center, an earthenware platter contains a chayote, three types of mushrooms, a poblano chili, and three open pitahayas. The sexual allusions are rendered with subtlety, humor, and impeccable pictorial quality.

Kahlo changed the bright blue sky of the background for a stormy one when Rivera asked her for a divorce.

Pitahayas, painted the same year, was included in the exhibition at the Julien Levy Gallery in New York [fig. 58]. André Breton wrote in the catalogue for the show, "I never imagined that world of fruits which encompasses such a marvel as the *pitahaya,* whose coiled pulp is like the colour of rose petals, whose skin is grey, and which tastes like a kiss blended of love and desire."[12]

Of all the metaphors of life painted by Kahlo through the medium of eroticized fruits, perhaps the most noteworthy is *Still Life (Tondo)* (1942), painted in oil on a round metal plate [fig. 59]. In the center of the composition, an open papaya looks like a uterus during the process of fertilization, when millions of sperm go in search of an egg that has just been released by an ovary. Only one spermatozoon will succeed in piercing the plasma membrane to fertilize the egg, which then becomes a zygote. This whole process is symbolized by the group of sexualized fruits, flowers, and vegetables that surround the papaya-womb. It is important to note the presence of two butterflies situated above the fruit-like uterus, symbols of the most wonderful and mysterious of the metamorphoses taking place inside the maternal womb: the engendering of a human being, a fusion of matter and spirit. Kahlo never enjoyed that privilege, but she did create eternal masterpieces like this one.

The president of Mexico at that time, Manuel Ávila Camacho, asked Kahlo for this painting to decorate the dining room of Los Pinos, the official presidential residence. A few days after it was delivered, the painting was returned to the artist because the president's prudish consort considered it obscene. The following year, Kahlo painted *The Bride Frightened at Seeing Life Opened,* probably a sarcastic allusion to the first lady's demureness [fig. 60]. It is generally considered the still life with the greatest erotic connotation, irony, and wit produced by Kahlo. Helga Prignitz-Poda has a different and more complex interpretation of this work's symbolic dimension, which we shall try to summarize here.[13] From this author's point of view, the work possesses a beauty intended to transmit the idea of the "transitory nature of all human beings." It is the representation through fruit of male and female genitals, united, like the yin and yang, "in a sumptuous feast." Colors and shapes complement one another to produce "a symphony of lushness and opulence." The presence of an owl and a grasshopper is associated with one of Aesop's fables, where the owl, a symbol of wisdom owing to its ability to see at night and thus know the underworld, ends up devouring the insect. "Just as the owl cannot see in the sun, the human being cannot understand things without conceptualizing them." The doll in a wedding dress reveals Kahlo's goal of disclosing the nature of desire: the bride is "frightened at the display of the things before her eyes: the wild longing of both sexes as part of nature." In conclusion, "with the two widely cut-open watermelons Frida offers to the observer a glimpse into the terrible territory of lushness, the greed for more

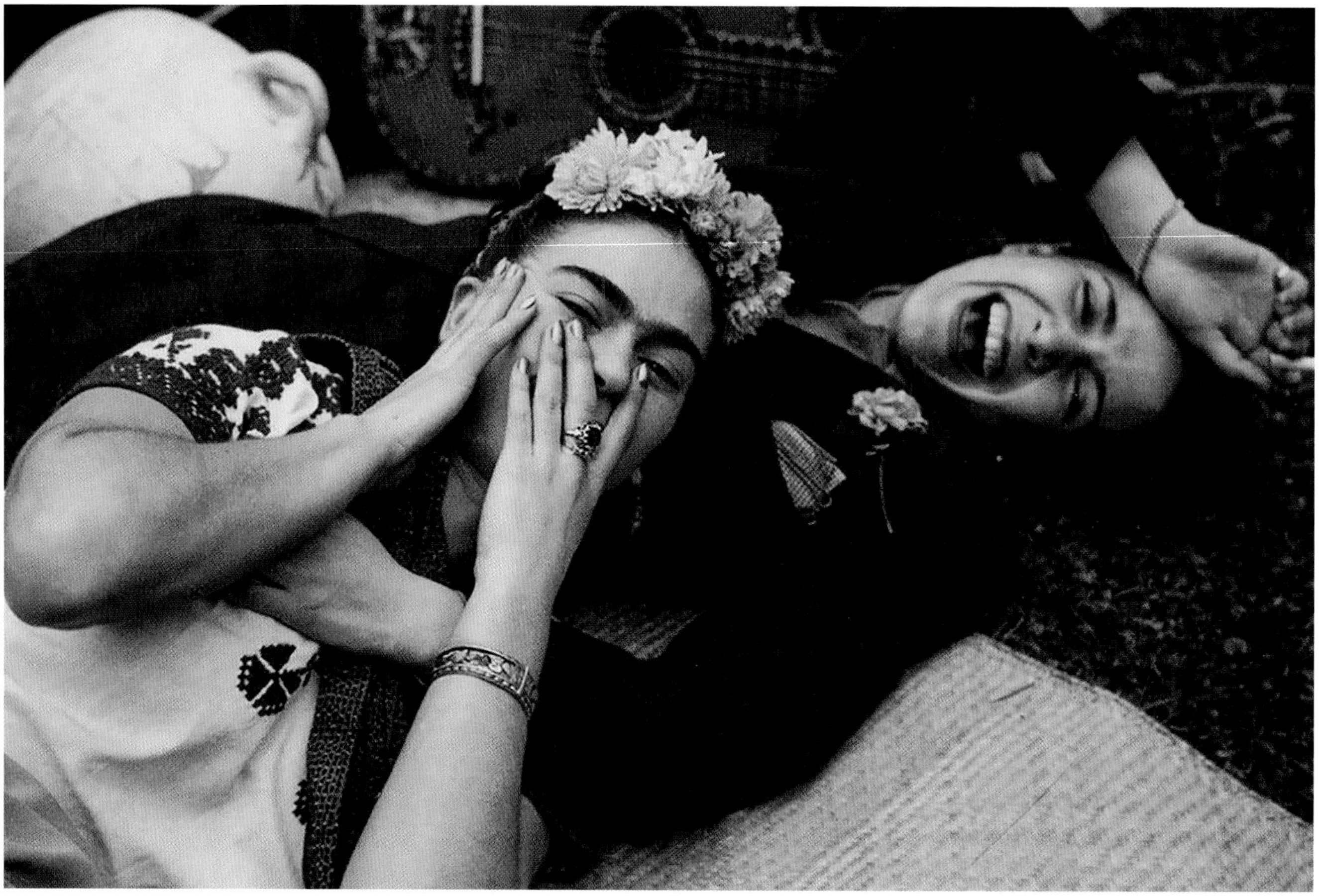

Frida Kahlo laughing with an unidentified person, c. 1945. Coyoacán (Mexico City), Museo Frida Kahlo

sensuousness, the insatiable desire for symbiotic closeness." Like poetry, good painting will always be open to different interpretations and inevitably reveals the mentality of the beholder.

Other eroticized still lifes worthy of mention are *Magnolias* (1945) [fig. 61], *Weeping Coconuts* (1951) [fig. 62], *Coconuts* (1951) [fig. 63], *Still Life (I Belong to Samuel Fastlicht)* (1951) [fig. 64], and *Still Life with Watermelons* (1953) [fig. 65].

Kahlo painted another testament to her bisexuality: *Two Nudes in the Forest* or *The Earth Itself* (1939) [fig. 66], painted the same year as *The Two Fridas,* in which she shows the couple that floats on a sponge in *What the Water Gave Me,* dating from a year earlier [fig. 27]. Two nude women, both with loose hair and Kahlo's face, one brown and the other white, rest in a landscape of contrasts, half barren plain and half vegetable exuberance, with more of the jungle than the forest. The brown figure is seated on a slope from which roots emerge, and her head is covered by a shawl that also serves as a cushion. She placidly rests her hand on the neck of the white Frida, who lies with her head in the other woman's lap looking out at the viewer. Her left arm embraces the right leg of the brown Frida, whose foot rests on her companion's thigh.

The scene is observed by a spider monkey, a symbol of lust, who also accompanies Kahlo in *Fulang-Chang and I* (1937) [fig. 22] and other self-portraits. *Two Nudes in the Forest* was sold for eight million dollars at an auction held at Christie's in New York in May 2016, the highest auction price paid for a Latin American artwork to that date.

Chavela Vargas, the great singer who made Mexican *rancheras* and *boleros* her own, gave an extremely elegant and moving account of her intimate relationship with Frida Kahlo in a documentary on her life:

> A painter friend of mine said, "There's a party tonight at Frida's house. Want to go?" So I went. There were so many people there. We sang and danced all night long. Everyone was drunk. She was like a vision. When I saw her face, her eyes, I thought she was from another world. Her eyebrows together were a swallow in mid-flight. I wasn't a woman yet. I was still very much a young girl. Yet, I knew I could love this person with the most devoted love in the world, the most ardent love in the world.[14]

Chavela Vargas, twelve years younger than Kahlo, lived for a time with Kahlo and Rivera in the Casa Azul, where she said she felt very happy and very much in love, as well as dearly loved by Kahlo: "She taught me many things and I learned a great deal, and without giving herself airs. I grasped heaven in my hands, with every word, every morning!"[15]

Nevertheless, Vargas suffered over having to share Kahlo's love with Rivera, and one day she decided to leave her:

> When I said I would leave her one day, my words probably hurt her deeply. But she said, "I know. It's impossible to tie you down to anyone's life. I can't bind you to my crutches or my bed. Leave." And one day, I opened the door and never returned.[16]

Vargas went on to have a roaring success at the Palacio de Bellas Artes in Mexico City, and with the support of the Spanish filmmaker Pedro Almodóvar, she also triumphed in Madrid, in Paris, and at New York's Carnegie Hall. Apparently, Vargas destroyed the letters sent to her by Kahlo.

Delving a little further into the subject of Kahlo's intimate life, Raquel Tibol relates an erotic experience that Kahlo had with the Mexican poet Carlos Pellicer:

> We know that the great poet Carlos Pellicer was a homosexual. He went to visit Frida, and she couldn't restrain herself and masturbated him. She thanked him afterward in a beautiful letter, where Frida indulges in no vulgarity after doing what she did. She thanks him in the letter "for letting her reach his sun." What a

> beautiful way of putting it, and what a poetic and respectful way to refer to a skin-to-skin act between two human beings! That happened in 1947, and when years later they amputated Frida's leg, Pellicer wrote three marvelous sonnets dedicated to Frida. In the last line [of the first verse] of one of them, he apologizes because "I was not able to be your Good Samaritan," meaning that Frida invited him to continue the relationship and he declined, because it wasn't his calling to be masturbated by a lesbian or a bisexual.[17]

Given the singularity of the occurrence and the artistic quality of the two actors in that peculiar scene, we quote here an extract from Kahlo's letter to Pellicer:

> I don't know how I dare to write you, but yesterday we said it would do me good. . . . Can verbs be invented? I want to say one to you: I *sky* you, so my wings stretch out enormously to love you without measure . . . in your extraordinary world, what I offer you is only one truth more that you receive and that will ever caress the deepest part of you. Thank you for receiving it, thank you for living, because yesterday you let me touch your innermost light, and because you said with your voice and your eyes what I had been waiting for all my life.[18]

We also offer a translation of the sonnet by Carlos Pellicer dedicated to Frida Kahlo, mentioned by Tibol:

> Like someone with flowers in his hand
> who stands gazing at an entire people
> to give it his heart, I love you.
> (I was not able to be your Good Samaritan.)
>
> Nothing in our grief has been in vain;
> let the brushes come: the first
> tinged in blood will tell you in warbles
> of its tears wandering over the plain.
>
> You are all nailed up with carnations.
> The brushes stick fire on the blood.
> A bloody child rises to heaven.
>
> I camp in an abyss of tenderness,
> dry with thirst. Your heart, in flight,
> dropped a little of its height.[19]

Kahlo enjoyed seducing and being seduced. Teresa del Conde remarked to us that later in Kahlo's life coitus must have been very difficult for her, perhaps spurring her to explore her erotic options further. Moreover, intimate relations with women made her feel maternally protected and cherished and soothingly caressed.

Diego Rivera was scornful of Kahlo's lesbian relationships, but he was infuriated by her love affairs with men. She knew it, and she also knew how to make use of her voluminous husband's wrath. It was part of the appeal of those erotic adventures for the artist. There was a famous story of a tryst Kahlo had with the sculptor Isamu Noguchi (1904–1988), who came to Mexico in 1935 on a Guggenheim fellowship with the hope of being able to paint a mural in the Abelardo Rodríguez Market in Mexico City, where several colleagues of his were working on other walls. He won the commission and finished his work in eight months: a relief in copper and silver tones entitled *History of Mexico*, with a combination of sculptures affixed to the wall and paintings of fists, swastikas, skeletons, and Albert Einstein's theory of relativity, $E = mc^2$. When the restoration of the murals in that market began in 2009, Noguchi's work was valued at two million dollars. Apart from his great talent, Noguchi was a very attractive man of considerable personality. Inevitably, he was captivated by Kahlo when he met her.

> I loved her very much. . . . She was a lovely person, absolutely marvelous person. Since Diego was well known to be a lady chaser, she cannot be blamed if she saw some men. . . . In those days we all sort of, more or less, horsed around, and Diego did and so did Frida. It wasn't quite acceptable to him, however. I used to have assignations with her here and there. One of the places was her sister Cristina's place, the blue house in Coyoacán. . . .
>
> I knew Frida well during an eight-month period. We went dancing all the time. Frida loved to dance. That was her passion, you know, everything that she couldn't do she loved to do. It made her absolutely furious to be unable to do things.[20]

One day, Rivera found out about the romance and immediately went to the house in Coyoacán. The lovers were in bed, and Kahlo's valet came to warn her of Rivera's arrival. Noguchi had to escape half-dressed through a window. A Xoloitzcuintli dog tore off one of his socks; he climbed a tree without it, and then he fled across the rooftop. Rivera, who was armed with a gun, found the lost sock and said to Kahlo, "The next time I see him, I'll kill him!"[21] That was the end of the romance between Kahlo and Noguchi.

After Rivera, Kahlo's greatest love was Nickolas Muray (1892–1965). Salomon Grimberg, the editor of the book *I Will Never Forget You . . .: Frida Kahlo and Nickolas Muray* (2006), tells the story of that long and intense relationship:

> Nickolas Muray, Miguel Covarrubias's best friend, arrived in Mexico in 1931. He was a very well-built engineer with an extraordinary personality, charismatic, handsome, intelligent, good-mannered, European. Moreover, Muray had done extraordinary things, as he had arrived in New York with twenty-five dollars and a fifty-word vocabulary, and in time had become one of the most important photographers in the United States. He took the first color photograph for an American magazine. When he arrived in Mexico in May 1931, he had just gotten divorced from his second wife, and he was looking for a torrid romance. He met Frida through Miguel Covarrubias, and Frida fell madly in love with Nick and wrote him her first love letter in Hungarian. In the letter, which is documented, she says to him, "I will love you forever, I will never forget you. Come to Mexico in August and we'll go to Tehuantepec together." Frida, who could be incredibly cruel, gave Nickolas Muray a drawing that's a self-portrait of her holding hands with Diego. That was her gift to her lover. Frida kept up a relationship with Nickolas Muray for ten years, and he took the most beautiful and exquisite color photographs that anyone had taken of Frida. The famous photo of Frida with her arms folded was taken by Nickolas Muray at the apex of their affair, and Diego said it was as gorgeous as a Piero della Francesca. She made Nick believe she was going to marry him. Finally, Diego asked Frida for a new marriage, and Frida broke up with Nick.[22]

The romance between Kahlo and Muray, which lasted a decade, survived the photographer's third marriage as well as the divorce and remarriage of Kahlo and Rivera. They remained friends until the painter's death in 1954, and the photographs taken of her by Muray survive as an additional facet of the immortal character called Frida Kahlo. The photograph mentioned by Grimberg and praised by Rivera is perhaps the most beautiful ever taken of Kahlo. Facing the camera, she wears a red shawl with pink highlights that covers her shoulders and breast, a bone necklace, and gilt earrings, and her hair is gathered back by a black headband with shining studs and a eaddress of purple wool. Kahlo's expression is one of absolute tranquility and—a rarity—a certain gentleness, like a contented lover. Her face, slightly turned and inclined to her right, displays her straight nose and the fleshiness of her clearly delineated scarlet lips to their best advantage, in harmony with the flying dove of her joined eyebrows and the color of her shawl. The down over her upper lip is barely perceptible. Her crossed forearms emphasize the proportion of her hands, whose fingernails are also painted red. The violet skirt with white flowers appears at the bottom of the frame.

In another of the magnificent photographs that Muray took of his talented lover, Kahlo is shown sitting frontally, wearing a black Tehuana dress and shawl. The blouse has red and yellow embroidery, and the skirt has a pattern of small flowers, a brocade strip fretted in saffron yellow, and a starched white flounce. She

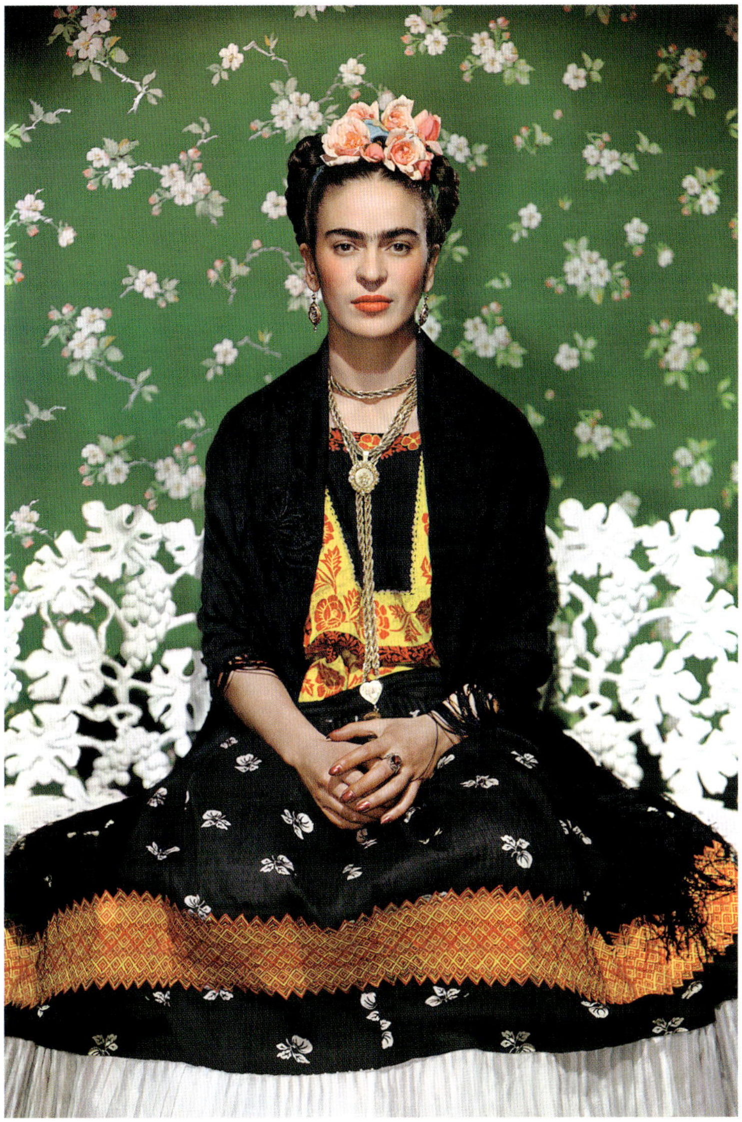

Kahlo on a white bench, New York, 1939. Photograph by Nickolas Muray. Alta (Utah), Nickolas Muray Photo Archives

wears a necklace and earrings of gilt filigree typical of Oaxaca. She has a serene gaze on her oval face, with its red lips and pink cheekbones. Her hair is gathered back in a headpiece of pink roses. The background wall is bright green with pink flowers, while the white-painted back of the cast-iron bench where she sits forms the shapes of known vegetable species, such as the Xanadu plant. Kahlo's elegance and the color of the composition make this photograph harmonious and attractive.

Illuminated by the force of Eros, Kahlo was the source and instrument of her own creation in both life and art. Through her prodigious imagination, she went about the gestation and invention of her persona and her oeuvre with iron resolution.

1 Octavio Paz, *The Double Flame: Love and Eroticism,* trans. Helen Lane (New York: Harcourt, 1996), 3.
2 Sor Juana Inés de la Cruz, *Buscan mis ojos tu presencia. Sonetos completos* (Mexico City: Verdehalago, 2006), 17.
3 Saint Augustine of Hippo, Homily 7 on the First Epistle of John to the Parthians, 8.
4 "Entrevista con Carlos Fuentes. Frida amada," in *Yo soy Frida*, ed. Héctor Tajonar (Mexico City: Milenio Diario, 2007), 5.
5 "Entrevista con Teresa del Conde. Frida pintura," in *Yo soy Frida*, 20.
6 Plato, *The Symposium*, trans. Walter Hamilton (Harmondsworth: Penguin, 1988), 87.
7 "Entrevista con Raquel Tibol. Frida poliédrica," in *Yo soy Frida*, 10.
8 Héctor Tajonar, "Soplo de luz," in *En esto ver aquello. Octavio Paz y el arte* (Mexico City: Consejo Nacional para la Cultura y las Artes e Instituto Nacional de Bellas Artes, 2014), 122.
9 "Entrevista con Salomon Grimberg. Frida inventada," in *Yo soy Frida*, 16.
10 Frida Kahlo, *Xóchitl Flower of Life*, 1938, oil on metal, 7 x 3¾ in. (18 x 9.5 cm), Mexico City, private collection.
11 Salomon Grimberg, "Xóchitl, or the Flower of Life," in *Frida Kahlo: National Homage, 1907–2007* (Mexico City: Instituto Nacional de Bellas Artes, 2008), 182.
12 André Breton, *Surrealism and Painting*, trans. Simon Watson Taylor (New York: Harper & Row, 1972), 143, quoted in Hayden Herrera, *Frida: The Biography of Frida Kahlo* (London: Bloomsbury, 2018), 224.
13 Helga Prignitz-Poda, "The Bride Frightened at Seeing Life Opened," in *Frida Kahlo: National Homage*, 226–30.
14 These words spoken by Chavela Vargas are taken from the documentary *Chavela*, directed by Catherine Gund and Daresha Kyi, based on an interview filmed in Mexico in 1991 (Aubin Pictures, 2017). It was made available on Netflix in August 2018.
15 Arturo Cruz Bárcenas, "Con Frida Kahlo toqué el cielo con las manos cada mañana: Chavela Vargas," *La Jornada*, June 14, 2011.
16 *Chavela*, 2017.
17 "Entrevista con Raquel Tibol. Frida poliédrica," in *Yo soy Frida*, 10.
18 Kahlo to Carlos Pellicer, November 1947, *Frida by Frida*, ed. Raquel Tibol and trans. Gregory Dechant (Mexico City: Editorial RM, 2003), 331.
19 Carlos Pellicer, *Obras. Poesía* (Mexico City: Fondo de Cultura Económica, 2003), 648.
20 Isamu Noguchi quoted in Herrera, *Frida*, 200.
21 Herrera, *Frida*, 201.
22 "Entrevista con Salomon Grimberg. Frida inventada," in *Yo soy Frida*, 14.

54

The Flower of Life

1944
Oil on Masonite,
11 x 7¾ in. (28 x 19.8 cm)
Xochimilco (Mexico City),
Collection Museo Dolores Olmedo

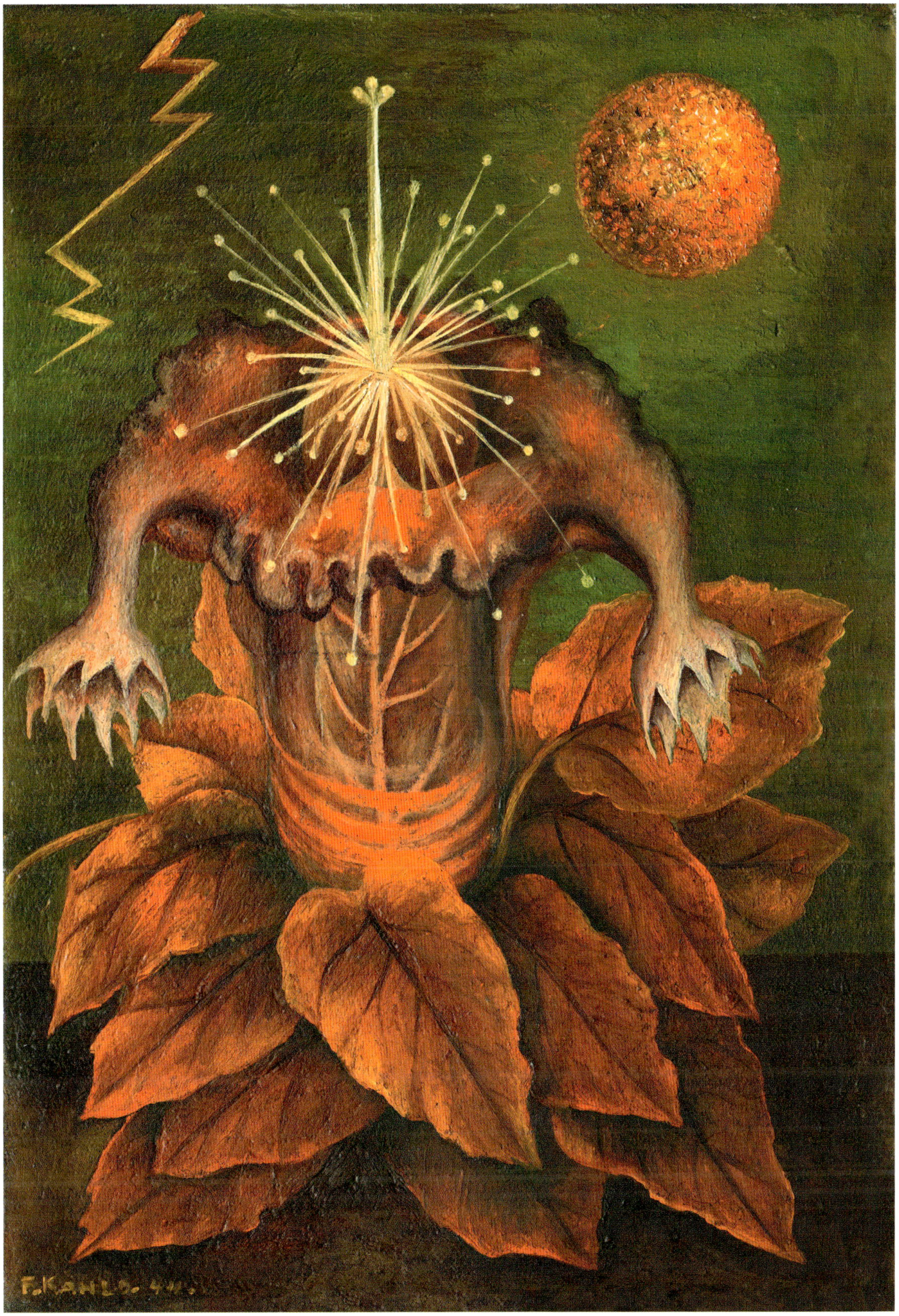

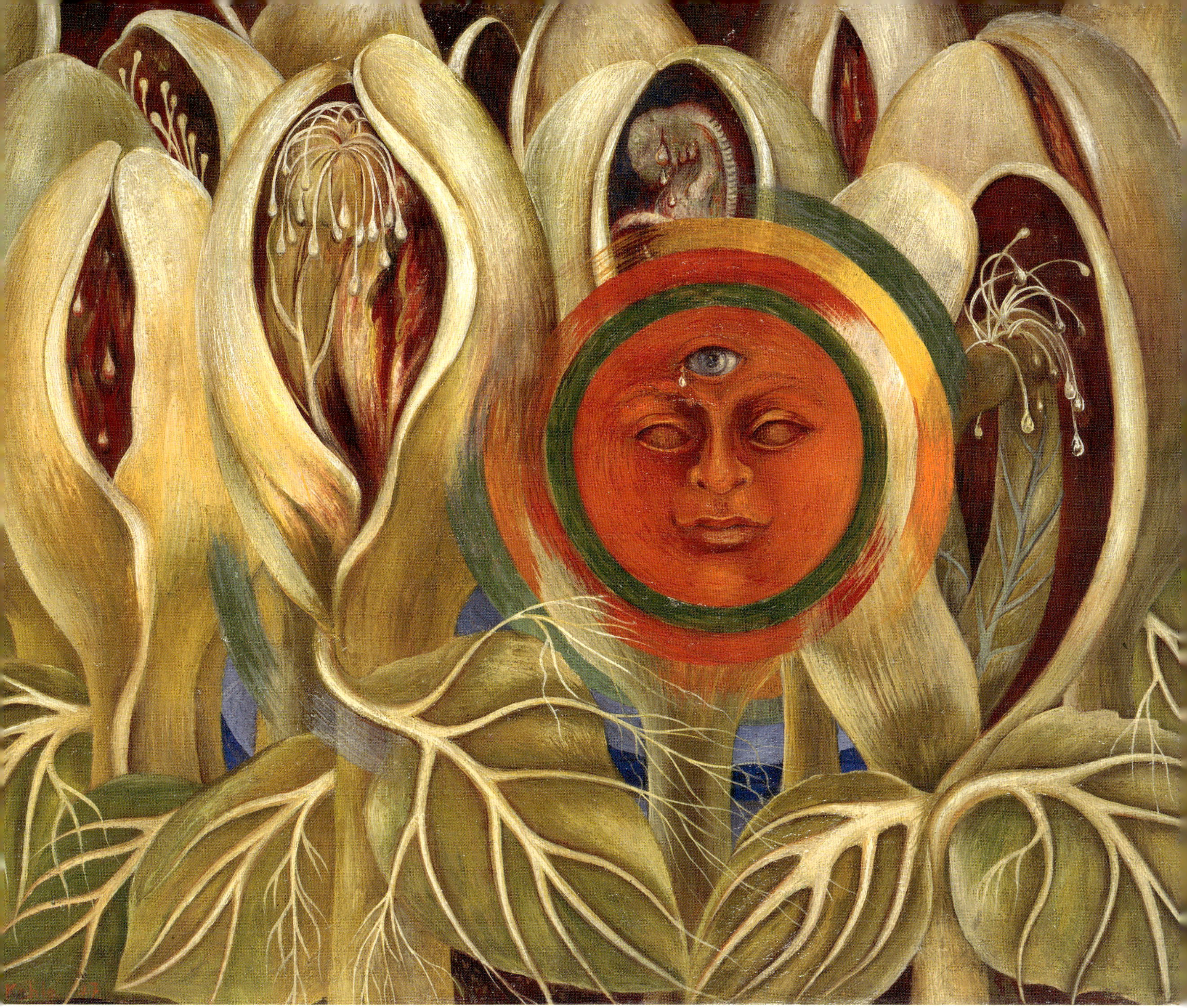

55

Sun and Life

1947
Oil on Masonite,
$15^{3}/_{4}$ x $19^{1}/_{2}$ in. (40 x 49.5 cm)
Mexico City, Galería Arvil Collection

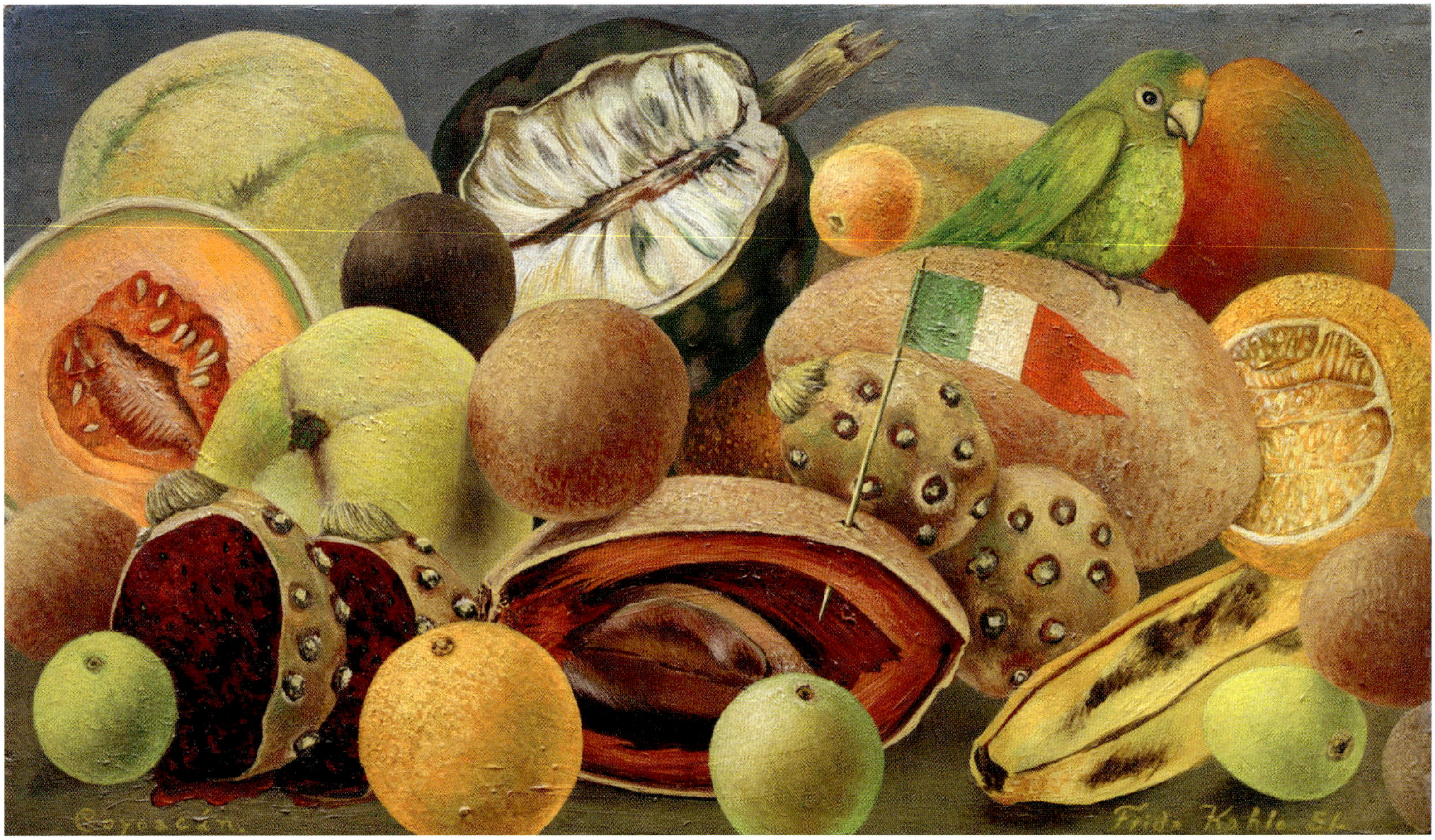

56
Still Life with Parrot and Flag

1951
Oil on Masonite, 11 x 15¾ in. (28 x 40 cm)
Mexico City, Galería Arvil Collection

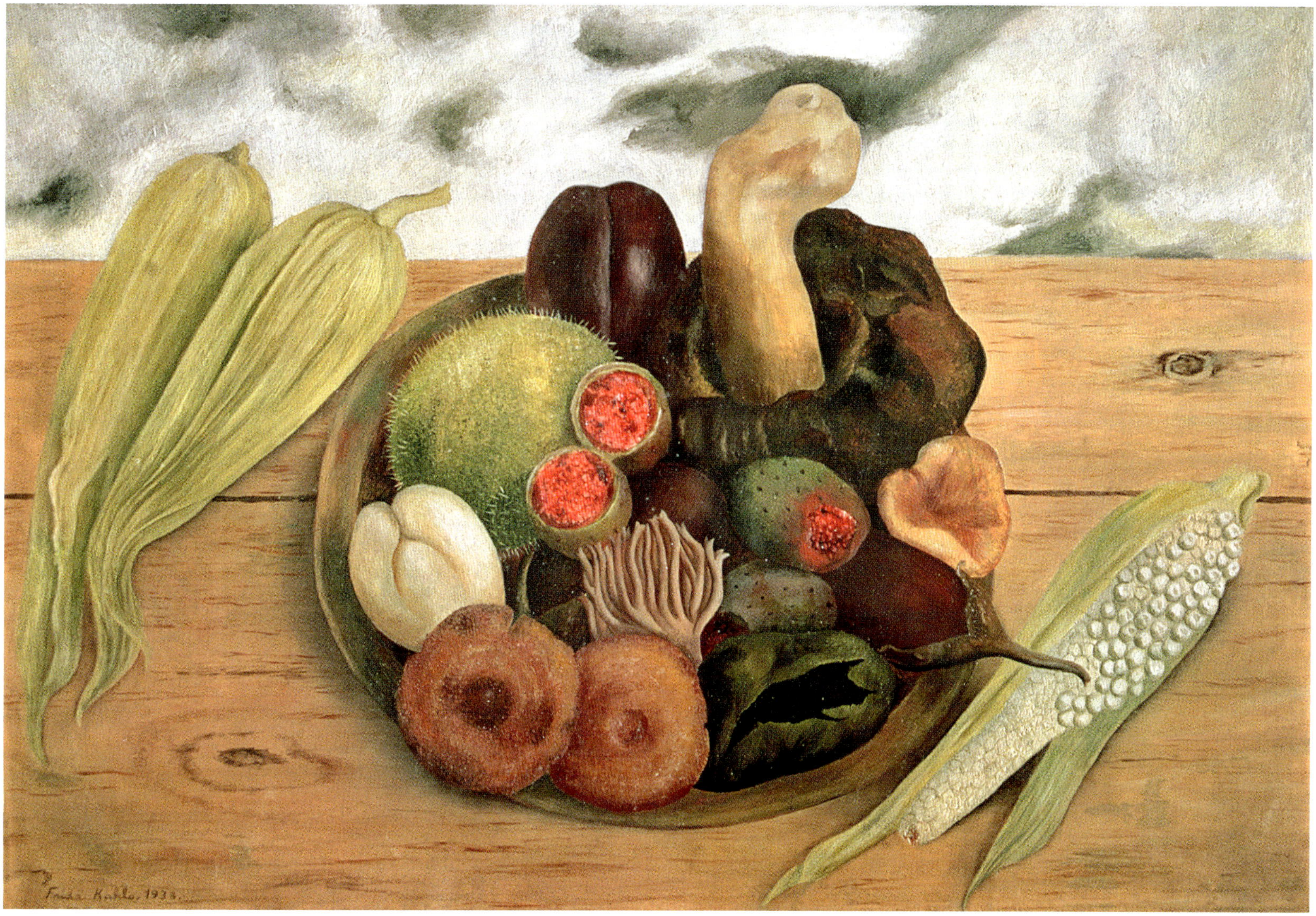

57

Fruits of the Earth

1938
Oil on Masonite,
16 x 23⅔ in. (40.6 x 60 cm)
Mexico City, Collection Banco
Nacional de México

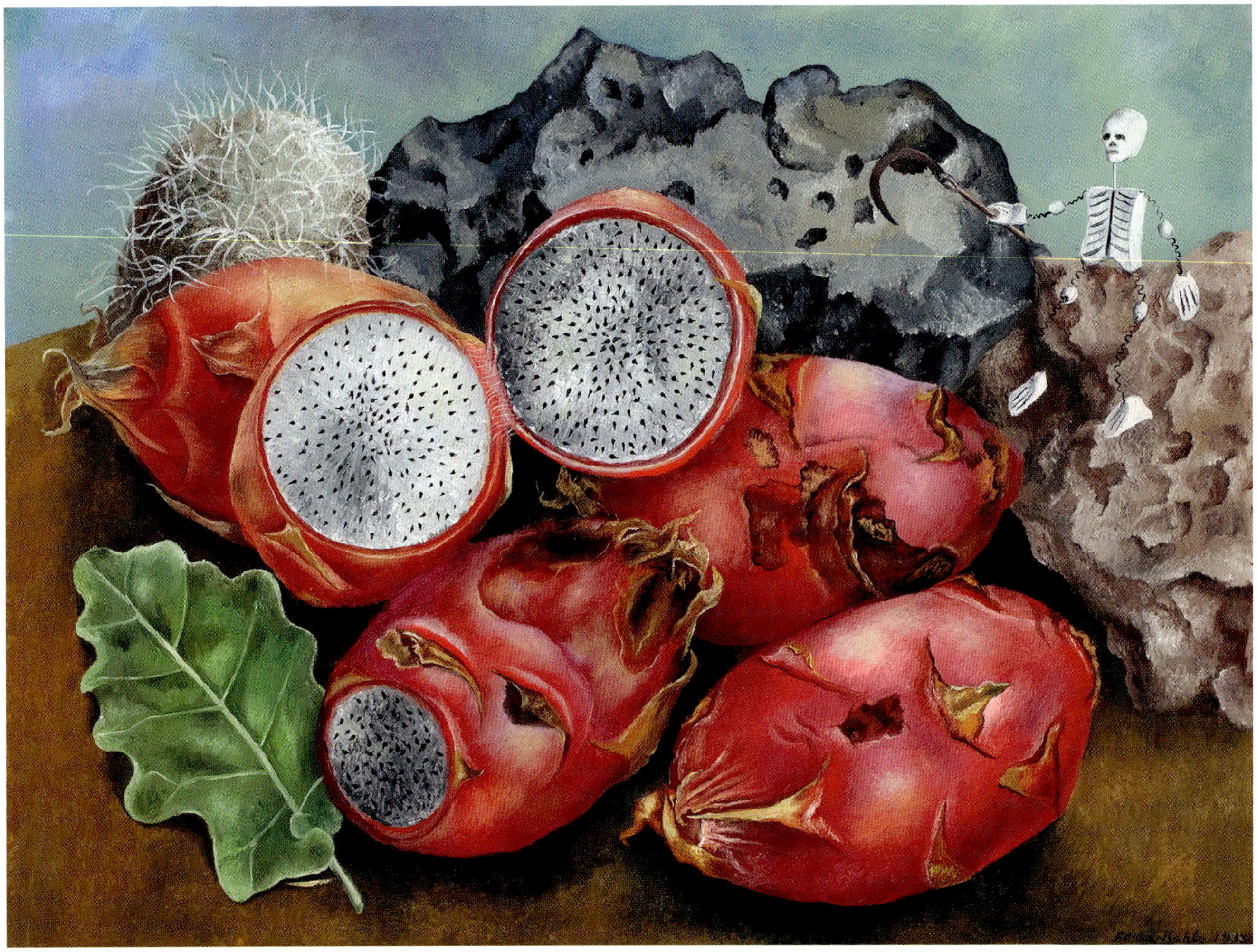

58

Pitahayas

1938
Oil on metal, 10 x 14 in. (25.4 x 35.6 cm)
Madison (Wisconsin), Madison Museum of Contemporary Art, Bequest of Rudolph and Louise Langer

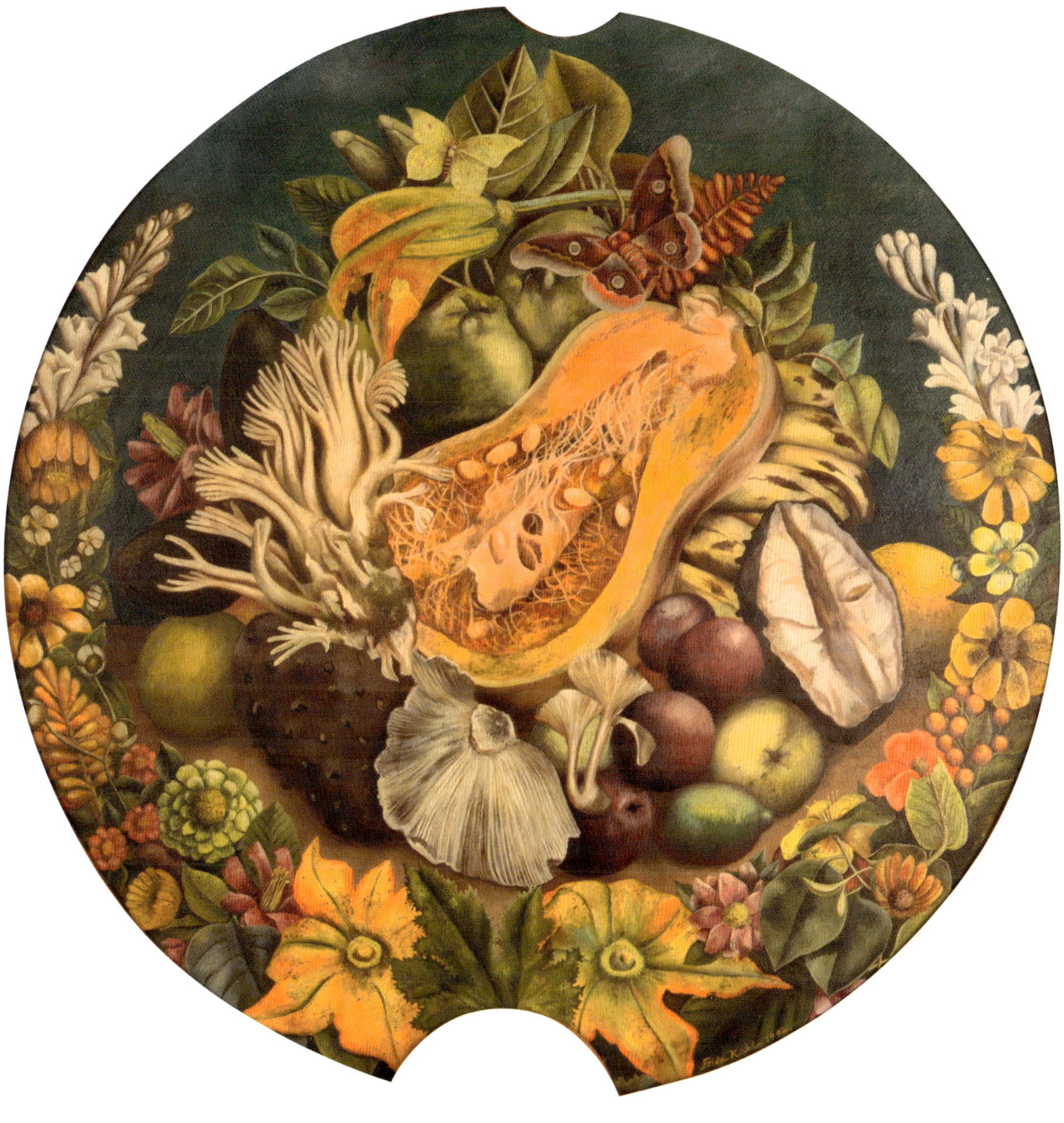

59

Still Life (Tondo)

1942
Oil on metal,
24¾ in. diameter (63 cm diameter)
Coayoacán (Mexico City),
Museo Frida Kahlo

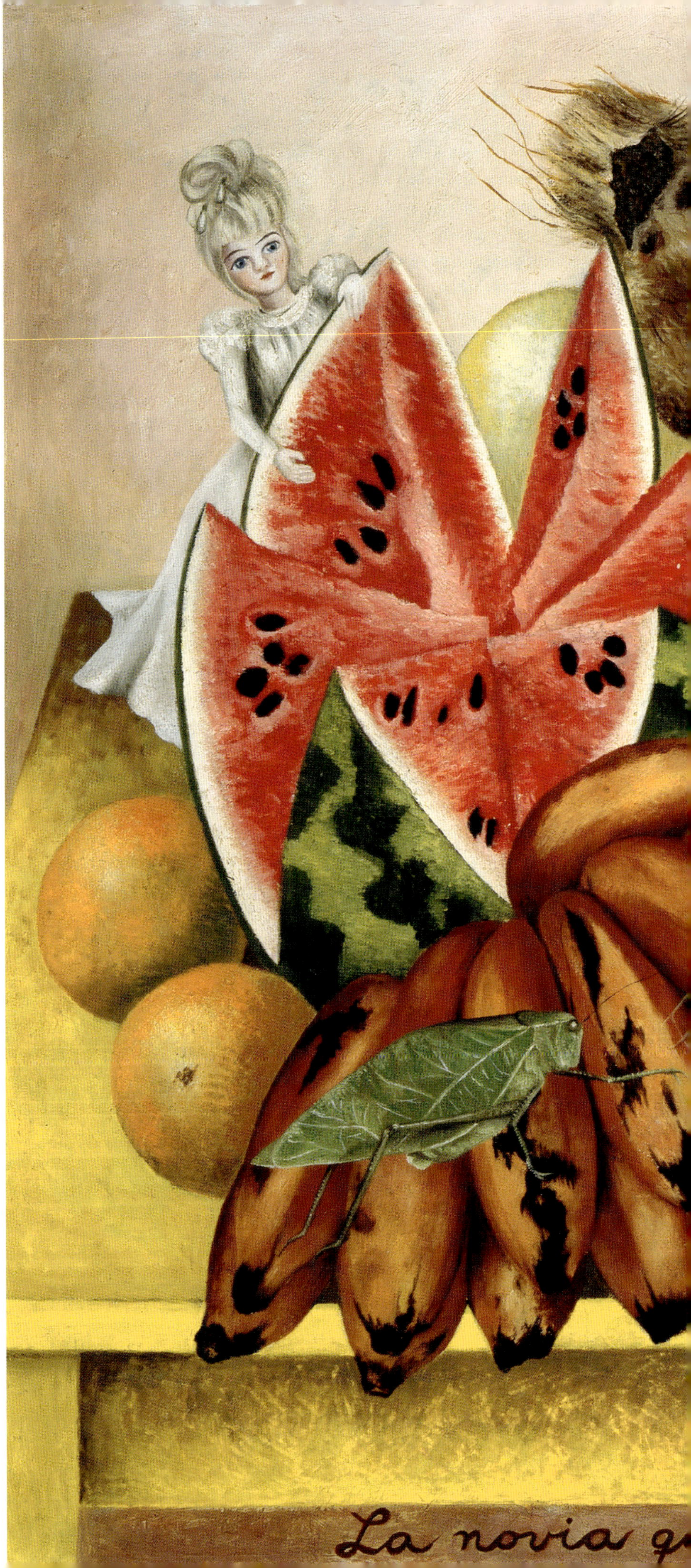

60

The Bride Frightened at Seeing Life Opened

1943
Oil on canvas,
24¾ x 32 in. (63 x 81.5 cm)
Gelman Collection

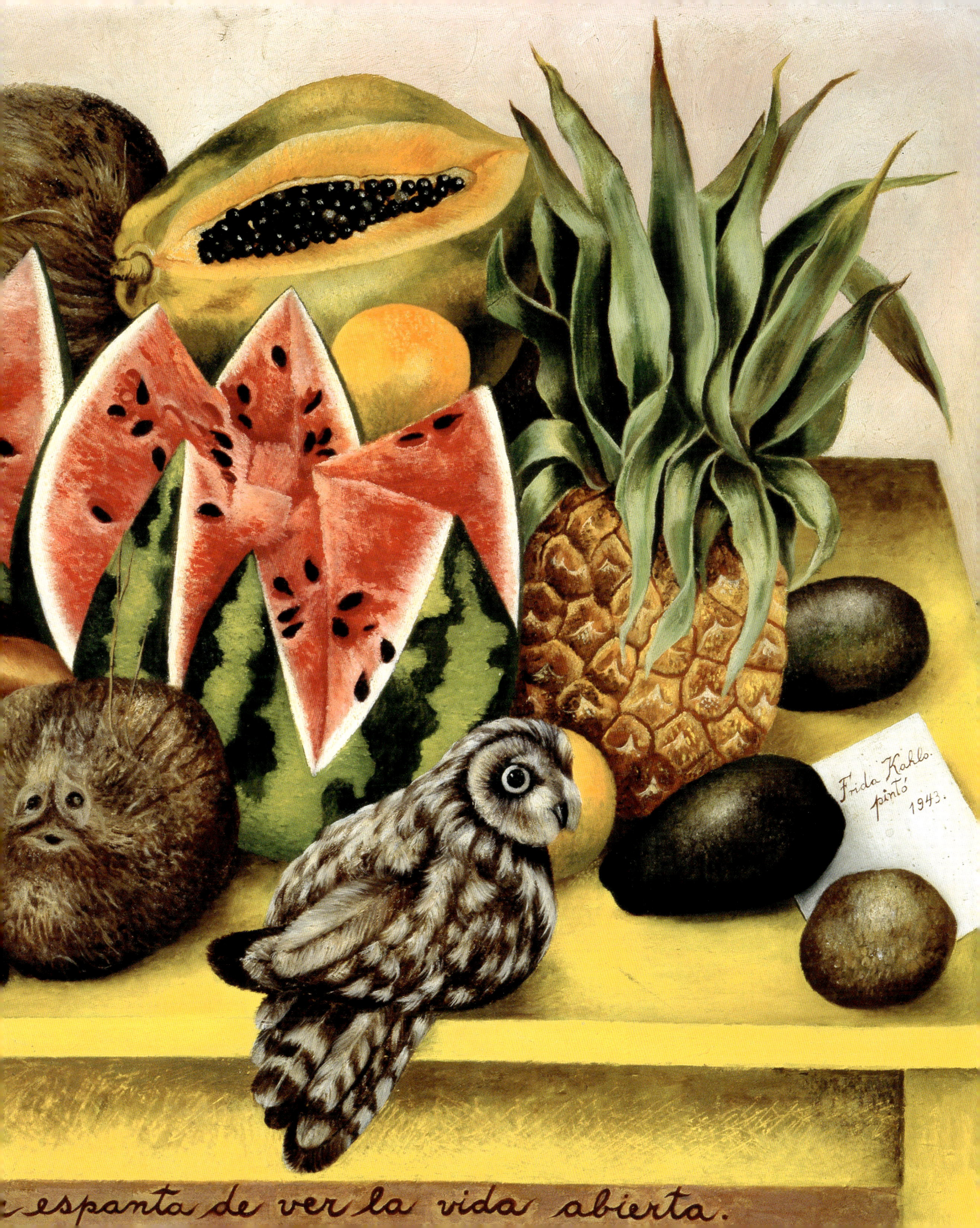
Frida Kahlo.
pintó
1943.
espanta de ver la vida abierta.

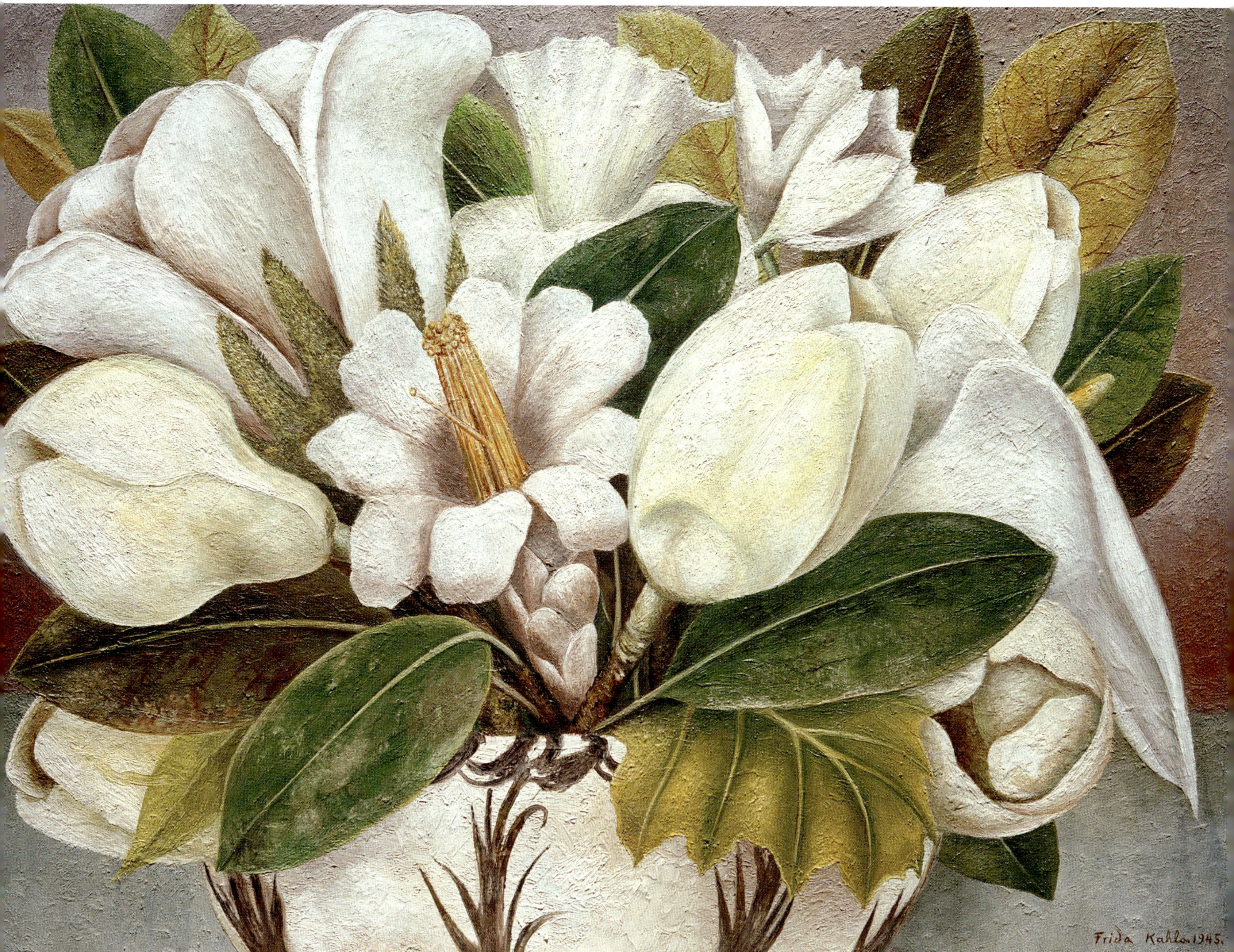

61
Magnolias

1945
Oil on Masonite,
16⅛ x 22½ in. (41 x 57 cm)
Balbina Azcárraga Collection

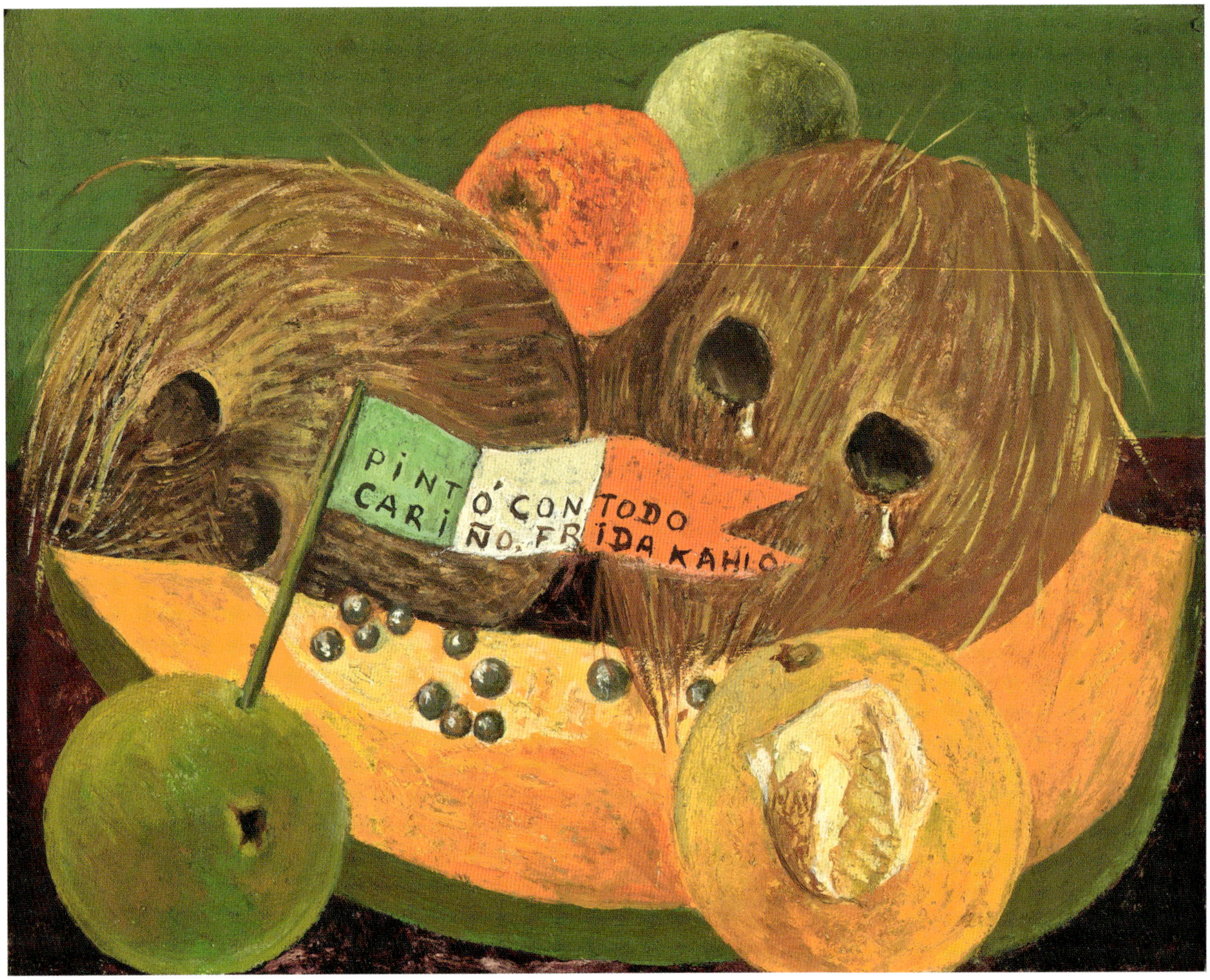

62

Weeping Coconuts

1951
Oil on Masonite, 9⅛ x 12 in. (23.2 x 30.5 cm)
Los Angeles (California), Los Angeles County Museum of Art, The Bernard and Edith Lewin Collection of Mexican Art, M.2004.283.2

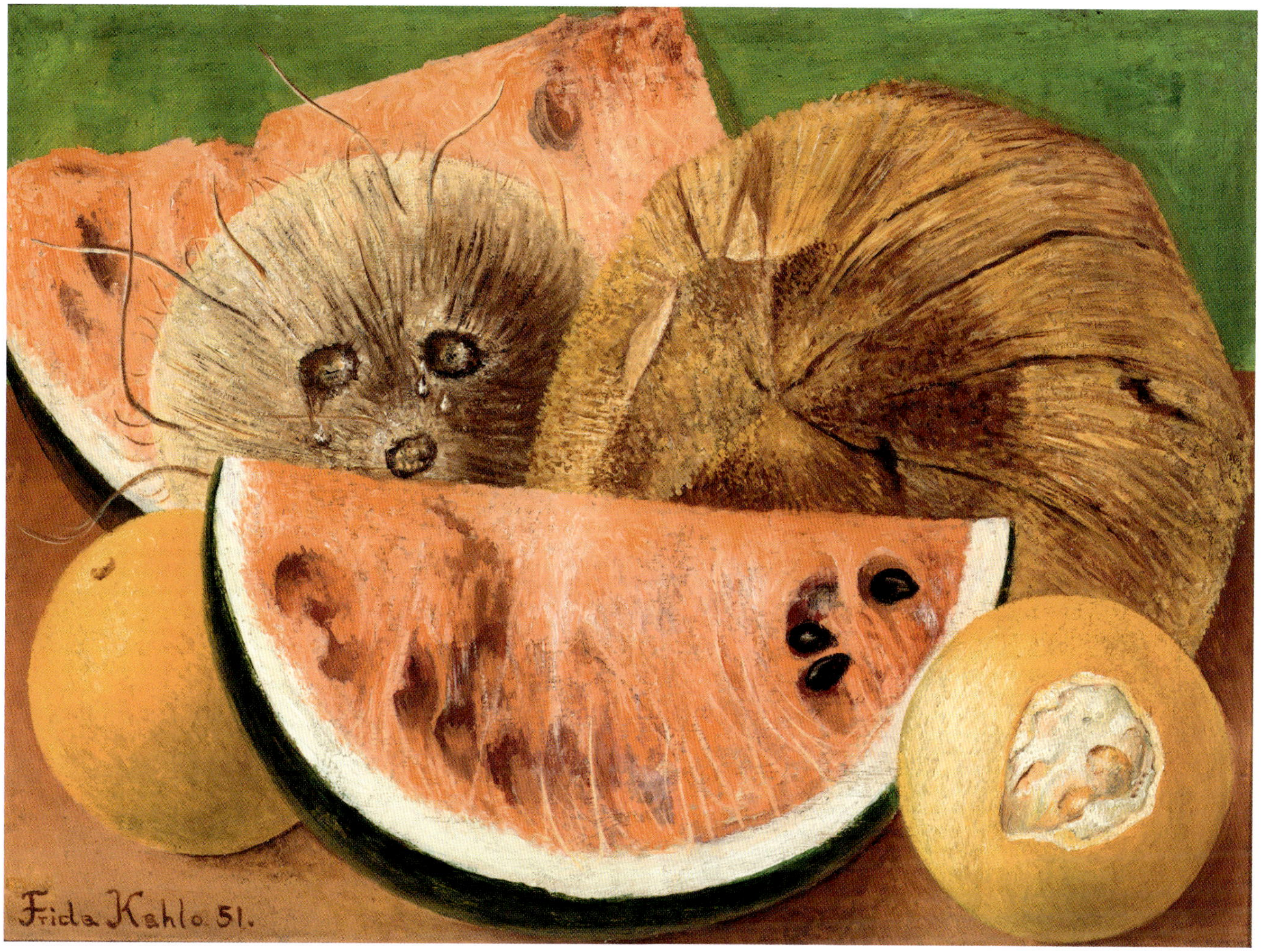

63

Coconuts

1951
Oil on Masonite,
10 x 13¾ in. (25.5 x 35 cm)
Mexico City, Museo de Arte Moderno, INBA

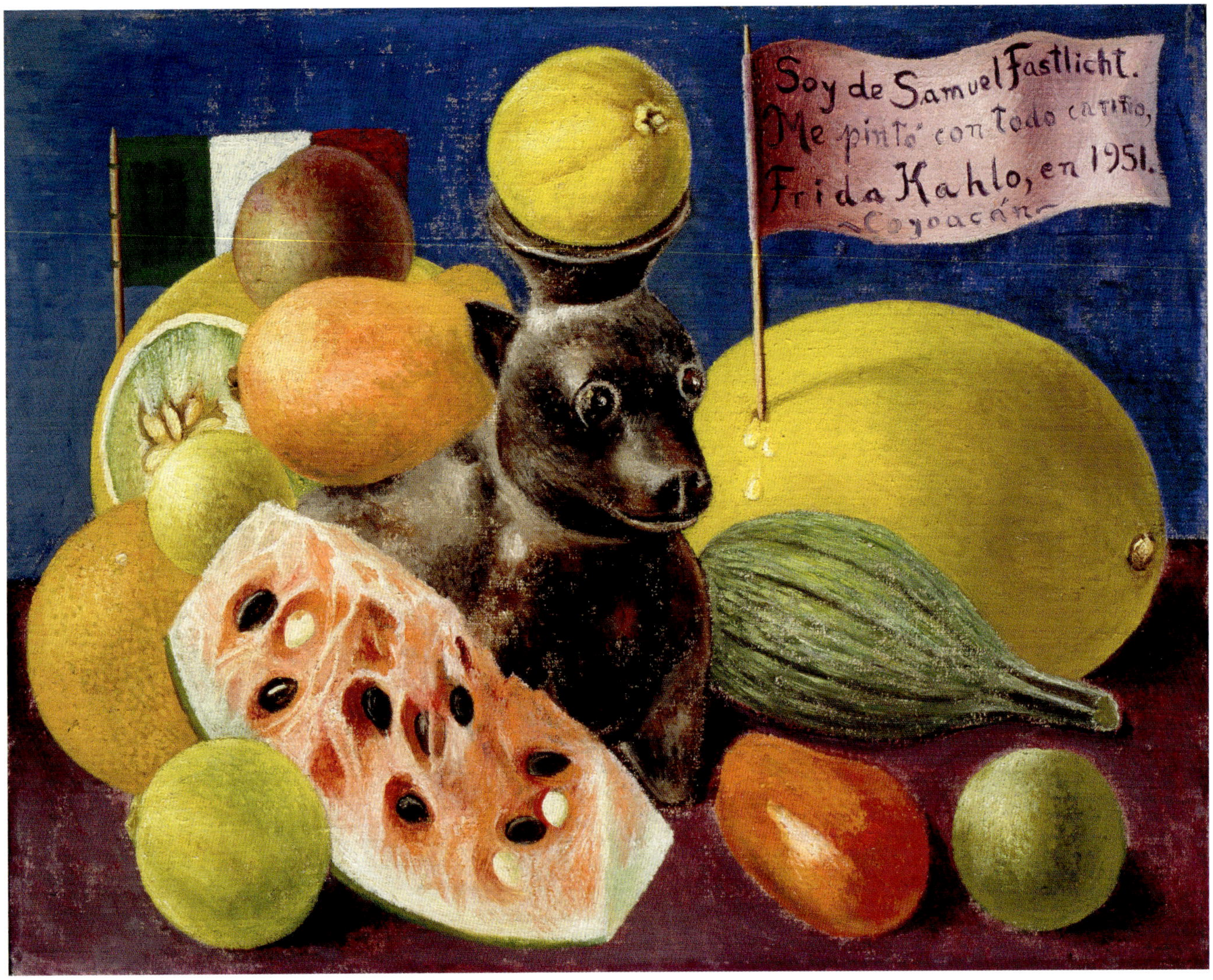

64

Still Life (I Belong to Samuel Fastlicht)

1951
Oil on Masonite, 11¼ x 14⅛ in. (28.6 x 35.9 cm)
Mexico City, Galería Arvil Collection

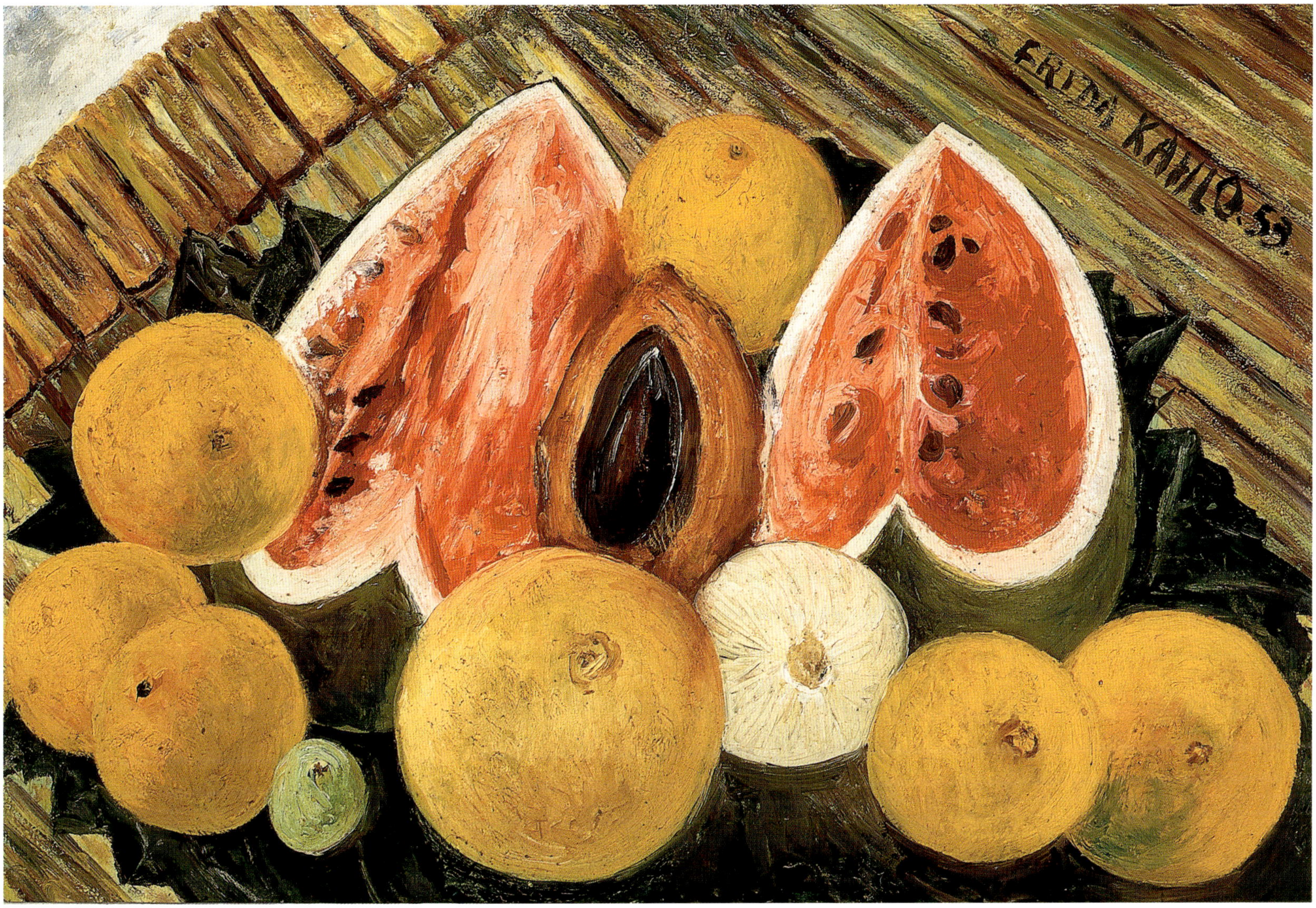

65

Still Life with Watermelons

1953
Oil on canvas, 15⅔ x 23½ in. (39.8 x 59.6 cm)
Mexico City, Museo de Arte Moderno, INBA

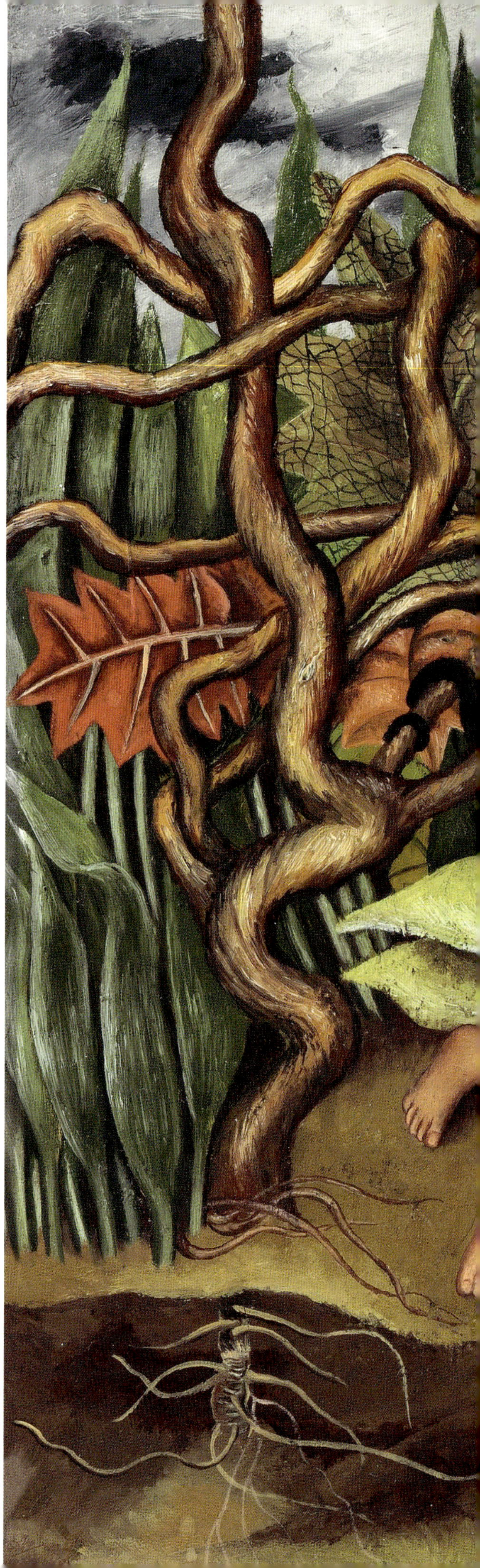

66

Two Nudes in the Forest
or **The Earth Itself**

1939
Oil on metal,
9⅞ x 11⅞ inches (21.1 x 30.2 cm)
Private collection

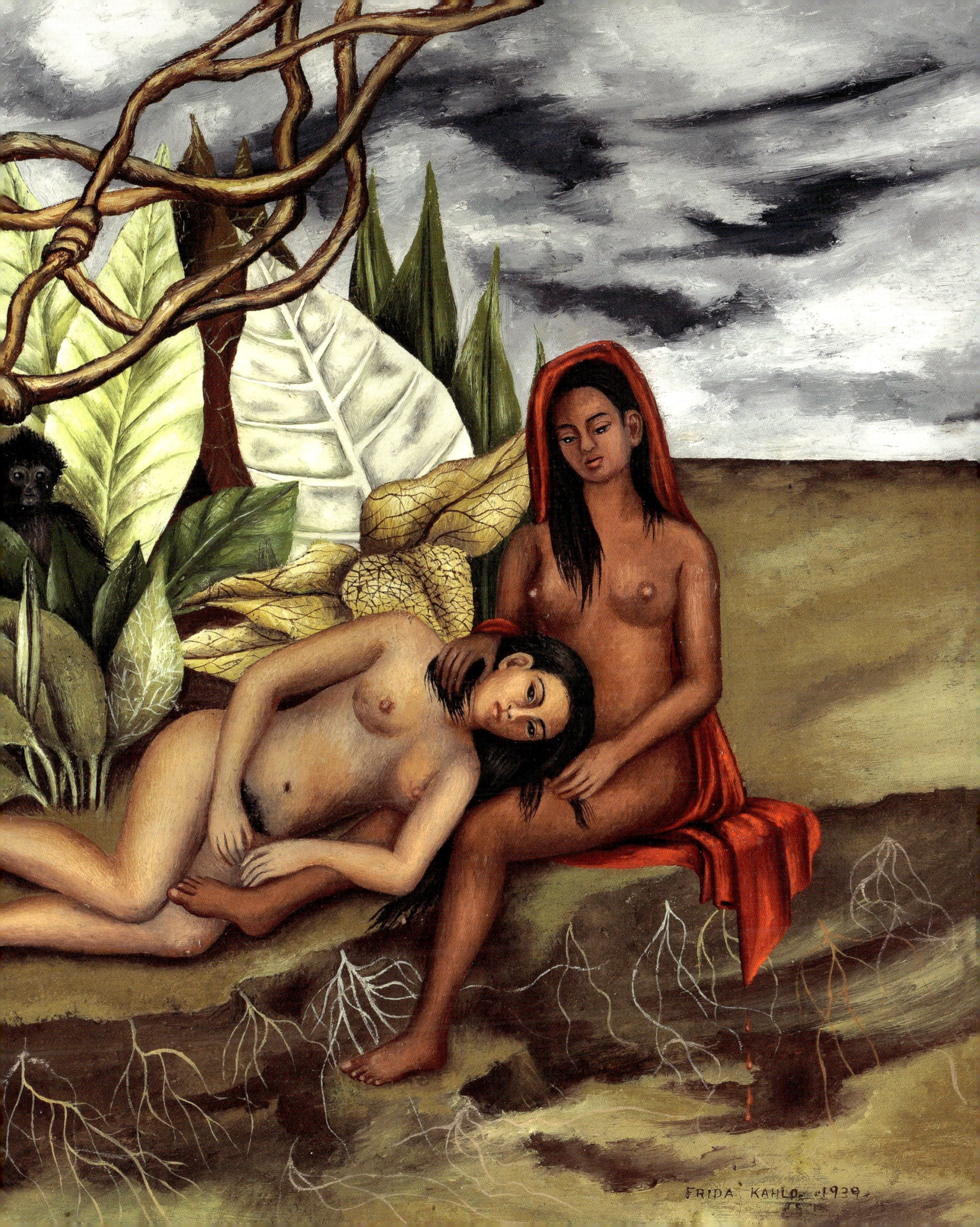
FRIDA KAHLO 1939

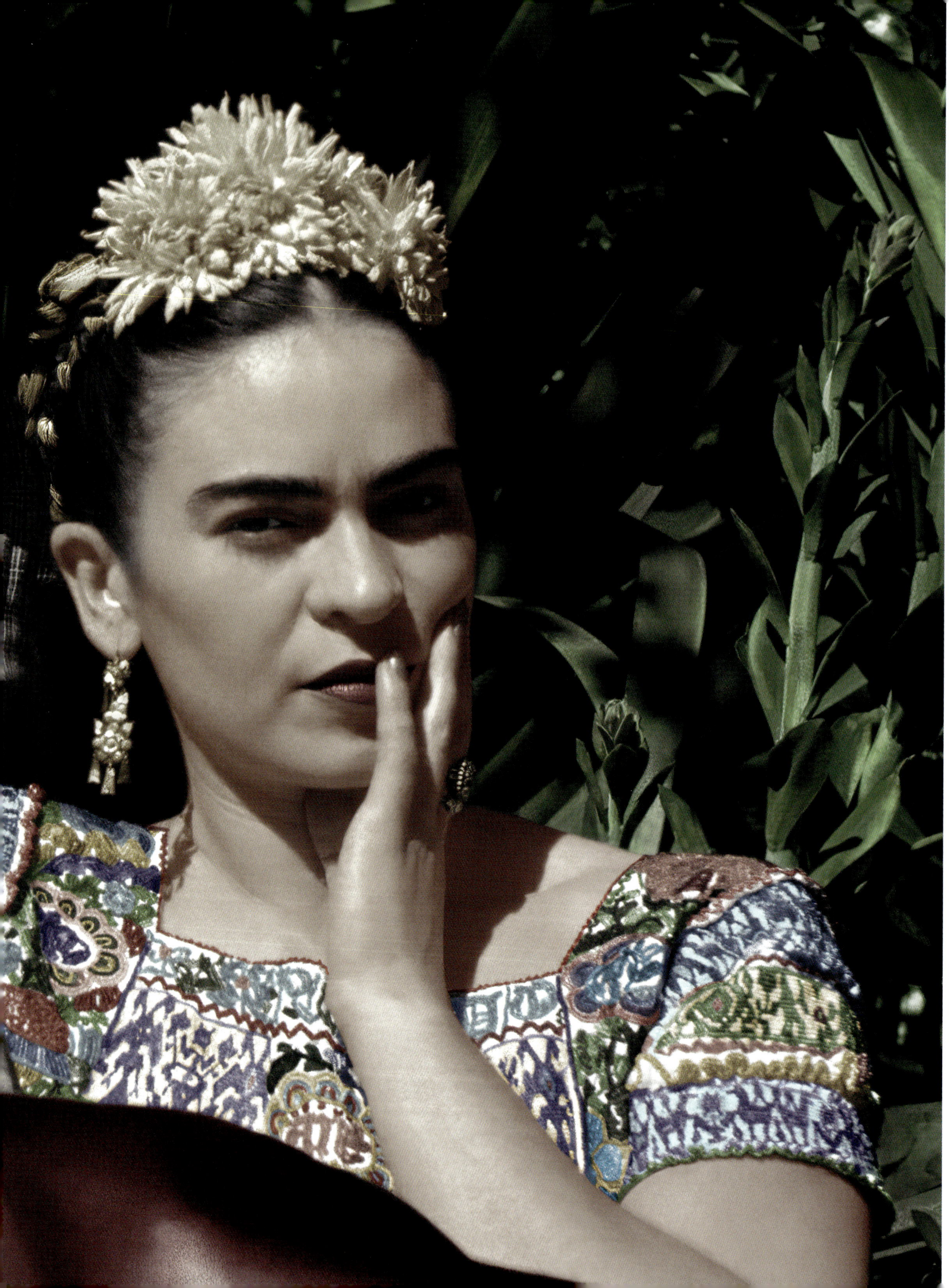

Metaphor for Herself

Painting is silent poetry and poetry is painting that speaks.

Simonides of Ceos[1]

Eternity is in love with the productions of time.

William Blake[2]

Of all the mysteries of the universe, none is deeper than that of creation. . . . It is sometimes given to us to witness this miracle, and it is given to us in one sphere only: that of art.

Stefan Zweig[3]

Pain is a mystery that instills a special knowledge in those who manage to sublimate it. Is there another artist who has suffered such intense and prolonged pain as Frida Kahlo? Her heartrending life is unflinchingly represented in her painting, her letters, and her diary. Kahlo shares her anguish and suffering with uncompromising realism while leading us into her inner world, illuminated by imagination and imbued with a love of life, nature, and beauty. To appreciate and understand Kahlo's work in its true dimension, one must analyze it not only within the context of the world history of art, but also within the field of aesthetic reflection that emerged in Classical antiquity. Such an approach allows us to evaluate the transcendence of her paintings and provide answers to the following questions: Can Kahlo's painting be considered silent poetry? Is there a tragic dimension to her life and oeuvre? Can beauty be ascribed to what has been called the "aesthetic of pain" in our artist's work?

One of the central themes in poetics and the philosophy of art is the link between poetry and painting. The poet Simonides of Ceos, quoted at the opening of this chapter, proposed a brotherhood between the art of the word and the visual arts, marking the historic beginning of the thought on the visual image and the metaphor that led to Horace's maxim *Ut pictura poesis* (as is painting so is poetry), a postulate that still spurs reflection today. Furthermore, the analogy between the two arts provoked a

Frida Kahlo in a garden, Xochimilco (Mexico City), 1941. Photograph by Leo Matiz. Mexico City, Fundación Leo Matiz

debate on whether these two artistic languages have the same capacity to create beauty or express the integrity of the human being as Greek tragedy does. We shall touch on these fascinating themes as concisely as possible.

In *Timaeus* and *The Symposium*, Plato defines the essential attributes of beauty: order and proportion, harmony and splendor. In varying forms, this concept of beauty governed Western art until the nineteenth century. However, in the ideal beauty of the Platonic *topos hyperuranios*, there is no room for ugliness or other defects consubstantial to concrete material reality. Aristotle agrees with the Platonic ideal of beauty, but with one fundamental difference: given that natural reality is not perfect, as Plato's world of ideas is, and that art must imitate nature to produce aesthetic pleasure, artistic beauty may include the imperfections of reality on the condition that the imitation is carried out with mastery. For Aristotle, beauty and ugliness are not mutually exclusive. It is possible to attain beauty if a terrible reality or something unpleasant is imitated with genius. Atrocity, suffering, and ugliness can be compatible with art. The clearest evidence of this is Greek tragedy. Greek theater expresses the human drama in all its complexity, depicting not only great physical pain but also pain resulting from the divine punishment inflicted on men who have fallen prey to hubris, or overweening arrogance in the face of the designs of the gods. It shows the fatality of misfortune that rules the destiny of man, the victim of divine wrath for transgressing the measures and limits imposed on earthly mortals by the gods. In his *Poetics*, Aristotle postulates that tragedy induces the spectator to identify with the passions of the protagonists, experiencing those passions together with them, but without suffering the fatal effects. He called this experience, one of emotional, bodily, and mental purification, "catharsis."

With Sophocles, the Athenian theater reached its full splendor and became a guidepost not just for the then-present time, but for posterity. In plays like *Oedipus Rex* and *Antigone*, and through their titular characters, tragedy was humanized. The aesthetic, ethical, and religious dimensions penetrated and complemented one another reciprocally, giving rise for the first time in the West to the conscious formation of man as the sum of body and *psyche* (soul). This, of course, includes woman, who appears, also for the first time, as a representative of humanity with a dignity equal to that of men in female characters of the stature of Antigone, Electra, Deianira, Jocasta, and Clytemnestra. In Sophocles, the tragedy is the impossibility of avoiding pain. Let us take the case of Antigone, destined to suffer due to her own nature. Her filial loyalty finds itself in confrontation with the law of the state, represented by Creon. Because of Antigone's civil disobedience in burying her brother in defiance of Creon's order, she is condemned to be buried alive. She decides to hang herself. A victim of injustice, Antigone personifies the full grandeur of the tragic human being who ascends to spiritual excellence through the destruction of her earthly happiness and her physical and social existence.

Mutatis mutandis, Frida Kahlo can be considered a tragic character because, like Antigone, a destiny of lifelong suffering was a part of her. This was not because of hubris or the Moira, who, Homer tells us, spins the thread of human life from birth, but owing to the whims of chance or the cruelty of nature. In contexts and for reasons that were very different from Antigone's yet analogous to them, Kahlo experienced the tragic self-knowledge of the human being, merged with her own destiny, and, in her own flesh, shared the grandeur of the sufferer as dramatized in the protagonists of Greek tragedy. The sublimation of her physical and emotional pain through her painting also had a cathartic impulse. Understanding Frida Kahlo's tragic dimension allows us to look more deeply at the poetic impulse of her creative process. Kahlo took the Delphic imperative—know thyself—to its ultimate conclusion and from it created an artistic oeuvre that is destined to transcend time.

The question of whether the poetic beauty of Greek tragedy can be expressed in the language of the visual arts without losing its standing as beautiful art still remains to be answered. Is the tragic compatible with pictorial or sculptural beauty? The paradigmatic work for debating this question is the Greek sculptural group *Laocoön and His Sons,*[4] which gave rise to a celebrated aesthetic controversy in the eighteenth century. This sculpture was created in the Hellenistic period (c. 40–30 B.C.E.) by three artists from Rhodes: Agesander, Polydorus, and Athenodoros. In the *Aeneid,* Virgil relates the myth of Laocoön, priest of Poseidon, who warned the Trojans not to allow the Trojan horse into the city. The Greeks managed to persuade Priam that the horse was a sacred image of Athena that they were presenting to them as a gift. Laocoön then tried to stop the horse from entering Troy, and at that moment his twin sons were attacked by two sea serpents. When he tried to save them, he suffered the same fate. Inspired by the myth, the sculpture *Laocoön and His Sons* is a marble representation of that terrible attack.

In his *Reflections on the Painting and Sculpture of the Greeks,* the archaeologist and art historian Johann Joachim Winckelmann (1717–1768) claimed that the sculpture of Laocoön is the paradigm of Greek art, and consequently postulated that pain and suffering are perfectly compatible with beauty. "Laocoön suffers, but suffers like the Philoctetes of Sophocles: we weeping feel his pains, but wish for the hero's strength to support his misery."[5] In the meantime, the philosopher, poet, and art critic Gotthold Ephraim Lessing (1729–1781), one of the leading representatives of the Enlightenment in Germany, wrote a study entitled *Laocoön, or on the Limits of Painting and Poetry* (1766). In this key work of eighteenth-century aesthetic theory, he counters Winckelmann's thesis with the argument that "painting, as an imitative power, can express ugliness; but painting as a fine art refuses to do so; as in the first capacity, all visible objects may be subjects for it; in the second, it is confined to those only by which pleasing sensations are awakened."[6] Lessing's blinkered argument shows that intelligence can occasionally betray the gaze.

It is difficult not to be awed by the majestic beauty of this masterpiece of three-dimensional art, perhaps equaled only centuries later by Michelangelo (1475–1564) and Gian Lorenzo Bernini (1598–1680). With consummate artistic skill, every muscle and tendon in the figures' bodies is reproduced with prodigious realism. Through virtuosity in their command of their material, the sculptors endowed this work with harmony and movement, rendering Laocoön's expression of suffering with a drama and beauty equivalent to those of the tragedies of Aeschylus, Euripides, and Sophocles. Like tragic poems, this magnificent sculpture is imbued with pathos, profound emotion, and passion—and a violent grief that makes an immediate and indelible impact on the viewer, producing an aesthetic experience of great intensity. With her broad artistic culture, Kahlo almost certainly knew the sculpture *Laocoön* from photographs and also from the pictorial version by El Greco (1541–1614), inspired by the same myth, for she was a great admirer of the Greek genius, who lies behind the dramatic skies of many of Kahlo's pictures.

In both literature and the visual arts, including cinema, pathos has the power to evoke a wide range of emotions in the reader or viewer: joy, passion, or love; sadness, rage, or jealousy; loneliness, anguish, or melancholy; fraternity, trust, or admiration; enthusiasm, fervor, or amazement. To be able to express this, the artist must be invaded by the feeling that is to be depicted in the work. In projecting herself onto a canvas or a panel, Kahlo evidently experienced not only a liberating relief from her ills but also a metamorphosis of her pain-ridden self into a creator of physical objects imbued with significance and pathos. The doubling up of Kahlo in her oeuvre is the vehement manifestation of a sublimation and a catharsis that have surged up from the depths of an existential combination of suffering and vitality, melancholy and festivity, imagination and carnality. Consequently, there is no doubt that Kahlo's painting is silent poetry, especially her most technically accomplished and symbolically complex works.

Can beauty be attributed to what has been called the "aesthetic of pain" in the work of our artist? From Classical antiquity until the nineteenth century, it should be recalled, the predominant concept of beauty was linked to the notion that one of the fundamental purposes of art is to please the eye of the viewer. Romanticism rebelled against these principles and their basis in the cult of reason, an Enlightenment ideal incarnated in the Neoclassical style, which took the canons of harmony and proportion to the extreme of generating formally rigid works lacking in vitality and expressive power. Against the decadent artifice of Neoclassicism, the Romantic movement exalted emotion and the imagination. It penetrated the depths of the human being, dreams, and the unconscious, in a prefiguration of Sigmund Freud and Surrealism. Rather than a style, Romanticism was a way of feeling and making inner life visible, a new form of self-knowledge as a means of exploring the enigmas of the cosmos. In Victor Hugo's words, Romanticism proposed entering "the forbidden, that effort to handle the impalpable and to see the invisible: . . . and thus it is that one penetrates into the impenetrable."[7] In this way there arose the greatest transformation in the conscience of the West since the Renaissance. It was a transition from distant observation of the daytime to immersion in the fantasies and discoveries of the nocturnal abyss. The cult of beauty did not disappear but was expanded, as in the hymn dedicated to it by Charles Baudelaire:

> What does it matter if you come from heaven or hell,
> O beauty! Immense, dreadful, ingenuous monster!
> If your eyes, your laugh, your foot open the door to me
> of an Infinite that I love and have never known?[8]

The author of *Les Fleurs du Mal*, a precursor of Romanticism and of modern art, did not want to limit beauty to a splendent or merely decorative appearance, but instead wanted to adore it in all its complexity and integrity, including horror and cruelty. *The Death of Sardanapalus*,[9] painted by Eugène Delacroix (1798–1863) in 1827, is considered the most explicitly Romantic work ever painted. The legendary king of Assyria disdainfully watches as his concubines and horses are massacred to prevent them from falling into the hands of the invader. Expressed in all its rawness, the scene of brutality and chaos represents an affront to Neoclassical values and an affirmation of the Romantic movement. "To say the word Romanticism is to say modern art—that is, intimacy, spirituality, color, aspiration toward the infinite," declared Baudelaire.[10] The Romantic spirit is present in Joseph Mallord William Turner (1775–1851) and William Blake (1757–1827) in Great Britain; Francisco de Goya (1746–1828) in Spain; Caspar David Friedrich (1774–1840) in Germany; and in French artists Théodore Géricault (1791–1824) and Delacroix, in Baudelaire's view the epitome of the Romantic artist. Another of the emblematic paintings of the Romantic rebellion is *Wanderer above the Sea of Fog* (c. 1817),[11] where Friedrich depicts himself on the peak of a mountain, his back to the viewer, in communion with himself while in ecstasy at the sublime mystery of nature. The essence of Romanticism is found in the expression of the poetic self of the artist as a means of exploring the labyrinths of his own existence, and of descending into the unfathomable abyss of eternity, the infinite, and the analogy of the universal.

While the Romantic movement made a profound change in the meaning of beauty and the purpose of art, a still more radical rupture was brought about by the European avant-garde movements that arose after the outbreak of World War I in 1914. At the close of the nineteenth century and the dawn of the twentieth, a new era revolutionized the way the world was seen and interpreted. Great scientific and technological discoveries, together with the emergence of psychoanalysis, seemed to confirm the unlimited power of man over himself and the universe. Such optimism was shattered by the violence and destruction of the Great War, leading to the total rejection of the cultural and artistic system in place until then. Cubism and Expressionism disfigured reality, Surrealism tried to change it, Marcel Duchamp (1887–1968) and Dadaism made fun of it, and abstract art erased it. With the emergence of the European avant-gardes and their epigones in America and around the world, the aesthetic canon and the history of art as a whole underwent a complete transformation, not always beneficial but inevitable. Beauty ceased to be the guiding concept of art to make way for what has been called "post-aesthetic" art. Nevertheless, beauty remains indissolubly linked to artistic thought and creation as a value, in spite of the violent shift in judgment parameters and the nearly always harmful influence of the art market on the definition of taste and quality. At the same time, it must be recognized that the modern and contemporary art begun by Romanticism and the European avant-gardes incorporated factors that proved fundamental to the adaptation of the concept of beauty, as well as the definition of art's function in the contemporary world: human pain and suffering, the imperfections of nature, the cruelties of what Borges deemed the "universal history of infamy," and human evil in its wide variety of manifestations.

All through the history of art, there are paradigmatic cases of great artworks that and artists who have visually contested the concept of beauty as restricted to the goal of pleasing the eye. Prominent among them was Hieronymus Bosch (c. 1450–1516), whose mental independence and portentous imagination enabled him to transcend the aesthetic conventions of the High Renaissance in the triptych *The Garden of Earthly Delights* (1490–1500), his best-known work.[12] Bosch was convinced that artistic intelligence and creativity should not be limited by conventions or aesthetic canons, but believed instead that they should be ruled by the inventions of the imagination. His pictorial genius prefigured Surrealism by four centuries and revolutionized the concept of beauty by elevating the terrible and the grotesque to the rank of great art. Another fine example is *The Triumph of Death* (1563),[13] a work by Pieter Brueghel the Elder (c. 1525–1569). The dire and desolate landscape of this painting leaves no room for hope, for all of human life and its social institutions are the victims of unavoidable destruction. Notwithstanding its moralizing message, this masterpiece possesses an undeniable and unforgettable pathetic beauty.

"The sleep of reason produces monsters," read the words on a celebrated Goya print that expresses the anguish of creative genius. Goya's *The 3rd of May 1808 in Madrid* (1814),[14] his series known as the Black Paintings, and his engravings recount the disasters and cruelties of war and human passions and vices with admirable artistic force, making an indelible impact on the viewer's sensibility. Perhaps the most radical expression of the aesthetic stigma attached to the communion of ugliness and beauty is *The Bearded Woman* (1631)[15] by José de Ribera, known as Lo Spagnoletto (1591–1652). With merciless realism, this portrait depicts an unusual phenomenon of nature: a woman with a thick black beard, and beneath it a voluminous breast with which she suckles the infant in her arms. The pictorial quality of the painting is indisputable, and patent, too, is the Caravaggesque influence on the handling of light and shadow, which makes the mysterious androgyne surge out of the darkness with all the expressive splendor of a bitterness assumed without resignation—an expression shared by the contrite husband who appears in the background. This is a case of hirsutism, or the appearance of excessive hair on a woman caused by adrenogenital syndrome due to a tumor or hyperplasia of the suprarenal glands. The illness of Magdalena Ventura, the subject of this haunting portrait, makes her one of the most horrendous women in the history of art. This contrasts with the energy and naturalness of this technically impeccable work, producing an enigmatic fusion of opposites. How to understand an aesthetic experience where surprise, aversion, and enjoyment all converge? Only art can produce that miracle.

In this discussion, it is impossible to ignore *Guernica*,[16] the origin and paradigm of twentieth-century art, created by Pablo Picasso (1881–1973) for the Spanish Pavilion at the Paris International Exposition of 1937 after the German aerial bombing of the Basque town of Guernica. It is the most radical fusion of monstrosity with art. It goes further than Greek tragedy because it represents a real catastrophe. *Guernica* changed the concept of beauty and art forever, uniting them with the darker aspects of humanity. The pleasure of the gaze is displaced by pathos, horror, and bewilderment. The aesthetic experience produced by this masterpiece is not a pleasant one, but it is both powerful and imperishable. It was not created to delight the gaze but to throw the soul into turmoil.

Kahlo felt a special admiration for the works of Bosch and Brueghel. If she is placed in this context, it becomes easier to understand the relationship between the so-called "aesthetic of pain" and the contemporary concept of beauty. Let us take Kahlo's *The Broken Column*, one of the most representative paintings of this aesthetic canon [fig. 7]. It was clearly not made to please the eye but to make an impact on it. This visual metaphor has pathos as well as impeccable technique, expressive power, and a symbolic dimension. A small masterpiece: silent poetry. This and other paintings by Kahlo can be related to the aesthetic of Romanticism and Surrealism, based on the expression of the artist's poetic self and the desire to engage the mind rather than the gaze of the viewer.

Kahlo's creative introspection never sought to go beyond herself. Perhaps the one exception is *Moses* (1945), also known as *The Nucleus of Creation*, a singular painting within the artist's production, and moreover a complex one because of its subject, its iconography, and the symbolism of the figures and works shown in it [fig. 67]. The oil was commissioned from her by the engineer José Domingo Lavín, who asked her to read Freud's book *Moses and Monotheism* before painting it. The composition is divided into three levels: gods, religious leaders and politicians, and the masses. In the upper center of the picture is a glowing sun from which rays that end in hands emerge.

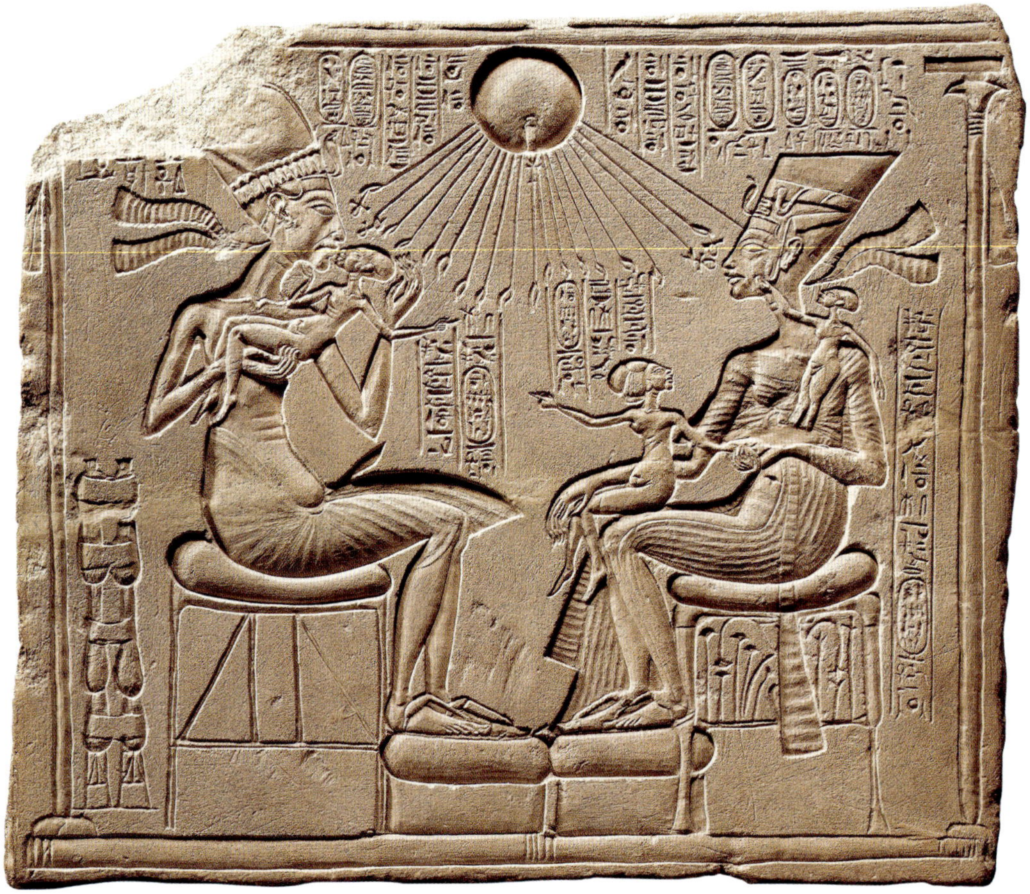

Akhenaton, Nefertiti, and Three of Their Daughters Worshipping the God Aton, c. 1340 B.C.E., relief on limestone, 13⅛ x 15½ x 1⅓ in. (33.5 x 39.5 x 3.5 cm). Berlin, Staatliche Museen zu Berlin, Ägyptisches Museum und Papyrussammlung, ÄM 14145

This was the representation of the god Aton, whose monotheistic cult was established by the pharaoh Akhenaton. Beneath this is a fetus inside a uterus from which drops fall onto the newborn Moses with a third eye in his forehead, floating in a shell on a river. At the far upper left of the picture are reproductions of pre-Hispanic sculptures: Coatlicue,[17] Tláloc,[18] and Quetzalcóatl with a human face emerging from the jaws of the serpent,[19] a selection that reveals Frida's knowledge of pre-Columbian art. In the upper right corner, we see a combination of gods from Egyptian and Greco-Roman mythology as well as the Judeo-Christian religious tradition. Also included is the eye of providence inside a triangle, a symbol of Egyptian origin that was appropriated by Christianity and Freemasonry. Seen under the sculptures on the left is the nude figure of a crowned man, while on the opposite side, a nude Venus reclines on a seashell. Beneath them are two skeletons; a devil's face emerges from the one on the feminine side. The central strip of the composition contains small portraits of those Frida called "the heroes," a mixture of thinkers and religious and political leaders: Buddha, Confucius, Jesus, Krishnamurti, Mohammed, Luther, Gandhi, Akhenaton, Nefertiti,

Julius Caesar, Alexander the Great, Napoleon, Hitler, Lenin, Stalin, Marx, Freud, and others. In the lower part of the picture, we see the faceless masses in front of a pyramid. Some are following apes; others are walking around aimlessly. A red sky burns in flames behind them. At the bottom right of the composition, a woman with drops of milk falling from her breasts—as in *My Nurse and I* [fig. 45]—carries a lamb in her arms in a position similar to that of the baby Diego Rivera in *The Love Embrace of the Universe, My Earth (Mexico), Diego, Myself and Señor Xólotl* [fig. 53], a picture that greatly resembles this portion. *Moses* represents Freud's thesis that the origin of monotheism was the religion established by Akhenaton in honor of the sun god Aton, and that Moses was an Egyptian, not a Hebrew.

With the exception of this picture, for which she was awarded a national prize for painting, the center of Frida Kahlo's life and work was the exploration, creation, and expression of her own persona. Perhaps impelled by the conviction that her physical disability made her different from others but also superior to them, Kahlo painted herself, photographed herself, thought herself, made herself up, dressed herself, and represented herself with a narcissistic enjoyment seldom equaled in the history of art. At a time when revolutionary nationalism dominated art in Mexico, Kahlo made her own persona into the prime subject of her art.

A metaphor for herself, the self-portraits of Frida Kahlo occupy a privileged place in the history of this fascinating genre, which includes some of the most outstanding works in the world history of painting, starting with *Self-portrait* (1500)[20] by Albrecht Dürer (1471–1528), the creator and summit of the genre. He marked the beginning of the Renaissance concept of the self as an individual subject and the author of its own life history. With him, too, arises the modern concept of what it means to be an artist. Dürer painted himself as Christ, the son of God, in the pose of the Savior of the World, except that the fingers of his right hand point not at heaven but at himself, in recognition of the painterly genius granted to him by divine grace. This self-portrait's realism, natural air, and expressive depth, deriving from its minute attention to detail, give it a pictorial perfection that has never been surpassed in the history of the genre. The monogram with his initials, "A.D."—which coincide with *Anno Domini* (in the year of our lord)—became his hallmark. This self-portrait is a bold affirmation of the artistic excellence of its own creator. There was one subject that fascinated Albrecht Dürer above all others: himself.

Frida Kahlo is a worthy heir to this artistic tradition, centered on a fascination with herself and the affirmation and awareness of her skill as a painter—and specifically, it is important to emphasize, as a woman painter. Lists of the most renowned self-portraitists in history contain an abundance of men: Albrecht Dürer, Leonardo da Vinci (1452–1519), Rembrandt (1606–1669), Goya, Diego Velázquez (1599–1660), Vincent van Gogh (1853–1890), Pablo Picasso, Egon Schiele (1890–1918), Max Beckmann (1884–1950), Paul Gauguin (1848–1903), and Francis Bacon (1909–1992), among others. Apart from

Frida Kahlo, who is never missing from such lists, it is rare to find the names of women painters included, despite the large number of self-portraits by female artists like Artemisia Gentileschi (1593–1653), Sofonisba Anguissola (c. 1532–1625), Élisabeth Louise Vigée Le Brun (1755–1842), Tamara de Lempicka (1898–1980), Remedios Varo (1908–1963), and Leonora Carrington (1917–2011). Strangely, little mention is made of the pioneering Caterina van Hemessen (1528–after 1587), not only the first painter of a female self-portrait, but the first artist, man or woman, to paint a self-portrait showing the artist in the act of painting before an easel. This talented young Flemish Renaissance woman painter represented herself at the moment when she was painting her self-portrait on the canvas, signed "ego caterina de hemessen me pinxi 1548 etatis suæ 20" (I, Caterina de Hemessen, painted myself in 1548 at the age of 20). Like Dürer, the painter reaffirms her creativity and invention of herself, and also expresses a spirituality contiguous with that of Christ. The complexity and profundity of this small oil prefigures Kahlo's attitude to her own work, excluding the religious aspect. Kahlo also communed with the valor of Van Gogh in resisting and expressing his own suffering, as we see in *Self-portrait with Bandaged Ear* (1889);[21] with Goya, in his domestication of the monsters that sprang from his mind; with the Expressionism of Beckmann and Schiele; with the pessimism of Bacon; and with the bitterness of James Ensor (1860–1949), reflected in his *Man of Sorrows* (1891),[22] an example of despair transformed into art that silently expresses the Belgian painter's words: "For me as well, art is born of pain and except in rare instances my life is bound up with bitterness and disillusions."[23]

With the artists who have given form to their anguished understanding of themselves, Kahlo shares the hope that such works will transcend the fugacity of life. These self-portraits survive as the energy made color and soul that is the art of painting. Besides melancholy, death was another constant presence in the painter's life, as seen in *Thinking about Death* (1943) [fig. 68]. In *Self-portrait with Loose Hair* (1947) [fig. 69], Kahlo abandons her stereotypical coiffure with adornments or headpieces and presents herself much more naturally, with no makeup, shortly after returning from New York, where she had undergone yet another operation on her spinal column, finally leading to complications and what some of her biographers have called the beginning of the end. Kahlo had just turned forty, although she made herself out to be three years younger. She looks thin and wan, and the sunken eyes and cheekbones denote the passage of time and increasingly poor health. Far from trying to hide her deterioration, whether for reasons of vanity or theatrical artifice, the artist emphasizes it with dignity and valor. If there is one thing that moves us about this portrait, it is its authenticity. She has recovered her full head of hair, which she cut off at the time of the divorce. Only in *Fulang-Chang and I* [fig. 22] and *Diego and I* [fig. 52] from 1949—when Rivera had fallen in love with María Félix and was at the point of asking Kahlo for another divorce—did she paint herself with the long, loose hair that her errant husband liked so much. The black hair falls like a cascade, as natural as the plant sprouting from the wall of volcanic stone in the background of the composition. Here I am and this is what I am like, Kahlo says to us with the eloquent silence of her profound gaze.

Two years earlier, in 1945, she had painted another of her peculiar self-portraits entitled *The Mask (of Madness)*, where the artist's face is covered by a grotesque mask with distraught, weeping eyes and an untidy mop of purple imitation hair that give the impression of acute dementia [fig. 70]. This is a dramatic element to symbolize the duality that inhabits her, expressed both in *The Two Fridas* [fig. 31] and in the tale she tells in her diary of her imaginary friend,[24] as well as to visualize her desire to hide the physical and internal suffering that has formed part of her own nature, like the characters of Greek tragedy.

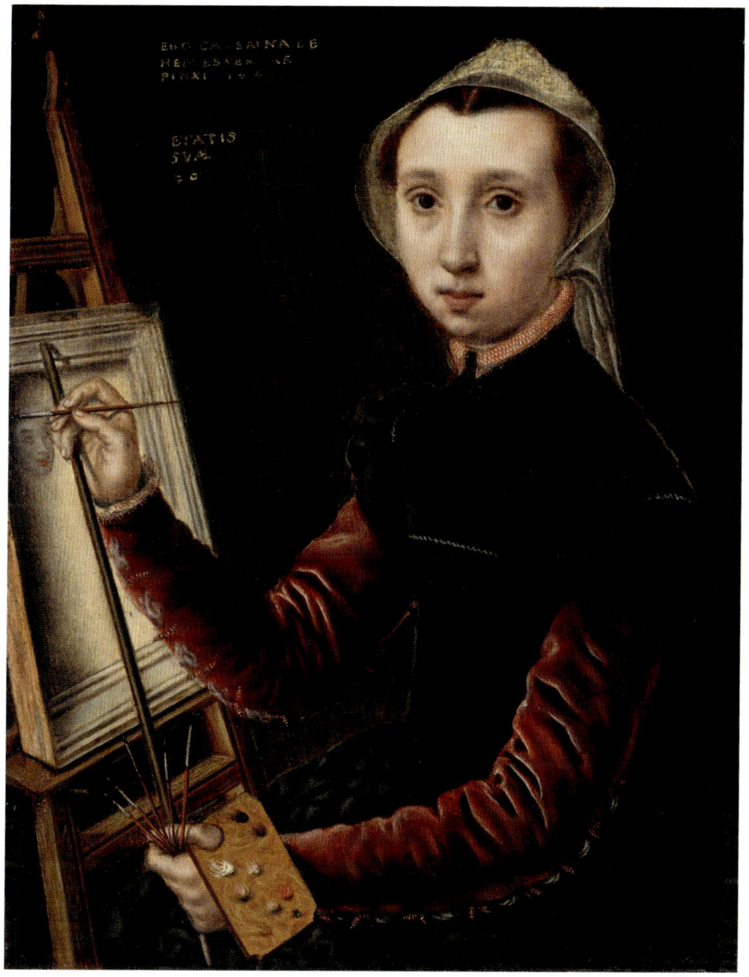

Caterina van Hemessen, *Self-portrait Seated at an Easel*, 1548, oil on oak panel, 12⅔ x 10 in. (32.2 x 25.2 cm). Basel, Kunstmuseum Basel, Schenkung der Prof. J. J. Bachofen-Burckhardt-Stiftung 2015, inv. 1361

In an interesting and controversial essay, art historian Oriana Baddeley posits that *The Mask (of Madness)* makes us doubt whether Kahlo's self-portraits really reveal her inner emotions, and asks: "Where does the mask fall? Does not the ritual repetition of those familiar features 'mask' far more than it uncovers?"[25] Baddeley's doubts arise from the following premises: first, that Kahlo's aesthetic interests spring from her fascination with the falsity of appearance; and second, that the conceptual basis of Kahlo's work is reduced to her personal adoption of a role in a masquerade. These conjectures are related in their turn to the author's analysis of the reports on Kahlo that appeared in the magazines *Elle* and *Vogue*. Yet there is no such falsity in Frida Kahlo's personality and oeuvre. On the contrary, there is an artistic authenticity that derives from the Romantic creation of the poetic self, and also from the defense of inner freedom, the supremacy of subjectivity, and the omnipotence of desire posited by the Surrealists. Those are the very things that raise Frida Kahlo's art to another level.

The word "persona" comes from the Greek *prosopon*, which means "mask" (*pros* = front, *opos* = face, so: "in front of the face"). In Latin, *persona* means an "actor's mask" or a "theatrical character." It was from this that Carl Jung derived his concept of the "persona" to designate the social face of the individual, meaning the mask or facade that is presented to the world in order to make an impression on others while hiding one's true nature. The persona thus represents the public personality, external, false, and distinct from the individual's genuine inner personality, which Jung calls the "anima." Modern English uses the term "persona" in a related sense to refer to the public image of a celebrity or some other person. In the case of Frida Kahlo, her "anima" and her "persona" are indissolubly linked, as are her life and work. Both are born of artistic creation.

Baddeley's interpretation reveals the confusion produced by the phenomenon of "Fridamania." Besides the marketing that has sprung up around Kahlo and the sharp increase in the price of her work on the art market, Fridamania has affected specialized studies on the biography and oeuvre of Frida Kahlo. Mixing an analysis of Frida's work with Fridamania generally leads to hasty and nearly always wrong conclusions. Of course, nobody has the last word on Kahlo and her painting, which, like all art, is open to diverse interpretations. Nevertheless, to doubt the authenticity of the artist's creative process, or of the human depth and complexity that is combined with the technical proficiency of her oeuvre, is a biased and incorrect view to say the least. We shall let the artist have her say:

> I wish . . . I could do whatever I liked—behind the curtain of "madness." Then: I'd arrange flowers, all day long, I'd paint, pain, love and tenderness, I'd laugh as much as I feel like at the stupidity of others, and they would all say: poor thing! she's crazy. (above all I'd laugh at my own stupidity) I'd build my world which while I lived, would be = in agreement = with all the worlds. The day, or the hour, or the minute, that I lived would be mine and everyone else's.[26]

To avoid confusion, we shall not go further into the phenomenon of Fridamania. This wave of international popularity sprang from interest in the artist's life and work prompted by Hayden Herrera's book *Frida: The Biography of Frida Kahlo*, first published in 1983, together with the extensive features on her in the magazines *Elle* (May 1989) and *Vogue* (February 1990); the films *Frida Still Life* (1983), directed by Paul Leduc and featuring Ofelia Medina, and *Frida* (2002), produced by and starring Salma Hayek; and the fact that the prices of her works have gone through the roof (mention has already been made of the works that have fetched the highest prices in international auctions). Fridamania is, above all, a marketing phenomenon supported by the popular fascination with the visual, symbolic, and vital values embodied by Frida Kahlo.

> Yes, Frida is good for Mexico because she is a lovable and engaging figure. People love her, and moreover she represents us very well abroad, she does us honor. I think Frida Kahlo's single eyebrow is a wing that flies us to other countries. They know us in Europe, in the United States, and even in the former Soviet Union, and what they know is a beautiful woman who in my view is a great painter, very original, very painstaking, very humble, very modest, because just as she painted

> every little hair in her eyebrows, she painted every little hair on her monkeys, too. She did everything like that, as if she were doing embroidery, because she didn't think she was the great genius who could splash on a stroke of paint and call it a masterpiece.[27]

What would Kahlo think if she came back and found out that one of her works (*Roots*) had sold for more than five million dollars?

> Behind all this success—which is a bubble, like all success—there also lies her suffering. And finally, what really mattered to her was Diego Rivera. Perhaps if Diego came back and didn't cheat on her, Frida might want to return, but she wouldn't come for the celebrity, as I think celebrity hangs very loose on her.[28]

Kahlo was never frivolous about her painting or the way she dressed. Both exemplified the fusion of her life and art and, to use Jung's concepts, her "anima" and her "persona," her inner self and her public image. She dressed as a Tehuana to reaffirm her Mexican identity, please Rivera, and distinguish herself from the ladies of Mexican high society. She spent hours dressing and arranging her hair as an act of self-assertion and strategic vanity, to attract attention and épater les bourgeois. The painting *The Suicide of Dorothy Hale* (1939) is a critique of New York society, whose values drove the former Broadway actress to suicide [fig. 71]. Depressed and ruined after her husband's death, Hale did not even have the money to pay the rent. A friend gave her five hundred dollars, a fortune at the time, and jokingly advised her to buy herself an evening dress to get a rich husband. She followed the first part of the advice, and then decided to throw herself out of the window of the Manhattan skyscraper where she lived. A friend of Hale's asked Kahlo to paint a picture to remember her by. When the friend received it, she was so taken aback that she thought of destroying it, but she fortunately restrained herself, and years later it was donated anonymously to the Phoenix Art Museum. Masterly in both form and content, the painting shows three moments in the actress's fall, with the high-rise building in the background and a dramatic sky of clouds covering the whole composition. At the foot, Hale's body appears intact, as if nothing had happened or the whole thing were a theatrical scene. Her elegant black dress is impeccable. She looks toward the viewer, like an actress waiting for the audience's applause. A little blood trickles from her ear and shoulder and invades the bottom of the frame. In the same tone of red, a brief handwritten inscription recounts the episode. As Oriana Baddeley observes, this work is "a poignant metaphor for the oppressive nature of the social values of New York and North America in general."[29] This is evidence of the critical profundity of Frida Kahlo's aesthetics, not a "fascination with the falsity of appearance,"[30] as the British scholar argues.

In the history of Mexican culture, Frida Kahlo shares the pinnacle of feminine creativity with Sor Juana Inés de la Cruz (1648/51–1695). The parallels between these two exceptionally gifted women are fascinating. Both geniuses, one a poet and the other a painter, they confronted adversity from an early age with admirable fortitude and perseverance. Both had difficult childhoods marked by solitude owing to their distinctiveness, which led them to introspection, self-analysis, and a determination to achieve prominence by being faithful to themselves. Their dignity manifested itself from their earliest youth, making them shine enough to achieve the goals they set for themselves. They also knew how to conquer their chosen ones: Kahlo won the heart of Diego Rivera, and Sor Juana that of the vicereines Leonor María de Carreto, marquise of Mancera (who gave her the title of "most beloved of the vicereine"), and her friend and patroness María Luisa Manrique de Lara, countess of Paredes de Nava and vicereine of New Spain. Both artists were beautiful, attractive, and brilliant, and so never lacked suitors. Each in her own way was able to charm anyone she met. Both expressed their affections with generosity and elegance, without excluding romances or flirtations with women. In the case of Sor Juana, there is no evidence that her proximity to Manrique de Lara ever reached the point of sensual or sexual intimacy, but there was undoubtedly love between them. No one should be scandalized at this passion, as:

> Being a woman, or being absent,
> is no impediment to loving you,
> for you know that souls
> ignore distance and sex.[31]

Sor Juana's loves, true or feigned, may have been chaste, and she may have tried to love the body through the soul, but how is this division to be established? Sor Juana did so by means of poetic metamorphosis:

> Halt, O faint shade of my elusive love,
> image of the enchantment I love best,
> fair illusion for whom I gladly die,
> sweet fiction for whose sake I live in pain.
>
> If th'attraction, the magnet of your charms
> draws my heart as if it were made of steel,
> why woo and win me over with flattery
> if then you will deceive me, turn and flee?
>
> But, satisfied and proud, you cannot boast
> that your tyranny triumphs over me:
> for though you escape and slip through the tight cords

> that bind your imagined form in fantasy,
> it matters not if you elude my arms,
> my dear, when thought alone can imprison you.[32]

There is another surprising analogy: both were self-taught. Both achieved excellence in their respective fields without formal education. Their intelligence, talent, and discipline were enough. Both Kahlo and Sor Juana achieved recognition for their art inside and outside of Mexico, winning fame and admiration at home and abroad. And there is another thing that unites them as creators of verbal and visual poetry: the mirror. In an exceptional essay entitled "Sor Juana Inés de la Cruz o Las trampas de la fe," Octavio Paz puts it admirably that

> the mirror turns the body into an image made of reflections. In the mirror, the body becomes simultaneously visible and untouchable. It is the triumph of eyes over touch. Subsequently, the image of the mirror is transformed into an object of knowledge. From eroticism to contemplation and from contemplation to criticism: the mirror and its double, the portrait, are a theater where seeing is metamorphosed into learning. . . .
>
> In many poems Juana Inés takes delight in the dialectic between the portrait and the model, the image in the mirror and the original, appearance and reality. The true reality is that of appearance. Both are copies of the essence, but appearance is more real than reality because it is more pure; I mean, less subject to accident and contingency.[33]

It is amazing how literally this text on Sor Juana's poetry can be applied to Kahlo's painting. And just as Kahlo revealed her soul through her self-portraits, Sor Juana was the author of the first autobiography of a woman in the history of world literature. Her 1691 intellectual biography is entitled *Respuesta a sor Filotea de Cruz*, a reference to the pseudonym of the Bishop of Puebla, the poet's confessor, with whom Sor Juana, known as the tenth muse of Mexico, maintained a running epistolary debate on theological matters. In her book, Sor Juana defends her vocation of attaining knowledge through the unveiling of her soul. Perhaps the most frequently remarked upon parallel between the two artists, however, is the fact that they were precursors to and paradigms of feminism—Sor Juana in the seventeenth century and Kahlo in the twentieth—as well as victims of patriarchal society and male chauvinism. Their example as defenders of the rights and dignity of women not only retains relevance, but is strengthened in the face of the challenges and injustices of today's world. As if all these parallels and similarities were not enough, it should be recalled that Sor Juana died at the age of forty-six and Kahlo at forty-seven. As a farewell, the poet nun wrote in the book of professions of the convent of San Gerónimo in Mexico City: "I, the worst in the world.

Sor Juana Inés de la Cruz."[34] In the meantime, the painter's parting words were "I hope the leaving is joyful—and I hope never to return—FRIDA."[35]

The miraculous connection between the poet and the painter could be strengthened still further if conclusive proof were found for a theory convincingly put forward by Josep Pascual Buxó, a leading specialist in Sor Juana. He argued that Sor Juana painted a self-portrait, missing to this day, that served as a basis for the many existing portraits of her, including the outstanding ones painted by Miguel Cabrera (c. 1715–1768) and Juan de Miranda (late seventeenth century–early eighteenth century). In an anonymous portrait acquired in Puebla in 1883 by an American collector, now at the Philadelphia Museum of Art, the painter wrote on the oil: "Faithful copy of another made of herself and painted by her hand by the Reverend Mother Juana Ynes de la Cruz."[36] Furthermore, Sor Juana alludes to the (presumed) self-portrait in several poems sent to her friend María Luisa Manrique de Lara, including this famous sonnet:

> This thing you see, a bright-colored deceit,
> displaying all the many charms of art,
> with false syllogisms of tint and hue
> is a cunning deception of the eye;
>
> this thing in which sheer flattery has tried
> to evade the stark horrors of the years
> and, vanquishing the cruelties of time,
> to triumph over age and oblivion,
>
> is vanity, contrivance, artifice,
> a delicate blossom stranded in the wind,
> a failed defense against our common fate;
>
> a fruitless enterprise, a great mistake,
> a decrepit frenzy, and rightly viewed,
> a corpse, some dust, a shadow, mere nothingness.[37]

The poetry of Sor Juana is painting that speaks, and the painting of Kahlo is silent poetry. What greater spiritual sisterhood could there be?

Sor Juana was a luminary of seventeenth-century Mexico and one of the greatest poets in the Spanish language. Kahlo was the greatest painter in Mexico and one of the most important women painters in world history. Octavio Paz, the author of the essay on Sor Juana quoted above, considered Kahlo a great artist who inherited the academic tradition and was influenced by Surrealism.

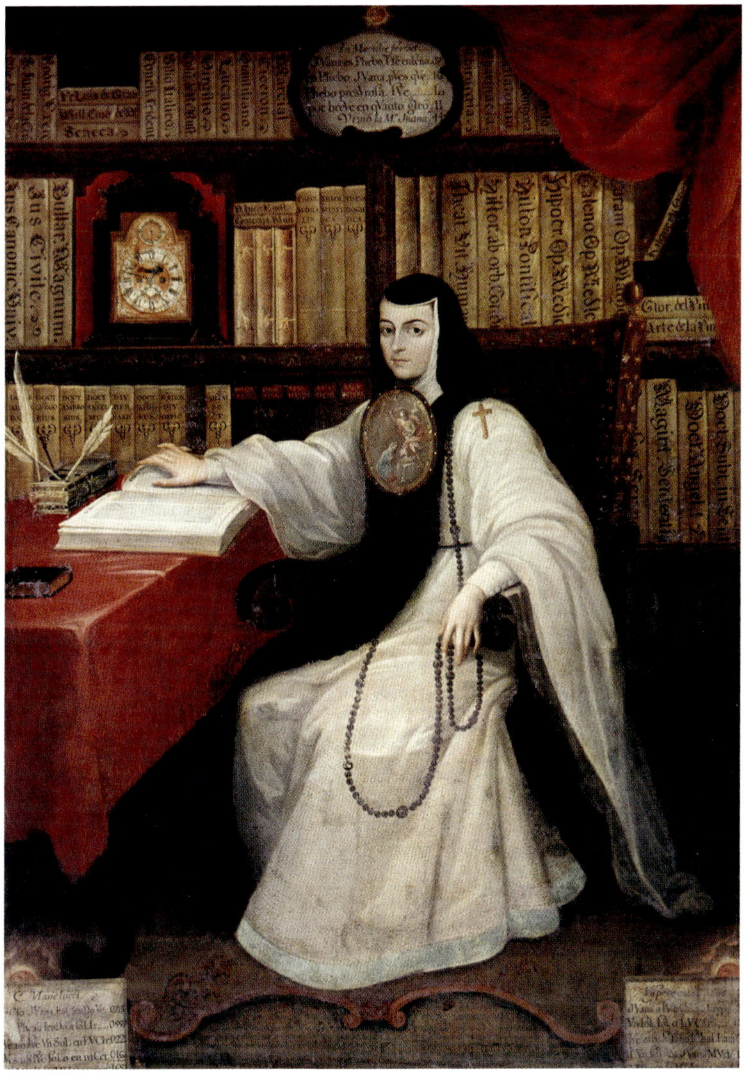

Frida Kahlo was not just an academically proficient artist: she was an intense visual poet . . . her form was nearly always perfect, and that perfection made the inflammable materials she contained—dreams, sex, death—burn with a sort of sumptuous violence. . . .

Her visual images were true explosions of the psychic subsoil, simultaneously paintings and revelations. Of very few artists can this be said. In Frida's visual metaphors, there is an astounding authenticity; looking at her pictures, we can say: this is true, this has been lived, suffered, and re-created. . . . Our painter is saved, nearly always, by the intervention of her two great gifts as a visual poet: humor and fantasy.[38]

Another thing the Mexican Nobel Prize winner shares with Kahlo is an impassioned knowledge of the pre-Columbian world. Both were heirs to the European avant-gardes, and both vindicated pre-Hispanic art by inserting it into their own works and the contemporary aesthetics of their day. A comparative study of the pre-Columbian images in the painting of Frida Kahlo and the poetry of Octavio Paz yields some surprising finds.[39]

Miguel Cabrera, *Portrait of Sor Juana Inés de la Cruz*, 1750, oil on canvas, 81½ x 58¼ in. (207 x 148 cm). Mexico City, Museo Nacional de Historia, Castillo de Chapultepec

Frida Kahlo never smiles in her self-portraits or in her photographs, not even in the ones taken of her by Nickolas Muray that appeared on the covers of *Elle* and *Vogue*. There was no smile on her public face, but there was in her writing and in her private life. Even in Kahlo's wounded carnality, blood and anguish are accompanied by black humor, giving rise to the highly personal song to life we find in her still lifes. Such a contrast is one of the great aesthetic values of her painting, occasionally reaching terrifying proportions as in *A Few Small Nips* [fig. 20]. In the midst of the dreams, the pain, and the distress of her invincible soul, there is another extremely important element in Kahlo's life: humor. She liked playing jokes as a little girl, and her gatherings with her friends were full of lighthearted laughter. Carlos Fuentes recalls that she loved the films of the Three Stooges and Laurel and Hardy.

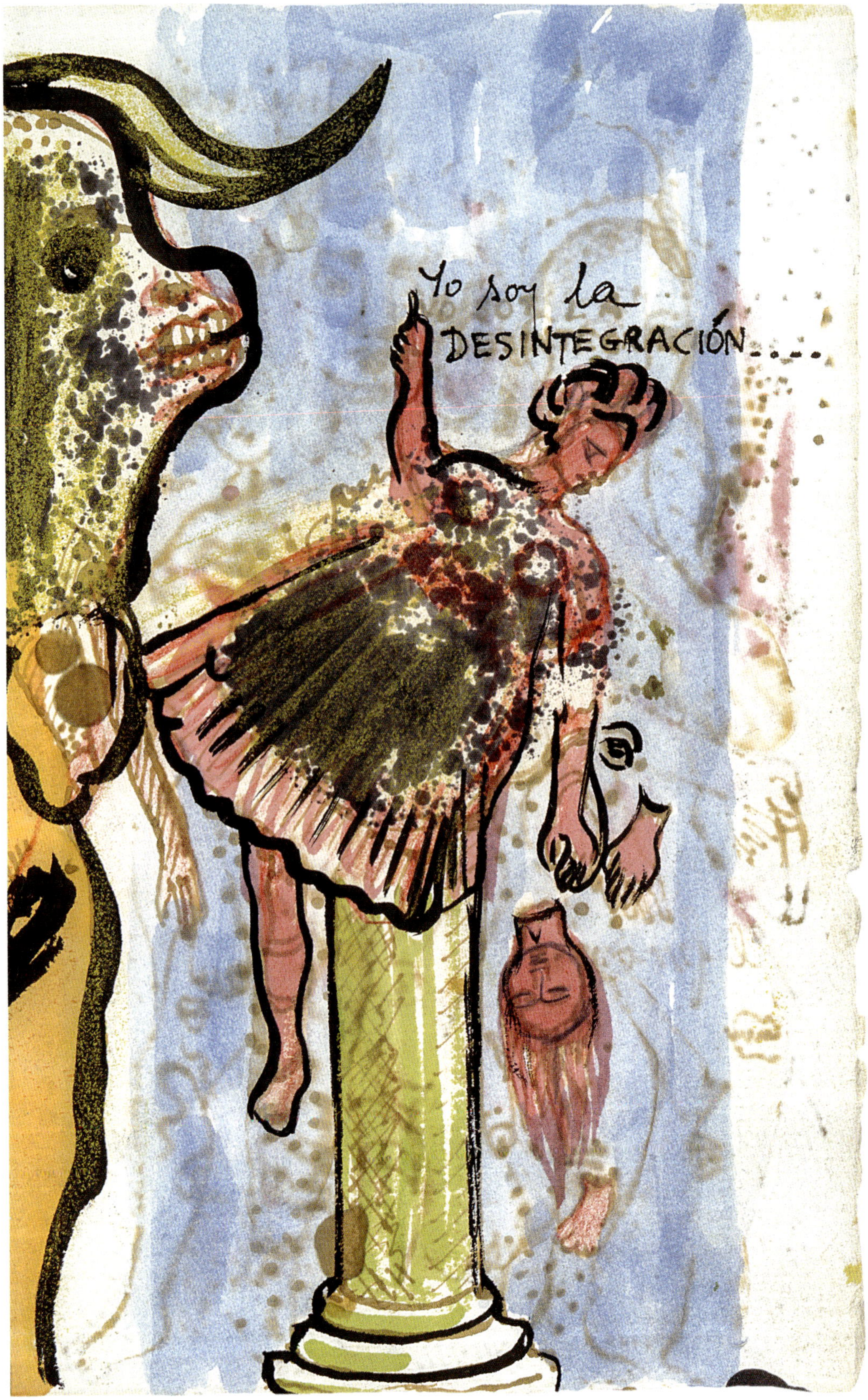

"I am DISINTEGRATION," page from Frida Kahlo's diary, c. 1944–54. Coyoacán (Mexico City), Museo Frida Kahlo

> [Frida] used to go to the cinema to kill herself laughing. She literally almost died watching Hollywood comedy, which is an anarchist cinema . . . where the comic actor dodges the law and the police, order is mocked, houses collapse, cars crash, and pies are thrown in faces. It's total disorder, and it made her die laughing. In the midst of pain, a great peal of laughter.[40]

Kahlo's characteristic humor diminished in the last years of her life with the progressive deterioration of her health. In 1950 and 1951, seven operations were carried out on her spine. She started to lose precision in her drawing and detail in her painting because her medicines affected her pulse and the steadiness of her hand. *Self-portrait with the Portrait of Dr. Farill* (1951) still preserves remarkable quality [fig. 72]. Kahlo shows herself in a wheelchair next to an easel bearing the portrait of her physician, which she has painted with the blood from her own heart, which we see as a palette on her lap.

The first retrospective exhibition on Kahlo's work in Mexico was organized at the initiative of the photographer Lola Álvarez Bravo (1907–1993), a friend of Kahlo's since high school. It was inaugurated in the spring of 1953 at the Galería de Arte Contemporáneo, owned by the photographer. The painter's health was delicate, and the doctors had forbidden her to attend the opening. Displaying her habitual boldness and resolve, Kahlo hired an ambulance and was carried on a stretcher into the opening of her exhibition, where she was received with surprise, joy, and great enthusiasm. The satisfaction and pleasure did not last long, as in August of that year, her right leg was amputated below the knee because the foot was totally gangrenous. "I am DISINTEGRATION," she wrote in her diary over a drawing that shows her as a doll tearing herself to pieces.[41] The pain was unbearable, and she could only calm it with Demerol, an opioid analgesic with an effect similar to that of morphine. On February 11, 1954, she wrote in her diary:

> They amputated my leg 6 months ago. It seemed to me centuries of torture and at times I nearly went crazy. I still feel like committing suicide. Diego prevents me from doing it in the vain belief that maybe he will need me. He has told me so and I believe him. But I have never suffered so much in my life.[42]

In these circumstances, her fervent support for Stalinist communism grew, as shown by paintings like *Marxism Will Give Health to the Sick* and *Self-portrait with Stalin*, both painted in 1954 [figs. 73 and 74]. Around that same time, by contrast, she wrote some lines of extraordinary quality and drama:

> Quietly, the grief
> loudly the pain.
> the accumulated poison
> love faded away.

Mine was a strange world
of criminal silences
of strangers' watchful eyes
misreading the evil.
darkness in the daytime
I didn't live the NIGHTS.
You are killing yourself!!
YOU ARE KILLING YOURSELF!!
With the morbid knife
of those who are watch-
ing. Was it
my fault?
I admit, my great guilt
as great as the pain
it was an enormous exit
which my love came through.
A very quiet passage
that was leading me toward death
I was so neglected!
that it would have been best for me.
You are killing yourself!
YOU ARE KILLING YOURSELF
There are some who will
never forget you!
I took their strong hands
Here I am, for them to live.
Frida.[43]

Kahlo's last public appearance was at a march organized by the Mexican Communist Party to protest the overthrow of the president of Guatemala, Jacobo Árbenz, planned by the CIA. A bust of Stalin is still on display at the Casa Azul, and the picture that Kahlo left unfinished on her easel was a portrait of Stalin. Weeks before her death, she painted some watermelons. On the one in the center, in the foreground, she wrote the phrase that gives the picture its title: *Viva la Vida* (1954) [fig. 75]. The last note in her diary was the sentence that has already been quoted: "I hope the leaving is joyful—and I hope never to return."

Frida Kahlo died on July 13, 1954, at the age of forty-seven. The official cause of death was pulmonary embolism, though the possibility of suicide has never been disproven. Kahlo's body lay in state at the Palacio de Bellas Artes in Mexico City. Her coffin was draped with the communist flag with the hammer and sickle, which led to

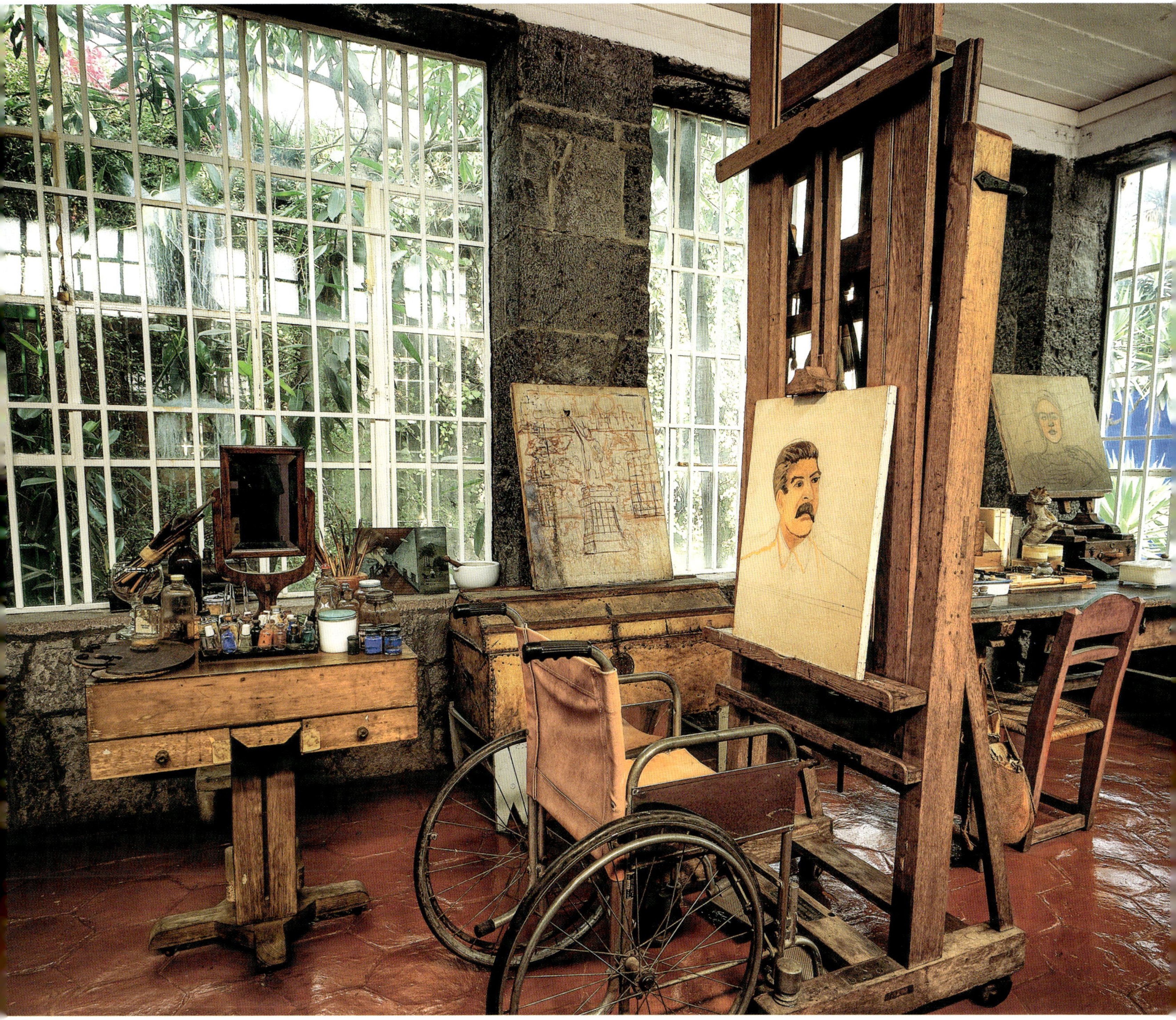

Frida Kahlo's studio in the Casa Azul, Coyoacán (Mexico City), with her unfinished portrait of Stalin on the easel

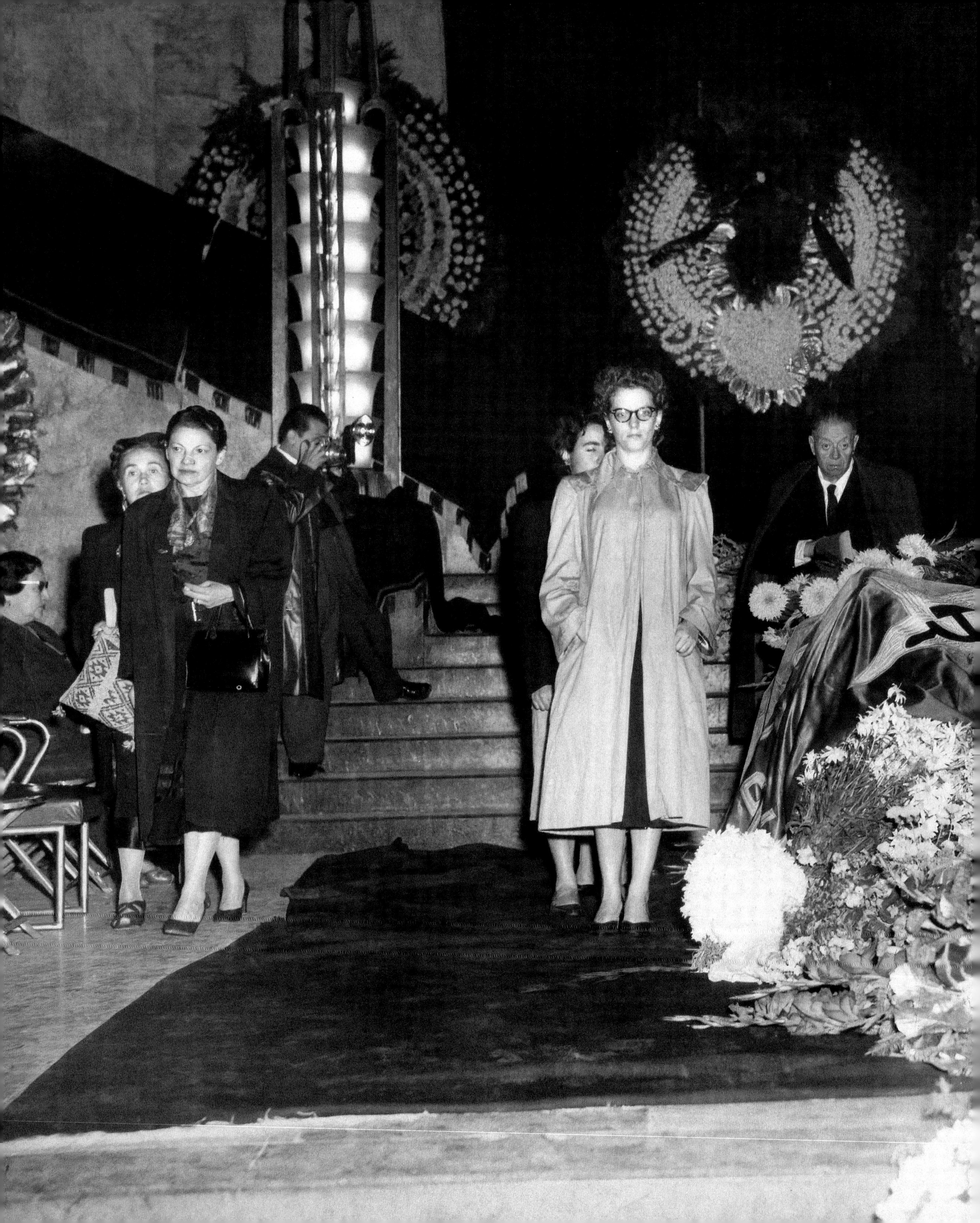

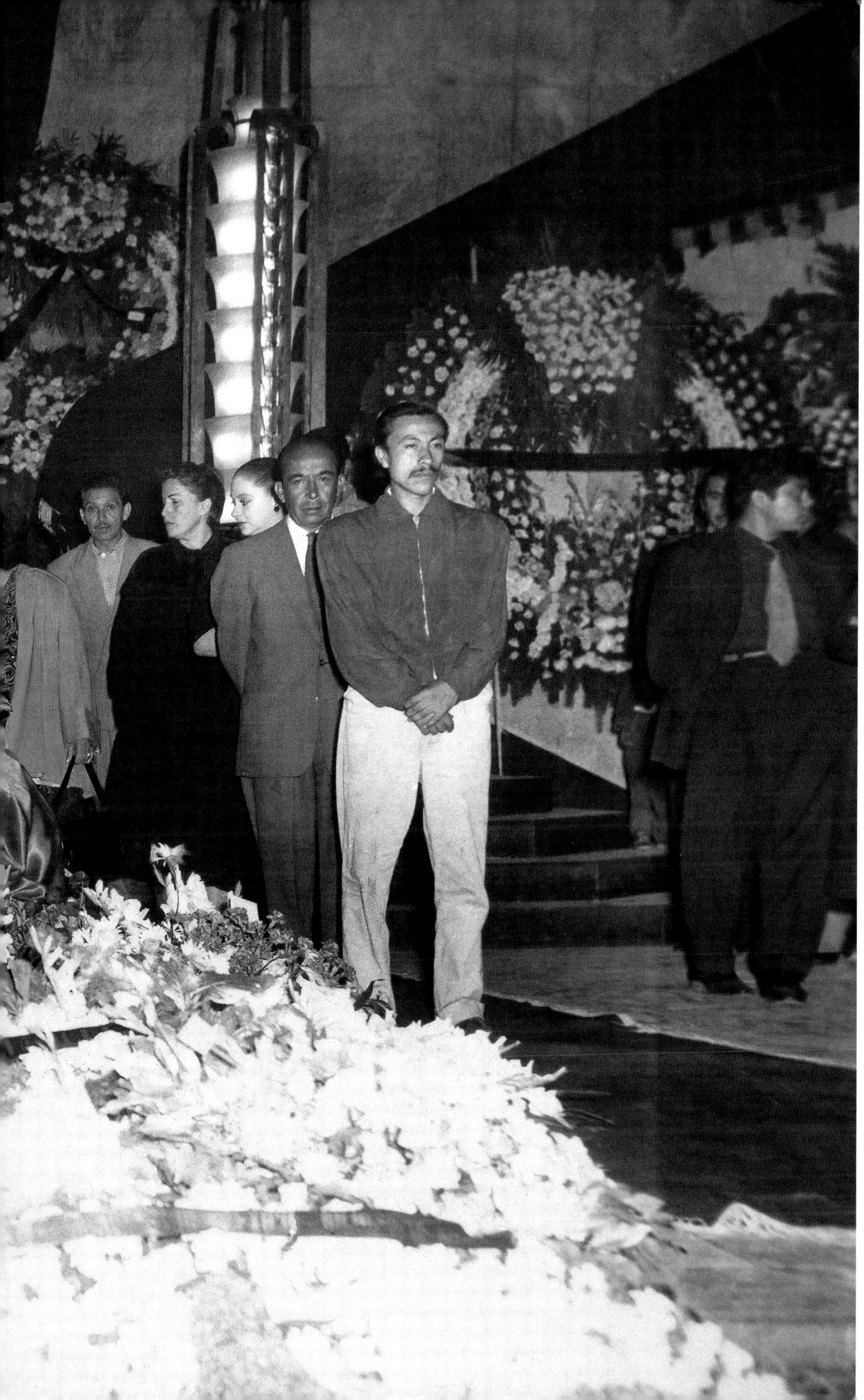

Frida Kahlo's body lying in state at the Palacio de Bellas Artes, Mexico City, after her death on July 13, 1954. Numerous people lined up on either side of the coffin to take turns standing vigil over her body. In the background, Diego Rivera. Courtesy Morton Subastas

the dismissal of the director of the Instituto Nacional de Bellas Artes, Andrés Iduarte. "The Internationale" was sung, and as a farewell, Diego Rivera, his face distorted with grief, asked those present to sing "La barca de oro" (The Golden Boat):

> I am going now to the harbor where
> the golden boat is waiting to take me away.
> I am going now, I have only come to say goodbye,
> Goodbye, my love, goodbye forever, goodbye.
> Your eyes will not see me again,
> nor will your ears hear my song.
> I am going to swell the seas with my weeping.
> Goodbye, my love, goodbye forever, goodbye.

In his autobiography, Rivera wrote: "July 13, 1954, was the most tragic day of my life. I had lost my beloved Frida forever. . . . Too late now I realized that the most wonderful part of my life had been my love for Frida."[44]

Today, Frida Kahlo is recognized as one of the most important artists of the twentieth century. She is regarded as the most famous woman artist in the history of art, and her life has been an inspiration for millions of women all over the planet. Her work has been shown in countless international exhibitions both before and since the artist's centenary. Frida, startling and luminous. Frida, tragic and cathartic. Frida, playful and stoic. Frida, melancholy and defiant. Frida, weeping and laughing. Frida, real and invented. Frida, polyhedral and heteroclite. Frida, critical of the Mexican Revolution and fanatical about the Russian Revolution: Frida, the devoted Stalinist. Frida, universal painter and icon of feminism. Frida, the paradigmatic. Frida, free in her sexuality. Frida in love with Frida and obsessed with Diego. Frida eroticized. Frida the genius. Eternal Frida. Frida Kahlo: metaphor for herself.

1 *Greek Lyrics*, trans. Richmond Lattimore (Chicago: The University of Chicago Press, 1960), 53.

2 William Blake, *The Marriage of Heaven and Hell* (Oxford: Oxford University Press, 1975), xviii.

3 Stefan Zweig, *El misterio de la creación artística* (Madrid: Ediciones Sequitur, 2015), 13.

4 Agesander of Rhodes, Athenodoros of Rhodes, Polydorus of Rhodes, *Laocoön*, c. 40–30 B.C.E., marble, 81⅞ x 64⅛ x 44 in. (208 x 163 x 112 cm), Rome, Musei Vaticani, inv. 1059.

5 Johann Joachim Winckelmann, *Writings on Art*, ed. David Irwin (London: Phaidon, 1972), 72.

6 Gotthold Ephraim Lessing, *Laocoön: An Essay on the Limits of Painting and Poetry*, trans. E. C. Beasley (London: Longman, Brown, Green, and Longmans, 1853), 168.

7 Victor Hugo, *William Shakespeare*, trans. Melville. B. Anderson (Chicago: A.C. McClurg and Company, 1887), 176.

8 Charles Baudelaire, "Hymne à la Beauté" in *Les Fleurs du Mal* (Oxford: Blackwell, 1966), 22.

9 Eugène Delacroix, *The Death of Sardanapalus*, 1827, oil on canvas, 195¼ x 154⅓ in. (496 x 392 cm), Paris, Musée du Louvre, RF 2346.

10 Charles Baudelaire, *Écrits sur l'art 1* (Paris: Éditions Gallimard, 1971), 146.

11 Caspar David Friedrich, *Wanderer above the Sea of Fog*, c. 1817, oil on canvas, 37⅓ x 29½ in. (94.8 x 74.8 cm), Hamburg, Hamburger Kunsthalle, inv. HK-5161.

12 Hieronymous Bosch, *The Garden of Earthly Delights*, 1490–1500, grisaille and oil on oak panel, 73⅛ x 128⅛ in. (185.8 x 325.5 cm), Madrid, Museo Nacional del Prado, P-2823.

13 Pieter Brueghel the Elder, *The Triumph of Death*, 1563, oil on panel, 46 x 63¾ in. (117 x 162 cm), Madrid, Museo Nacional del Prado, P-1393.

14 Francisco de Goya y Lucientes, *The 3rd of May 1808 in Madrid*, oil on canvas, 105½ x 136⅔ in. (268 x 347 cm), Madrid, Museo Nacional del Prado, P-749.

15 José de Ribera, *La mujer barbuda*, 1631, oil on canvas, 76⅓ x 49⅝ in. (194 x 126 cm), Fundación Casa Ducal de Medinaceli.

16 Pablo Picasso, *Guernica*, 1937, oil on canvas, 137½ x 305¾ in. (349.3 x 776.6 cm), Madrid, Museo Nacional Centro de Arte Reina Sofía, DE00050.

17 *Coatlicue*, c. 1400s, andesite, 99¼ inches (2.52 m) (height), Mexico City, Museo Nacional de Antropología.

18 *Tláloc*, c. 1500s, stone, 15¾ x 10⅝ x 8⅔ in. (40 x 27 x 22 cm), Berlin, Staatliche Museen zu Berlin, Ethnologisches Museum, IV Ca 3721.

19 *Quetzalcóatl*, 1400–1521, andesite, 5⅞ x 11 x 9⅞ in. (15 x 28 x 25 cm), Paris, Musée du Quai Branly-Jacques Chirac, 71.1878.1.59.

20 Albrecht Dürer, *Self-portrait*, 1500, oil on panel, 26⅜ x 19⅓ in. (67.1 x 48.9 cm), Munich, Bayerische Staatsgemäldesammlungen, Alte Pinakothek München, inv. 5396.

21 Vincent van Gogh, *Self-portrait with Bandaged Ear*, 1889, oil on canvas, 23⅞ x 19⅔ in. (60.5 x 50 cm, London, The Courtauld, Samuel Courtauld, bequest, 1948, P. 1948.SC.175.

22 James Ensor, *Man of Sorrows*, 1891, oil on panel, 8½ x 6⅓ in. (21.5 x 16 cm), Antwerp, Koninklijk Museum voor Schone Kunsten Antwerpen, inv. 3320.

23 James Ensor quoted in Ulrike Becks-Malorny, *James Ensor, 1860–1949: Masks, Death and the Sea* (Cologne: Taschen, 1999), 83.

24 Frida Kahlo, *The Diary of Frida Kahlo: An Intimate Self-portrait* (New York: Harry N. Abrams, 1995), 245–47.

25 Oriana Baddeley, "'Her Dress Hangs Here': De-frocking the Kahlo Cult," *Oxford Art Journal* 14, no. 1 (1991): 12.

26 Kahlo, *Diary*, 242.

27 "Entrevista con Elena Poniatowska. Frida color," in *Yo soy Frida*, ed. Héctor Tajona (Mexico City: Milenio Diario, 2007), 36.

28 "Entrevista con Elena Poniatowska. Frida color," in *Yo soy Frida*, 36

29 Baddeley, "Her Dress," 14.

30 Baddeley, "Her Dress," 12.

31 Sor Juana Inés de la Cruz, *Obras completas de sor Juana Inés de la Cruz. I. Lírica personal* (Mexico City: Fondo de Cultura Económica, 1951), 57.

32 Sor Juana Inés de la Cruz, *Sor Juana Inés de la Cruz: Selected Works*, trans. Edith Grossman (New York: W. W. Norton & Company, 2014), 66.

33 Octavio Paz, *Sor Juana: Or, the Traps of Faith*, trans. Margaret Sayers Peden (Cambridge: Harvard University Press, 1988), 84.

34 Guillermo Schmidhuber de la Mora, "El Libro de profesiones del Convento de San Jerónimo de México: la profesión de sor Juana Inés de la Cruz," *eHumanista* 19 (2011): 540.

35 Kahlo, *Diary*, 285.

36 José Pascual Buxó, "Los retratos de Sor Juana: pintura y poesía," in *En esto ver aquello. Octavio Paz y el arte* (Mexico City, Consejo Nacional para la Cultura y las Artes e Instituto Nacional de Bellas Artes, 2014), 239.

37 *Sor Juana Inés de la Cruz: Selected Works*, 59.

38 Octavio Paz, *Obras completas, vol. 7: Los privilegios de la vista II. Solitarios e independientes* (Mexico City: Fondo de Cultura Económica, 1994), 291–92.

39 Luis Roberto Vera, "Octavio Paz y Frida Kahlo: La herencia precolombina," *Casa del Tiempo* 2–3 (2007–8): 41–56.

40 "Entrevista con Carlos Fuentes. Frida amada," in *Yo soy Frida*, 3.

41 Kahlo, *Diary*, 225.

42 Kahlo, *Diary*, 278.

43 Kahlo, *Diary*, 273.

44 Diego Rivera with Gladys March, *My Art, My Life: An Autobiography* (Garden City: Dover Publications, 1991), 178 and 180.

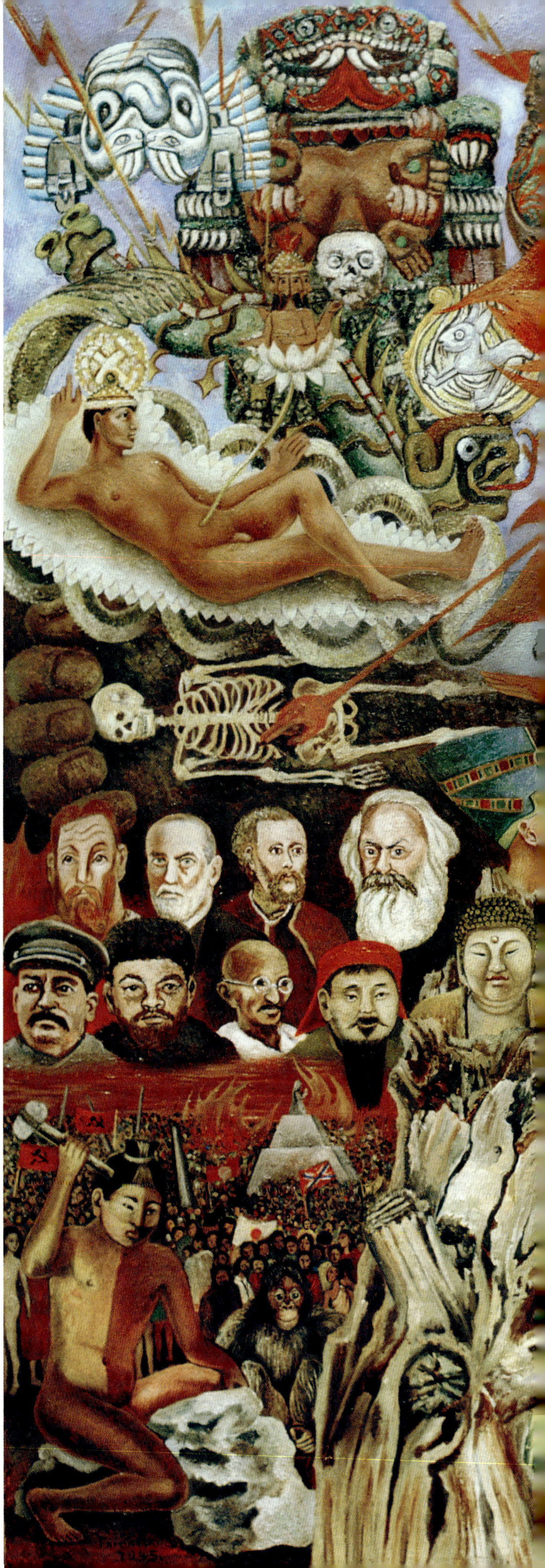

67

Moses or The Nucleus of Creation

1945
Oil on Masonite,
24 x 29¾ in. (61 x 75.6 cm)
Private collection

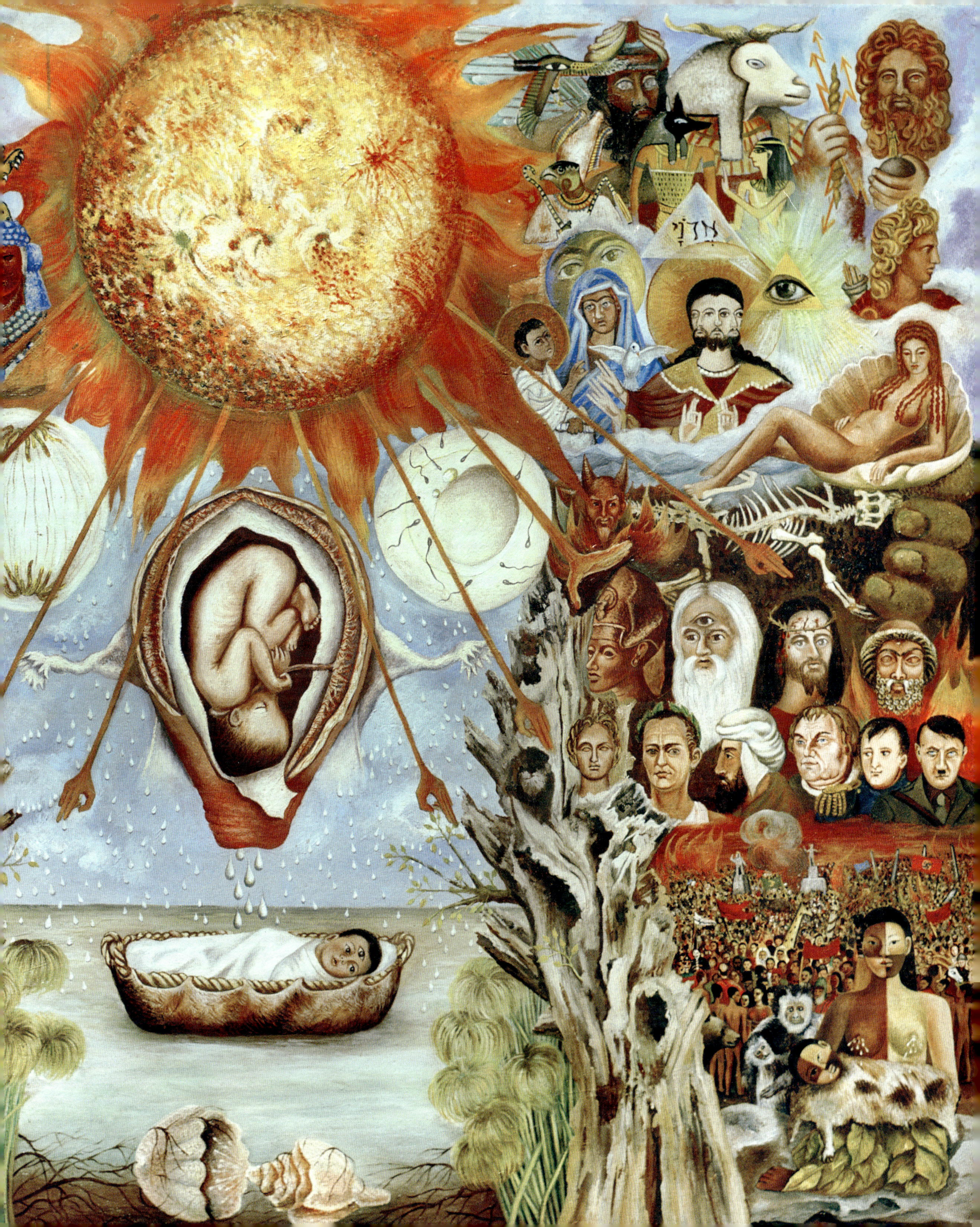

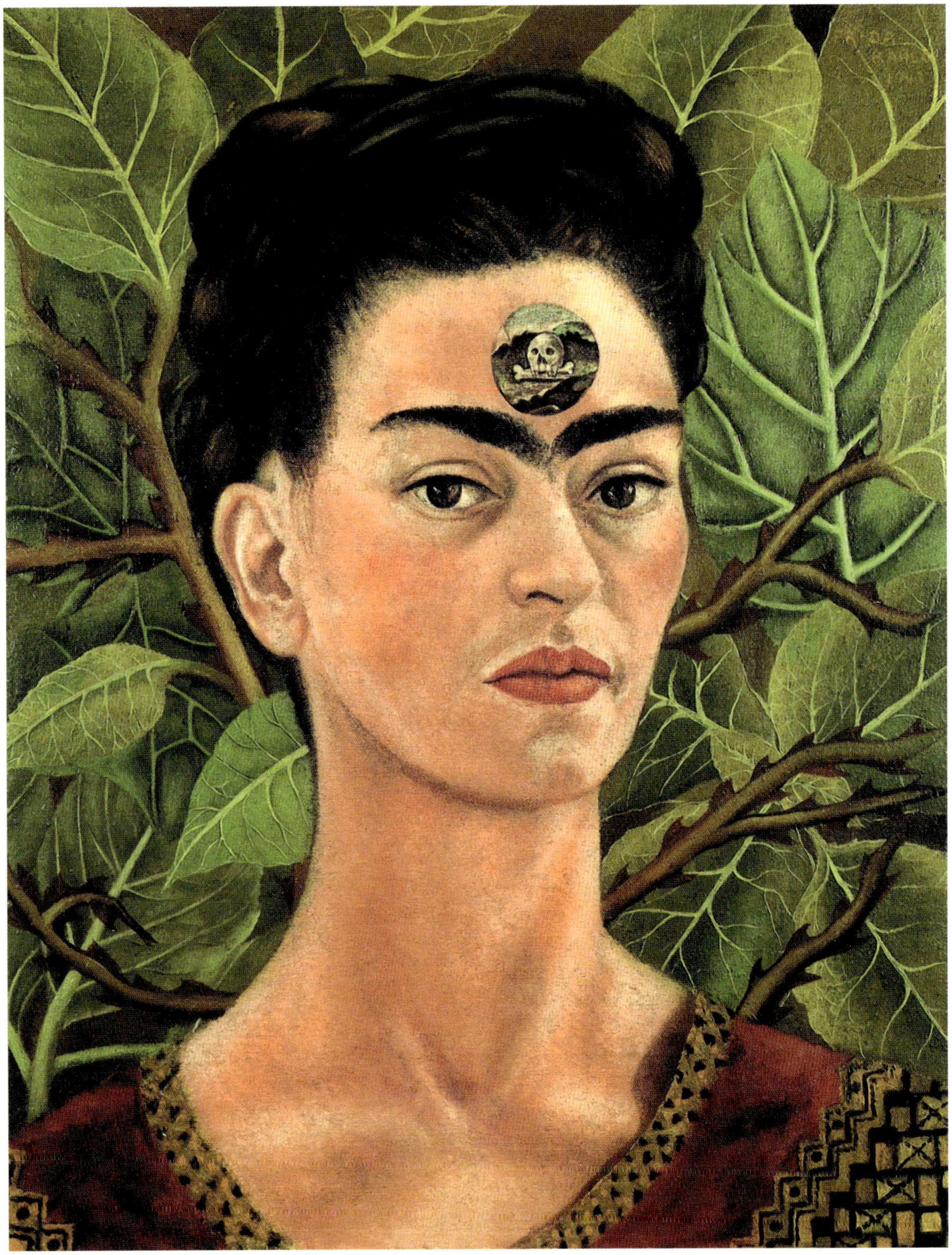

68

Thinking about Death

1943
Oil on canvas,
17½ x 14⅓ in. (44.5 x 36.3 cm)
Private collection

69

Self-portrait with Loose Hair

1947
Oil on Masonite,
24 x 17¾ in. (61 x 45 cm)
Des Moines (Iowa), private collection

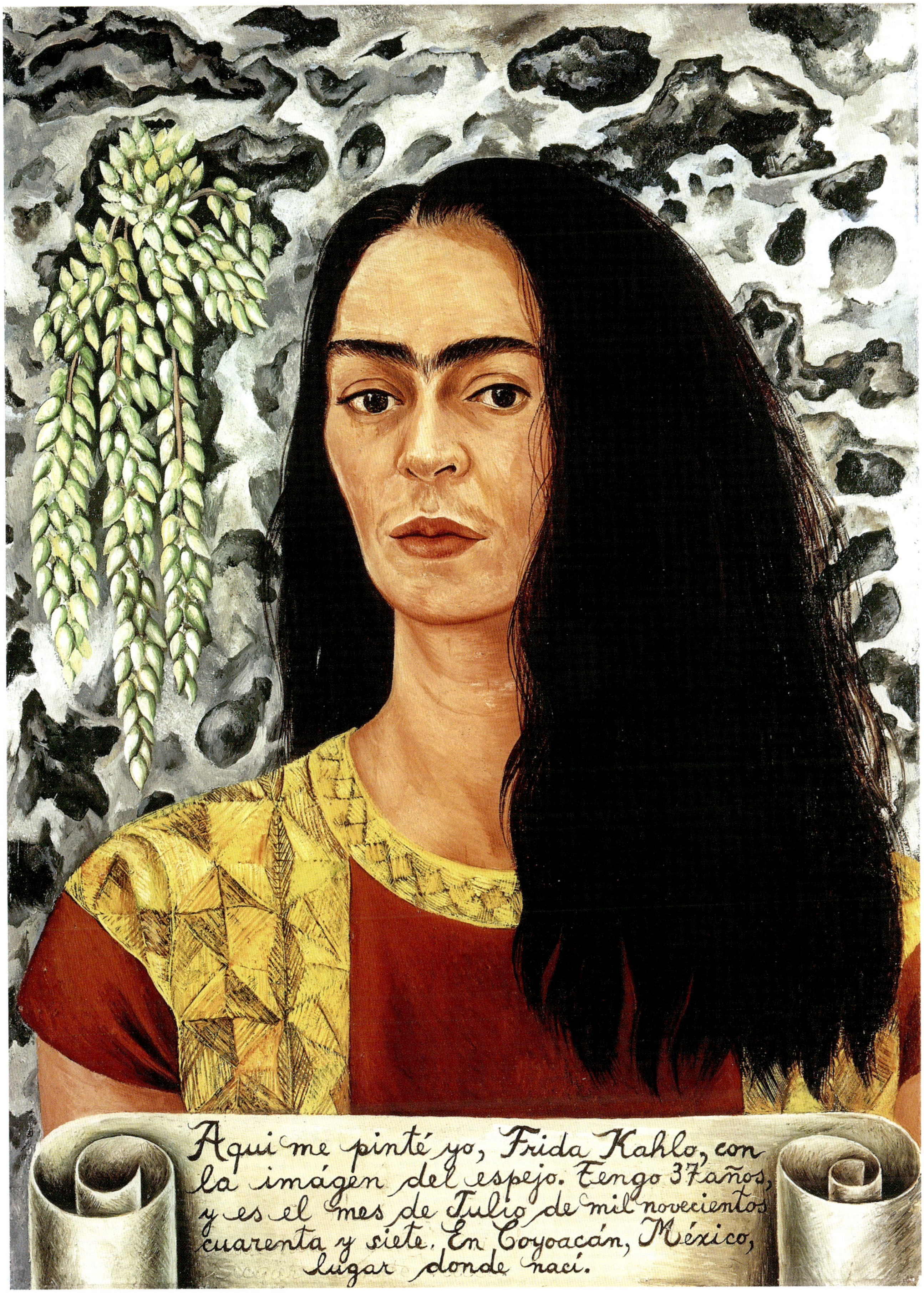
Aqui me pinté yo, Frida Kahlo, con
la imágen del espejo. Tengo 37 años,
y es el mes de Julio de mil novecientos
cuarenta y siete. En Coyoacán, México,
lugar donde nací.

70

The Mask (of Madness)

1945
Oil on canvas,
15¾ x 12 in. (40 x 30.5 cm)
Xochimilco (Mexico City),
Collection Museo Dolores Olmedo

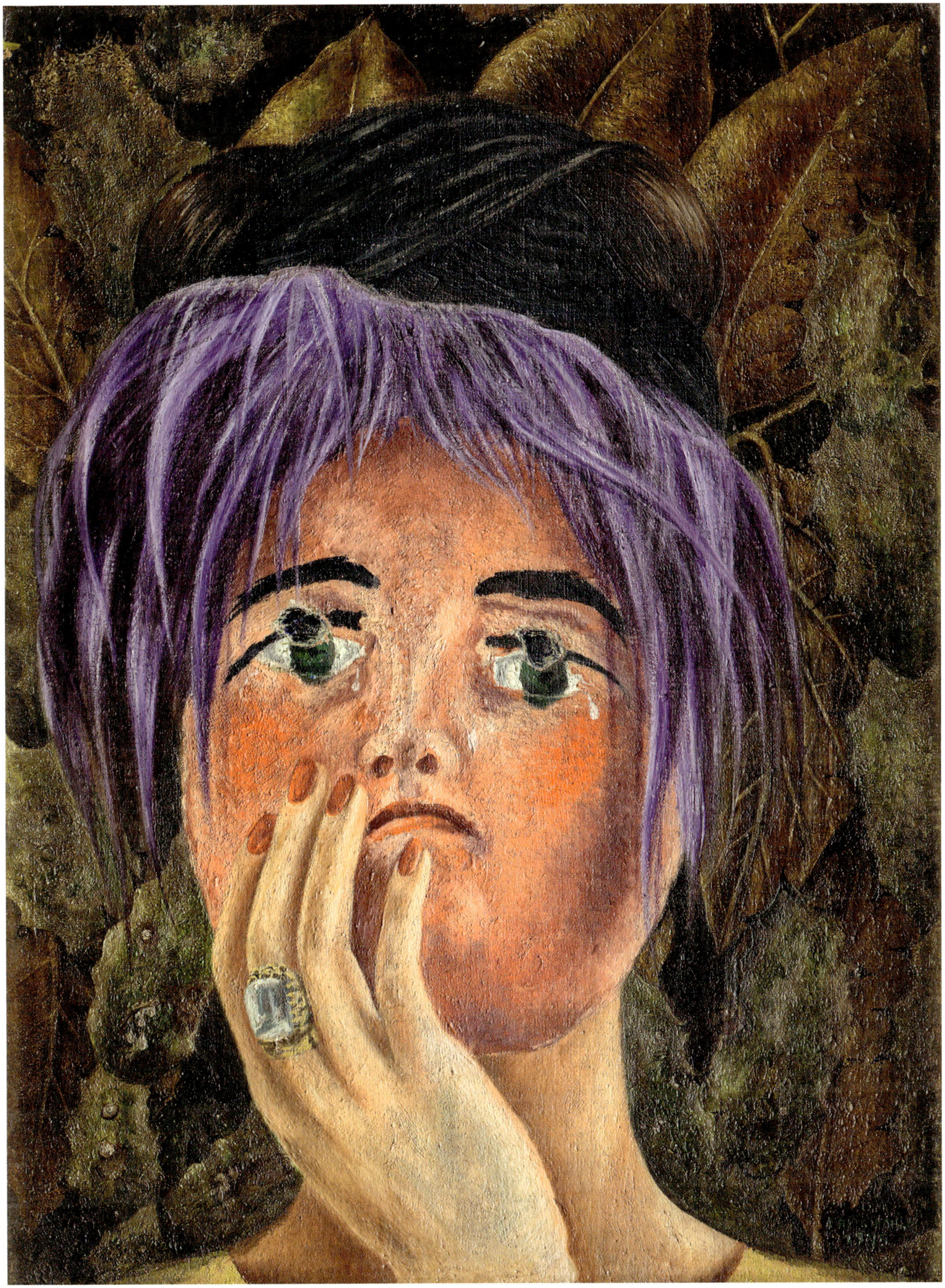

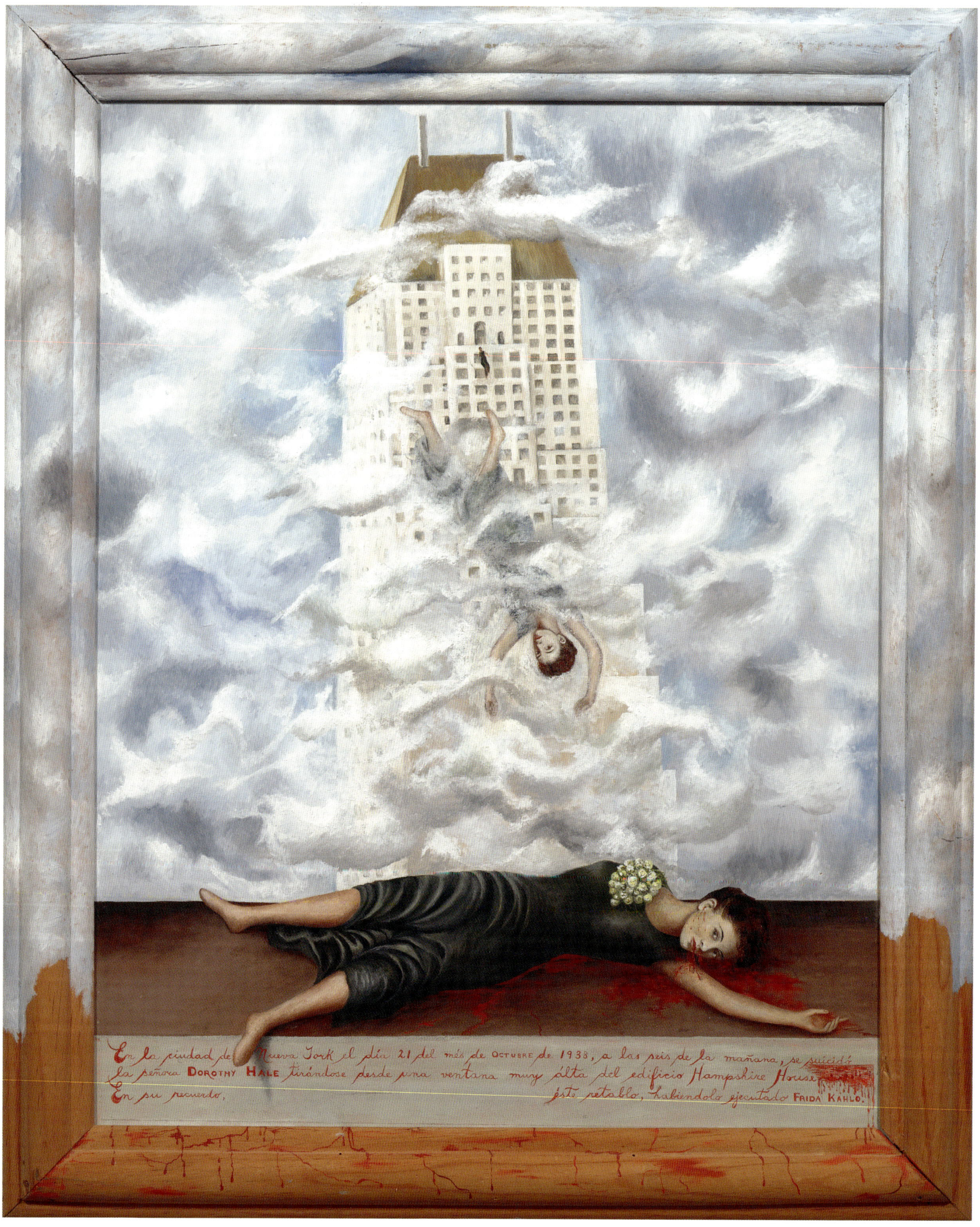
En la ciudad de Nueva York el día 21 del més de OCTUBRE de 1938, a las seis de la mañana, se suicidó
la señora DOROTHY HALE tirándose desde una ventana muy álta del edificio Hampshire House.
En su recuerdo, éste retablo, habiendolo ejecutado FRIDA KAHLO.

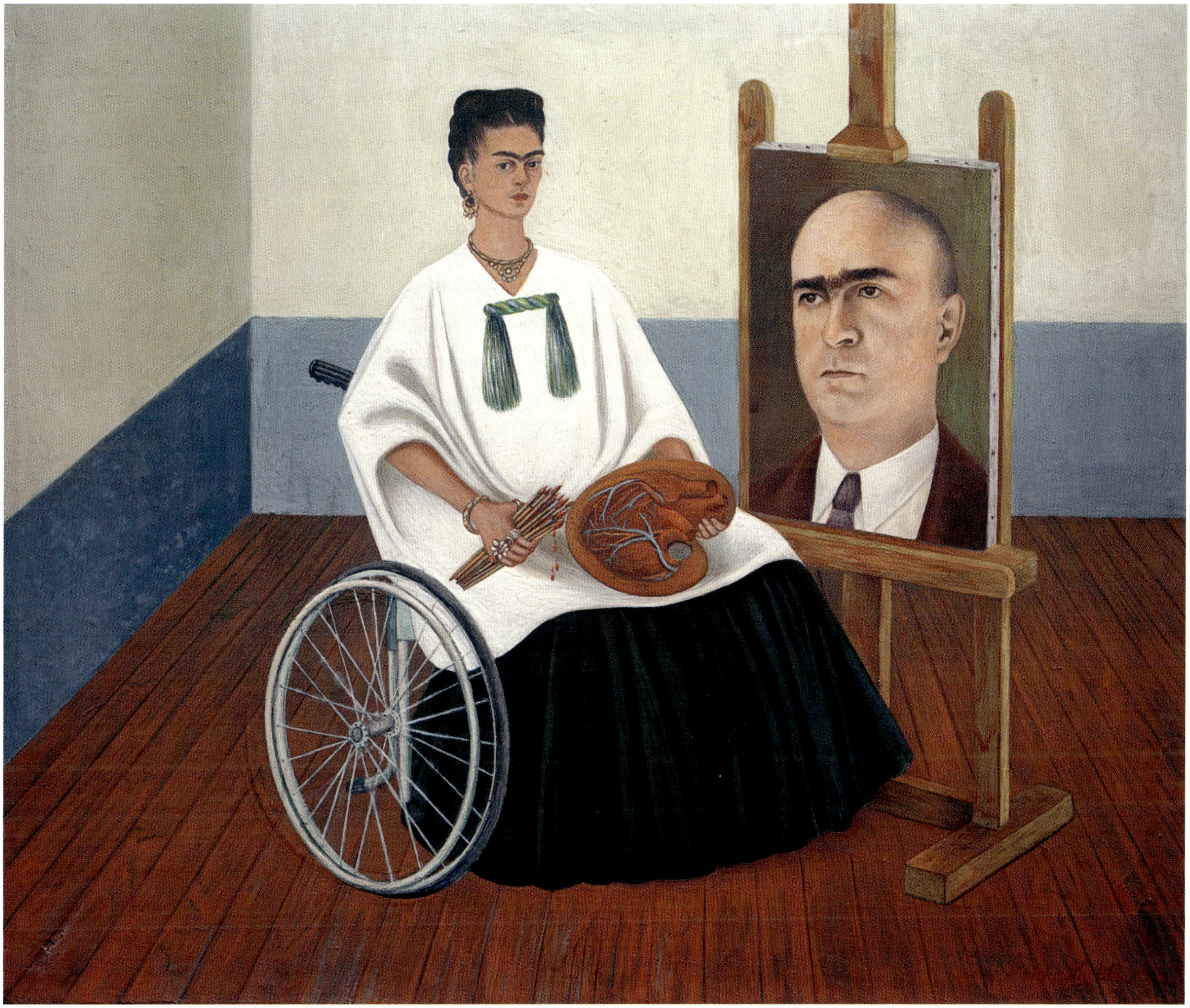

71
The Suicide of Dorothy Hale

1939
Oil on Masonite with painted frame,
23½ x 19½ in. (59.7 x 49.5 cm)
Phoenix, Phoenix Art Museum,
Gift of an anonymous donor, 1960.20

72
Self-portrait with the Portrait of Dr. Farill

1951
Oil on Masonite,
16⅓ x 19⅔ in. (41.5 x 50 cm)
Private collection

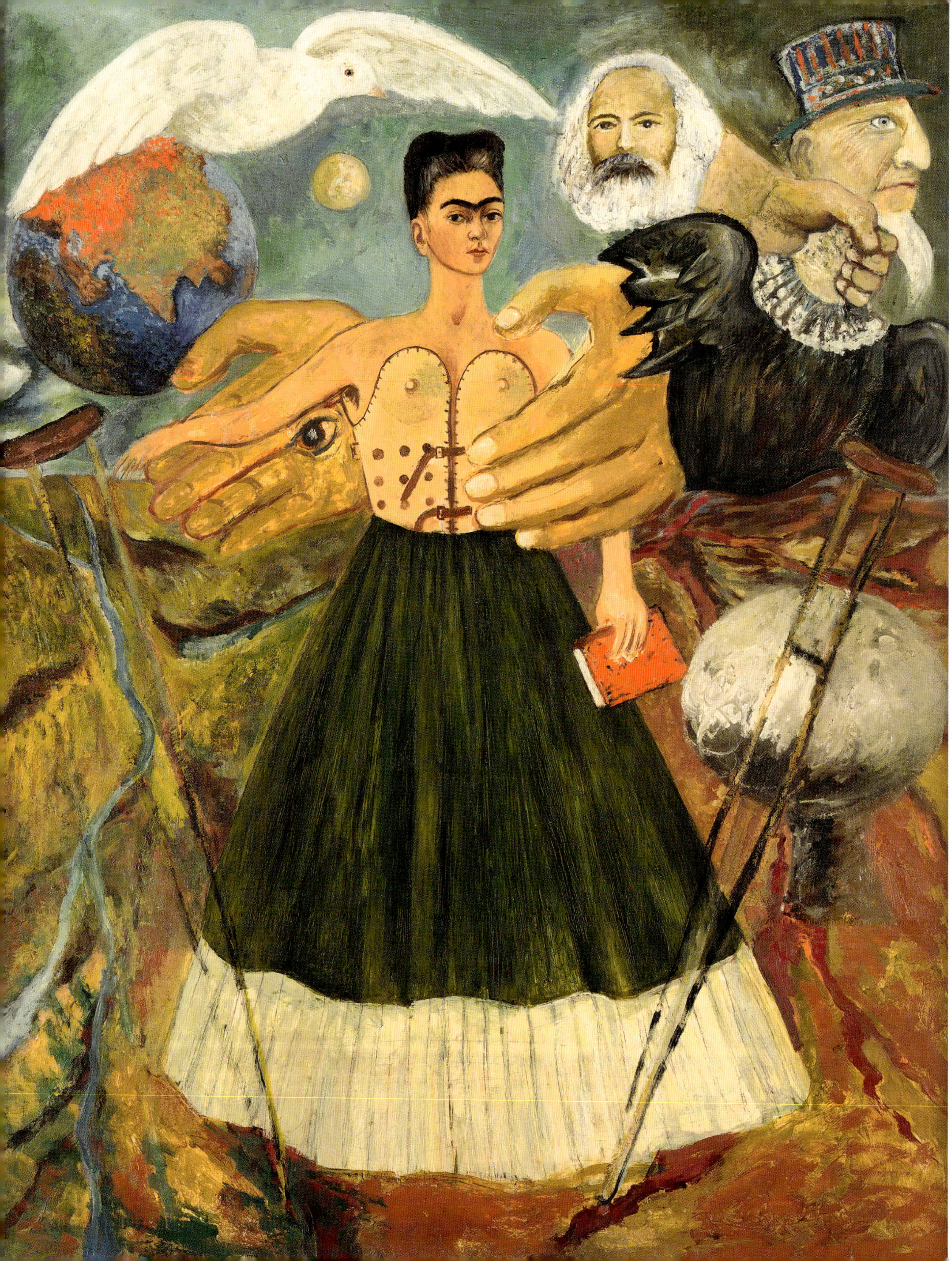

73
Marxism Will Give Health to the Sick

1954
Oil on Masonite,
30 x 23⅔ in. (76 x 60 cm)
Coyoacán (Mexico City),
Museo Frida Kahlo

74
Self-portrait with Stalin

1954
Oil on Masonite,
23¼ x 15⅜ in. (59 x 39 cm)
Coyoacán (Mexico City),
Museo Frida Kahlo

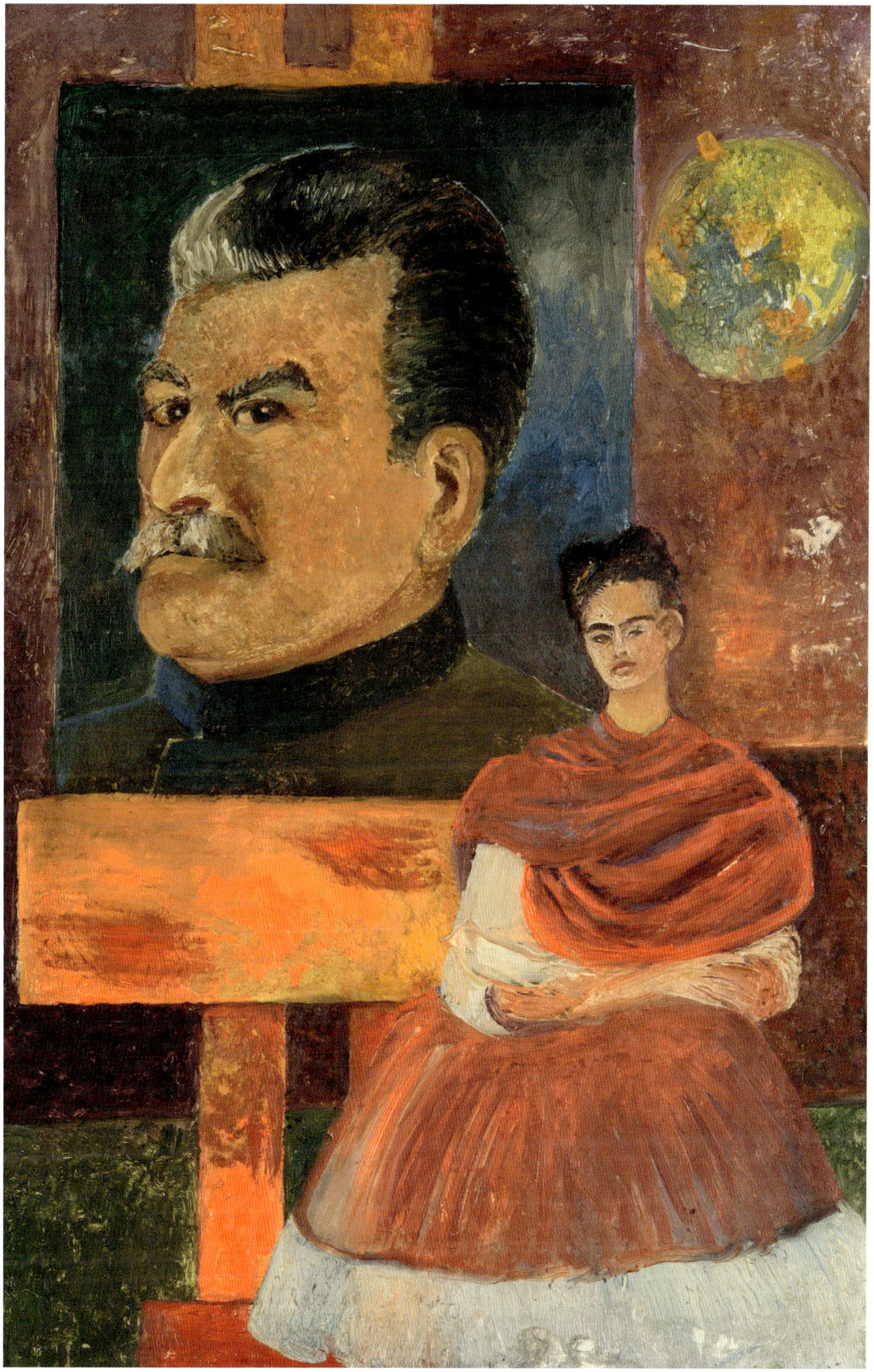

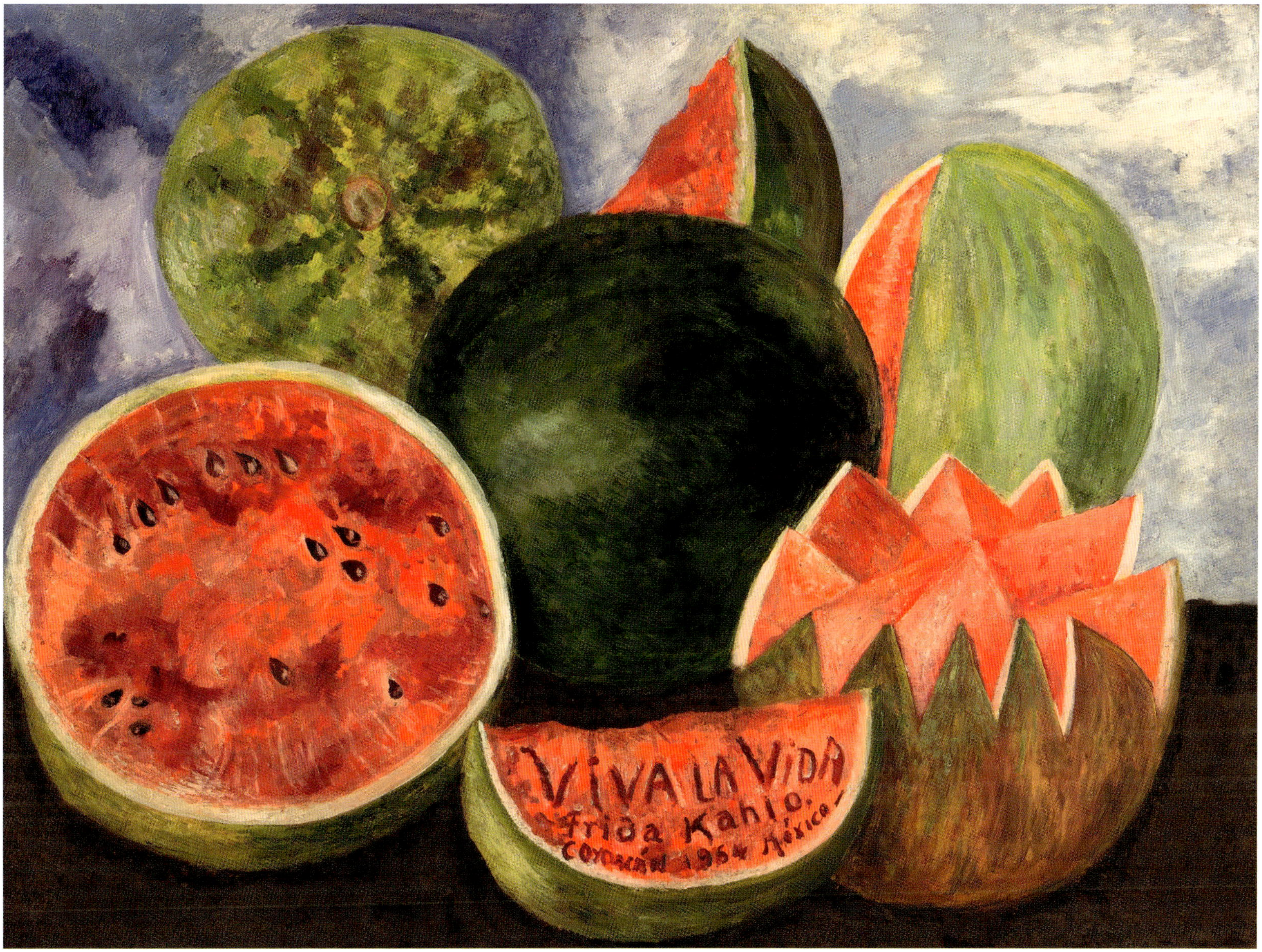

75

Viva la Vida

1954
Oil on Masonite,
20½ x 28⅓ in. (52 x 72 cm)
Coyoacán (Mexico City),
Museo Frida Kahlo

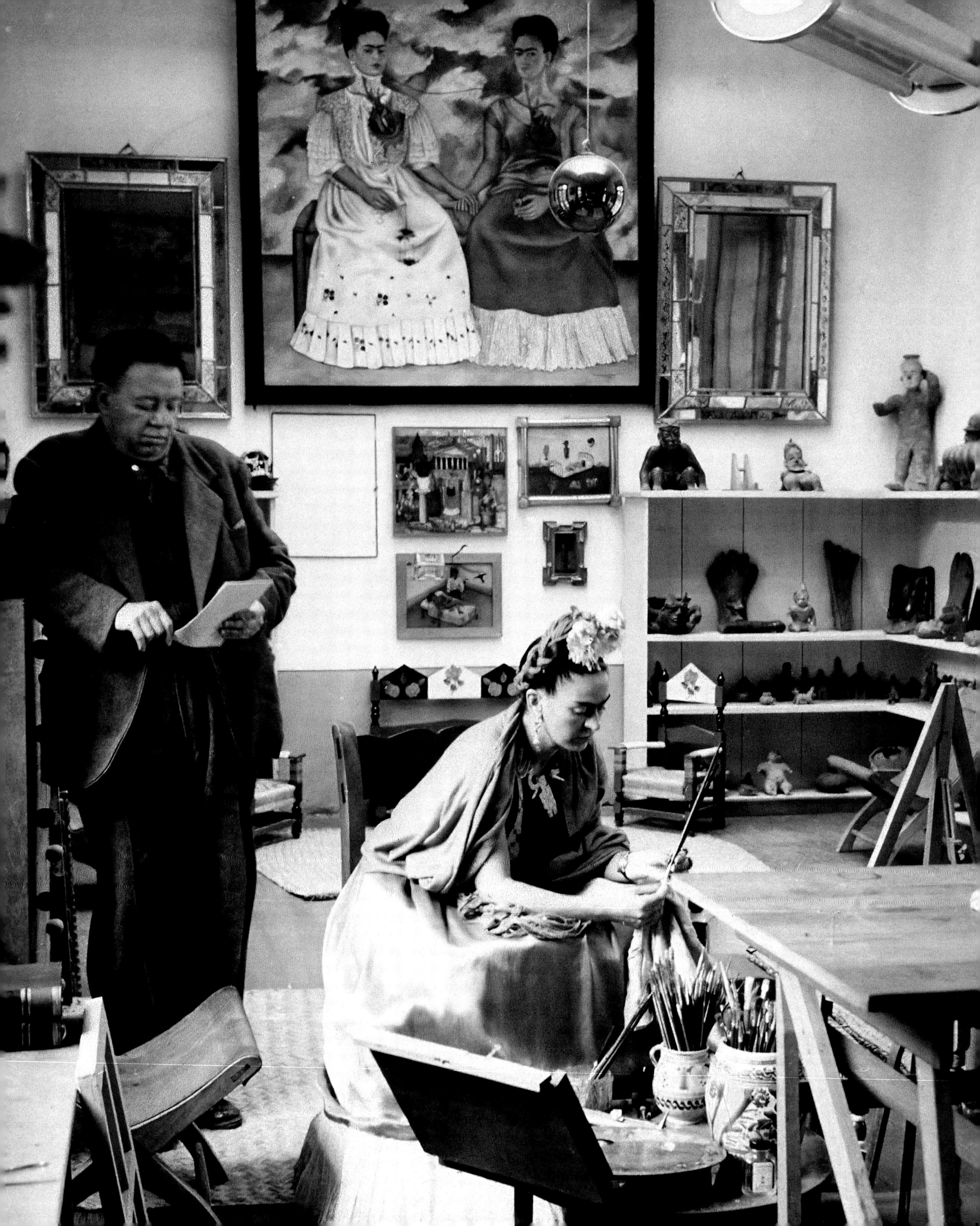

Chronology

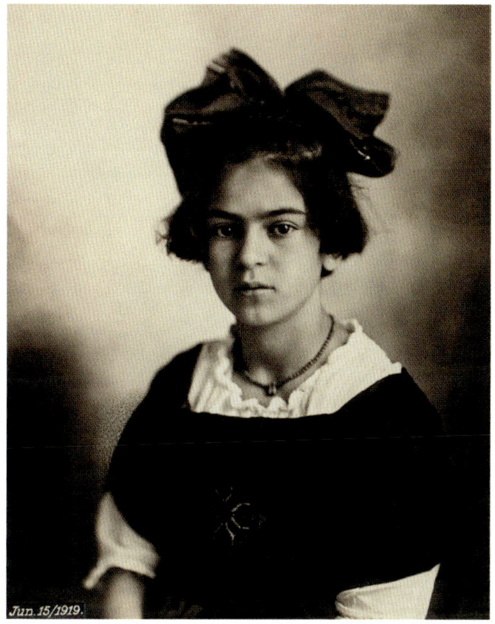

Frida Kahlo, June 15, 1919. Photograph by Guillermo Kahlo. Coyoacán (Mexico City), Museo Frida Kahlo

1907

Magdalena Carmen Frieda Kahlo Calderón is born on July 6 in Coyoacán, a suburb of Mexico City. She is one of three daughters born to Guillermo Kahlo, a photographer of German origin, and his second wife, Matilde Calderón, a Mexican.

1910

On November 20, the Mexican Revolution, led by Francisco I. Madero under the slogan "effective suffrage, no reelection," begins with the aim of deposing dictator Porfirio Díaz. Later Frida Kahlo will change her date of birth to make it coincide with this occasion.

1913

She suffers poliomyelitis that makes her right leg shorter and thinner than the left. Even so, encouraged by her father, to whom she is increasingly close, she skillfully plays various sports.

1921

After attending a German school in Mexico City, where her schoolmates nickname her "Frida Kahlo, *pata de palo* (wooden leg)," she is awarded her junior high school diploma.

1922

Intending to study medicine, Kahlo enrolls at the National Preparatory School in Mexico City, a prestigious institution housed in the former College of San Ildefonso, the cradle of the Mexican muralism movement. There she meets future Mexican artists and intellectuals and joins the group called "Los Cachuchas."

Kahlo first meets Diego Rivera while he is painting the mural *Creation* in the school's auditorium, the Simón Bolívar Amphitheater.

Frida Kahlo with Diego Rivera in her studio at the Casa Azul, c. 1945

1923

Diego Rivera begins the murals at the Public Education Secretariat, which he will finish in 1928.

1925

Kahlo works as an apprentice in the studio of the printer and engraver Fernando Fernández, who teaches her to draw.

On September 17, Frida Kahlo is the victim of a terrible accident that causes multiple fractures in her spinal column and pelvis and other extremely serious injuries that leave her disabled for life and incapable of having children. She is traveling with Alejandro Gómez Arias, her first great love, on a city bus that collides with a streetcar. She remains in the Red Cross Hospital for one month, and when she returns home, she spends nearly a year in bed.

Frida Kahlo, Coyoacán (Mexico City), February 7, 1926. Photograph by Guillermo Kahlo

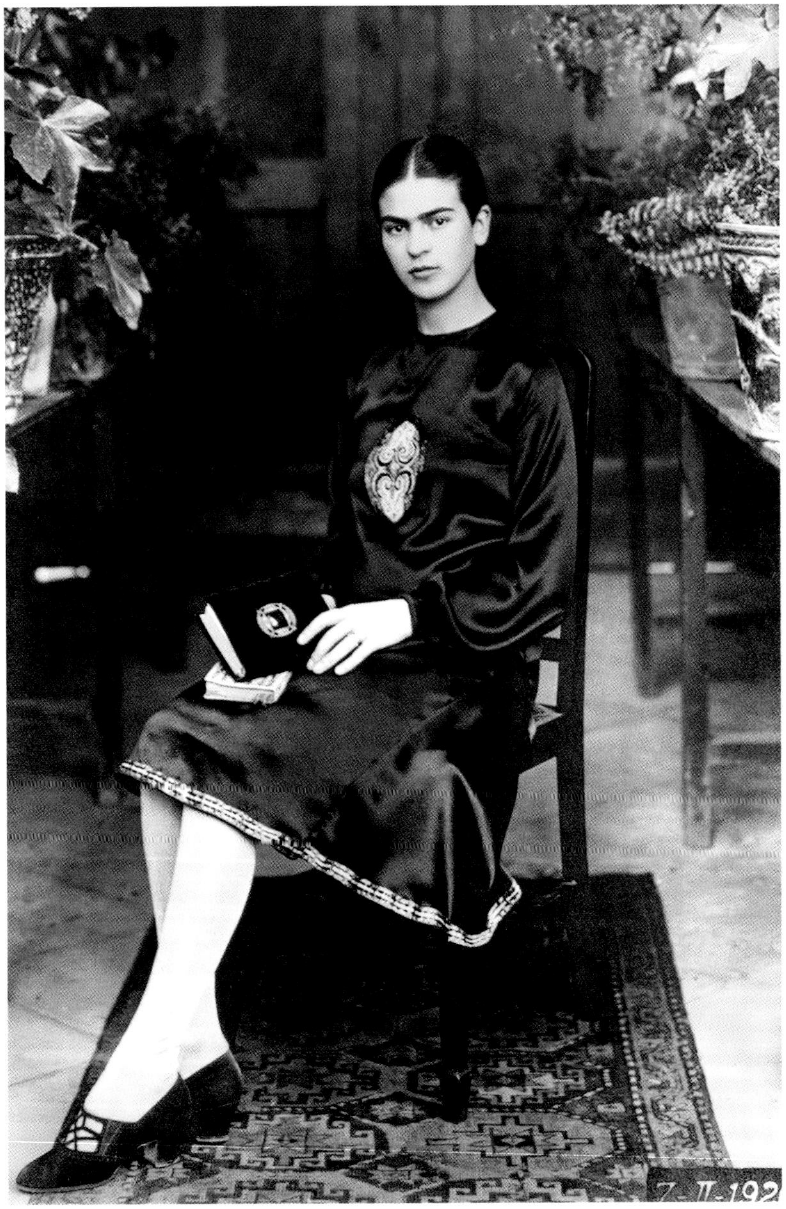

1926

Kahlo starts to paint during her convalescence because her mother places a mirror and an easel for her on the canopy of her bed. Her father teaches her to retouch his photographs, and she thus learns to work in painstaking detail with short and precise brushstrokes, a technique she will use and perfect throughout her career as a painter.

Astonishingly, her first masterpiece, *Self-portrait in a Velvet Dress,* dates from this year [fig. 6]. Technically impeccable, it denotes the influence of Italian Mannerism and of Amedeo Modigliani (1884–1920).

1927

Kahlo paints another great work, *Portrait of Miguel N. Lira* [fig. 4]. To her considerable technical dexterity, she now adds the use of symbols and a humor associated with eroticism. The painting has echoes of Stridentism.

Diego Rivera paints the murals in the Rivera Chapel at the Autonomous University of Chapingo.

1928

Through her friend Tina Modotti (1896–1942), an Italian photographer who came to Mexico with Edward Weston (1886–1958), Kahlo joins the Mexican Communist Party. Through her participation she again encounters Diego Rivera, who has been a militant since 1922. Kahlo and Rivera fall in love. The strong attraction between them, strengthened by their ideological affinity, will make them inseparable.

Rivera includes Frida Kahlo as the central figure in the mural *The Arsenal* at the Public Education Secretariat.

1929

On August 21, Frida Kahlo and Diego Rivera are married. "A marriage between an elephant and a dove," as Kahlo reported her parents described it.

Kahlo's style undergoes a shift, and she paints two pictures inspired by popular Mexican painting: *Time Flies* and *The Bus* [figs. 8 and 9].

Rivera is expelled from the Communist Party and Kahlo turns in her card out of solidarity with her husband. They go to live in Cuernavaca, where Diego paints a mural in the Palace of Cortés commissioned by the American ambassador in Mexico, Dwight W. Morrow.

Diego Rivera starts to paint murals in the National Palace.

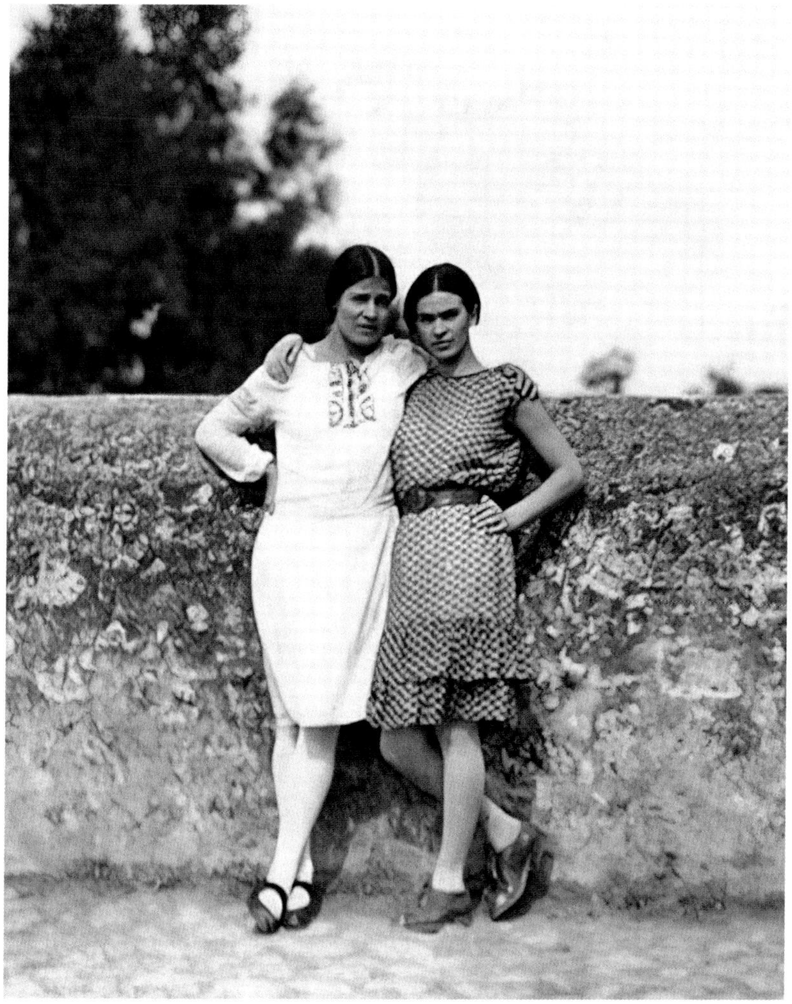

Tina Modotti and Frida Kahlo, c. 1928

1930

Due to Rivera's work commitments, the couple move to the United States. They live for three years in San Francisco, Detroit, and New York.

This is a very difficult year for the painter, as she becomes pregnant and then loses the baby. Her suffering gives rise to a series of dramatic and essential self-portraits, the first of which is *Self Portrait* [fig. 10].

1931

The Museum of Modern Art in New York presents a retrospective on Diego Rivera. Kahlo encounters the art of the twentieth-century avant-garde movements. Rivera and Kahlo consort with leading members of America's high society.

Kahlo paints *Frieda and Diego Rivera* [fig. 11] and the magnificent *Portrait of Luther Burbank* [fig. 12].

These are the years of the Great Depression in the United States. Kahlo resents the marked social differences caused by capitalism and expresses this through her work.

Kahlo meets doctor Leo Eloesser, who becomes her physician and trusted confidant.

1932

On July 14, Kahlo has another miscarriage in Detroit, where Rivera is working for Edsel Ford and the Detroit Institute of Arts.

Matilde Calderón, Kahlo's mother, dies on September 15.

Kahlo and Rivera move to New York so that Rivera can fulfill a commission at Rockefeller Center.

Kahlo paints four pictures: *My Birth*, in response to the death of her mother [fig. 2]; *Henry Ford Hospital*, a heartrending metaphor for the suffering produced by her miscarriages [fig. 14]; *Window Display in a Street in Detroit* [fig. 17]; and *Self-portrait on the Border Line between Mexico and the United States*, in which she reveals her existential dilemma over the differences between the two countries [fig. 16].

1933

Kahlo produces one of the most important works of her career, *My Dress Hangs There* (1933–1939), a devastating critique of New York capitalism linked to the artist's existential emptiness in that city [fig. 18].

1934

Rivera's mural at Rockefeller Center, *Man at the Crossroads, Looking with Hope and High Vision to the Choosing of a New and Better Future*, causes a scandal because the artist refuses to remove the face of Lenin. Nelson Rockefeller breaks the contract with Rivera and destroys his mural.

That same year, Rivera paints a mural on the same subject at the Palacio de Bellas Artes in Mexico City.

Frida Kahlo and Diego Rivera, March 19, 1932. Photograph by Carl Van Vechten

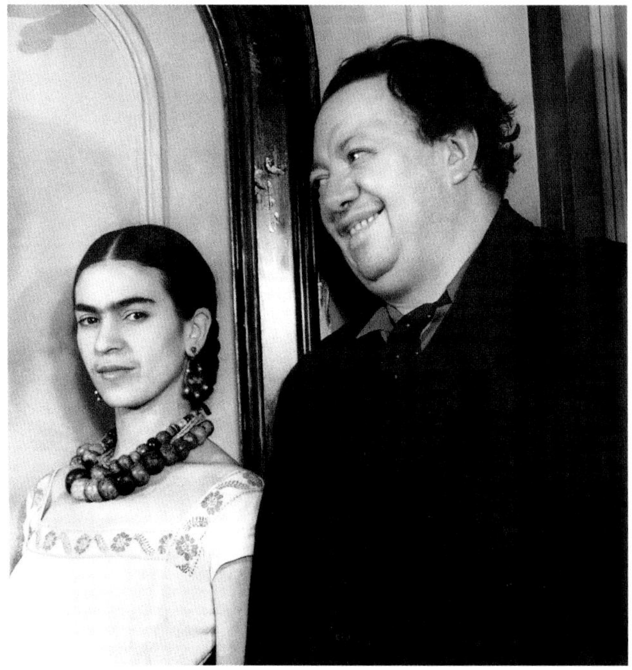

Diego Rivera and Frida Kahlo arrive in San Francisco, 1930. Photograph by Manuel Álvarez Bravo

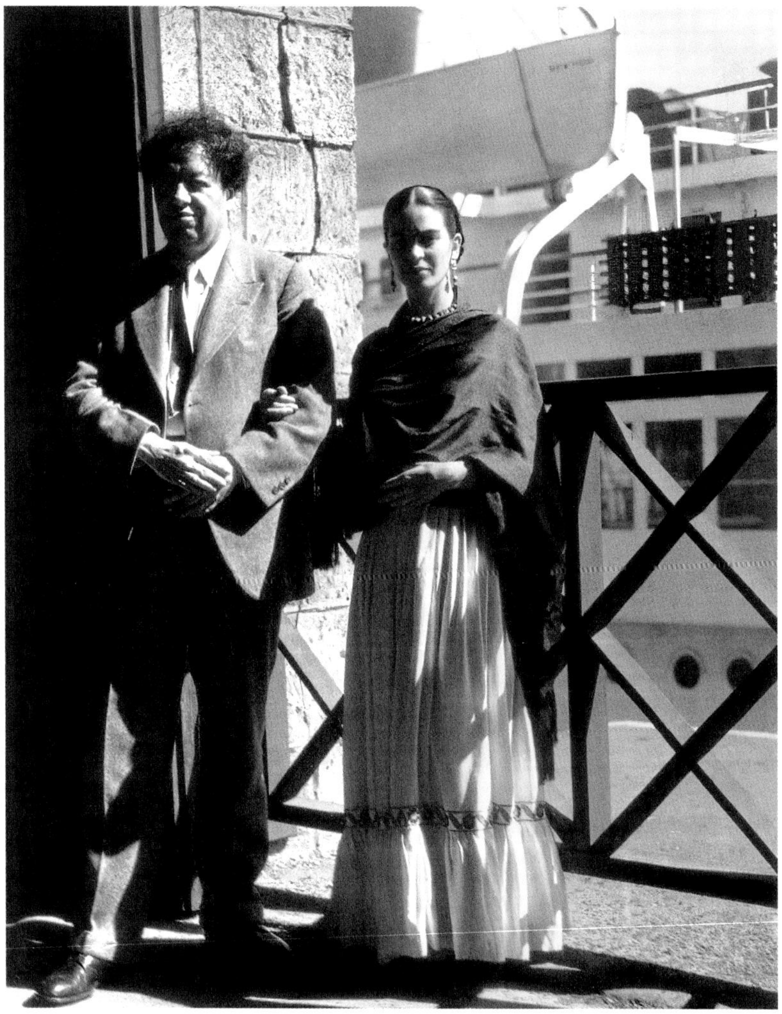

Distant from each other, the couple return to Mexico to live in the Casa Estudio (San Ángel), recently built for them by the architect Juan O'Gorman (1905–1982). With a Mexican touch, the house is influenced by the functionalism of Le Corbusier (1887–1965) and the Bauhaus of Mies van der Rohe (1886–1969).

Kahlo has another miscarriage, and some of her toes are amputated.

Rivera feels greatly frustrated at having been obliged by Kahlo to return to Mexico and starts a relationship with Cristina, Frida's younger sister. Devastated, the painter separates from her husband.

1935

Kahlo paints *A Few Small Nips* or *Passionately in Love*, an expression of her emotional grief mixed with gory black humor [fig. 20].

She begins a love affair with the sculptor Isamu Noguchi (1904–1988), who is in Mexico to paint a mural at the Abelardo Rodríguez Market. Gun in hand, Diego Rivera chases Noguchi out of Kahlo's house.

Arrival of Leon Trotsky and his wife, Natalia Sedova, in Mexico, where they are welcomed by Frida Kahlo and escorted by the police, Tampico, January 9, 1937

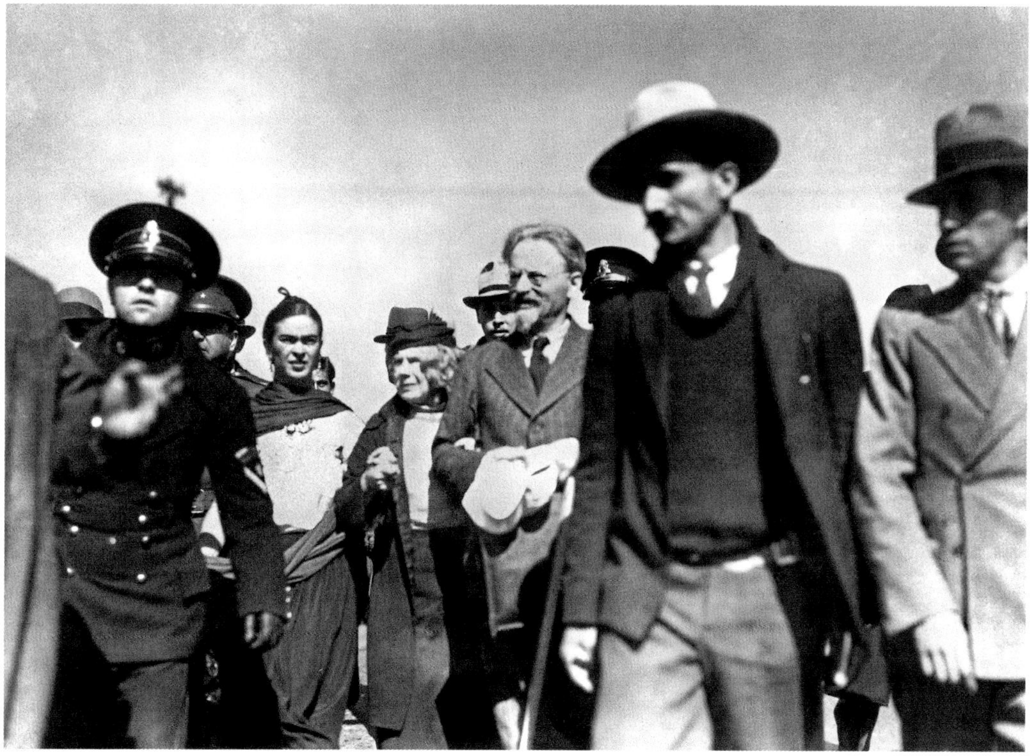

1936

The Spanish Civil War begins; it will last until 1939. Rivera and Kahlo support the Republicans.

1937

Leon Trotsky comes to live in Mexico thanks to the intervention of Rivera, who persuades President Lázaro Cárdenas to grant asylum to the leader of the Fourth International. Rivera asks Kahlo to go to Tampico to welcome Trotsky and his wife, Natalia Sedova. Kahlo and Rivera put up Trotsky and Sedova at the Casa Azul.

Kahlo begins a love affair with the Soviet ideologue and gives him *Self-portrait Dedicated to Leon Trotsky* [fig. 25].

Kahlo paints *My Nurse and I* [fig. 45].

1938

André Breton (1896–1966), the leader of the Surrealist movement, travels to Mexico with his wife, Jacqueline Lamba (1910–1993), to meet Trotsky. Lamba and Kahlo become great friends. Breton marvels at Kahlo's painting *What the Water Gave Me*, painted that year [fig. 27]. He heaps praise on her work, declaring her a born Surrealist, although Kahlo rejects the label. Even so, Breton becomes Kahlo's most important promoter, organizing the two major exhibitions of her work in New York and Paris that lead to her international recognition.

The opening of the exhibition of Kahlo's painting at the Julien Levy Gallery, the epicenter of New York Surrealism, is a great success. *The Frame*, painted that year, is one of the few works that is not sold in the exhibition [fig. 28].

The photographer Nickolas Muray (1892–1965) buys *What the Water Gave Me*. A relationship starts between Muray and Kahlo that will last a decade.

Kahlo paints *Girl with Death Mask* [fig. 46].

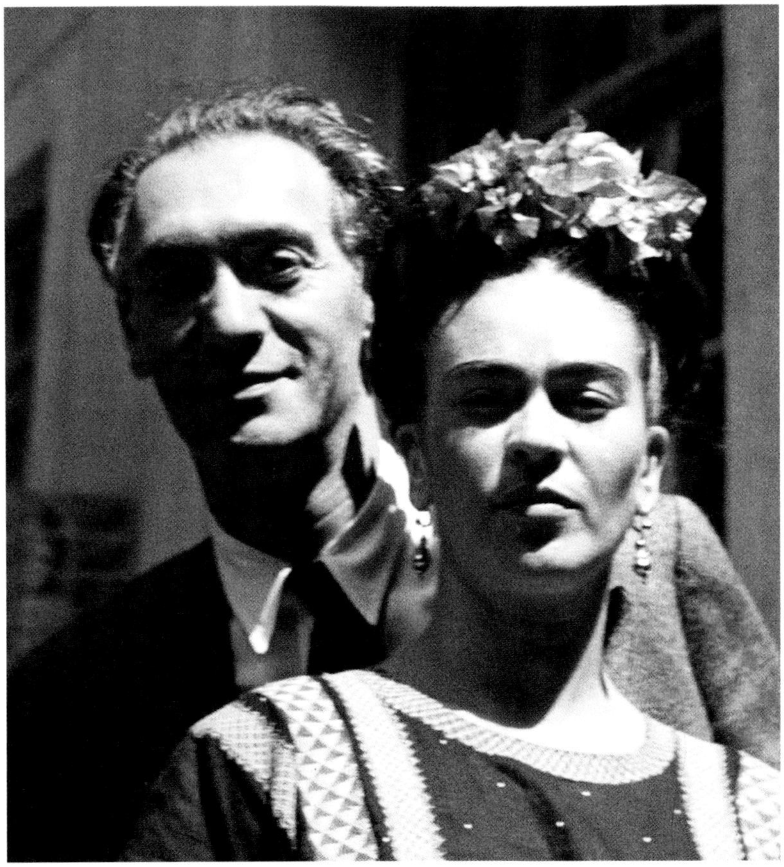

Nickolas Muray and Frida Kahlo, 1939. Private collection

1939

Opening of the exhibition *Mexique*, featuring works by Frida Kahlo, at the Galerie Renou et Colle in Paris, the cradle of Surrealism. Breton neglects his organizational duties and Marcel Duchamp (1887–1968) steps in to help Kahlo collect her pictures from customs so that they can be included in the show. A success for the artist, the exhibition is visited and praised by Wassily Kandinsky (1866–1944), Joan Miró (1893–1983), Yves Tanguy (1900–1955), Wolfgang Paalen (1905–1959), and Pablo Picasso (1881–1973).

The Musée du Louvre, through the Jeu de Paume, buys the painting *The Frame* for France's national collection.

In the magazine *La Flèche*, the critic L. P. Foucaud writes that Kahlo's works are "a door opened on the infinite and on the continuity of art."

Elsa Schiaparelli designs the Robe Madame Rivera, a dress inspired by Frida Kahlo.

Kahlo returns to Mexico and Diego Rivera asks her for a divorce. The papers are signed in November.

She paints *The Two Fridas* [fig. 31].

1940

On January 17, the International Surrealist Exhibition, organized by André Breton, Wolfgang Paalen, and César Moro (1903–1956), opens at Inés Amor's Galería de Arte Mexicano in Mexico City. Kahlo participates with two works, *The Two Fridas* and *The Wounded Table*. The latter, painted that same year, has now been missing for nearly seven decades.

In May, there is a failed attempt to assassinate Leon Trotsky under the command of David Alfaro Siqueiros (1896–1974).

On August 20, Leon Trotsky is attacked on Stalin's orders at his home in Coyoacán, Mexico City; he dies the next day. The crime is perpetrated by Ramón Mercader, a Soviet spy of Spanish origin, who will spend twenty years in jail. Frida and Cristina Kahlo are interrogated and spend two days in prison but are released because they have nothing to do with the murder.

Rivera, who had broken his ties with the Soviet leader, goes to San Francisco, where he is participating in the Golden Gate International Exhibition. There he happens by chance upon Kahlo, who has gone there to be operated on by Leo Eloesser. The couple remarry on December 8.

Kahlo paints *Self-portrait with Thorn Necklace and Hummingbird*, one of her most celebrated works [fig. 30].

1941

The couple returns to Mexico and take up residence in the Casa Azul, where Kahlo was born. The second marriage is bound by several rules: separate bedrooms and no physical contact.

Guillermo Kahlo dies on April 14.

Kahlo's physical and emotional health develops further complications. In these years, her production of self-portraits and still lifes intensifies.

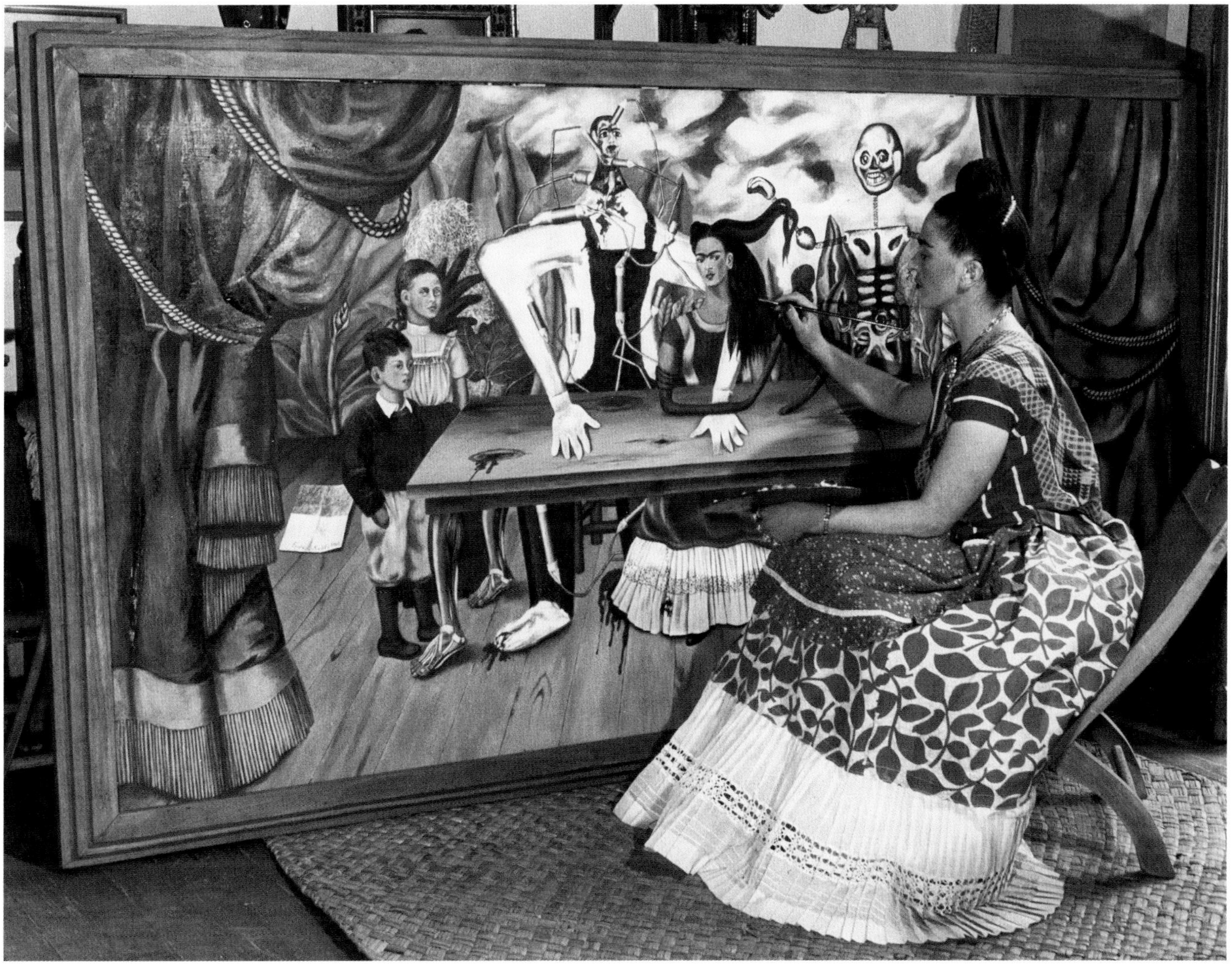

Frida Kahlo painting *The Wounded Table* (whereabouts unknown), 1940. Photograph by Bernard G. Silberstein. Detroit Institute of Arts, Gift of the artist, F81.489

1942

Kahlo paints *Still Life (Tondo)* [fig. 59].

1943

Kahlo paints *Roots*, sold at Sotheby's in 2004 for 5.6 million dollars [fig. 44].

Kahlo teaches painting at La Esmeralda, an art school. Because of her delicate health, most of the lessons are held at her home. She calls her pupils "Los Fridos."

1944

Kahlo paints *The Broken Column* [fig. 7] and finishes *Double Portrait of Diego and I*, begun in 1929, the year of their first wedding, to give it to her husband to mark their fifteenth year of marriage [fig. 51].

She starts to write her diary, which will cover the last decade of her life. It contains thoughts, poems, dreams, drawings, and watercolors. It will be published in its entirety many years later under the title *The Diary of Frida Kahlo: An Intimate Self-portrait.*

1945

Kahlo paints *Moses* [fig. 67], a complex and original work based on Sigmund Freud's book *Moses and Monotheism* (published in 1939). The same year, she also paints *Without Hope* [fig. 33].

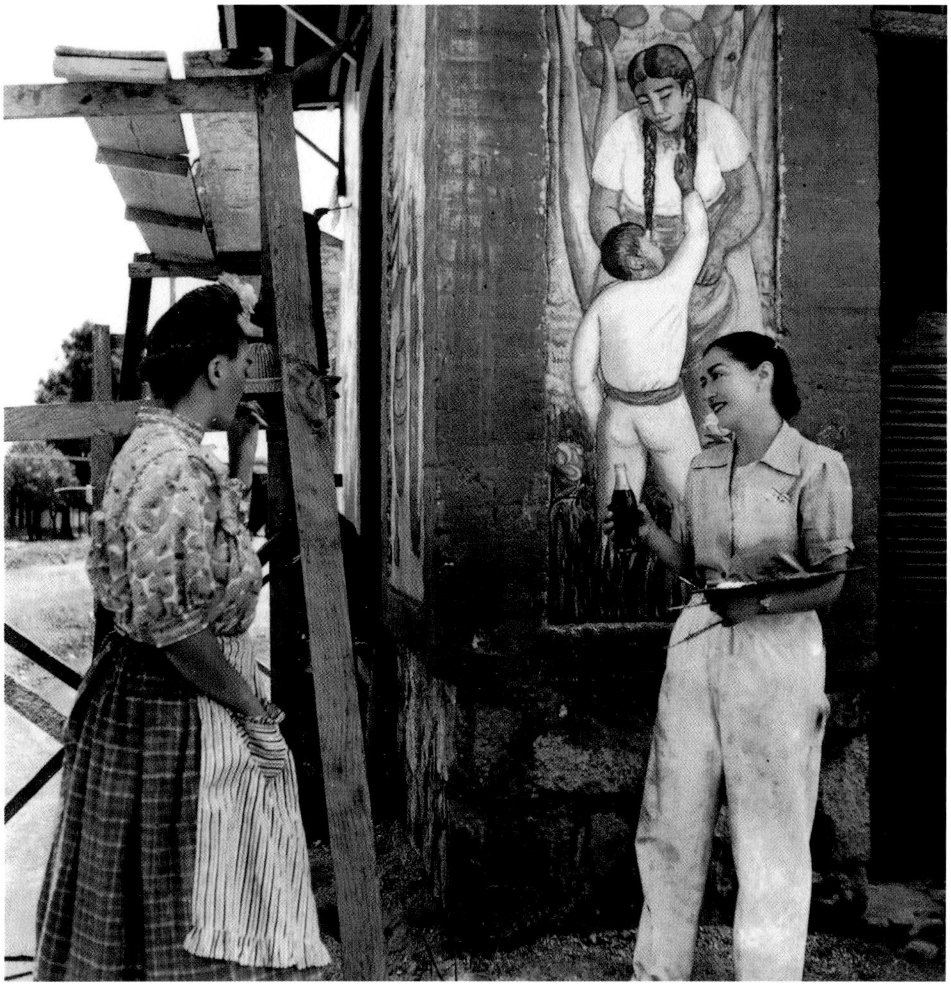

Frida Kahlo and one of her pupils from La Esmeralda, María de los Ángeles Ramos, in the Pulquería La Rosita, where Los Fridos painted some murals, Coyoacán (Mexico City), 1943. Photograph by Leo Matiz. Mexico City, Fundación Leo Matiz

1946
Kahlo is awarded a national prize for painting for her work *Moses*.

She paints *Little Deer* [fig. 48].

1947
Kahlo paints *Self-portrait with Loose Hair*, which reveals the progressive deterioration of her health [fig. 69].

1948
Kahlo rejoins the Mexican Communist Party. Her Stalinism starts to be reflected in her work.

1949
Kahlo writes a text entitled "Portrait of Diego" for the catalogue of the tribute exhibition to Diego Rivera inaugurated in the Palacio de Bellas Artes on August 1. Raquel Tibol described this text as one of the best written on a Mexican artist in the twentieth century.

1950–52
Kahlo's health worsens. In 1951, she spends nine months in treatment at the English Hospital in Mexico City. Between 1950 and 1951, seven operations are carried out on her spinal column. Her pulse starts to weaken, and the quality of her paintings is consequently diminished.

In 1951, she paints *Self-portrait with the Portrait of Dr. Farill*, perhaps her last great self-portrait [fig. 72]. She continues to paint still lifes, while her Stalinist fervor grows more acute and expresses itself in her painting.

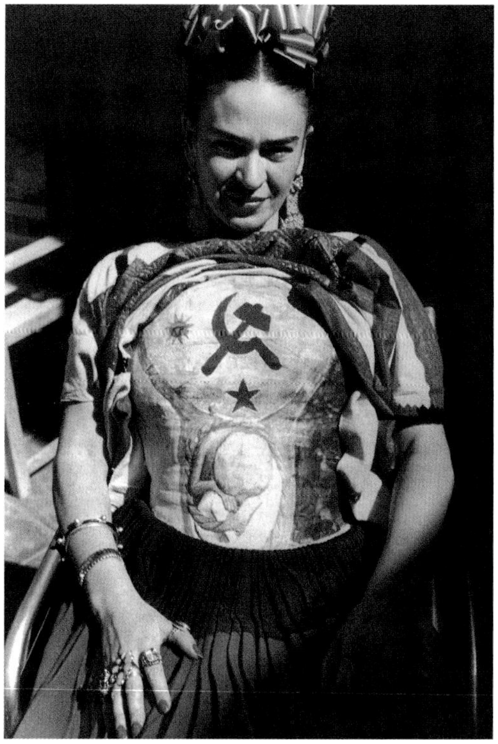

Frida Kahlo, 1951. Photograph by Florence Arquin. Private collection

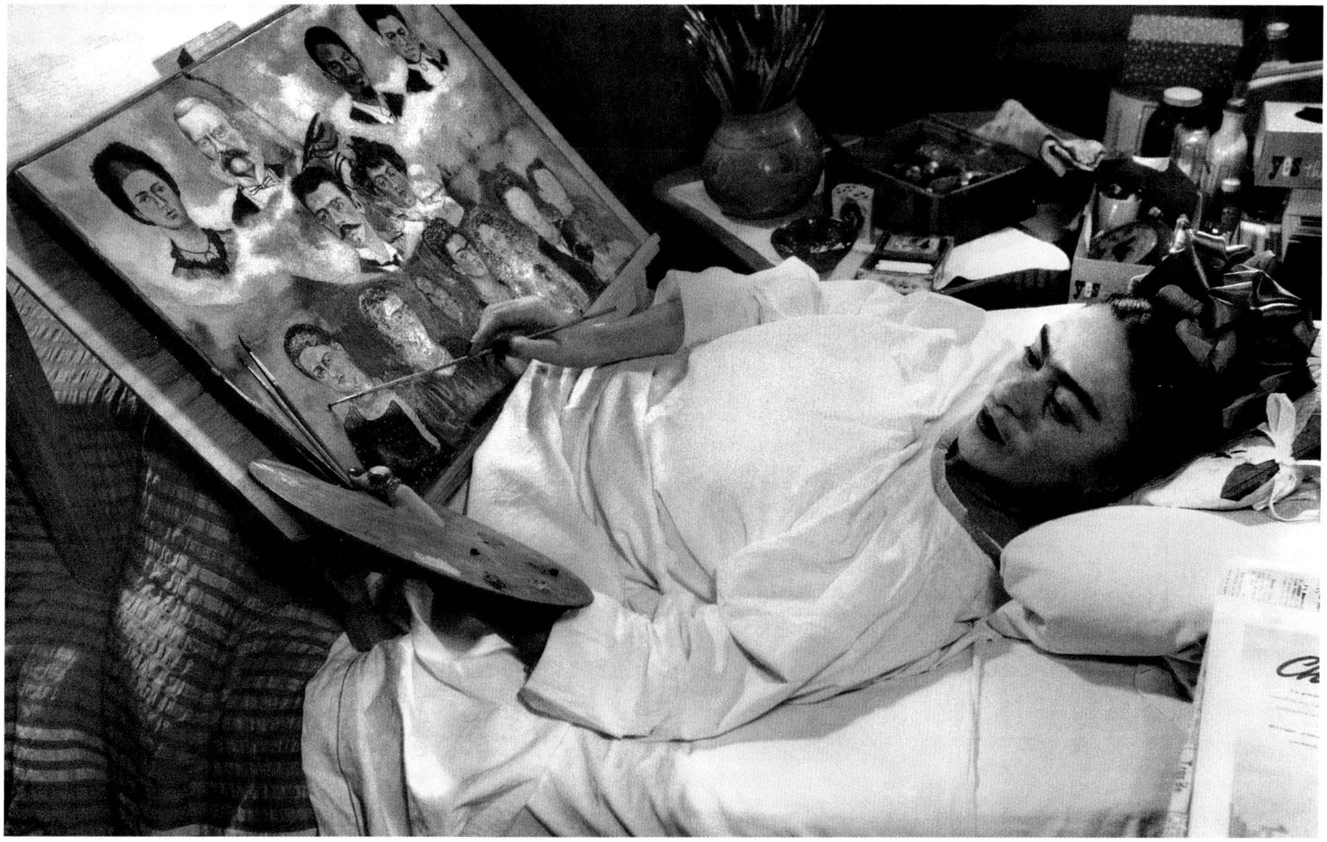

Frida Kahlo painting *Portrait of Frida's Family*, 1952. Photograph by Juan Guzmán

1953

In the spring, the first solo exhibition dedicated to Frida Kahlo in Mexico is inaugurated. It is organized by the photographer Lola Álvarez Bravo (1907–1993), her friend since high school, at the Galería de Arte Contemporáneo, which is owned by the photographer. Although the doctors forbid her to attend the opening of the exhibition, she hires an ambulance and is carried into the gallery on a stretcher.

In August, Kahlo's right leg is amputated below the knee due to gangrene. The pain is dreadful, and she can only calm it with very strong opiates. "I am DISINTEGRATION," she writes in her diary.

Diego Rivera begins the construction of Anahuacalli, designed by himself with the collaboration of the architect and painter Juan O'Gorman, to house his collection of more than 50,000 pieces of pre-Hispanic art. It is currently a museum.

1954

In July, Kahlo attends a political demonstration with Rivera to protest the intervention of the CIA in Guatemala. It is her last public appearance.

She paints her last still life, entitled *Viva la Vida* [fig. 75]. The last line in her diary reads: "I hope the leaving is joyful—and I hope never to return." On her easel, she leaves an unfinished portrait of Stalin.

Frida Kahlo dies on July 13. The official cause of death is pulmonary embolism.

Her body lies in state at the Palacio de Bellas Artes. Her ashes are now in an urn at the Casa Azul, now the Museo Frida Kahlo.

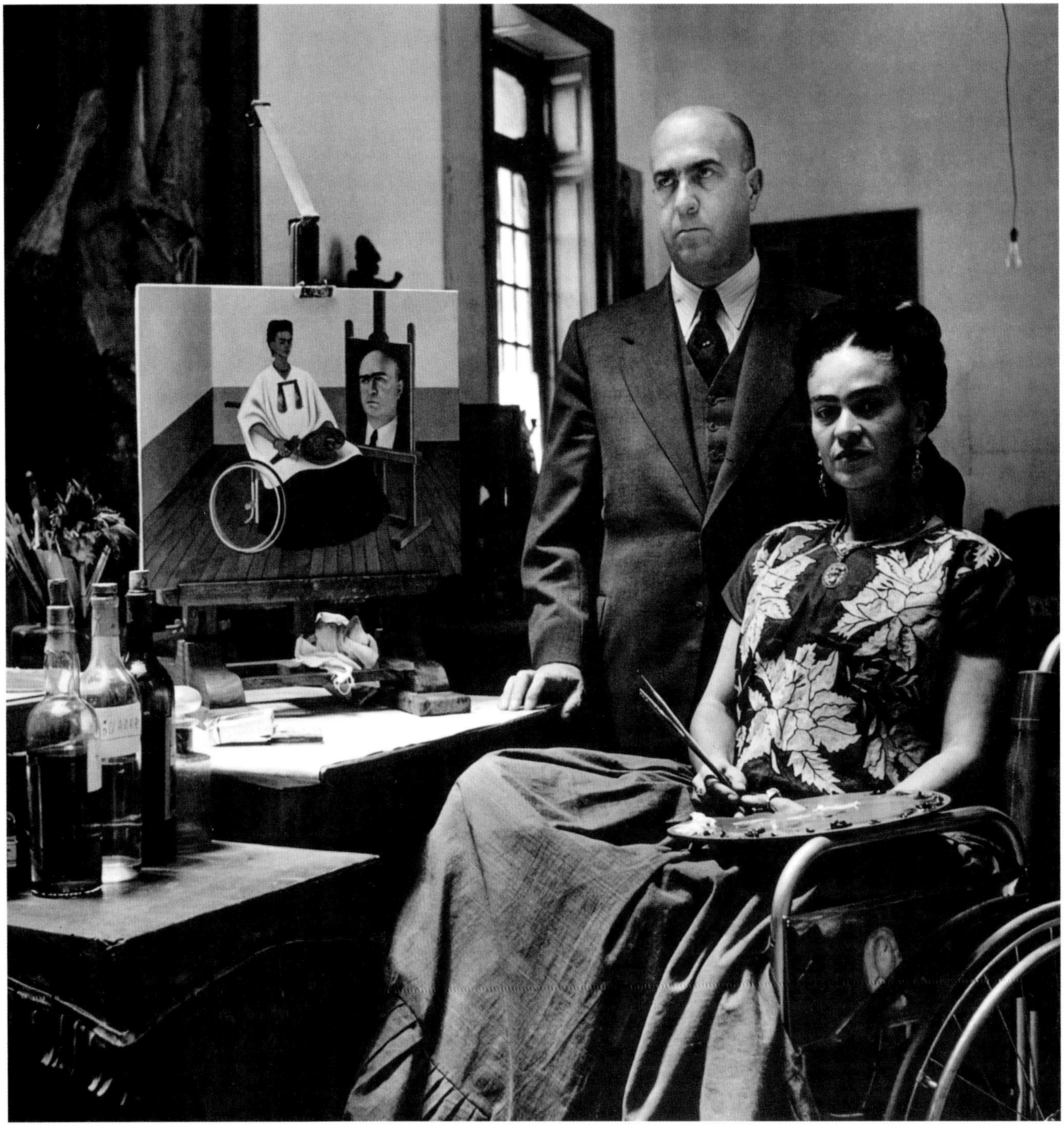

Frida Kahlo with Juan Farill in front of *Self-portrait with the Portrait of Dr. Farill*, 1952. Photograph by Gisèle Freund

A bedridden Kahlo attends the opening of her first solo exhibition of paintings in Mexico City in 1953. On the left is the singer Concha Michel, and on the right the painter and writer Gerardo Murillo, known as Dr. Atl.

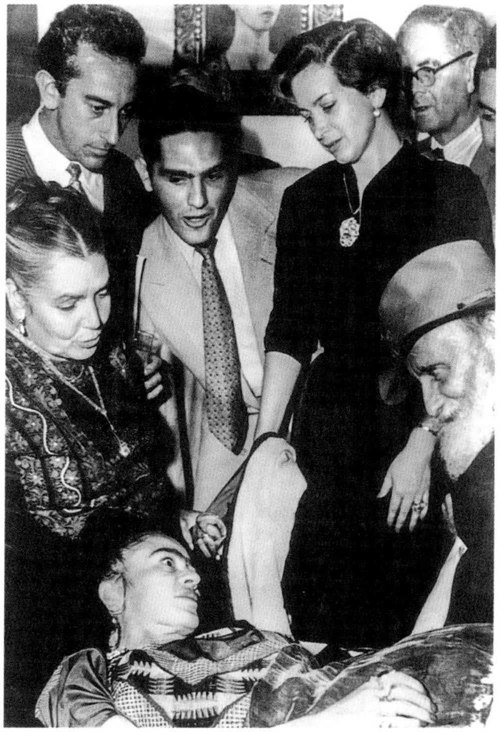

1957

Diego Rivera, suffering from cancer of the pancreas, dies. Before he dies, he and his friend Dolores Olmedo organize the constitution of a trust with the Bank of Mexico to administer the rights of both painters, manage the Casa Azul, and complete the Museo Anahuacalli.

Rivera is buried in the Rotunda of Illustrious Men in Mexico City.

1958

The Casa Azul opens as the Museo Frida Kahlo.

1964

The Museo Anahuacalli, specializing in pre-Hispanic art, opens.

Funeral cortège of Frida Kahlo on the way to the Panteón Civil de Dolores in Mexico City, where her body was cremated, July 14, 1954. Diego Rivera walks alongside the engineer César Martino, former president of Mexico Lázaro Cárdenas, and the director of the Instituto Nacional de Bellas Artes, Andrés Iduarte, who holds Rivera's arm. Courtesy Morton Subastas

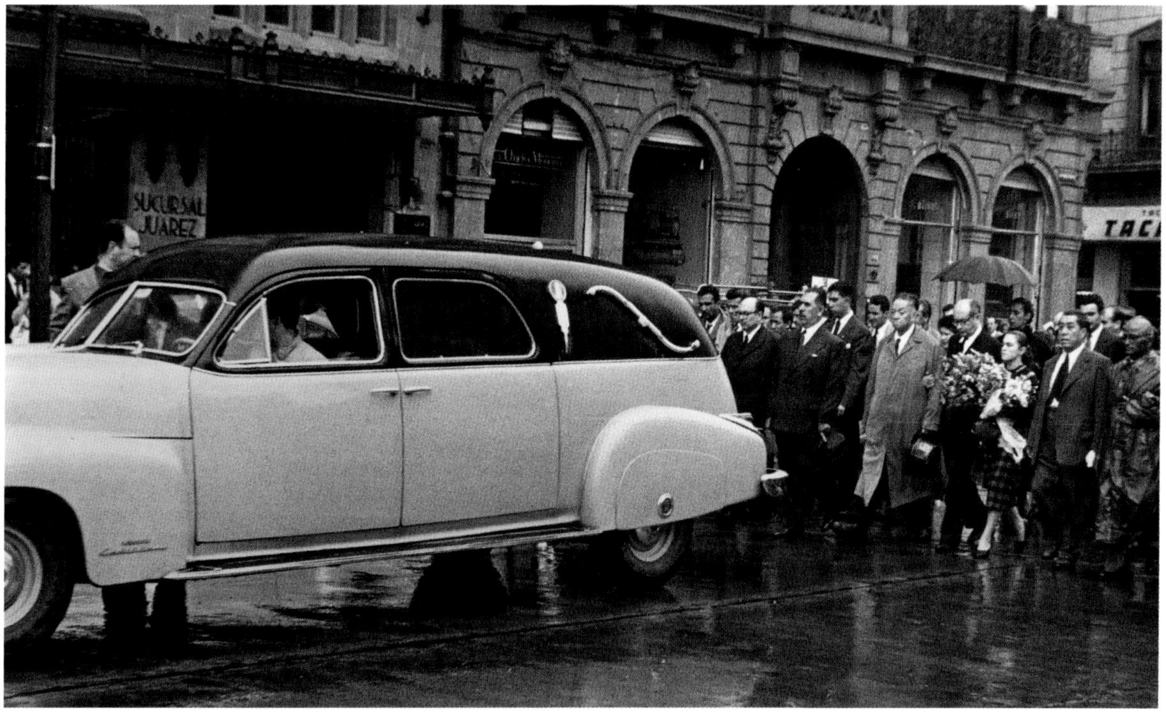

Garden courtyard
of the Casa Azul

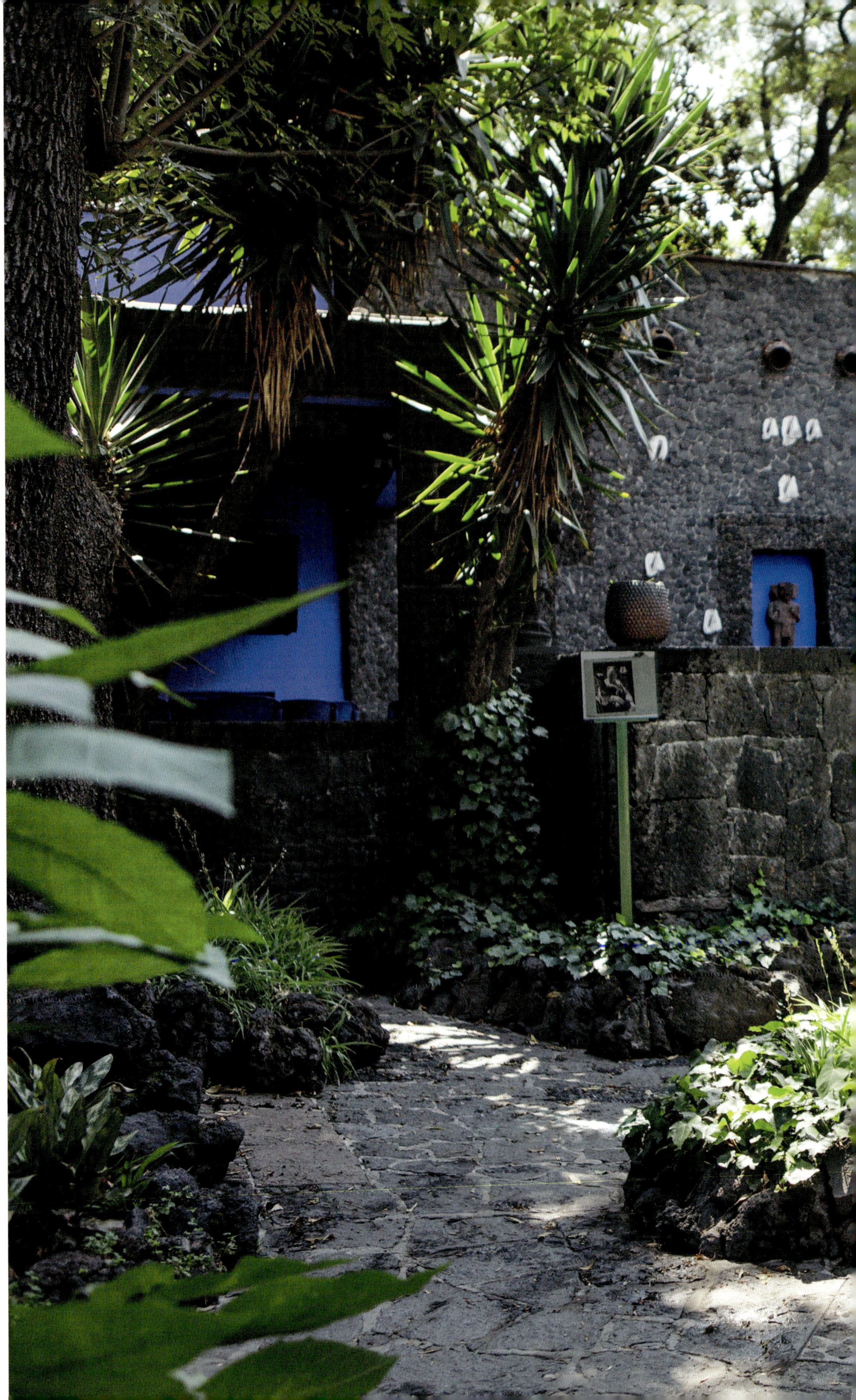

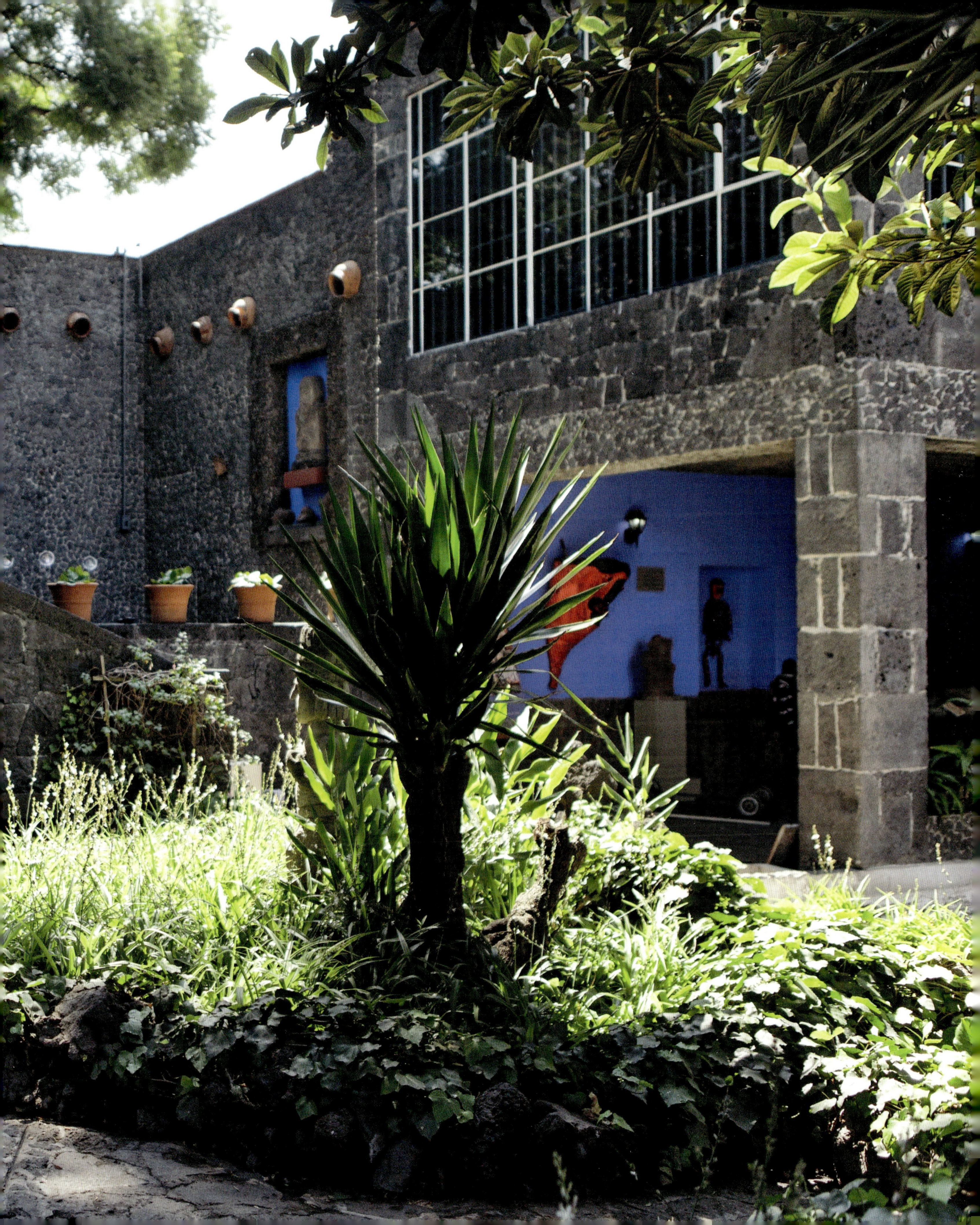

Produced by
Ediciones El Viso

Coordination
Gonzalo Saavedra
Lucía Varela

Design
Subiela Bernat

Translation
Philip Sutton

Photo Research
Manuela Docampo

Typesetting
Ana Martín

Prepress
Emilio Breton

Printing and Binding
Printer Trento S.r.l., Trento

For Rizzoli Electa
Charles Miers, Publisher
Margaret Rennolds Chace, Associate Publisher
Gloria Nantz, Editor

First published in the United States of America in 2022 by
Rizzoli Electa, A Division of
Rizzoli International Publications, Inc.
49 West 27th Street
New York, NY 10001
www.rizzoliusa.com

Printed in Italy
Fifth printing, 2025
2025 2026 2027 / 10 9 8 7 6 5
ISBN: 978-0-8478-7147-6
Library of Congress Control Number: 2021944652

MIX
Paper | Supporting responsible forestry
FSC® C015829

The authorized representative in the EU for product safety and compliance is Mondadori Libri S.p.A., via Gian Battista Vico 42, Milan, Italy, 20123, www.mondadori.it

Visit us online:
Facebook.com/RizzoliNewYork
Instagram.com/RizzoliBooks
Youtube.com/user/RizzoliNY

Jacket front: *Self-portrait with Thorn Necklace and Hummingbird*, 1940 (detail of fig. 30)
Jacket back: *Girl from Tehuacán, Lucha María* or *Sun and Moon*, 1942 (detail of fig. 47)
Page 2: *What the Water Gave Me*, 1938 (detail of fig. 27)
Page 3: *Sun and Life*, 1947 (detail of fig. 55)
Page 4: *Viva la Vida*, 1954 (detail of fig. 75)
Page 5: *Portrait of Diego Rivera*, 1937 (detail of fig. 23)
Page 6: *Portrait of Luther Burbank*, 1931 (detail of fig. 12)
Page 7: *My Dress Hangs There*, 1933–39 (detail of fig. 18)
Page 8: *Self-portrait in a Velvet Dress*, 1926 (detail of fig. 6)

Photography credits

Album: fig. 68; pp. 18, 22, 23, 193, 210, 211
Album / akg-images: figs. 5, 9, 10, 12–15, 20, 26, 32, 33, 35, 38, 39, 50, 52, 54, 61, 67, 72; pp. 6, 214 (top), 215
Album / Fine Art Images: figs. 1, 6, 23, 29, 40–42, 45, 48, 60, 66; pp. 5, 8, 20, 74, 180, 216, 218 (bottom)
Album / Granger, NYC: pp. 143, 189, 214 (bottom), 219, 220, 221 (top)
Album / quintlox: p. 183
Archivart / Alamy Stock Photo: fig. 34
Archivo Diego Rivera y Frida Kahlo, Banco de México, Fiduciary in the Diego Rivera and Frida Kahlo Museum Trust: figs. 3, 59, 73–75; pp. 4, 148
© Art Collection / Alamy Limited / agefotostock: p. 212
© Association Atelier André Breton, 2021: p. 88
© Centre Pompidou, MNAM-CCI, Dist. RMN-Grand Palais / Jean-Claude Planchet: fig. 28
© Christie's Images/Bridgeman Images: figs. 16, 19, 21, 27, 46, 69; p. 2
© Jorge Contreras Chacel/Bridgeman Images: figs. 2, 43
Courtesy Albright-Knox Art Gallery: fig. 36
Courtesy Collection Banco Nacional de México: fig. 57
Courtesy Collection of the Madison Museum of Contemporary Art, Wisconsin: fig. 58
Courtesy FEMSA Collection (photography by Humberto Tachiquín «Tachi»): fig. 18; p. 7
Courtesy Galería Arvil: figs. 51, 55, 56, 64; p. 3
Courtesy Gary Nader Fine Art: fig. 17
Courtesy Morton Subastas: pp. 194–95, 221 (bottom)
Courtesy Museo de Arte Moderno, INBAL/Secretaría de Cultura. Mexico City, Mexico: figs. 31, 63, 65
Courtesy Pérez Simón Collection, Mexico (© Rafael Doniz): fig. 47; jacket back
Courtesy private collection: fig. 8
Courtesy San Francisco Museum of Modern Art (photography by Ben Blackwell): fig. 11
Detroit Institute of Arts, USA © Detroit Institute of Arts/Gift of the Artist/Bridgeman Images: p. 217
Digital image Museum Associates/LACMA/Art Resource NY/SCALA, Florence: fig. 62
Digital image, The Museum of Modern Art, New York/Scala, Florence: fig. 22
© Galerie Bilderwelt/Bridgeman Images: p. 41
Granger / Bridgeman Images: p. 68
Harry Ransom Center. The University of Texas at Austin: fig. 30; jacket front
© IMEC, Fonds MCC, Dist. RMN-Grand Palais - © Gisèle Freund: pp. 10–11
© Sara Janini/agefotostock: pp. 222–23
Erich Lessing / Album: figs. 4, 24, 49, 53, 70
© Alejandra Matiz. Acervo de la Fundación Leo Matiz: pp. 100, 140, 172, 218 (top)
Museo Dolores Olmedo Patino, Mexico City. Photo © Leonard de Selva/Bridgeman Images: fig. 7
Museum of Fine Arts, Boston. All rights reserved/Scala, Florence: p. 38
National Museum of Women in the Arts, Washington, D.C., (Image by Google): fig. 25
© The New York Times Archives / Redux / Contactophoto: p. 45
© Phoenix Art Museum. All rights reserved: fig. 71
Photo Art Resource/Scala, Florence: fig. 37
© 2021. Photo Georgia O'Keeffe Museum, Santa Fe/Art Resource/Scala, Florence: p. 145
Photo by Nickolas Muray; © Nickolas Muray Photo Archives: p. 153
Photo Scala, Florence: p. 26
Photo Schalkwijk/Art Resource/Scala, Florence: p. 42
Smithsonian Institution (photography by Chester Dale): p. 107
© Sotheby's/Bridgeman: fig. 44
La Vaca Independiente (photography by Bob Schalkwijk): p. 190
Vintage_Space / Alamy Stock Photo: p. 213